The Chinese in America

Critical Perspectives on Asian Pacific Americans Series

Books in the series will educate and inform readers in the academy, in Asian American communities, and the general public regarding Asian Pacific American experiences. They examine key social, economic, psychological, cultural, and political issues. Theoretically innovative, engaging, comparative, and multidisciplinary, these books reflect the contemporary issues that are of critical importance to understanding and empowering Asian Pacific Americans.

Series Titles Include

Diana Ting Liu Wu, *Asilace* (1997)

Juanita Tamayo Lott, *Asian Americans: From Racial Category to Multiple Identities* (1997)

Jun Xing, *Asian America through the Lens: History, Representations, and Identity* (1998)

Pyong Gap Min and Rose Kim, editors, *Struggle for Ethnic Identity: Narratives by Asian American Professionals* (1999)

Wendy Ho, *In Her Mother's House: The Politics of Asian American Mother Daughter Writing* (2000)

Deborah Woo, *Glass Ceilings and Asian Americans: The New Face of Workplace Barriers* (2000)

Patricia Wong Hall and Victor M. Hwang, editors, *Anti-Asian Violence in North America: Asian American and Asian Canadian Reflections on Hate, Healing, and Resistance* (2001)

Pyong Gap Min and Jung Ha Kim, editors, *Religions in Asian America: Building Faith Communities* (2001)

Pyong Gap Min, editor, *The Second Generation: Ethnic Identity among Asian Americans* (2002)

Submission Guidelines

Prospective authors of single or co-authored books and editors of anthologies should submit a letter of introduction, the manuscript or a four- to ten-page proposal, a book outline, and a curriculum vitae to:

Critical Perspectives on Asian Pacific Americans Series
AltaMira Press
1630 North Main Street, #367
Walnut Creek, CA 94596

The Chinese in America

A History from Gold Mountain to the New Millennium

EDITED BY SUSIE LAN CASSEL

ALTAMIRA
PRESS

A Division of
ROWMAN & LITTLEFIELD PUBLISHERS, INC.
Walnut Creek • *Lanham* • *New York* • *Oxford*

ALTAMIRA PRESS
A Division of Rowman & Littlefield Publishers, Inc.
1630 North Main Street, #367
Walnut Creek, CA 94596
www.altamirapress.com

Rowman & Littlefield Publishers, Inc.
4720 Boston Way,
Lanham, MD 20706

12 Hid's Copse Road
Cumnor Hill, Oxford OX2 9JJ, England

Copyright © 2002 by ALTAMIRA PRESS

British Library Cataloguing in Publication Information Available

Library of Congress Cataloging-in-Publication Data

The Chinese in America : a history from Gold Mountain to the new millennium / edited
by Susie Lan Cassel.
    p. cm.
    Papers from the Sixth Chinese American Conference, held July 9–11, 1999 and
hosted by the Chinese Historical Society of Greater San Diego and Baja California.
    Includes index.
    ISBN 0-7591-0000-4 (cloth : alk. paper)—ISBN 0-7591-0001-2 (pbk. : alk. paper)
    1. Chinese Americans—History—Congresses. I. Cassel, Susie Lan, 1966–

E184.C5 C4928 2002
973'.04951—dc21   2001045990

Printed in the United States of America

♾™ The paper used in this publication meets the minimum requirements of American
National Standard for Information Sciences—Permanence of Paper for Printed Library
Materials, ANSI/NISO Z39.48-1992.

Contents

Figures

Tables

Acknowledgments

The Chinese Historical Society of Greater San Diego and Baja California (now the San Diego Chinese Historical Society and Museum) was proud to host the Sixth Chinese American Conference on July 9–11, 1999. We were pleased to present the conference to our fellow Chinese historical societies and Chinese American communities across the nation, as well as to the faculty, students, and supporters of Asian American studies programs. We hope that you, the reader, will be able to sense from these essays the passion and dedication of the presenters during the conference and find their expertise useful in your studies and pursuits.

We are indebted to Dr. Susie Lan Cassel for her effective efforts to turn this outstanding collection of papers into a valuable publication. Her skills are a credit to California State University, San Marcos, to our organization, and to the San Diego region.

The planning committee was among the best I've ever worked with. We thank Murray Lee, curator of Chinese American history at the San Diego Chinese Historical Museum, for his persistence and hard work as the driving force behind the program. Significant leaders included Donna Lee, Gladys Lee, Dr. Judith Liu, and Susie Quon. Other key planning team members were Paul Chace, Norman Fong, Beverly Hom, Dorothy Hom, Tom Hom, Sawyer Hsu, Virginia Kim, Robin Low, Al Ong, Dr. Youwen Ouyang, Markus Quon, Carmen Tom, and Dr. Richard Wang. Dorothy Hom has sadly passed away, and we miss her enthusiasm and soul. The support of the Chinese Historical Museum executive director, Dr. Alexander Chuang, is especially appreciated.

We are grateful to the Chinese Historical Society of America and the Chinese Historical Society of Southern California for their support and sponsorship. Outside San Diego, the advice of Dr. Lorraine Dong and Munson Kwok, along with Stephanie Fan, Gilbert Hom, Dr. Victor Jew, Dr. Marlon Hom, Stanley Mu, and Ying Zeng, was appreciated. Locally, Dr. Lilly Cheng, Dr. Kenji Ima, Yosh Kawahara, and Dr. Leland Saito were a significant help.

Our cosponsors assisted with vital financial support for expenses or scholarships. This included our major sponsors—Sempra Energy, University of San Diego (President Alice B. Hayes), and California State University (CSU), San Marcos (President Alexander Gonzalez). Other cosponsors were Viejas Casino and Turf Club, City of San Diego Commission for Arts and Culture, San Diego Chinese Women's Association, University of California, San Diego (UCSD) Chinese Studies Program, Chinese Consolidated Benevolent Association (CCBA) of San Diego, House of China in San Diego's Balboa Park, UCSD Ethnic Studies Program, San Diego State University Department of Asian Studies, San Diego Mesa College, Humanities Institute at San Diego Mesa College, Buddha's Light International Association, Chinese Historical and Cultural Project (San Jose), Organization of Chinese Americans (OCA), Chinese American Citizens Alliance (CACA), Related Capital Company, Union Bank of California, San Diego Chinese American Science and Engineering Association, Asian Buying Consortium, and Nine Dragons, Inc. Individual cosponsors were Dr. Alexander Chuang, Michael Lee, and David Du. Official supporters included the Society for California Archaeology, Chinese Historical Society of New England, CSU San Marcos Computing & Telecommunications, and the Wing Luke Asian Museum in Seattle.

For help specifically with this volume, we thank Murray Lee, Him Mark Lai, Munson Kwok, Dr. Kathleen Moore, Dr. Christopher D. Johnson, Dr. Leland Saito, Dr. Anibal Yañez-Chavez, Sunny Liang, Chuck Allen, Susie Quon, Donna Lee, and Dr. Richard Wang.

Best wishes and happy reading.

Michael Yee
Chair, Sixth Chinese American Conference
President, San Diego Chinese Historical Society and Museum

Introduction: One Hundred and Fifty Years of Chinese in America: The Politics of Polarity

Susie Lan Cassel

On March 8, 1999, a Chinese American scientist was summarily dismissed from his job after twenty years at a U.S. nuclear weapons research facility, following an unfounded allegation in the *New York Times* that he had leaked the "crown jewels" of nuclear secrets to China. For nine months after the media made this allegation, Wen Ho Lee was harassed, intimidated, and interrogated by two hundred FBI agents and sixty computer specialists, while he, his family, his colleagues, and his friends were kept under twenty-four-hour surveillance. Dr. Lee was eventually charged not with spying or transferring secrets, as he was originally alleged to have done, but with the far lesser offense of the "mishandling of classified data," a crime most often left unprosecuted and endemic to the agencies that handle this kind of information.[1] Dr. Lee had already spent 278 days in solitary confinement, enduring unusually cruel conditions, when a high-level FBI official recanted key testimony in the case. All but one of the fifty-nine charges against Lee were immediately dropped[2] and, in an unprecedented move, the judge apologized to Lee, while the *New York Times* issued a full-page explanation that expressed regret for some of its coverage and the president of the United States told reporters he had "always had reservations" about some aspects of the case.

The special attention Dr. Wen Ho Lee received from the media, the FBI, and the politicians stems directly from the fact that he was an American of Chinese descent in an election year when the United States was experiencing increased tensions with China.[3] Said differently, his case was front-page news—for months—because it underscored already existent racial paranoia, which became politicized in the interest of certain domestic and international agendas.[4] Invoking the kind of racial essentialism that earlier in the twentieth century

1

had led to the imprisonment of over 100,000 people of Japanese descent in the western United States, the headline that ignited this fiasco set the stage for its coverage: "China Stole Nuclear Secrets for Bombs, U.S. Aides Say."[5] Of note, the word "China" in this title is a play on words that refers simultaneously to Lee, an American citizen, and to China, a rogue nation, in an essentialist collapse of ethnicity and political allegiance. Furthermore, the evidence that this article relied upon for its allegation of spying was the testimony of *U.S.* aides, positioned as the voices of legitimacy and credibility, in contrast to China and thus Lee, who, even though a U.S. citizen, was positioned as enemy (and) alien. From the moment that the story broke, the deck was already stacked against Dr. Lee. No wonder the *New York Times* questioned its own objectivity and regretted some of its coverage. The fact that the U.S. government apologized at the end of both sagas—that of Japanese American Internment and the Wen Ho Lee case—transforms these incidents into historical tragedies. The magnitude of the issues; the suffering, pity, and fear elicited; and the recognition of wrongdoing make these instances of systematic and institutionalized racism tragedies of Aristotelian proportion. But unlike characters in Aristotelian dramas, the real-life protagonists in these cases do not have the opportunity to correct their "tragic" flaws—their race cannot be changed.

W. E. B. DuBois is famous for noting that the problem of the twentieth century is the "problem of the color line." When considering the inescapable issue of race in the context of the history of Chinese in America, the tragedy of Wen Ho Lee, perched as it is on the cusp of the twenty-first century, is an appropriate symbol for the experiences of Chinese Americans past and present. On the one hand, Chinese, above other immigrant and racial groups, have been courted by the American economic establishment as diligent (and often knowledgeable) "model" workers who can contribute meaningfully to the development of a prosperous nation. On the other hand, Chinese have been perpetual foreigners whose welcome in America has been unduly retracted when economic or international circumstances shift. A persistent image of the Chinese as favored workers has been followed historically by a record of legalized and institutionalized racism, suggesting two contradictory threads of reception that are difficult, at best, to reconcile. What is fundamental to both views is the fact that Chinese have been consistently set apart from other immigrants and racial groups in America. Whether Chinese are "othered" as better or as worse than their immigrant and racialized counterparts, resulting in favoritism or discrimination and exclusion, they have been caught in an endemic display of politics, expressed in terms of polar extremes that, after 150 years, still appear to be inescapable. While the historical record displays an oscillation that occurs over decades, with waves of Chinese invited to work on the railroads then excluded twenty years later, or courted to high-tech specialties then faced with glass ceilings in upper management, both themes are embodied in the case of the highly specialized scientist who was enticed to work in a secret weapons lab only to be likened to spies like the Rosenbergs (who, incidentally, were executed for leaking nuclear secrets from the very same lab). When it concerns the Chinese in America, the treatment has not fit the crime and the promise of honest wages for honest work has been retracted on the whim of the political moment. Why have the Chinese, among all of America's immigrant and racial groups, fallen prey to such extreme political maneuverings? How have the Chinese survived and thrived in a racially hostile environment for over a century and a half? Who were the early immigrants, who are their descendants, and who are the Chinese immigrants now? These are just some of the important questions this volume attempts to address.

Building upon an established canon, this collection brings together new knowledge from a variety of disciplines that contributes to our understanding of the themes and issues that have shaped Chinese American studies, covering the period since the arrival of Chinese gold miners in 1849. It is not comprehensive, for no collection is, but through a careful examination of recent findings it attempts to add a new layer of information to our historical palimpsest that promises to broaden, deepen, and perhaps even shift our current assessment of the experiences of the Chinese. Arranged in six sociohistorical units, this volume traces Chinese immigration to Canada, to the United States, and to Mexico. As we embark upon the "Pacific Century," an age in which the increasingly large presence of Asians in America reflects continuing global ruptures and unexpected alliances, we take this opportunity to pause and trace the changes, note the heterogeneity, and admire the tenacity of immigrants who continue to live in a racially hostile world. As the Wen Ho Lee case shows, a pervasive and simultaneous politics of polarity has come to define the Chinese experience in America.[6]

DEFYING STEREOTYPES: THE EARLIEST ARRIVALS

From the 1370s to 1893, China's official imperial policy outlawed emigration. Chinese who migrated outside of China were considered vagabonds, outlaws, and fugitives, unless their leave was formally approved, in which case they were considered temporary guests of another country. If travelers dared to return to China without having proper approval for being outside the country, law dictated that they be punished as criminals.[7] While these official policies probably dissuaded some Chinese from emigrating, the lack of strict enforcement, along with the growing incentive to develop business and trade enterprises in Southeast Asia, in particular, meant that emigration patterns were slowly being established, despite laws to the contrary. By the nineteenth century, China witnessed its greatest outflow of emigrants to North and Central America and, by the end of the century, the Qing court realized that Chinese living outside the country might not threaten China by mounting oppositional forces to the government but could, instead, be an asset to the empire.

In contrast to traditional China, modern China encouraged emigration because it eased domestic unemployment tensions, created business and investment linkages between China and overseas communities, and guaranteed a significant national income from international sources, due to the cultural practice of sending home remittances.[8] Reciprocally, China oversaw education and identity-retention programs for overseas Chinese and served as their diplomatic protectorate, negotiating the Burlingame Treaty with the United States in 1868 to ensure the "free migration and emigration of their citizens and subjects respectively, from one country to the other, for the purpose of curiosity, of trade, or as permanent residents"[9] and successfully pressuring the United States during World War II to repeal the Chinese Exclusion Laws as part of a wartime alliance with China, just to name two examples.[10]

Southeast Asia served as host to the first main group of Chinese émigrés, and North America was their second regional target. The history of Chinese in America conventionally begins with the discovery of gold at Sutter's Mill, California, in 1849 and the ensuing wave of immigrants who were "pushed" from war, flood, and political turmoil in Guangdong, the southernmost province of China, and "pulled" to a New World that promised streets lined with gold (a unique commodity in Chinese culture that is considered fiscally inviolate). Historians tell us that there were four waves of Chinese immigration to the United States but that the first two waves (from 1849 to 1882 and from 1882 to 1943) consisted primarily of illiterate and unskilled "sojourners" who traveled to California with the intent of striking it rich and returning to China.[11] These bachelors worked in some of the only industries open to them at the time—working as miners, railroad workers, and farmers—and these jobs as laborers unfortunately contributed to a perception of the Chinese as peasants and opportunists who had few alternatives besides immigration. This impression proved damaging when, in 1882, an Exclusion Law was passed that explicitly barred Chinese laborers from immigrating into the United States (diplomats, tourists, merchants, teachers, and scholars were exempted). This law specifically discriminated according to class and was the first and only law passed in the United States that explicitly prohibited immigrants on the basis of race. Notably, the core provisions of the law were renewed ten times before being abolished sixty years later.

New research that considers global perspectives in addition to domestic trends reveals a more complex profile of the early Chinese in the United States. Haiming Liu suggests that many Chinese who immigrated were not from the poorest and lowest echelons of society with few options for earning a living besides leaving their homes. Using immigration theory, he reveals a more heterogeneous profile of the early Chinese, arguing that many nineteenth-century Chinese travelers to America were skilled workers and ambitious businessmen who immigrated to improve their social standing. David Valentine's chapter on placer mining demonstrates through case study what Liu's paper suggests through historical analysis. Based on archaeological evidence, Valentine argues that some Chinese immigrants to American Canyon, Nevada, during the gold mining period may not have been novice miners, as commonly believed. Some Chinese were likely experienced miners who brought with them water management technology and unique placer mining expertise. My chapter on Ah Quin raises questions about the stereotype of an illiterate Chinese workforce through the study of a nineteenth-century, ten-volume diary written mostly in English. The length, grammar, and mastery of the language displayed in this personal narrative confounds assumptions that the Chinese could not speak or write in English, further supporting Liu's assertion that some Chinese immigrants were both literate and skilled.

Together, the chapters in the first section of this book complicate the profile of the early Chinese immigrants, helping to question the stereotype of Chinese immigrants as exclusively from the lowest echelons in Chinese society while suggesting a more heterogeneous and talented workforce that possessed job skills and literacy in English.

DISCRIMINATION AND EXCLUSION ACROSS AMERICA
During the century and a half of Chinese presence in America, the three nation-states that make up the geographical territory of North America—Canada, the United States, and Mexico—enacted parallel legislation that discriminated specifically against the Chinese, even as the repercussions of that legislation adversely affected neighboring nation-states. For instance, the tax

that made manifest California's desire to discourage Chinese from immigrating to the gold mines (the 1850 and 1852 Foreign Miner's Tax) was mirrored in Canada with the 1853 Head Tax, which forced Chinese to pay a surcharge of Can$50 to enter Canada.[12] When mining and immigration fees were not sufficient to quell the flow of Chinese, both the United States and Canada enacted more severe legislation in the form of exclusion laws that expressly forbade Chinese entrance to these countries.[13] Forbidden or banished from Canadian and U.S. territories, many Chinese traveled south of the border to Mexico and particularly to Baja California, where they were initially welcomed as diligent workers but later expelled as threats to an emerging indigenous economy.[14] By the early twentieth century, Chinese from Canada and the United States (and new immigrants from across the Pacific) were migrating further and further south, from Sonora and Sinaloa, Mexico (where exclusion laws were eventually enacted), to Cuba and the Caribbean. When immigration laws in the United States opened up again in 1965, the domino effect of migration brought the Chinese north again.

Given the tomes of laws that fined, excluded, expropriated, and exiled the Chinese from Canada to Mexico, one theme in studies of Chinese emigration to America has remained resoundingly and regrettably the same: racial discrimination. Despite their success—or perhaps as a result of it—Chinese have been the targets of legislative bias and the victims of social violence. Admittedly, anti-Chinese legislation may be easier to track than Chinese hate crimes; however, the number and brutality of attacks against Chinese recorded for the last half of the nineteenth century are still astonishing. Robert Chang estimates that more than 300 Chinese were murdered between 1860 and 1887. According to Victor Jew, in the United States alone from 1850 to 1908, there were 153 recorded instances of anti-Chinese violence. Of those, 143 Chinese were murdered and 10,525 were displaced from their homes.[15] The degree of violence not only calls attention to the severity of these crimes and the hostility of the communities into which many Chinese immigrated, but it also serves to highlight the tenacity and perseverance of those who continued to live in a racially hostile world.

The second section of this book attempts to build upon the well-established narrative of Chinese discrimination and forced migration by exploring these themes in uncharted territories east of California and north of the U.S. border. Anti-Chinese riots are not new to Chinese American history. They have been well documented, primarily on the West Coast, in places like Seattle, Tacoma, and San Francisco, but also in Denver and Rock Springs, Wyoming.[16] The chapters in this section show that even in regions such as the Midwest and Southwest, where relatively few Chinese resided, deep-seated prejudice was expressed publicly and violently as a part of complex social and cultural factors regarding threats to labor, economics, and sexual morality. Victor Jew recovers a long-forgotten anti-Chinese riot in Milwaukee, Wisconsin, in 1889 that is noteworthy for its location as well as for its stimulus. Although most anti-Chinese riots were ignited as a result of a perceived threat to white labor, this incident was sparked by alleged cases of illicit, interracial, pedophilic intercourse. Despite its front-page coverage in the newspapers of the time, the Milwaukee riot has been forgotten in the annals of Asian American and Midwestern history. Elmer Rusco gives a familiar account of anti-Chinese armed expulsion in the less familiar mining town of Unionville, Nevada. Rusco argues that, despite good-faith intentions to prosecute the anti-Chinese vigilantes, a myriad of judicial and political forces stood in the way, ironically resulting in increased rather than decreased discrimination. The recovery of these little-known yellow peril events helps flesh out the breadth and degree of injury inflicted upon the Chinese. In both cases, we see genuine efforts for criminal prosecution, but we also see a judicial system rendered futile by cultural bias and political influence.

Nancy Lee continues this exploration of discrimination and exclusion into Canada. She approaches the study of history by focusing on a Chinese Canadian novel, Denise Chong's *The Concubine's Children: Portrait of a Family Divided,* and discusses the use of biography and the literary tropes that it accommodates as a way of recounting a Chinese Canadian history filled with racism. Comparing the way events are narrated in Canadian school history books to excerpts from the novel, Lee unearths deep-seated prejudice institutionalized in Canada's educational system. This historiographical approach, she argues, offers an unconventional but more realistic way to process some of the stories that history confronts.

That Chinese were consistently and violently persecuted is not news, but the fact that many Chinese immigrants prospered even while living in a racially hostile world is impressive by any standard. That a model minority legacy, however problematic,[17] could eventually emerge even in the face of such past violence is remarkable. The success of the Chinese, especially when measured against their despicable treatment, calls attention again to the polar extremes that have come to define their experience.

LIVELIHOOD IN THE NEW WORLD

Like other immigrant groups, Chinese were enticed to America by the promise of honest work for honest wages. Taking advantage of the credit-ticket system, many Chinese came to America to work on the railroads, and they composed as much as 90 percent of the labor force of the Central Pacific Railroad at one time.[18] When the railroad was complete, Chinese moved into agriculture (tenant farming and irrigation development), manufacturing (shoes, woolens, and cigars), and small business, where they established laundries, restaurants, and garment factories, just to name a few enterprises. It is clear, however, that widespread racism and discrimination severely restricted job access.

The exclusion of the Chinese from the photograph that memorialized the completion of the Transcontinental Railroad at Promontory Point, Utah—despite the fact that the railroad was built owing much to Chinese labor—is representative of their continued debarment and dismissal in the American workplace. From the Foreign Miner's Tax to the fourteen laundry ordinances passed in San Francisco to fine and curtail Chinese establishments, discriminatory measures drove the Chinese from one workplace to another. As labor unions and legislative bodies successfully exiled them from an increasing array of employment opportunities (mining, railroads, farming, factories), they were forced into more and more self-contained industries, often in service to other Chinese, in local Chinatowns or via export to China. Of note is the renewed theme of a versatile and knowledgeable workforce that, even under duress, proved itself viable in a variety of fields.

To understand how such an oppressive level of discrimination could be legally and perpetually instituted in the workplace, it is necessary to interrogate the widespread cultural perceptions that led to such legislation and bias. To this end, Shirley Tam explores the depiction of the coolie image in turn-of-the-century periodicals. Tam demonstrates how underlying prejudices are often manifested in constructions of race, with the Chinese being depicted overwhelmingly in condescending or derogatory ways—even by those who were ostensibly sympathetic. Interestingly, she argues that the Chinese became scapegoats for two opposing camps: their image was manipulated to advance the arguments of exclusionists as well as sympathizers in a double-edged sword in which their portrayal was exploited at the same moment that their low status was reconfirmed. Linda Bentz and Robert Schwemmer provide us with an example of how the derogatory and politicized cultural perceptions of Chinese identified by Tam were enacted to destroy the productive Chinese fishing industry in California. They explore the nineteenth-century history of Chinese fishing and junk building and argue that Chinese were skilled fishermen who imported industry knowledge from China and exported goods back to China. Legislation against them in the fishing, shrimp, and abalone industries demonstrates, once again, the pervasiveness of their oppression.

Excluded from mainstream work, the Chinese exercised a diligent work ethic and vocational ingenuity that allowed them to develop new occupations, one of which is explored by Dolores Young. In her case study of seaweed gatherers in the Central Coast of California, Young shows how a small number of Chinese for almost a century used the seaweed *Ulva* to generate a new local food product that became an industry for export. In spite of the labor-intensive work, she suggests (like Valentine with placer miners) that these rugged individualists brought with them specialized knowledge and skills that allowed them to earn a living while contributing uniquely to their communities.

Finally, we turn to an essay that documents a vocation from an Old World past that continues to attract New World attention. William Bowen, an anthropologist, studies the Chinese medicinal industry and shows how, unlike the seaweed gatherers' self-containment, the Chinese medicinal industry prospered by opening up to non-Chinese in terms of both patients and practitioners. Bowen analyzes advertisements, case histories, and career trends, particularly with reference to San Diego, to show that Chinese medicine is an important industry that has survived from the earliest immigrants to the present. He argues that like those in other industries, Chinese practitioners of medicine experienced legalized discrimination and that they persevered to make important contributions to the treatment of psychological and physical ailments.

The chapters in this section expand the canon of Chinese livelihood to tell the stories of some of the lesser-known vocations that were viable in the past and, in Bowen's case, that remain prevalent today. These stories help us fill out the history of a skilled and diversified Chinese workforce that developed even in the face of pervasive labor discrimination.

INFLUENCES: FROM OLD WORLD TO NEW WORLD

Wang Gungwu, in *The Encyclopedia of the Chinese Overseas*, writes, "There is a tendency among many Chinese to attribute every success they have to the uniqueness and superiority of Chinese culture. This is sometimes exaggerated to the point of incredulity, notably by those with chauvinist or nationalist agendas. . . . On the other hand, it is not possible to avoid the question of Chinese culture."[19] In the academic world, however, Asian American studies has historically shied away from discussions that link Asian immigrants (and their descendants) to their ancestral homelands in favor of explorations that link these travelers to their adopted countries. This disciplinary penchant exists for a number of good reasons, among them a more immediate desire to help erase unfair and derogatory assumptions about Asians who have been linked stereotypically to the Old World and a concomitant dedication to promoting Asians as legitimate—instead of prohibited—members of their adopted nations. The fourth section of this book is a particularly valuable contribution to the scholarship, since it takes as its organizing theme the often avoided but inescapable influences carried from Old World into New World.

Without trying to prioritize or favor Old World or New World values, the chapters in this section inquire into the social organizations and cultural attributes that the Chinese brought with them to the New World. In response to the *myth* of immigration—that travelers to a New World are greeted with a cultural carte blanche that can be consciously and deliberately inscribed with the worthy values of the Old World while not being contaminated by the unworthy values of the New World—the chapters here suggest that sociocultural transformation is dynamic: it is neither wholly conscious nor unconscious, wholly controlled nor controllable. It proceeds, instead, according to circumstance, often resulting in surprising medleys and mélanges.

The first two chapters explore two different Chinese social organizations that developed branches in America. Although both were originally formed for political ends in China, these organizations made important contributions to Chinese American politics and culture. More specifically, Jane Leung Larson describes Chinese American political activism as initiated by the Baohuanghui. This international conglomerate, made up mostly of overseas Chinese, was originally formed to help establish a modern constitutional monarchy in China; however, it soon catalyzed a variety of other political actions and played a crucial role in mobilizing an anti-American boycott in China to protest the American exclusion of Chinese. Their effective organizing led to the growth of Chinese civil society both in China and abroad and solidified the place of the Chinese in America as a political interest group. Sue Fawn Chung explores a related organization, the Zhigongtang, and shows how Chinese immigrants without family or friends in frontier America at the turn of the century entrusted their fate in the afterlife to this "Chinese Free Mason Society." A close examination of several Zhigongtang funerals shows that their burial practices were an amalgamation of traditional Chinese and modern American rituals. Accordingly, Chung argues, the Chinese were not unassimilable foreigners, as was often maintained. The Zhigongtang funerals demonstrate an increasing degree of acculturation to common American practices.

The next set of essays explore gender from male and female perspectives and demonstrate the relevance of traditional Chinese culture, even for second-generation, American-born Chinese. Sheldon Zhang focuses on the Chinese American delinquent boy and applies family stress theory and criminology theory to argue that traditional Chinese familial and cultural values, even in the United States, can be effectively used for social control. In contrast to Chung, whose essay demonstrates increased accommodation to U.S. values, Zhang reminds us of the reverse—that even in an environment that might encourage acculturation, traditional Chinese values can have a powerful impact on second-generation immigrants. Bonnie Khaw-Posthuma's study of Chinese (American) women serves as a nice complement to Zhang's research. She bridges the gap between Old World and New World by taking footbinding as the symbol of Old World patriarchy and showing how this practice has been appropriated in Chinese American literature as a symbol for the new Asian American woman. Interrogating the trope of footbinding as it appears in texts by Maxine Hong Kingston, Jade Snow Wong, Ruthann Lum McCunn, and Pang-Mei Chang, Khaw-Posthuma argues that footbinding is deployed as a metaphorical symbol for a freer Asian American female subjectivity. Her interdisciplinary study draws on sociological, historical, and literary findings to demonstrate that a new and improved gendered paradigm can arise from the "unwrapping" of the Old.

Zhiwei Xiao's piece complicates this theme of Old World influences by including a third layer of discussion: he examines Chinese perceptions of American film renditions of Chinese, specifically in the case of the film *The Good Earth* (based on the Pearl Buck novel). Although this film was lauded in the United States for its "sympathetic" portrayal of Chinese characters, Xiao argues that this film's poor reception amid protests in China testifies to the difficulty of filmic translations of cultural and identity politics. In problematizing the influences of Old World upon New, film is seen as an international vehicle for representing contemporary cultural issues, such as stereotyping, censorship, and national politics.

As bookends for this section, the Larson and Xiao pieces call attention to the complicated global dimensions of identity politics. From Larson's examination of America's perception of a Chinese overseas organization in America, to Xiao's analysis of the Chinese perception of American renditions of Chinese, the critical gaze in this section turns full circle to more completely realize the paradigmatic possibilities of Old World and New World influences. These multiple vantage points underscore the overlapping themes of nationalism and ethnocentrism entrenched within global identity politics. As a result, the chapters in this section ultimately display the unavoidable influences of China on (Chinese) America, while simultaneously suggesting the notable distance between the two.

ESTABLISHING A CHINESE AMERICAN IDENTITY

Perhaps the most difficult issue with which immigrants (and those who study them) must struggle is the issue of identity. What we can be sure of is that Chinese Americans are indisputably different from Chinese in China, but how they are different is far less clear. The section on identity mirrors the multidisciplinary concern borne by this topic and includes essays based both on praxis and in theory. Informed by the bicultural and assimilationist models of identity formation, these chapters explore and then build upon these conventional paradigms, suggesting increasingly diverse possibilities for Chinese American subjectivity. Viewing identity as centrally located in ancestry, community, politics, culture, and family, these chapters make clearer the complexity involved in identity negotiations and give us a sense of the different means and models currently available for conceiving of and arriving at a bicultural and heterogeneous Chinese American self.

We begin with Albert Cheng and Him Mark Lai's report on the success of the "In Search of Roots" program. This eleven-year-old community-based program accepts students into an intensive study about Chinese ancestry that culminates in a visit to their ancestral villages in China. This chapter demonstrates how the recovery of family history aids in the development of biculturalism through resinicization. Murray Lee addresses the issue of community patriarchy and its role in establishing an ethnic enclave in his chapter on Ah Quin. As a role model and founding father of San Diego's Chinese American community, Ah Quin raised twelve children and served as a cultural ambassador and go-between in affairs between Chinese and non-Chinese in San Diego's early Chinatown district. Together, these chapters lay a firm foundation of conventional bicultural and assimilationist scholarship, respectively.

The next three chapters attempt to complicate the "either/or" and "blended" paradigms for identity formation by examining different case studies that reveal the politics of selfhood. Echoing Larson's study of political activism, Chiou-ling Yeh looks at Chinese American youth who protested against the inclusion of only "model minority" stereotypes in the festivals celebrated within Chinatown. Yeh's analysis of the San Francisco Chinatown New Year Festival establishes heterogeneity as central to Chinese American community politics and takes as its point of departure the intergenerational conflicts that are typical in areas with continuing waves of new immigrants.

Two theoretical explorations, both based in literature, follow. Yuan Yuan's exploration of subjectivity takes as its focus a literary configuration that he calls the "China narrative" as it is depicted in two of Amy Tan's novels. He provides a sophisticated analysis of the concept of recollection as a translation and distortion of experience. The mothers' China narratives, he argues, occupy a semiotic space of recollection that is perceived by mothers as a loss of history and identity while simultaneously used by mothers to enact authoritative dominion over their daughters. For daughters, the China narrative is a historical and cultural construction that they can only see from the point of view of their mothers (who are notably unreliable sources). Yuan suggests that the inherent disjuncture between mothers and daughters in terms of their perceptions of China and Chineseness is at the heart of the tensions in Tan's mother-daughter relationships. Vivian Chin interrogates another Chinese American novel, Fae Myenne Ng's *Bone*, and posits that rituals are not simply products of cultural identity, but are complicit in shaping it. In *Bone*, Chin proposes that performance acts say more than speech acts. Instead of the assimilationist paradigm where a Chinese American's goal is to become American, Chin argues that the end-goal in *Bone* is to become a certain kind of acceptable Chinese American. This controversial perspective presumes heterogeneous Chinese American identities that are set against the more monolithic and homogeneous archetypes often discussed.

Taken together, these chapters offer a set of paradigms for the exploration and discovery—in praxis and in theory—of a self-assured, uncompromised Chinese American self.

CHINESE AMERICA: SETTLED

China's labeling of its emigrants as "overseas Chinese," or *huaqiao*, implies an unquestioned loyalty to the homeland that suggests that Chinese are always rooted to China and that they have a patriotic obligation to return from overseas and help to enrich "their" country.[20] According to historians, this perception of Chinese as sojourners (rather than settlers) was shared, at least in intent, by a majority of early Chinese immigrants, about half of whom actually returned to China and many more of whom wanted to return but lacked the necessary resources.[21] China's presumption that its emigrants would return to China has been encouraged by host countries in the form of social violence and legislative action that demonstrate that the citizenry of the Americas has wanted nothing less than the dismantling of Chinese ethnic enclaves and the return to China of Chinese living abroad.

Against pressure from China and from host countries, Chinese formed overseas settlements almost from the beginning. Even the passage of the Page Law in 1875, which effectively prevented Chinese women from immigrating to the United States, truncating efforts to establish Chinese families and settlements (miscegenation laws would make it illegal for Chinese to marry non-Chinese), did not keep the Chinese from establishing multigenerational communities, many of which existed for decades. The development of these ethnic enclaves has, for the most part, followed a recognizable pattern: communities have evolved from bachelor labor groups to relatively homogeneous Chinatown societies, to the heterogeneous, multilingual, and multiethnic Chinatowns we see today. Chinese community members eventually participate in local politics, engage in factionalism, and reflect alliances from China in their adopted countries.

The final unit in this book helps to demonstrate that many Chinese in America were not simply sojourners, but from the beginning were settlers who made interesting and long-lasting contributions. Arranged in rough chronological order, the chapters in this section demonstrate a solidification of the Chinese penchant for settling, from some of the earliest Chinatowns to the more contemporary and suburban Chinese American communities. Based on archaeological evidence recovered from the site of Woolen Mills Chinatown (established in 1887), Scott Baxter and Rebecca Allen piece together a picture of what life was like for its inhabitants prior to the destruction of their community by arson in 1902. Baxter and Allen's archeological findings demonstrate through material history a theme similar to one echoed throughout this volume, that Chinese were not, as locals thought, unclean and unsophisticated. They created for themselves a well-planned and highly functional city.

Catalina Velázquez Morales reminds us that Chinese immigrants to America settled not only in northern California, but also in Baja California. Her chapter is interesting not only for its recounting of a typical settlement pattern in a less typical region, but for the fact that it has been translated from Spanish and relies almost entirely on Spanish-language primary and secondary sources. These Spanish-language sources interestingly confirm that Chinese experiences in Baja roughly paralleled the discrimination and dislocation experienced to the north. Despite these hardships—or perhaps as a result of them—the Chinese there were also able to found successful ethnic communities. As they grew in prosperity, Velázquez Morales asserts, the Chinese in Baja followed a typical progression by migrating from the fields to the cities, from agricultural work to entrepreneurial work, largely as the result of savvy business alliances and reliable social organizations.

marie rose wong gives a contrasting paradigm to Velázquez Morales's more conventional pattern by exploring the unique spatial arrangement of the Chinatown in Portland, Oregon, the largest Chinatown prior to 1900. Wong argues that this community's arrangement and accommodation of urban as well as rural areas distinguishes it from other Chinatowns, and she questions whether it can be called an ethnic enclave at all. And Ying Zeng continues this theme by focusing on the San Diego Chinese community in the contemporary time period and exploring its geographical and political diversity. Analyzing two case studies, Zeng demonstrates how, in the absence of a geographically defined Chinatown, ethnic ties join Chinese groups together to form productive solidarities.

Significantly, the focus of this volume has been the Chinese who stayed in America and who, over a century and a half, founded a legacy of community and history even in the face of miner's taxes, exclusion laws, social violence, and criminal prosecution. According to the most recent census, at 2.4 million, the Chinese are the largest Asian immigrant group in the United States; and they inhabit perhaps the most extensive ethnic settlements. These settlers have made their homes in urban and remote locations, from east to west and north to south. Yet in the same year that we can celebrate the appointment of the first Asian American to the U.S. president's cabinet,[22] we see a fellow Asian American, Fu Manchu-like, being prosecuted by administrators in that very same cabinet. The story of Wen Ho Lee reminds us that Chinese are unusual in the annals of American immigrant history in the sense that they have been considered so esteemed and so despicable, so desired and so repudiated. The fact that a highly skilled Chinese scientist can be hired in a nuclear weapons lab and then made into a political scapegoat is, in many ways, a natural extension of a past filled with the paradoxes of orientalism and exclusion. In uncovering new layers of knowledge concerning the lives and experiences of Chinese from Canada to Baja California, from California to Washington, D.C., this collection complicates and in some cases resists the received wisdom of the 150-year history of the Chinese in America.

For the future, we can predict with certainty only one unfortunate reality: Asia's position on the world stage will, as always, affect Asians abroad, who have been persecuted when relations between Asia and host countries are poor and favored when those relations are good. As this book goes to press, another incident has hit the front pages that confirms this fact again: an American spy plane has collided with a Chinese fighter plane and has been forced to make an emergency landing in China. The twenty-four American crew members were held by China for eleven days before being allowed to return home, and China has yet to release the plane itself. During those eleven days, the Organization of Chinese Americans published a report citing increased domestic hostility toward Chinese in America, including calls by radio announcers for Chinese American internment and the boycott of Chinese restaurants. These continuing incidents ultimately remind us of the tenuousness of acceptance in a land where the domestic economy and overseas relations may have more to do with success (and failure) than hard work and skill. These international events demonstrate that racial discord is not simply rooted in the color of one's skin or the accent of one's speech, but in complex historical, economic, and political circumstances. As we usher in a time when optimists predict favor for Asian countries (and by extension their immigrants and their descendants) and pessimists fear the worst, we can rest on this cusp of the millennium assured of one hopeful conclusion: that understanding the past may help us to improve the future.

NOTES

Thanks are due to Ling-chi Wang, whose keynote address at the 1999 Chinese American Conference in San Diego remarked upon Wen Ho Lee and the Democratic campaign finance scandal and inspired this essay. My thanks also to Haiming Liu, Jane Leung Larson, and Robert Chang for their invaluable comments on an earlier version of this introduction. I would like to dedicate my work on this book to my mother and father, who taught me what it is to be Chinese (and) American and to the memory of my uncle Sunny Liang who drew the characters for the cover of this book. He would have been proud to see this work in print.

1. Notably, he's the first person ever to be charged with violating certain U.S. statutes that protect classified information, and these charges could have led to life imprisonment. As a former nuclear missile launch officer with the U.S. Air Force, I can attest to the fact that it is highly unusual to publicly prosecute security infractions, not only because of the possible additional compromise of classified information that might be necessary for such prosecution, but also because commanders and managers placed in the position to report security infractions risk damage to their reputations and careers as a result of those reports. Often, violators are given internal warnings or reprimands so as not to draw additional attention to

an already sensitive and embarrassing situation. Against this backdrop, the very public prosecution of Dr. Wen Ho Lee can be seen to be even more unusual.

2. Dr. Lee pled guilty to a single felony count of mishandling national-defense information.

3. For a sense of the tense political climate between the United States and China from 1999 to 2000, consider that within the space of about one year Wen Ho Lee was arrested and accused of espionage based on the flimsiest of evidence; the United States (mistakenly) bombed the Chinese embassy in Belgrade, Yugoslavia; Taiwan elected a president from the Democratic Progressive Party (which supports Taiwanese independence); and renewed fears of a Taiwanese declaration of independence provoked saber rattling from China and pressured American politicians (again) to choose between a controversial alliance with Taiwan, as suggested by the 1979 Taiwan Relations Act, or alliance with China, as encouraged by its "most favored nation" status (now called "normal trade relations"). Taken together, these events provide a backdrop for an election year filled with anti-Chinese American sentiment.

4. Specifically, Democratic vice president Gore was accused of accepting illegal foreign contributions from Chinese donors and Republican representative Christopher Cox issued the "Cox Report" alleging China had a vast spy network in the United States. As one journalist has argued, Wen Ho Lee was the fulcrum of a Republican attempt to show that the Democrats were soft on communism because, according to the theory, the Clinton presidency was soft on Chinese nuclear espionage. See Anthony Lewis, "Abroad at Home," *New York Times* on the web, 16 September 2000, www.nytimes.com.

5. James Risen and Jeff Gerth, "Breach at Los Alamos: A Special Report. China Stole Nuclear Secrets for Bombs, U.S. Aides Say," *New York Times*, 6 March 1999, www.nytimes.com

6. I use "America" advisedly to refer to the geographical territory of the North American continent, including Canada, the United States, and Mexico. By contrast, I use "United States" to refer to the American nation-state.

7. Wang Gungwu, *The Chinese Overseas: From Earthbound China to the Quest for Autonomy* (Cambridge, Mass.: Harvard University Press, 2000), 43–44.

8. One study shows that between 1871 and 1931, remittances from overseas Chinese accounted for 41 percent of China's international balance of payments. See Leo M. Douw, "Overseas Chinese Remittances," in *The Encyclopedia of the Chinese Overseas*, ed. Lynn Pan (Cambridge, Mass.: Harvard University Press, 1999), 110.

9. As quoted in Roger Daniels, *Asian America: Chinese and Japanese in the United States since 1850* (Seattle: University of Washington Press, 1988), 37.

10. Of note, the repeal included all or the core parts of the fifteen exclusionary statutes passed between 1882 and 1913.

11. The third wave covers 1943–1965 and the fourth wave 1965 to the present. See Sucheng Chan, *Entry Denied: Exclusion and the Chinese Community in America, 1882–1943* (Philadelphia: Temple University Press, 1991), preface. Note that Gary Okihiro argues that Western perceptions of Chinese must take into account a prehistory that begins with Hippocrates in the fifth century B.C.E. If this is the case, then we may speak of five eras of Chinese American history. See Gary Okihiro, *Margins and Mainstreams* (Seattle: University of Washington Press, 1996). On sojourners, see Ronald Takaki, *A Different Mirror* (Boston: Little, Brown, 1993).

12. From 1885 to 1923 Canada imposed a series of head taxes on Chinese entrance to Canada that started at Can$50 in 1885 and grew to Can$500 by 1903.

13. In 1923, Canada passed the Chinese Immigration Act, which set a quota for Chinese so low (twenty-four) that it effectively excluded entry.

14. Mexican states, like Sonora in 1930, passed a series of laws that effectively limited Chinese labor and thus immigration.

15. See Robert Chang, "Why We Need a Critical Asian American Legal Studies," in *Asian American Studies: A Reader,* ed. Jean Yu-wen Shen Wu and Min Song (New Brunswick, N.J.: Rutgers University Press, 2000), 368. Note that "Robert" is misprinted as "Richard" in the article itself. See also Jew, chapter 4 in this volume.

16. See Sucheng Chan, "Hostility and Conflict," in *Asian American Studies,* Wu and Song ed., 47–66.

17. On the problematics of the model minority hypothesis, see Sucheng Chan, *Asian Americans: An Interpretive History* (New York: Twayne, 1991), 167–71.

18. See Takaki, *A Different Mirror,* 197.

19. Wang Gungwu, "Introduction," in *Encyclopedia,* Pan ed., 11.

20. For a thorough discussion of the huaqiao, see Wang Gungwu, *The Chinese Overseas.*

21. See Philip Q. Yang, "Sojourners or Settlers: Post-1965 Chinese Immigrants," *JAAS* 2, no. 1 (1999): 61–91.

22. Norm Mineta, a Japanese Hawaiian, was appointed secretary of commerce under President William J. Clinton.

I

Defying Stereotypes:
The Earliest Arrivals

1

The Social Origins of Early Chinese Immigrants: A Revisionist Perspective

Haiming Liu

INTERPRETATIONS OF CHINESE IMMIGRATION

Much of what was once assumed about the early Chinese immigrants now seems stereotypical. Stereotypes die hard. This chapter aims to reject the long-accepted assumptions that nineteenth-century Chinese immigrants came from the lowest social class, and that Chinese emigration to the United States was a desperate escape from poverty and hunger—that Chinese were considered part of the "huddled masses" bound to the United States for mere survival. Apparently, such stereotypes bear the influence of the assimilationist school of immigration studies.

The assimilationist model of immigration studies arose in the 1920s with Thomas and Znaniecki's *The Polish Peasant in Europe and America,* and with the work of Chicago school sociologists, such as Robert Park.[1] According to assimilationist scholars, immigration to the United States is a process of social disorganization, adjustment, and Americanization. Immigrants were poverty-driven, illiterate, and socially unrelated individuals uprooted from traditional societies. As traditional ethnic and family or kinship ties to the home country quickly dissolved, mainstream society gradually absorbed immigrants who suffered alienation after their entry into U.S. society. Assimilation is seen as the ultimate goal for all immigrants. This model, readily applied to Irish, Polish, Greek, and Italian immigrants, viewed the United States as the final destination of immigrants, treated human migration as a one-way trip, and defined U.S. society as a "melting pot."

Most writings on Chinese immigration published before the 1970s viewed Chinese in terms of the classical assimilationist school, focusing on the mainstream U.S. response to Chinese immigrants and the Chinese adaptation to the new country. A key concept in assimilationist interpretations of early Chinese immigrants is "sojourner." According to Gunther Barth, a typical assimilationist scholar, the Chinese came to the United States to earn quick cash and had no desire to settle down in America. Their cultural linkage to China and loyalty to traditional values prevented them from becoming part of U.S. society.[2] In her study on the origins of Chinese emigration, June Mei also concluded that Chinese immigration to California generally consisted of "poor men of rural background," and their uprooting was out of necessity rather than choice.[3] Kil Young Zo also insists that Chinese immigrants, different from Europeans, were poor and illiterate peasants from poverty-stricken villages in Taishan County who came with the sole purpose of making money and who had no desire to make permanent homes in a strange country. Chinese culture traditionally discouraged the Chinese from emigrating overseas.[4]

Since the 1980s, the study of Chinese in the United States has entered a new stage. Discrimination, community, and identity have become major issues of focus as more and more Asian American scholars have entered the field. The most influential scholars include Sucheng Chan and Ronald Takaki. These scholars see the experiences of Chinese as comparable to those of African or Latino immigrants to the United States, and they emphasize how the Chinese, like other Asians, became a racial minority group in the United States. The right for Asians to claim their Americanness is the dominant theme in their writings. In rejecting the "sojourner" concept, for example, Sucheng Chan and Ronald Takaki have convincingly demonstrated that the Chinese were also settlers and active participants in U.S. economic and social life. Their major criticism of mainstream U.S. historiography is its exclusion of Asians. However, few of the studies on Chinese Americans in the 1980s challenged the stereotypes of Chinese culture.

Ironically, assimilationalist interpretations of Chinese immigrants often begin by stereotyping Chinese culture. In such writings, Chinese culture is viewed as static and conservative in contrast to a modern, dynamic Western society. Chinese society is perceived as a self-contained agricultural world with a landbound rural population. Chinese emigration to the United States is described as an exotic adventure that collides with traditional Chinese values; and the Chinese immigrants are viewed as people who take little initiative in controlling their own destinies. Chinese tradition is even held responsible for discouraging women from coming to the United States together with Chinese men.

The long-standing Western view of Chinese civilization as isolationist and conservative—and Chinese society as backward and poor—may even influence some Asian American scholars' understanding of Chinese culture. For example, in his 1998 edition of *Strangers from a Different Shore: A History of Asian Americans,* Ronald Takaki describes Chinese immigrants as people "driven by harsh economic conditions to seek survival elsewhere"; he says they were "generally illiterate or had very little schooling. . . . Moreover, Chinese tradition and culture limited the possibilities of migration for women."[5] Defining Chinese immigration as a survival strategy implies that poverty is the major push factor in immigration to the United States. Treating Chinese immigrants as an undifferentiated low-class group fails to explain the dynamics and complexity of the Chinese immigration process. Though Takaki's book rejects assimilationist viewpoints, his own assumption about the social origin of Chinese immigrants still leads people to think of Asian immigration in terms of a linear progression from traditional culture toward Americanization.

A REVISIONIST PERSPECTIVE

Having recognized the limitations of the classical assimilationist paradigm, revisionist scholars like Samuel Baily, Philip Curtin, Roger Daniels, Virginia Yans-McLaughlin, and Ewa Morawska have posed new perspectives about immigrants and the immigration process. As a result, a new synthesis that begins to address the complexity of human migration has emerged. For instance, most revisionist scholars agree that immigrants tend to come from a variety of social backgrounds rather than solely from the lowest economic class and the poorest region.[6] Morawska points out that, contrary to the well-established stereotype of the "huddled masses," most U.S.-bound migrants, while certainly poor by absolute and relative standards, did not originate from the poorest regions and were not members of the lowest economic classes, but rather came from the lower and lower-middle ranks of their home societies.[7] Many immigrants from the south of Italy, according to Yans-McLaughlin, were more energetic and better-educated than those who stayed behind.[8] Immigrants appear to have possessed levels of education and labor skills above the average in their home countries.

In general, immigrants are people with strong desires to maintain or improve their social and economic status at home by seeking opportunities overseas. Immigration is also a family-oriented, group-sustained, and socially embedded migratory activity that involves people in kinship or other social relations. Once reaching its momentum, an immigration movement can sustain itself for several generations. In such circumstances, human migration becomes a local tradition.

Examining the social origins of early Chinese immigrants through a revisionist paradigm, I found substantially different results when compared to existing conclusions about this subject, especially regarding the immigrants' class background, literacy, and immigration motivations. I believe that most early Chinese immigrants probably belonged to the middle- and lower-middle-class ranks of Chinese society rather than the lowest social classes. The nineteenth-century emigration region in Guangdong was a place with a tradition of migration, diversified commercial activities, prevalent lineage organizations, and a competitive environment. A highly motivated people with considerable literacy had lived in the region for generations. Developing a revisionist perspective on the social origins of early Chinese immigrants renders a more accurate description of them and is crucial to shattering some of the deep-rooted stereotypes of Chinese immigrants.

EARLY CHINESE IMMIGRATION

Beginning in the mid-nineteenth century, the Chinese became the first large stream of Asian immigrants to arrive in the United States, with approximately 370,000 arriving between 1840 and 1880 from Guangdong Province.[9] In Hawaii, Chinese immigrants worked on sugar plantations. More diversified occupations existed in California, where the Chinese mined gold; built railroads; grew wheat, vegetables, and fruits; worked in cigar, clothes, and shoe-making factories; opened laundries, restaurants, groceries, and gift shops; and provided herbal medicine services in California (see Bowen, chapter 10 in this volume). In the Northwest, in addition to these occupations, the Chinese also worked in salmon canneries. In pursuing these economic opportunities, Chinese immigrants played a vital role in the social and cultural development of the American West.

Chinese emigrated across seven thousand miles of the Pacific Ocean as a result of overlapping domestic and international factors. The domestic factors included population pressure, continuous peasant uprisings, a worsening social and political order, disintegration of a traditionally self-sufficient rural economy, and internal decay of the Qing Dynasty (1644–1911). International factors arose from the growing impact of Western and Japanese invasion of and domination over China. Foreign encroachment of China ranged from active recruitment of Chinese laborers, missionary activities, and commercial activities to open trade and the labor markets, military interference, unequal treaties, extraterritorial privileges, and foreign settlements. Chinese emigration to the northern United States in the nineteenth century was also closely connected to domestic U.S. capitalist expansion in Asia. The internal situation explains why the Chinese emigrated, while the external situation helped to determine where they went.

Their immigration patterns, community life, and participation in the U.S. economy demonstrate how the Chinese collectively and creatively coped with structural limitations and adapted themselves to their new environments. Said differently, the immigrants played a vital role in the making of their own histories. When the Chinese began emigrating to the United States in the 1850s, the majority were young, able-bodied males. Though half of them were married, most came without their wives and children. Mining, farming, and building the railroads often required laborers to move from place to place. Working conditions in factories were harsh; and wages for Chinese laborers were too low to support a family. While some immigrants saw their lives in the United States as transitory and intended to return to China after a short stay, others found it difficult to establish family life in the American West.

The immigrants' initial responses to the frontier lifestyle could have changed once they became more familiar with U.S. society and living conditions improved, but they did not. For example, while the male to female ratio of Chinese was 18.58 in 1860, it dropped to 12.84 by 1870.[10] A skewed sex ratio among Chinese communities persisted in the continental United States until the 1930s, mainly due to Chinese Exclusion Laws. Lack of family life in Chinese immigrant communities was a consequence of the U.S. racial environment and not of Chinese culture. Had Chinese immigrants been treated similar to European immigrants, Chinese women no doubt would have joined Chinese men as immigrants. Today, after racist and sexist immigration laws have been abolished, Chinese immigrant women outnumber immigrant men.[11]

I do not differ from most Asian American scholars regarding the use of structural determinants, such as political and economic conditions, to delineate the broad geographical boundaries of mass migration. However, I emphasize that immigration is not merely a result of external forces, but that it also requires powerful motivation from the immigrants themselves. Most Chinese immigrants came to the United States to improve their economic status or to avoid downward social mobility. As their motivation is closely linked to the social environment in which they lived, we need to pursue an in-depth discussion of the emigration region in Guangdong Province.

EMIGRATION REGION IN GUANGDONG

In the nineteenth century, Guangdong was characterized by its diversified commercial activities, prevalent lineage organizations, and a competitive social environment. In agriculture, cash crops began to replace self-sufficient farming. While the Zhujing (Pearl River) Delta produced silk and sugarcane, hilly areas grew tea, tobacco, and various fruits. The delta was "one of the richest agricultural areas in China where immigrants were probably upwardly mobile people who saw emigration as a way to obtain the funds that would enable them to benefit from the expansion of commercial agriculture."[12] According to William Skinner, some speculative agribusiness men were able to expand their landed property and became rich within a short time because the commercial marketing system was well developed and organized in rural Guangdong.[13] Though suffering from population pressure, natural disasters, ethnic conflicts, Western colonialism, and peasant rebellion movements, Guangdong Province was not the poorest place in China.

More significantly, participation in and exposure to the market economy increased villagers' knowledge of the outside world, complicated the economic calculations of individual households, and "sharpened the competitive environment in which the villagers lived."[14] Due to the economic ecology of Guangdong, the rural population consisted of people who professed various occupations and labor skills. In the rural villages of nineteenth-century Guangdong, there were clerks, salesmen, merchants, fruit dealers, carpenters, doctors, tailors, teachers, and many others in addition to farmers. Meanwhile, Guangzhou, the capital city of Guangdong, had been the main port to foreign commerce since the eighteenth century.

The interplay of all these factors—the coexistence of cash and household agricultural patterns, diverse occupations and social classes among the villagers, access to coastal transportation, and exposure to outside influence—could affect the dynamics and intensity of Chinese emigration. These factors are probably critical in explaining who the Chinese immigrants were and their motivations for migration. For most Chinese, immigration, instead of being an exotic adventure, was a rational choice based on aspirations for social advancement. Coming from such an environment, Chinese immigrants were by no means land-bound, conservative, and inward-looking people with no potential to settle down overseas. Many of them were not the impoverished and needy peasants who would take whatever jobs were available, but they were highly motivated people aspiring to upward mobility.

Their kinship organization and system of inheritance also mattered. Chinese culture disapproved of primogeniture. Equal inheritance of family property among the male siblings was the root cause for the continual fragmentation of family land. Such a system often caused bitter conflicts between brothers. To avoid fragmentation, clans, instead of nuclear families, sometimes claimed ownership of the land. But competition for the control of clan affairs sometimes led to further conflicts and the splitting of kinship organizations. Thus, land fragmentation and reorganization of the Chinese extended family resulted in numerous clan organizations in Guangdong. The clan system was so prevalent that most rural inhabitants in that area belonged to one or two lineage societies.[15]

Given the prominence of the kinship system in Guangdong, Chinese immigration to the United States was often a group, rather than an individual, decision. Pioneer merchant immigrants passed on information about the new country to their kin, encouraged them to emigrate, and even paid the transportation costs for clansmen who could not afford it. Immigration decisions were made through social networks that extended from the home villages to Chinese communities in the American West. Immigrants usually headed to locations where they could find accommodations or jobs through the assistance of relatives or friends. Following this pattern, most Chinese immigrants came from seven counties in Guangdong Province. Chinese immigrant social organizations such as the Six Companies were based on kinship and districts. If poverty was the major cause of Chinese emigration abroad, the emigrants would have come from any area that was poor, and they would have consisted mainly of people from the lower classes.

Since kinship formed the basis for social relationships in Guangdong, Chinese immigration followed the "chain migration" phenomenon. When this kinship network was transplanted to North America, it provided for the initial accommodation of new immigrants, helped them find jobs, or simply offered them jobs through family businesses. Pooling resources, relatives shared risks and profits and were able to expand family businesses. As Yans-McLaughlin points out, "The network structure that originally functioned as the grid connecting Old World kin might, for example, transform itself in ethnic subeconomies to providing jobs, housing, or even business opportunities."[16] An obvious divergence of Chinese immigration history from the assimilationist model is the strengthening rather than weakening of family and kinship ties through the migration process. With relatives assisting each other and the bonds between parents and children remaining strong, transplanted kin networks expanded and created new possibilities. Kinship networks probably played a far more significant role than just life necessity in immigration decisions.

LITERACY OF CHINESE IMMIGRANTS

Chinese immigrant networks involved people on both sides of the Pacific. An important means of communication to maintain and operate the networks was letter writing. In order to pass information to relatives and friends at home or obtain news from China, many early Chinese immigrants probably had a functional reading and writing ability, especially those who were from the middle or lower-middle classes. Thus, lack of literacy was merely another mistaken perception about the Chinese immigrants.

The education system in China was partially responsible for the literacy of Chinese immigrants. In traditional Chinese society, education gave people hope and opportunity. As a famous Confucian epigram states, fine scholarship leads to high officialdom. A son from a poor peasant family could become a court official if he passed the imperial examinations. Ping-ti Ho has noted that to effectively perpetuate the hierarchy system, Confucius and his exponents advocated selecting members of the ruling class on the basis of individual merit. Equal opportunity for education was the basis of such selection.[17] To evolve from a scholar to an official was a Chinese dream. To realize that dream, parents paid careful attention to their children's education and a clan or big family often supported one or several family members in their educational pursuits.

A school in a rural village was called a *shushi* (reading house). A larger and better-equipped school in the rural town was usually referred to as a *shuyuan* (academy). The *shuyuan* system originated in the Tang Dynasty (618–906), as it provided private places where scholars could store books and study, and became popular in the Song Dynasty (960–1279), following the rise of the neo-Confucian movement. As education still led to wealth and prestige during the late Qing period, there existed in Guangdong numerous county or district schools called *shuyuan* and family and clan schools called *shushi* (reading room). These schools not only helped aspiring young scholars to reach official positions but also enabled the Chinese rural population to achieve functional literacy.

According to Ping-ti Ho's research on social mobility in imperial China, Chinese peasants achieved a high degree of literacy. He observes that literacy was essential for the peasant families not only for pursuing scholarly titles but also for successful farm management.[18] Evelyn S. Rawski also argues for a high degree of literacy among the Chinese rural population. She points out that "information from the mid- and late nineteenth century suggests that 30 to 45 percent of the men and from 2 to 10 percent of women in China knew how to read and write."[19] Sinologist Herrlee Creel wrote of his observations during a trip to China: "Late in 1935 I traveled somewhat extensively through rural sections of several Chinese provinces, and was quite surprised at the degree of literacy I encountered even among those who made their living by manual labor."[20] No doubt, in the feudal hierarchy of Chinese society, the social statuses of gentry and peasant were distinct. But if any Chinese peasants hoped to change their social status through education, they could send their sons to the village schools, county schools, and then provincial schools until they could not afford it or their sons proved to be poor scholars. Many people in rural areas in China could probably read and write minimally as a result of the long-existing civil service examination system. Total illiteracy is a stereotypical image of the Chinese rural population.

As education was an important cultural value in Chinese society, Chinese immigrants brought this tradition to the United States. Schools in the early Chinese communities in North America followed the *shuyuan* tradition. The first community-sponsored school in San Francisco was set up in 1884 and was called *Daqing shuyuan* (the Great Qing School). When Chinese immigrants formed their social organizations, they sent for scholars who passed the civil service examinations to serve as organization officials. For example, the Six Companies had four *juren* (provincial examination degree holders) as presidents in 1906. Of the fourteen presidents from 1881 to 1927, the Sanyi Company had three *jinshi* (national examination degree holders), nine *juren*, and one *gongsheng* (district examination degree holder).[21] Though merchants rather than scholars eventually became leaders of the Six Companies, the above examples demonstrate the importance of education in Chinese culture.

A few studies on Chinese immigrants note the considerable degree of literacy among early Chinese immigrants. In his book, *The Chinese of America*, Jack Chen writes, "As for literacy, Charles Nordhoff states emphatically, not once but twice, in his book *California*, that most of the Chinese there in 1872 could read in Chinese—at least, I suppose, to the extent of what is now called 'functional' literacy."[22] Rawski also notes that the 1896 census for Hawaii reported that 25 percent of Chinese female immigrants were literate.[23] Neither Chen's nor Rawski's observations have received adequate attention from Asian American scholars. Conventional scholarly explorations of immigration are

often conducted within national contexts. As most scholars are mainly preoccupied with Chinese immigrant adjustment to U.S. society, English-language
ability probably became the criterion to judge whether the Chinese were literate or not.

Literacy is important for Chinese immigrants or any immigrant group
since letter correspondence, as mentioned above, between them and their
families in the home country was the only means of communication. In order
to exchange information among themselves, Chinese communities also published Chinese-language newspapers. The first Chinese newspapers appeared
in San Francisco's Chinatown as early as 1854.[24] After that, Chinese-language
newspapers became an indispensable part of Chinese U.S. communities.
There are numerous other examples and evidence to prove that Chinese immigrants were not illiterate, however, the civil service exam system serves as a
sufficient indicator.

"SOJOURNERS" WITH A MIGRATION TRADITION

The stereotype of Chinese as illiterate and impoverished peasants also led to a
stereotypical image of them as "sojourners." According to assimilationist views,
sheer poverty forced many poor Chinese to seek quick money in the United
States in order to return to their home villages as wealthy men. If it had not
been for the hopeless situation in rural Guangdong, this argument suggests, the
Chinese would not have gone overseas in search of economic opportunities.
The Chinese were seen as conservative and inward-looking in nature, so that
Chinese society would not encourage emigration. Though most Asian American scholars reject this "sojourner" concept, many also assume that Chinese
immigration began in the nineteenth century, when Western nations opened
up a hitherto closed China. However, newly published studies on Chinese society convincingly demonstrate that long before the nineteenth century China
had participated in a complex network of international exchanges that
stretched from Syria in the west to Japan in the east and from Korea in the
north to Indonesia in the south. By the sixteenth century, their commercial and
cultural exchange activities included Europe and the New World.[25] Historically,
China has not been a closed nation.

As a coastal province, Guangdong had long been exposed to foreign cultures. The first Muslim mosque was established in Guangzhou (Canton), its
capital city, as early as 672. During the Tang Dynasty (618–906), "Canton's
foreign population ran into the tens of thousands. . . . From Canton it was
possible to travel all over China by an extensive network of roads and water-

ways, many newly built to accommodate the burgeoning traffic." Informative travel accounts of foreign countries like *Zhufan Zhi* (Records of foreign peoples) were published as early as 1225.[26] Partly due to the extensive exchange activities with the outside world, seeking opportunities overseas became a tradition and a cultural heritage in Guangdong Province. In fact, Chinese trans-Pacific emigration was a continuation of overland migration in China proper. Chinese civilization originated in the Yellow River Valley in the north and gradually expanded into the south and southwestern parts of China, which include present-day Guangdong, Guangxi, and Fujian Provinces. During 1402–1424, led by Zheng He, a Muslim eunuch, a Chinese fleet of three hundred ships—some up to 400 feet long and 180 feet wide—traveled as far as East Africa. Chinese society interacted with other cultures and peoples much more than many have realized.

In their voyages overseas in the nineteenth century, the Chinese were, in fact, not much different from European immigrants. Immigration patterns indicate that many immigrants, after years of hard work, accumulate sufficient capital to return to their home countries. Return is typical rather than unique in the immigration experience. In his study of seventeenth-century British immigration to the United States, David Cressy calculated that as many as one in six British immigrants returned to England either permanently or temporarily.[27] According to Ronald Takaki, the return rate of the Chinese between 1850 and 1882 was 47 percent. But the return rate was equally high for many European immigrant groups—55 percent for Englishmen, 46 percent for Scots, 42 percent for Irish, 40 percent for Polish, and 50 percent for Italians.[28]

Since most immigrants came to the United States with an economic motive, emigration was not a simple, two-step, unidirectional movement in which immigrants were driven out of their home countries and drawn to the United States. In the process of immigration, returning home was normal. The United States should not be assumed to be the immigrant's final destination. When economic opportunities became available elsewhere, including in their home countries, immigrants often moved again. In fact, many immigrants returned to the home country when disappointed by their U.S. experiences. *They Remember America,* by Theodore Saloutos, for example, is a book about returned Greek immigrants.[29] While Virginia Yans-McLaughlin finds repatriation an alternative to Americanization, Roger Daniels views returning to the homeland as a rejection of U.S. society.[30] In short, the revisionist perspective does not view immigration as a one-way trip.

In the nineteenth century, with improved and cheaper transportation, travel back and forth between the sending and receiving countries was also normal. Chinese emigration to the United States occurred in an era when ocean transportation had been greatly developed and improved. When British emigrants went to the New England colony in the seventeenth century, they typically waited four weeks at the dock and then took another eight to ten weeks to cross the furious Atlantic Ocean.[31] But an average trip from Hong Kong to San Francisco took thirty-five days in the nineteenth century. U.S. transportation companies were among the powerful influences promoting Chinese immigration. In 1866, the Pacific Mail Steamship Company entered the trade under a government subsidy, and soon the Occidental and Oriental Steamship Company joined in the competition. The ship companies actively distributed placards, maps, and pamphlets about the United States. The Pacific Mail Company provided bimonthly sailings with comfortable service. Many of the crew were also Chinese.[32] As Sandy Lydon argues, for Asian immigrants, California was not the end of the continent but the nearest shore of a land stretching eastward: "Seen from our perch above Hawaii it is the European presence in California which becomes extraordinary (and even tenuous)."[33] From the perspective of immigrants, conceptions of emigration probably included staying, sojourning, returning, and emigrating elsewhere. It makes little sense to describe the Chinese as different because of their return rate.

Furthermore, high return rates could be interpreted as an indication that immigration was a long-existing tradition among the Chinese in Guangdong. Since the seventeenth century, millions of Chinese have left China to go overseas. Chinese immigrants usually had specific purposes, such as exploring job, business, or educational opportunities. Most of them merely tried to improve or avoid loss of their social status at home by going overseas. Depending on whether they could achieve such goals, and their perceptions of the host country, they would decide whether to stay or to migrate to another place. Symbolically, China was the home country. Return to the home country was normal. In the immigration process, some immigrants stayed, others returned, still others remained in the receiving country for a while and then left. The immigrants' experiences indicate that sojourn and return are among various conceptions of immigration, rather than the criteria to judge whether a person is an immigrant or not.

CONCLUSION

When we revisit the social origins of Chinese immigrants, we see that a cash-crop economy, the inheritance system, the fragmentation of land, the popularity of schools, Western influence, and a migration tradition were all elements responsible for Chinese immigration. The interplay of these elements made villagers in Guangdong less earth bound, more competitive minded, and sensitive to opportunities for social mobility elsewhere. These are the very qualities immigrants tend to possess. Early Chinese immigrants are precisely people of this kind.

However, the assimilationist school often assumes that immigrants are mostly disadvantaged members of poorer countries who are willing to participate in international labor migration. Immigration flow from Asian or other countries to America arises out of the sheer existence of economic inequalities. Completely uprooted from the old traditional society, immigrants are thought to be eager to settle down and take the United States as their new home. Since the United States is imagined as the final destination in the immigration process, such studies focus only on one geographic point of a worldwide social movement. But immigration studies need to go beyond the national context.

Immigrants are people who travel overseas with their culture intact. A solid understanding of Chinese culture is the key to enhancing an understanding of Chinese immigrants. If we assume that Chinese culture is conservative, backward, and inward looking, we tend to view Chinese immigrants as different from European immigrants. If we imagine that Chinese culture is inferior to Western culture, we expect Chinese immigrants to abandon partially or entirely their Chinese heritage in order to absorb fully U.S. ideas and cultures. Following such a paradigm, we fail to make a significant departure from the assimilationist approach, which defines the immigration process as a linear progression from traditional culture toward Americanization. Since the old paradigm in immigration studies views immigrants as "the poor, needy, and uneducated," we must shift to a new paradigm with "acknowledgment of the ideas, skills, expertise, capital, and other benefits (of the immigrants) provided to the country."[34] Internationalism has to move the immigration paradigm away from the nation-state context toward a global field.

NOTES

I would like to thank Susie Lan Cassel and two anonymous readers for their extremely helpful comments and suggestions on early drafts of this chapter.

1. William I. Thomas and Florian Znaniecki, *The Polish Peasant in Europe and America* (Boston: Knopf, 1927); Robert Ezra Park and Herbert A. Miller, *Old World*

Traits Transplanted (New York: Harper, 1921); and Robert Ezra Park, *Race and Culture* (Glencoe, Ill.: Free Press, 1950).

2. Gunther Barth, *Bitter Strength: A History of Chinese in the United States* (Cambridge, Mass.: Harvard University Press, 1964).

3. June Mei, "Socioeconomic Origins of Emigration: Guangdong to California, 1850–1882," in *Labor Immigration under Capitalism: Asian Workers in the United States before World War II,* ed. Lucie Cheng and Edna Bonacich (Berkeley: University of California Press, 1984), 235.

4. Kil Young Zo, *Chinese Emigration into the United States* (New York: Arno, 1978), 4, 54–59.

5. Ronald Takaki, *Strangers from a Different Shore: A History of Asian Americans,* rev. ed. (Boston: Little, Brown, 1998), 32–36.

6. Roger Daniels, *Coming to America: A History of Immigration and Ethnicity in American Life* (New York: Harper Perennial, 1991), 16–22; Ewa Morawska, "The Sociology and Historiography of Immigration," in *Immigration Reconsidered: History, Sociology, and Politics,* ed. Virginia Yans-McLaughlin (New York: Oxford University Press, 1990), 187–240; Alejandro Portes and Ruben G. Rumbaut, *Immigrant America: A Portrait* (Berkeley: University of California Press, 1990), 8–14; and Virginia Yans-McLaughlin, *Family and Community: Italian Immigrants in Buffalo, 1880–1930* (Ithaca, N.Y.: Cornell University Press, 1971), 34–35.

7. Morawska, "The Sociology and Historiography of Immigration," 193.

8. Yans-McLaughlin, *Family and Community,* 35.

9. Sucheng Chan, *Asian Americans: An Interpretive History* (New York: Twayne, 1991), 3.

10. Evelyn Nakano Glenn and Stacey G. H. Yap, "Chinese American Families," in *Minority Families in the United States: A Multicultural Perspective,* ed. Ronald L. Taylor (Englewood Cliffs, N.J.: Prentice Hall, 1994), 120.

11. Bill Ong Hing, "Making and Remaking Asian Pacific America: Immigration Policy," in *The State of Asian Pacific America: Policy Issues to the Year 2020,* ed. Leadership Education for Asian Pacifics (LEAP) Asian Pacific American Public Policy Institute and the University of California, Los Angeles, Asian American Studies Center (Los Angeles: LEAP Asian Pacific American Public Policy Institute and UCLA Asian American Studies Center, 1993), 130.

12. Sucheng Chan, "European and Asian Immigration," in *Immigration Reconsidered,* Yans-McLaughlin ed., 44. Here Chan differs from her views in her *Asian Americans: An Interpretive History.*

13. G. William Skinner, "Chinese Peasants and the Closed Community: An Open and Shut Case," *Comparative Studies in Society and History* 13, no. 3 (1971): 270–81.

14. Evelyn S. Rawski, "Economic and Social Foundations of Late Imperial Culture," in *Popular Culture in Late Imperial China,* ed. David Johnson, Andrew Nathan, and Evelyn S. Rawski (Berkeley: University of California Press, 1985), 7.

15. Han-sheng Chen, *Landlord and Peasant in China* (New York, International, 1936), 37.

16. Yans-McLaughlin, introduction to *Immigration Reconsidered,* 12.

17. Ping-ti Ho and Tang Tsou, ed., *China's Heritage and the Communist Political System,* vol. 1 (Chicago: University of Chicago Press, 1968), 26.

18. Ping-ti Ho, *The Ladder of Success in Imperial China* (New York: Columbia University Press, 1962), 314.

19. Evelyn S. Rawski, *Education and Popular Literacy in Ch'ing China* (Michigan: University of Michigan Press, 1979), 149.

20. Herrlee G. Creel, "Supplementary Notes," in *China's Heritage,* Ping-ti Ho and Tang Tsou eds., 1:69.

21. Liu Boji, *Meiguo Huaqiao Shi* (A History of the Chinese in the United States of America) (Taibei: Commission of Overseas Chinese Affairs, Republic of China, 1976), 174–75.

22. Jack Chen, *The Chinese of America* (San Francisco: Harper & Row, 1980), 120.

23. Rawski, *Education and Popular Literacy in Ch'ing China,* 7.

24. Him Mark Lai, *Cong Huaren Dao Huaqiao* (From Overseas Chinese to Chinese Americans) (Hong Kong: Joint Publishing [K.K.], 1992), 46.

25. Joanna Waley-Cohen, *The Sextants of Beijing: Global Currents in Chinese History* (New York: Norton, 1999), 5.

26. Waley-Cohen, *The Sextants of Beijing,* 24, 34, 38.

27. David Cressy, *Coming Over: Migration and Communication between England and New England in the Seventeenth Century* (Cambridge: Cambridge University Press, 1987), 212.

28. Takaki, *A History of Asian Americans,* 11, 116.

29. Theodore Saloutos, *They Remember America: The Story of the Repatriated Greek Americans* (Berkeley: University of California Press, 1958).

30. Daniels, *Coming to America*, 20; Yans-McLaughlin, introduction to *Immigration Reconsidered*, 7.

31. Cressy, *Coming Over*, 54.

32. Robert Schwendinger, "Investigating Chinese Immigrant Ships and Sailors," and Dorothy Perkins, "Coming to San Francisco by Steamship," in *The Chinese American Experience: Papers from the Second National Conference on Chinese American Studies*, ed. Genny Lim (San Francisco: Chinese Historical Society of America and the Chinese Culture Foundation of San Francisco, 1980); also Robert J. Schwendinger, "North from Panama, West to the Orient: The Pacific Mail Steamship Company, As Photographed by Carleton E. Watkins," *California History* 57, no. 1 (spring 1978): 46–57.

33. Sandy Lydon, *Chinese Gold: The Chinese in the Monterey Bay Region* (Capitola, Calif.: Capitola Book Company, 1985), 14.

34. Shirley Hune, "An Overview of Asian Pacific American Futures: Shifting Paradigms," in *The State of Asian Pacific America*, 6.

2

Chinese Placer Mining in the United States: An Example from American Canyon, Nevada

David Valentine

The discovery of gold at Sutter's Mill attracted Chinese to California and the U.S. West Coast as much as it attracted any other group. Chinese argonauts, lured by the promise of easy wealth and pushed by deplorable conditions at home, joined the California gold rush. In the early 1850s, 85 percent of California Chinese, some twenty thousand immigrants, were placer mining,[1] but they supposedly did not have any mining experience when they arrived. Evidence in defense of this statement includes the fact that no distinctive Chinese placer mining tools have been found and that the bulk of the Chinese were from Guangdong Province, an area where the economy was based on fishing and rice paddy agriculture instead of mining. As it concerns mining, this deductive reasoning is problematic and potentially erroneous. Chinese immigrants were considered unskilled miners in part because no distinctly Chinese mining tools or mine features have been observed in the United States. There is a problem, however, in relying on artifacts in this case, because many of the placer mining grounds in the western United States were remined during the Depression era of the 1930s.[2] This activity destroyed many of the earlier mining artifacts and features that might have been created by Chinese miners. Haiming Liu also points out that Guangdong's economy was very diverse, and a wide variety of professionals worked in Guangdong and immigrated to the United States.[3] Experienced miners could have partly constituted that group of professional immigrants.

China and Guangdong have a long mining history. This mining history includes gold and placer mining and suggests that some mining methods employed in China were in place long before any Chinese left for foreign lands. A study of the archaeology and history of American Canyon, a Chinese placer mining village in northern Nevada, shows that many of the mining ruins there have a distinct Chinese signature. Therefore, it is clearly possible that some Chinese argonauts were skilled miners at their arrival in the United States.

PLACER MINING

Gravel deposits containing gold or other minerals (such as cinnabar, diamonds, garnets, jade, platinum, tin, tungsten, and turquoise) are known as placer deposits. The gold discovered in 1849 at Sutter's Mill in California was a placer deposit. To mine placer deposits, water and gravity are used to separate out desired minerals, which have a high specific gravity, from undesired gravel. The search for placer gold often led to the discovery of "mother lodes"—the original gold veins from which placer deposits derive. Lode mining requires machinery and extra labor to tunnel through hard rock and to separate gold from rock and other minerals. A substantial outlay of capital is required to procure necessary machinery and extra labor prior to commencement of lode mining. Lacking large sums of money for the initial outlay, most Chinese were prevented from starting hard-rock gold mines. Antagonism from Euro-American miners and mine laborers also deterred many Chinese from acquiring jobs at hard-rock mines. Due to these pressures, many Chinese switched from mining-related jobs to service jobs such as cooking or running laundries. Chinese who stayed in the mining industry specialized in placer mining.

Furthermore, to avoid antagonism with Euro-American miners, Chinese specialized in reworking placer claims believed to be "worked out" by Euro-American miners. Late-nineteenth-century Euro-American miners generally expected a claim to pay a minimum of four dollars per day. Once Euro-American miners removed the easily obtainable gold, they declared their claims "worked out" and willingly sold or leased them to patient Chinese miners who willingly recovered the smaller nuggets and gold dust.[4]

The tool kit most often used by the Chinese placer miner consisted of the "pan" and "rocker." A gold pan is a large pan in which gold-bearing gravel and water are swished around in an effort to separate lighter sand and gravel from the heavier gold particles. It is most often used in initial prospecting efforts when the miner is looking for pockets of gold. The rocker, also known as a cradle, was first developed by Mexican miners in California.[5] It generally consists of an open wooden box mounted on rocker legs, and vaguely resembles an infant's cradle (figure 2.1). Inside the box is a screen for removing large material, a deflecting apron to direct the flow of water and gravel, and a riffled bottom to catch the gold (figure 2.2). The device is rocked to keep the gravel

FIGURE 2.1
The rocker or "cradle" used in nineteenth-century Chinese placer mining to screen large material from gold (side view) (Copyright © David Valentine. Reprinted with permission.)

FIGURE 2.2
The rocker in Chinese placer mining (top view) (Copyright © David Valentine. Reprinted with permission.)

moving through the box and to concentrate the gold in the riffles.[6] Materials to construct a rocker were inexpensive, and the rocker was very portable, contributing to its desirability for thrifty and mobile Chinese placer miners (figure 2.3). Chinese placer miners are identified with the use of rockers.[7]

CHINESE MINING, ESPECIALLY IN GUANGDONG

How did thousands of Chinese rice farmers and fishermen, supposedly ignorant in the ways of placer mining, gain such immediate success in the United States? The Chinese are credited with bringing water management technology to U.S. goldfields. Ditching, damming, and pumping are believed to be a legacy of rice paddy agriculture and canal building practiced in Guangdong Province.[8] Water management is very important in most placer mining endeavors to assist in sorting out gold from clay, sand, and gravel, and Chinese expertise in this area directly affected success in mining.

For instance, Heidhus indicates that Chinese pumping technology was applied to mining early on in Malaysia.[9] Another source supporting the use of Chinese water technology in mining is Brelich, who states, "During the rainy season, the surface water which accumulates in the lower workings, is forked by means of bamboo or wooden chain pumps *similar to those used for irrigation purposes*" (emphasis added).[10] Steeves also mentions that water engineering was important to mining in Yunnan.[11] This demonstrates that Chinese water management technology was not just applied to agricultural needs in China. Many Chinese miners would have been familiar with the construction and use of pumps, ditches, etc. that were also used in agriculture. For instance, in American Canyon and in California, agricultural techniques were transferred to mining when water was poured into a shaft from a nearby can and gold-bearing gravel was hoisted out of the shaft by use of a windlass (figure 2.4).

Fredlund et al.[12] recognized that the Guangdong Chinese had some knowledge of placer mining, though it was for tin (cassiterite) instead of gold, and they speculate that this knowledge was acquired during Chinese tin mining in Malaysia.[13] Ritchie, Steeves, and Zhu note that the Chinese have a long history of metal working, and thus of mining, however, they still credit Chinese miners' success to three other things: first, their social organization; second, their knowledge of other engineering principles (mainly water management, as mentioned above); and third, an ability to work long, hard hours with minimal rewards.[14] Zhu notes an additional factor: superior diets and medical support.[15]

China has an important mining industry based on a long history of mining and metallurgy dating back to well before 4000 B.C.E., when copper was

FIGURE 2.3
Chinese miner transporting rocker (Copyright © Nevada Historical Society. Reprinted
with permission.)

first worked in China. Even today, China is the sixth largest producer of gold
in the world, with placer deposits accounting for 10 percent of China's production.[16] Bronze metallurgy was developed in China between 2500 and 2000
B.C.E., years before it was developed in Europe or other parts of the world.[17]
Chinese miners and metallurgists developed piston bellows to assist with met-
allurgical endeavors, and were the first to use stamp mills.[18]

From antiquity, Chinese had prospecting experience that included knowledge of associated minerals and rock types[19] and the use of plants as possible
indicators of mineral concentrations.[20] Sung's account of seventeenth-century
Chinese technology demonstrates that the Chinese had a thorough knowledge
of mining technology, including placer mining principles such as sluicing and
panning, used in exploiting placer deposits of gold, silver, iron, and jade.[21]
Sing also demonstrates that stream washing was used as a benefaction process
during lode mining and milling.

This early knowledge of mining was passed down through the ages. Willis
states:

> A mining proposition in China is unlike one in any other country; there's noth-
> ing new about it. American mines are new and so are methods. In Europe, new
> methods are applied to old mines. But in China, mines and methods are those

FIGURE 2.4
California Chinese placer miners using an agricultural water management technique also employed in American Canyon

of the ancestral Chinese. Inhabited for several thousand years by a people skilled in the use of metals, China has but little unprospected territory. Practically all her metalliferous deposits are known and have been worked to the level where pumping became necessary; but they have not been worked with effective appliances for deep mining or with an intelligent understanding of ore deposits, and their future productiveness depends upon the application of modern machinery, business methods, and scientific knowledge.[22]

It follows that having mines, one also has miners. Sun reports on Chinese miners during the Qing period (1644–1911 C.E.).[23] He notes that miners were generally considered of low status, and that they could be grouped into three categories: those from regions without sufficient agricultural resources who were forced into mining to make a living; those without some other "proper" occupation; and those who were local farmers, earning extra income during the off-season. Miners were a closed group, with their own jargon, gods, charms, and *tongs* (associations). Professional miners were restless and rootless, and would readily abandon an area to pursue work or to act on rumors of a new strike elsewhere. They participated in many mining rushes throughout China and adjoining regions. Full-time miners tended to make Chinese officials nervous. They believed miners when unemployed caused civil unrest through their vagabond ways or through *tong* conflicts. Many miners came from the provinces of Yunnan, Sichuan, Jiangxi, and Hunan, where agriculture played a lesser role and mining was less strictly controlled by the Chinese administration, but miners worked throughout the empire.

A cursory examination of Chinese mining in the late nineteenth and early twentieth centuries is possible, with information specific to Guangdong Province, due in large part to reports by European and U.S. geologists looking for mineral deposits in China for Western companies to exploit following the Opium Wars (1839–1850). These reports indicate that the Chinese mining industry was in disarray for many of the same reasons that China was in political and economic chaos, such as the Opium Wars (1839–1850), the Taiping Rebellion (1851–1864), the Punti-Hakka conflict (1854–1867), the Muslim Rebellion (1858–1873), and a variety of floods and famines.[24]

While it is true that a very important part of the Guangdong economy consists of rice paddy agriculture, it is also true that Guangdong is mountainous. The mountainous regions contain mineral deposits that were mined. The types of mineral deposits specific to Guangdong that were being exploited through the late nineteenth and early twentieth centuries are antimony (and possibly associated mercury),[25] bituminous coal,[26] gold,[27] iron,[28] lead,[29] silver,[30] and tin.[31]

Many of these deposits are mined by hard-rock methods (that is, the metals are still bound up with other minerals in unweathered bedrock), but iron, gold, mercury, and tin (cassiterite) all might have been placer mined (weathered and eroded out from bedrock). The references to Guangdong gold mines are limited, and it is not known if they are hard rock or placer,[32] however, cassiterite and iron sand deposits were definitely placer mined in Guangdong.[33]

The placer mining techniques used to recover iron sand, tin, and other minerals were identical to those used to recover gold. Wagner describes placer mining of iron sand in Henan Province.[34] In this region, a wooden sluice board is made and water is diverted (with ditches and dams) to run over it. Iron sand is carried to the sluice for washing. Wagner states that "iron sand sluicing requires no special tools or skills, is outdoor work, requires less physical strength than [hard-rock] mining, and involves no danger."[35] After being washed, the sand is smelted using charcoal to produce iron. Although Henan Province is distant from Guangdong, extensive iron sand exists along the southeast coast of China in the provinces of Zhejiang, Fujian, and Guangdong.[36] Tegengren did not consider iron sand economically important, but he was searching for large deposits for use in heavy industry.[37] He acknowledged that locals in Fujian used low-technology methods. Iron sand was important where there was sufficient population to create a demand for iron tools that could not be cheaply supplied from other sources, and there was sufficient iron sand and fuel for smelting. In these cases, iron sand mining and smelting was done by the local population. Many people, including women and children, were familiar with the processes, since most sluiced iron sand for extra income when not engaged in farming.[38] Therefore, many Chinese farmers had knowledge of sluicing and other placer mining techniques.

Additional placer mining was done by Guangdong Chinese who recovered cassiterite. No reference describing the methods used was found, possibly since turn-of-the-century European and U.S. geologists working in China were more interested in iron and mercury. Heidhus, however, describes Chinese placer tin mining on Bangka Island in Malaysia.[39] The methods she describes are similar to those used for iron sand sluicing, in which a sluice board or box was made, water was diverted to run over it, and the tin ore was carried to the board for sluicing. Many of the Chinese who arrived to mine tin were described as being knowledgeable and experienced, and it was speculated that many of them were Hakka from Guangdong.

Evidence from geologic and mining reports from China at the turn of the twentieth-century indicate that China has had a long and active mining history. More specifically, Guangdong Province has a documented history of mineral exploitation, including placer mining. Water management technology cannot be considered a strictly agricultural technology, since it was also applied to mining in China. This suggests that the hypothesis that Chinese were inexperienced miners when they arrived in the United States is false.

THE AMERICAN CANYON MINES

American Canyon is unusual among nineteenth-century Chinese mining sites in that it still retains Chinese mining features. Located in Pershing County, northern Nevada in the Humboldt Range, it was the site of a Chinese village from 1884 to circa 1906 and had an economy based on gold placer mining. The site is impacted by modern mining, but still retains large, undisturbed areas. These portions of the site have enough archaeological information to yield significant information on Chinese mining practices.

Mining-related archaeological features at the site include ditch and dam remnants and hundreds of narrow mine shafts with associated mine tailings.

Mining-related artifacts include shovel heads, rocker screens, and cans modified into buckets and dippers.

In the latter part of the nineteenth century, American Canyon (as it was known to the Euro-American population) was the largest Chinatown in Humboldt County (Pershing County was created out of Humboldt County in 1919), with a population of between 100 and 125 Chinese miners. At least two, and often as many as four, Chinese stores operated in American Canyon. The site was also home to a Chinese butcher, a Chinese teamster, and a Chinese wood merchant.[40]

By 1900, American Canyon's population had declined to roughly fifty-eight Chinese. The decline was probably brought about by a number of factors, including an aging population (few young Chinese men were able to enter the United States after passage of the Chinese Exclusion Act in 1882), depletion of much of the easily accessed gold, and increasing Euro-American hard-rock mining activity.[41] In 1905, less than a dozen Chinese were left. The last store closed early in 1908, and only four aged Chinese miners were enumerated there during the 1910 census.[42]

In American Canyon, Chinese merchants leased claims from Euro-Americans, and then subleased small twenty-by-twenty-foot plots to individual Chinese miners, assigning plots through a lottery.[43] The merchants also constructed ditches and a dam that brought water down to American Canyon for use in placer mines and homes. Water appears to have been distributed by selling buckets of water to individuals, as they needed it.[44]

In contrast to Euro-American placer miners, who traveled in groups but quickly dispersed into individual miners or very small groups when reaching the goldfields,[45] the Chinese replicated the kind of organization practiced in China. Namely, a group of professional miners acted under the leadership of a "manager" who furnished capital, mining expertise, and knowledge of local conditions. Occasionally, no wages were paid, but profits from the mine were shared among members of the group.[46] In American Canyon, the managers were the local merchants who put up money for claim leases and ditch systems and had the means and knowledge for dealing with local Euro-Americans.

Unfortunately, little evidence of the ditch system remains, since it was largely replaced with buried iron pipe after the abandonment of the area by the Chinese. The dam still remains, but appears to have been recently repaired with modern heavy equipment.[47] The dam might have been constructed using *hang-tu*, or tamped-earth methods. Steeves found many dams made this way at Chinese placer mining sites in Oregon.[48] Not many other cultures created dams using *hang-tu,* and this can be viewed as an indicator of a Chinese presence.

Another indicator of Chinese mining practices in American Canyon are the notches found in the sidewalls of some of the shafts. These notches are 20 x 10 cm. Sets of them are arranged vertically, with regular spacing, on opposing sidewalls of the shafts (figure 2.5). This appears to be remnants of a shoring method (a means of propping up sidewalls and roofs in mines to prevent cave-ins) used by the Chinese. A few discussions or illustrations that allude to similar shoring used in Chinese mines are in the literature. Yang mentions timber props in an ancient copper mine.[49] Timber props found in vertical and inclined shafts of the copper mine are 5–10 cm in diameter. The props used in deeper, "horizontal galleries" are 20 cm in diameter. An illustration of this comes from Sung (figure 2.6), which shows wooden poles used to prop up the roof of a coal mine.[50] This is in contrast to the practice of Euro-American miners in the late nineteenth century, who built wooden frameworks to support mine shafts and adits.

Relatively small shaft size is another apparent indicator of Chinese mining. Small shaft sizes appear to be the norm in China. Penhallurick mentions shafts averaging 80 cm square at a Chinese copper mine.[51] Yang mentions shafts ranging from 0.95 to 1.3 m square.[52] The largest Chinese shafts mentioned are coal shafts described by Hommel[53] that are around 1.8 m square. It is not known if the Chinese excavated smaller shafts because they tend to be smaller people, or if they did so to reduce the amount of material that needed to be moved. Shafts in American Canyon believed to be excavated by Chinese range from 0.5 m to 1 m square. Shafts believed to be constructed by Euro-Americans range from 1.5 m square up to greater than 2.5 m square. This size range is consistent with Euro-American–mined shafts observed elsewhere in Nevada.

McGowan, Ritchie, and Steeves have speculated that well-sorted placer tailings might be an indicator of Chinese placer mining.[54] Placer mine tailings are piles of gravel excavated out of the mine and discarded after gold was removed, or if the miner believed it contained no gold. Careful miners washed all the gravel and sorted it into piles of different sizes. The tailings associated with the majority of the placer shafts throughout American Canyon are very well sorted. This is reported to be because the Chinese washed and sorted all of the gravel excavated from a shaft. Euro-Americans would prospect the gravel as they excavated and only wash "paystreaks" (zones of gravel containing high amounts of gold), and their tailings piles often look disorganized and

FIGURE 2.5
Sidewall notches in mining shafts, with shoring method used by Chinese (Copyright
© David Valentine. Reprinted with permission.)

FIGURE 2.6
Pole-shoring method of mining, to prop roof of mine with wooden poles (From *Chinese Technology in the Seventeenth Century: t'ien kung k'ai wu*, translated by E-tu Zen Sun and Shiou-chuan Sun [Mineola, N.Y.: Dover Publications, 1997]. Copyright © 1997 Dover Publications, Inc. Reprinted with permission.)

unsorted. One Chinese merchant, Wong Kee, alluded to this practice of washing all the gravel (eighteen bucket loads to a rocker) in a quote from Bragg, "some time he catch em $10, some time $20, some time $50, some time $90 and some time too bittie to rockerful."[55] LaLande, however, cautions against using sorted placer tailing piles to determine ethnicity in mining districts, as some Euro-Americans eventually mined as efficiently as the Chinese.[56] In the United States, this could be an indication that placer grounds were reworked during the Great Depression.

CONCLUSION

Several points are important in understanding Chinese mining in American Canyon, and possibly elsewhere in the United States. They are (1) the Chinese have a long history of mining that includes placer mining; (2) miners from China included professional groups that regularly followed mining rushes all over China and other parts of the world; (3) other miners found in China were farmers who mined during the off-season for extra income; (4) water management practices (i.e., pumping and ditching) cannot be considered strictly agricultural technology, since they were also applied to mining in China; (5) a wide variety of mining was carried out in Guangdong Province, including placer mining of iron sand and tin; and (6) many of the peasant farmers may have practiced placer mining for these commodities. Therefore, it is likely that a significant portion of the Chinese were familiar with placer mining practices and principles when they arrived in the United States. It may even be possible that some of the first Chinese to join the gold rush were experienced, professional miners whose employment opportunities in China were restricted due to civil unrest. Chinese mining equipment from the gold rush era might not be readily recognized as Chinese since it is similar to the equipment used around the world—there are only so many ways to make a sluice box. Adaptation to technology available in the United States was likely due to experienced Chinese miners recognizing a workable, available tool and making good use of it.

Chinese placer mining technology, though generally elusive and often not acknowledged, can be recognized archaeologically. In the past, this has largely consisted only of the acknowledgment of Chinese water-management practices, such as dam and ditch construction. In American Canyon, a Chinese presence is evident in the arrangement of the placer shafts (created through Chinese social organization) and the presence of Chinese shoring methods. The well-sorted character of the tailings piles, the small size of the shafts, and the presence of a possible *hang-tu* dam also allude to the Chinese presence.

NOTES

1. Randall E. Rohe, "After the Gold Rush: Chinese Mining in the Far West, 1850–1890," *Montana: The Magazine of Western History* 32, no. 4 (1982): 2–19.

2. Charles W. Miller, *The Automobile Gold Rushes and Depression Era Mining* (Moscow: University of Idaho Press, 1998).

3. Haiming Liu, "The Social Origins of Early Chinese Immigrants: A Revisionist Perspective," chapter 1 in this volume.

4. Daniel Liestman, "The Chinese in the Black Hills, 1876–1932," *Journal of the West* 27 (1988): 74–83.

5. Jeffrey M. LaLande, "Sojourners in the Oregon Siskiyous: Adaptation and Acculturation of the Chinese Miners in the Applegate Valley, Ca. 1855–1900" (master's thesis, Oregon State University, 1981), 312–13.

6. William O. Vanderburg, "Placer Mining in Nevada," *Nevada Bureau of Mines and Geology Bulletin* 27 (1983), 37–41.

7. Jeffrey M. LaLande, "Sojourners in Search of Gold: Hydraulic Mining Techniques of the Chinese on the Oregon Frontier," *Industrial Archaeology* 11 (1985): 29–52. Randall E. Rohe, "Chinese River Mining in the West," *Montana: The Magazine of Western History* 46, no. 3 (1996): 14–29.

8. LaLande, "Sojourners in Search of Gold"; Neville A. Ritchie, "Archaeology and History of the Chinese in Southern New Zealand during the Nineteenth Century: A Study of Acculturation, Adaptation, and Change" (Ph.D. diss., University of Otago, 1986), 54; Randall E. Rohe, "The Chinese and Hydraulic Mining in the Far West," *Mining History Association Annual* 1: 73–91; Rohe, "Chinese River Mining in the West"; Liping Zhu, *A Chinaman's Chance: The Chinese on the Rocky Mountain Mining Frontier* (Niwot: University Press of Colorado, 1997), 105.

9. Mary F. Somers Heidhus, *Banka Tin and Mentok Pepper: Chinese Settlement on an Indonesian Island* (Singapore: Institute of Southeast Asian Studies, 1992).

10. Henry Brelich, "Chinese Methods of Mining Quicksilver," *Transactions of the Institute of Mining and Metallurgy* 14 (1905): 483–95.

11. Laban R. Steeves, "Chinese Gold Miners of Northeastern Oregon, 1862–1900" (master's thesis, University of Oregon, 1984), 161.

12. Lynn Fredlund et al., "Archaeological Investigations in the German Gulch Historic Mining District (24SB212): A Historic Chinese and Euroamerican Placer Mining Area in Southwestern Montana, Vol. 1" (Butte, Mont.: GCM Services, 1991; photocopy).

13. However, Heidhus's account of Chinese placer tin mining on the island of Bangka in Malaysia indicates that the Chinese greatly improved mining and smelting techniques when they arrived around 1750.

14. Ritchie, "Chinese in Southern New Zealand"; Laban R. Steeves, "Chinese Gold Miners," 161; Liping Zhu, "No Need to Rush: The Chinese, Placer Mining, and the Western Environment," *Montana: The Magazine of Western History* 49, no. 3 (1999): 42–57.

15. Zhu, "No Need to Rush," 48–50.

16. James P. Dorian, *Minerals, Energy and Economic Development in China* (Oxford: Clarendon Press, 1994).

17. R. D. Penhallurick, *Tin in Antiquity* (London: Institute of Metals, 1986).

18. Paul T. Craddock, *Early Metal Mining and Production* (Washington, D.C.: Smithsonian Institution Press, 1995).

19. Joseph Needham, *The Sciences of the Earth*, vol. 3 of *Science and Civilisation in China* (London: Cambridge University Press, 1971); Yang Wenhang, "Rocks, Mineralogy and Mining," in *Ancient China's Technology and Science*, comp. the Institute of the History of Natural Sciences, Chinese Academy of Sciences (Beijing: Foreign Language Press, 1983), 258–69.

20. Needham, *Sciences of the Earth*.

21. Sung Ying-Hsing, *Tien-Kung K'ai-Wu: Chinese Technology in the Seventeenth Century*, trans. E-tu Zen Sun and Shiou-Chuan Sun (1637; reprint, University Park: Pennsylvania State University Press, 1966).

22. Bailey Willis, "Mineral Resources of China," *Economic Geology* 3 (1908): 1.

23. Sun E-Tu Zen, "Mining Labor in the Ch'ing Period," in *Approaches to Modern Chinese History*, ed. Albert Feuerwerker, Rhoads Murphy, and Mary C. Wright (Berkeley: University of California Press, 1967), 45–67.

24. Henry Brelich, "Chinese Methods of Mining Quicksilver," 487; Thomas T. Read, "The Mineral Production and Resources of China," *Bulletin of the American Institute of Mining Engineers* (1912): 293–343; Felix R. Tegengren, *The Quicksilver Deposits of China*, Geological Survey of China, Ministry of Agriculture and Commerce, Bulletin 2 (Peking: Geological Survey of China, Ministry of Agriculture and Commerce, 1920), 8–11; Felix R. Tegengren, *The Iron Ores and Iron Industry of China, Part II*, Memoirs of the Geological Survey of China, no. A(2) (Peking: Geological Survey of China, Ministry of Agriculture and Commerce, 1923).

25. Philip Scalasi and David Cook, *Classic Mineral Localities of the World: Asia and Australia* (New York: Van Nostrand Reinhold, 1983), 14–20; Read, "Mineral Production and Resources," 339.

26. Read, "Mineral Production and Resources," 297, 307.

27. Read, "Mineral Production and Resources," 332.

28. Jean Chesneaux, Marianne Bastid, and Marie-Claire Bergere, *China from the Opium Wars to the 1911 Revolution*, trans. Anne Destenay (New York: Pantheon Books, 1976), 226; Read, "Mineral Production and Resources," 312, 326; Sun, "Mining Labor in the Ch'ing Period," 59; Tegengren, *Iron Ores and Iron Industry*; Donald B. Wagner, *Dabieshan: Traditional Chinese Iron-Production Techniques Practised in Southern Henan in the Twentieth Century*, Scandinavian Institute of Asian Studies Monograph 52 (London: Curzon Press, 1985).

29. Sun, "Mining Labor in the Ch'ing Period," 52; Read, "Mineral Production and Resources," 337.

30. Chesneaux et al., *China from the Opium Wars*, 226; Read, "Mineral Production and Resources," 334.

31. Penhallurick, *Tin in Antiquity*; Sun, "Mining Labor in the Ch'ing Period," 52; Read, "Mineral Production and Resources," 336–37.

32. Read, "Mineral Production and Resources," 332.

33. Read, "Mineral Production and Resources," 312, 326; Tegengren, *Iron Ores and Iron Industry*.

34. Wagner, *Dabieshan*.

35. Wagner, *Dabieshan*, 28.

36. Wagner, *Dabieshan*, fig. 14.

37. Tegengren, *Iron Ores and Iron Industry*.

38. Wagner, *Dabieshan*.

39. Heidhus, *Banka Tin and Mentok Pepper*.

40. David W. Valentine, "Historical and Archaeological Investigations at 26PE2137: American Canyon, Pershing County, Nevada" (master's thesis, University of Nevada, Las Vegas, 1999).

41. David W. Valentine, "American Canyon: A Chinese Village," in *Community in the American West*, ed. Stephen Tchudi, 107–30 (Reno: University of Nevada Press, 1999), 123–124.

42. Valentine, "American Canyon: A Chinese Village."

43. William G. Emminger, "Our Neighbors: Spring Valley Mining District" (1966), Emminger Collection, vol. 3, Nevada Room, Pershing County Library, Lovelock, Nevada.

44. Valentine, "Historical and Archaeological Investigations."

45. Martin Ridge, "Disorder, Crime, and Punishment in the California Gold Rush," *Montana: The Magazine of Western History* 49, no. 3 (1999): 12–27.

46. Sun, "Mining Labor in the Ch'ing Period," 45–67.

47. Valentine, "Historical and Archaeological Investigations," 94.

48. Steeves, "Chinese Gold Miners."

49. Yang, "Rocks, Mineralogy and Mining," 264–66.

50. Sung, *Tien-Kung K'ai-Wu*, fig. 11-3.

51. Penhallurick, *Tin in Antiquity*, 41.

52. Yang, "Rocks, Mineralogy and Mining," 264–66.

53. Rudolf P. Hommel, *China at Work: An Illustrated Record of the Primitive Industries of China's Masses, Whose Life Is Toil, and Thus an Account of Chinese Civilization* (1937; reprint, Cambridge, Mass.: MIT Press, 1969), 3.

54. Barry McGowan, "The Typology and Techniques of Alluvial Mining: The Example of the Shoalhaven and Mangarlowe Goldfields in Southern New South Wales," *Australasian Historical Archaeology* 14 (1996): 34–45; Ritchie, "The Chinese in Southern New Zealand"; Steeves, "Chinese Gold Miners."

55. Allen C. Bragg, *Humboldt County 1905* (Winnemucca: North Central Nevada Historical Society, 1976), 20.

56. LaLande, "Sojourners in the Oregon Siskiyous," 332.

3

To Inscribe the Self Daily: The Discovery of the Ah Quin Diary

Susie Lan Cassel

Tom Ah Quin was born in Guangdong Province in 1848, the oldest son of farmers who, with hopes for an improved future, sent their son to an American missionary school in China where he learned to read and write in Chinese and English. Around 1863 Ah Quin, as he came to be called, emigrated to the United States and lived in Santa Barbara, Alaska, and San Francisco, before making his home in San Diego.[1]

On June 12, 1877, on the eve of his departure from Santa Barbara to Alaska, Ah Quin began his diary with the following entry: "See all the Friends and Teachers good by to them they feel sorry and some cry because they may not see me no more." Did Ah Quin know then that these prophetic first words would lead to literally thousands of entries and result in a bicultural narrative that may be considered the greatest achievement of his life? Did he imagine that the daily record of his life, as a cook in Alaska, as a domestic in San Francisco, as a railroad labor recruiter and businessman in San Diego, would fascinate family members and scholars alike and be considered the most significant extant writings by a nineteenth-century Chinese immigrant to the United States? Could he have known how much his writings would contribute to our understanding of the life of Chinese in a bachelor society during the Chinese Exclusion Era? What Ah Quin might not have known, but what his prolific narrative makes clear, is that his diary is representative of a growing body of nonfiction writing by first-generation immigrants that functions as a unique and invaluable repository of information about the bicultural experience.

Like all writers, Ah Quin is bound by the limitations, conventions, and revelations that accompany the form he selects for his writing. Notably, he used the form of a diary—not a journal, a memoir, an autobiography, an epistle, or a collection of informal scribblings. His writing consists of a daily, systematic record of the events of his life as they are recalled, more or less, day-by-day. His work (unfortunately) doesn't have the journal's penchant for self-reflection and internal inquiry; it is not an epistle written for a particular audience. In contrast to the autobiography and memoir, it is not an act of recollection in which he recounts the significant events of his life using a viewpoint or perspective formulated later. Memory, so central to the autobiography, is not an essential concern of the diary, which privileges the immediate rather than the re-collected, the diurnal rather than the historical. As such, the diary represents an act of antimemory, positioned in contrast to the autobiography, and the diary's quotidian nature arguably provides us with the best approximation of the objective life as it is lived.

The particular brand of objectivity put forward by the diary makes it an unusual source for knowledge. Its autobiographical nature (note that the diary, as a form, is not an autobiography, but it is clearly autobiographical) underscores three broad areas of significance embedded within the text itself and echoed in the Greek roots of the term *autos-bios-graphe* or "self-life-writing." For the Ah Quin diary, these areas of importance can be interpreted as follows: first, it is a psychological record of the development of a *self* over most of a man's adult life; second, it is a sociohistorical account of a Chinese immigrant's *life* during the age of Chinese exclusion; and finally, it is an act of *writing* that must be considered within the context of other acts of writing, specifically nonfiction writing and writing by other Chinese Americans. Taken together, these intertwining threads of significance call attention to the valuable insight that can be gleaned from a personal document like a diary, especially when it is authored by a member of an oppressed group who, more often than not, has been (mis)represented by the media machinery of the dominant society.

AUTOS: THE SITUATIONAL SELF

As a vehicle through which to view the self, the diary represents the developing self, not a unitary self created from a (supposedly) fully realized position and written in retrospect for clear economic or political gain. Since diaries often go on for many years (Queen Victoria is said to have kept a diary for over sixty years),[2] the reader is in a unique position to see the whole trajectory of a written life in relatively few hours, and to have a perspective on the development, the subtle changes, and the shifts in consciousness that the writer, barring a systematic reading of his own text, might not himself realize. The burden for the reader is to distinguish, from among thousands of entries and numerous volumes, the more important events and periods from those more mundane and to assemble a representative profile of the self that dedicated so much to the act of writing. Privy to secrets known only to the diarist and the person fortunate enough to encounter his thoughts, the reader is in a privileged position to know the writer better than he may know himself.

Simply to inscribe the self, to fix the self actively within the world one inhabits, within the pages of history, takes a certain sense of what Marxists might refer to as "bourgeois individualism." That is, even though a working-class laborer when he began the diary, Ah Quin must have had a certain sense of his own importance in order to spend endless hours recording for some nameless posterity the events of his individual existence, including the time that he awoke each morning, the time he consumed his meals, and the time he went to bed each night. The rigorous and devotional attitude that he brings to writing—in ten diary volumes, in at least three copy books, in accounting ledgers, in numerous translations, and in countless letters—suggests that Ah Quin saw writing as an act of production in which he took pride. The sheer volume of his work implies that his prolific writing was one avenue through which he produced meaning and self-satisfaction in his life, as if to say, "I write, therefore I am."

To explore the self produced by the writing, a sometimes artificial distinction must be drawn between Ah Quin the author and producer of the text and Ah Quin the character who is produced by the writing. Admittedly, there are times when the two are inseparable or easily collapsed, but there are other times when the gap between them helps to draw attention to the constructedness of the self that is fashioned. For instance, one of the most striking things about the diary is its persistent, multilayered representation of cultural double consciousness. The measure of time, so important for a diary, is put forward by Ah Quin the author in bicultural terms. In the day books that he uses, he always scrawls the Chinese Empire date next to the preformatted Roman calendar date, as if to show an ever present location in two very different worlds. He primarily writes in English, but he code switches at interesting and sometimes inexplicable moments, invoking Chinese characters, for instance, to document items in the appendixes (e.g., recipes, loans and repayments, addresses). The cultural double consciousness enacted at the textual level is mirrored at the character level. Within the same year, Ah Quin the character celebrates holidays from both cultures, including Christmas, the Fourth of July, and the Buddhist Day of the Dead, and he regularly cooks and consumes both American and Chinese food.

From the surface-level issues of language and time, to the content-laden levels of cultural holidays and culinary practices, one theme reflected by Ah Quin the author and Ah Quin the character is a knowledge and allegiance to Chinese as well as American cultural traditions.

The enormous impact of this cultural double consciousness on first-generation immigrants means that biculturalism furthermore becomes the central lens through which to examine the diary's developing self. In fact, three different but related selves emerge from a systematic study of the diary—the Alaska Ah Quin, the San Francisco Ah Quin, and the San Diego Ah Quin— and the differences among these bicultural personas can be attributed in large part to social and situational roles.

The Alaska Ah Quin is found in the first two volumes of the diary, dated 1877–1878, when Ah Quin works as a cook for the superintendent, foreman, and workers of a coal mine on one of the Alaskan islands. This Ah Quin is portrayed as a skilled and well-versed cook, a devout and industrious Christian, and a genuine friend and companion to the whites for whom he works. As a hardworking and responsible cook, he awakes each morning around 4 A.M. to bake biscuits for what he calls "breakfast," cooks three meals a day for between four and twenty men, and cleans the house, studies, goes on a walk, or digs for clams in the afternoons. His pride in the sheer array of American foods he concocts is demonstrated by his constant mention of them, including pot pie, cornmeal pudding, sheep-head cheese, omelets, hotcakes, clam chowder, roast halibut and cod, stewed goose, venison stew, and corned beef, as well as deserts such as ginger cakes, graham biscuits, pie, rice pudding, muffins, angel food cake, and doughnuts.[3] He is dedicated to quality, staying up all night, for instance, to watch bread that isn't rising properly, and he is almost boastful about his industriousness, making mention often of the number of fish he cleans in a prescribed amount of time (the best is forty-seven fish in three hours) or the number of cookies he bakes in a day (sometimes 100, sometimes 170). The Alaska Ah Quin is resourceful, making a fan out of a bird's wing; he is disciplined, taking baths and combing his hair every Saturday; and he is a bit romantic, taking walks on the beach, into the mountains, and into the coal mines. With a wide range of skills and competencies, the Alaska Ah Quin is depicted as so competent that he regularly has hours each day to devote to his studies.

The most studious and seemingly religious Ah Quin that appears in the diary, the Alaska Ah Quin often spends five or six hours a day reading or studying from among a variety of texts, including the newspaper, a grammar book, a letter-writing primer, or especially the Bible (mostly the gospels). The second volume of the diary stands out from among the rest in its unrelenting focus on the Bible (it is also the only extant volume that Ah Quin the author copied into beautiful calligraphic script).[4] Each day, the reader is told which biblical verses the Alaska Ah Quin reads, which he reproduces into a separate copybook (or into the diary), and which Christian hymns he works to translate. The pervasiveness of the Christian Bible in volume 2 of the diary seems to paint this Ah Quin as an unusual devotee of Christianity, yet there is little commentary on Christianity besides the repetition of the verses themselves, and there is no rationale given for their reading, selection, or duplication. With the exception of a scene or two in which this Ah Quin hints at his internalization of Christian principles (in one entry he dreams that he converts his grandmother to Christianity: she was "lost like dead" until he tells her about the Christian religion, after which she "lives again" and is "joyful" [May 18, 1878]), the randomness, pervasiveness, and cursory appearance of biblical verses invite a degree of curiosity. What role did Bible study play in the life of the Alaska Ah Quin? How is this biblical presence relevant to Ah Quin the author? One humorous passage provides some insight. Here, as was often the case, Ah Quin the author transcribes a single biblical verse and then shifts to record the mundane activities of the day, "Lev—12:1 And the Lord spake unto Moses saying. clam soup and starch pud[ding]—for din[ner]" (June 16, 1878). This blending of two separate ideas, the sacred with the profane, suggests that the author and/or the character had little regard for the meaning behind the biblical words. Why did Ah Quin the author copy so prolifically from the Bible if he was paying so little attention to the words? What kind of a Christian was Ah Quin the author or Ah Quin the character? Whether Ah Quin copied biblical verses in the diary to affirm his belief system or to improve his handwriting, or to practice his English remains to be decided. In the absence of a more conclusive study, the Alaska Ah Quin represents a provocative paradigm of transnational Christianity put forward by a Chinese diarist who attends an American missionary school in China and then immigrates to the United States to live in a Judeo-Christian culture.

One final trait deserves mention regarding the Alaska Ah Quin. Given the historical context in which the Alaska Ah Quin emerges—a few years before the 1882 Chinese Exclusion Law, when hostilities toward Chinese in the United States were reaching their peak—this Ah Quin seems to enjoy a surprisingly friendly relationship with his white employers. They look after his welfare by giving him a new room to sleep in and poison for his bed bugs, and they intercede when he has a fight with his kitchen helper, Ah Tan. More importantly, the white employers, especially the foreman, Mr. Gourley, spend hours "chitchatting" with this Ah Quin in "my ketchen," and telling him "good stories" in the front room—and Ah Quin reciprocates. After he wanders into the coal mine and falls into a wet hole, Ah Quin returns home and tells them about it so all can laugh together. In the words of the author, "I said Mr. Gourley you want laugh at me so he say what is it I told him about I fall in the [hole] of the tunnel . . . so he laugh and make fun to me . . . after Mr. J. P. Stearns heard me fall in that hole then he come see me and make fun at me say I am baptism" (Sept. 15, 1877). Once, a white man calls to Ah Quin while riding a sled and he loses his balance and falls over. The author writes, "I laugh Mr. Thompson again at 2 o'clock this afternoon he drive the mule with the sled and hold few poles going up the tunnel and he see me out off the kitchen he call on me want me take a ride and just he fall down then I laugh greatly" (Jan. 14, 1878). When the men return after a night out, they tell Ah Quin in the morning about dancing with their shoes off, including the Alaska Ah Quin in the laughter as they revisit each other's fooleries. To be able to share *equally* in the kind of laughter that pokes fun at the individual members of a group means that the power differential within the group must be all but erased. Said differently, in a group that has an inherent unequal distribution of social and economic power, the fact that Ah Quin could offer his own mistakes up for laughter and participate in the laughter at white men's mishaps means that the asymmetrical power dynamic so common between Chinese and whites at this time must have been all but leveled—at least for the moment.

If laughter shared among whites and Chinese in pre-Exclusion Era Alaska is unexpected, then gift exchanges are even more surprising. Signaling thoughtfulness, narcissism, or business savvy, the Alaska Ah Quin occasionally delivers photographs of himself to whites he hopes will remember him. With more important figures, he offers more substantial gifts, like a red silk apron in one case and, after cutting it off, strands of his queue in another case. Apparently, the Alaska Ah Quin means these strands of his hair to be mementos to the foreman and superintendent of the mine—and the employers respond in kind. On the Chinese New Year, the Alaska Ah Quin feels "very alonesome" and Mr. E. T. Gourley asks him "why don't you burn any firework today then I laugh and when he have his dinner he give me the picture for the new year present and I say thank [you] forever that [the] only thing I received for the present this year 1878" (Feb. 1, 1878). Later, another man gives him "whiskers" that are nearly fifteen inches long and which he keeps "to remember the

friend" (May 15, 1878).[5] Although the Alaskan Ah Quin nearly always addresses whites by the respectful title "Mister," denoting an understanding of
his place in the social hierarchy, the laughter and gifts he shares with his white
employers suggest a friendly, if more approximate relationship. Like the
mimic men of colonial India, to use Homi Bhabha's words, the Alaska Ah
Quin can be said to be "Almost the same, but not quite. Almost the same, but
not white."

Depicted as a successful cook, a devout Christian, and a friend to whites,
the Alaska Ah Quin makes earnest efforts to adapt to American culture and
society. Perhaps it is no surprise that this is the persona who cuts off his queue
in a symbolic gesture of assimilation that makes him "look like the white people not like our china any more" (June 1, 1878). Even if he uses the Western
form of the diary, and finds his most satisfying social relationships in the
company of whites, his biculturalism is still always evident. He cooks the pork
in "our style" (Chinese style) for dinner and continually feels guilty that he has
abandoned his filial responsibility to care for his parents in their old age,
lamenting that "I may not see them no more" (Dec. 10, 1877).

When Ah Quin finds himself in San Francisco, after a short stay in Santa
Barbara, his Alaska identity all but disappears. The easygoing, playful, and studious Ah Quin gives way in San Francisco to an identity that is more typical
of nineteenth-century Chinese laborers who are treated as subservient in a
culture that is largely alien. The San Francisco Ah Quin works as a cook and
domestic for U.S. military officers from 1879 to 1880, first on Angel Island and
later at the Presidio. Gone are the four and five free hours in the afternoons
when he can record in the diary and study biblical verses. In fact, he feels so
rushed to get the cooking, cleaning, ironing, shoe polishing, and laundry done
that he complains that "the work is very hurry in every morn[ing]" (Feb. 14,
1879) and there is "no time rest 1 minute" (Feb. 21, 1879). Gone are the long
talks filled with "good stories" and laughter with his employers. Here, he is
scolded for not doing acceptable work. The title "Mister," used to describe his
employers in Alaska, slips on occasion in San Francisco to become "Master,"
reconfirming Ah Quin's acknowledgment of his own altered and more subservient status.

Of note, the San Francisco Ah Quin has a particularly tentative relationship with one white man, Mr. H. G. Otis, who eventually serves as a house
manager in both houses where Ah Quin works. Otis is the only white man up
to this point in the diary not regularly addressed by a title, and he scolds Ah
Quin on one occasion for cooking food that Mr. Otis claims is unfit for con-

sumption. Interestingly, the first time Ah Quin is scolded by a white man, for not having the man's shoes polished in time, the diary registers a feeling of remorse. The author writes, "I have no time to black the shoes of Mr. Dyer. Then he scold me Christ what I do. whole morning I felt very sorry about it" (Apr. 7, 1879). When Otis scolds him, however, the remorse is replaced by an implicit challenge. The author writes, "Otis [s]cold me. he say the potatoes is not fix [fit] to eat. but he like fry potatoes" (Nov. 18, 1879). The last phrase, "but he like fry potatoes," signals Ah Quin's reluctance this time to admit to the error, and suggests a note of defiance. Ah Quin's logic, however, is not foolproof. Just because Otis likes fried potatoes does not necessarily mean that this batch of fried potatoes was to his liking. Instead, the gap in Ah Quin's logic reveals his sense of resistance. (One wonders if this insolence was uttered only in the diary.) In addition, a few other unusual events involve Otis. He is the only person who presumes to instruct Ah Quin on how to cook for guests (Ah Quin regularly studies an American cookbook) and, on at least eight occasions when Otis is not home, Ah Quin goes into Otis's room and sleeps in his bed, sometimes only for an hour. Does Ah Quin appreciate or resent Otis's cooking instruction? Is sleeping in the white man's bed a liberty that was permitted, an act of eroticism, or an act of subversion? Does he sleep there because his own quarters were less than adequate? Does he write about it to subvert a power structure that doesn't favor him? For Ah Quin, does the absence of a title for Otis imply the presence of resistance or, worse, defiance? Nowhere else in the diary do we get this sense of persistent and unspoken tension from Ah Quin; therefore the relationship between Otis and Ah Quin serves as an interesting case of interracial relations that highlights, among other things, one kind of agency or willfulness available to a nineteenth-century Chinese immigrant in Ah Quin's position.

When the San Francisco Ah Quin isn't working, on Wednesday and Thursday evenings, he often travels to the San Francisco Chinatown, where he frequents theaters, restaurants, gambling halls, church services, and whorehouses. Many Chinese depended upon the infrastructure of the Chinese enclave for financial assistance and support, so, as was common, Ah Quin is hounded by Chinese associations for dues and sought after by friends and relatives for loans. In one case, when he doesn't have enough money to extend a loan, he takes the watch off of his wrist and gives it to his friend (relation?) to pawn. Generosity like this places Ah Quin at the center of his social circle, and people search him out for help with English translations, visit him often in his quarters, and fill his social calendar with outings.

Far from the studious and religious Alaskan cook, the San Francisco Ah Quin lives in a racially divided world where his work environment is alien and his social interactions are limited. Popular in his Chinese community but estranged in the white world, this Ah Quin represents a split model of biculturalism in which Chinese and white worlds resist blending and subjects are seemingly forced to choose between being forever alien and living forever at the margins.[6]

In San Diego, we find a third characterization. Ah Quin comes to San Diego in 1880 to work as a labor recruiter for the California Southern Railroad (C.S.R.R.). Unfortunately, three years go by between his departure for San Diego and the next diary entry (it is unclear whether volumes of the diary were lost or never existed) and great changes take place in the intervening time: Ah Quin marries, he has the first of twelve children, he opens a store to supply goods to the Chinese working on the railroad, and the 1882 Chinese Exclusion Law is passed. The 1884 diary opens to a new Ah Quin, whose lifestyle resembles the modern professional in its pace, stress level, and achievements.

The San Diego Ah Quin begins high-pressure, managerial-type work in his recruitment of Chinese laborers for the California Southern Railroad. When his employers give the word, Ah Quin travels immediately to all areas of southern California, from Riverside County to Orange County to Los Angeles County and sometimes even to San Francisco, in search of workers. He is an effective recruiter, bringing in as many as ninety-two workers at one time, but he still curses himself on days when other recruiters fill the demands more quickly. The author writes, "William got all the men supply to C.S.R.R. that make me not felt well" (Sept. 21, 1884) and "not felt well. bec[ause] I lost the chance to get all the men what is the C.S.R.R. take" (Sept. 25, 1884). We can imagine that with over 160 Chinese working on the railroad, Ah Quin sees a captive audience for (Chinese) food import, so he sets up a store and begins shipping goods, like rice and fish, from San Francisco and San Diego to southern California railroad gangs. After the southern segment of the railroad is complete, Ah Quin continues informally as a labor recruiter, being called upon by local growers, for instance, when Chinese workers are needed to clear lands for agriculture.

In addition to recruiting Chinese workers and supplying railroad gangs with goods, the San Diego Ah Quin forms a company (companies?) with other Chinese investors and expands his business interests to include several farms (which he calls "gardens"), a restaurant, a Japanese store, and a pawnshop, among other enterprises. He leases or buys land in the San Diego areas of Fallbrook, San Miguel, Sweetwater Junction, and Bonita; he buys horses and wagons to work the land; and he hires Chinese to oversee production, planting, and harvesting of crops—namely, potatoes and lima beans. As an involved manager, Ah Quin regularly visits the farms himself, remarking upon the "salt spots" in the land where little will grow. With his restaurant, he is similarly active, and complains about the chief cook, who is often drunk. Notably, Ah Quin says little about the other investors except to mention their occasional quarrels.

This Ah Quin is also regularly hired as a Chinese translator for the San Diego courthouse, which in addition to income gives him access to and knowledge about the American judicial system. On at least two occasions, Ah Quin enacts a surprising degree of agency by filing suit against two American businesses: he sues the railroad company for cutting into a lot he owns in Riverside County (it is settled in his favor) and he sues the San Diego paper for slander. Even though he eventually drops the case against the paper, the suit is interesting because it highlights the gap between the perception of nineteenth-century Chinese in America as unskilled, heathen laborers who come to America to exploit opportunities and return to China, and Ah Quin-the-man, an ambitious and successful Christian who is well established in San Diego and is so concerned about his reputation that he sues the paper to preserve his honor. The gap is even more manifest in an incident that Ah Quin likely considers the greatest mistake of his life. He co-signs on a loan for a white lawyer friend, who eventually defaults and ironically leaves Ah Quin, too honest to flee the responsibility, to melt his wife's and children's gold jewelry to help to pay the debt. In contrast to the stereotype of early Chinese immigrants as insidious or passive laborers who were fearful of the courts, Ah Quin is fearless in his approach to matters of personal justice and unflinching in his dedication to responsibility and sacrifice. As a respected businessman, he goes to great lengths to protect his honor and uphold his good name, perhaps precisely because he is aware of the rampant negative assumptions about the Chinese.

Finally, we see in the San Diego Ah Quin the husband and father who takes his family by wagon out to inspect his farms and dresses his children in the American style to send them to church on Sundays. While his business practices seem to dominate the San Diego diary entries, Ah Quin makes some mention of his wife, Ah Sue, remarking upon her "seasickness" (morning sickness) and her willingness to forgive him when he comes home drunk and belligerent. In the author's words, "in home very late I full drunk but I bad temper broken the globe. and scold my Wife bad. I am sorry it made her sorry also she take care me and put me in bed . . . my Wife excuse me about last night. I fool her she is very good act" (July 27–28, 1891). Self-reportedly drunk and full of temper on some occasions, Ah Quin also seems attentive to his wife in his own ways, making a special dinner for her birthday and helping her with the sewing and with the children. In short, we know relatively little from the diaries about the personal relationship between Ah Quin and Ah Sue, but what can be seen is a fairly typical relationship in its alternating currents of struggle and understanding.

With little time for church services or personal study, the San Diego Ah Quin is presented as the consummate entrepreneur and respectable community member who is equally conversant in Chinese and white societies: he is hired by white railroad administrators and he exercises his ability to hire white lawyers; he gives and takes loans from whites and Chinese alike; and he helps to settle cases for the U.S. court system and is called upon informally to settle disputes within the Chinese community. Although he is much wealthier in San Diego than in Alaska or in San Francisco, he falls on hard times in the early 1890s and has to sell off a number of his business ventures to satisfy his creditors. But in a remarkable display of talent and tenacity, he eventually regains his fortune and resumes his role as a bicultural patriarch.

From the laughter-filled laborer in Alaska, to the split subject in San Francisco, to the bicultural community citizen in San Diego, we see three manifestations of Ah Quin emerge from the diary, each largely the result of situational forces. An examination of a life over twenty-five years of daily history can uncover subtle shifts and changes of perspective over years and locations, and can ultimately remind us again of the dynamic—rather than static—nature of identity formation.

BIOS: A CHINESE LIFE DURING THE AGE OF EXCLUSION
If diarists are historians of the self, then the documents they produce have important private and public dimensions: in the private domain, a diary is an unusual narrative of a psychological history that bears the bumps and bruises of personal growth that may or may not be representative of the experience of others in the same time and place; in the public domain, it serves as a historical and anthropological record that contributes uniquely to the cultural heritage. Ideally, scholars would study a wide range of diaries from a particular group at a particular moment to extract truths common

to all, but in the absence of such rich materials, the examination of a single written life is still beneficial. As Georges Gusdorf argues, the individual is an interdependent unit in a community; "the individual does not oppose himself to all others, . . . [he lives] *with* others in an interdependent existence that asserts its rhythms everywhere in the community."[7] As such, a diary is to some degree representative of the community from which it stems, but *how* representative is the life that is written? This is a more difficult question to answer.

The existence of Ah Quin's diary itself helps to challenge the stereotype of an illiterate nineteenth-century Chinese workforce (see Liu, chapter 1 in this volume). It certainly doesn't prove that all early Chinese immigrants were literate in Chinese and in English, but the fact that one person could be so proficient in both languages opens the possibility that others had access to a similar level of education. Yong Chen, in his article about Ah Quin, makes the point that Ah Quin's Chinese-language proficiency is greater than his English-language proficiency, as demonstrated by his ability to use more sophisticated and nuanced terms in Chinese,[8] but it deserves mention that Ah Quin regularly uses the wrong Chinese character, just as he regularly misspells words in English. He seems to use a phonetic system in English, relying heavily on the sound of language in order to inscribe it. For instance, "cherry pie" is spelled "cheely pie"; "crowd" is spelled "clowed"; and "little" is spelled "lettle." In English, he also uses minimum and arbitrary punctuation, with sentences unpredictably continuing on or ending. Words are capitalized based on their importance, so "Wife," for instance, is almost always capitalized, as are terms like "Because" (when he wants to provide an explanation for something), or "Big thief" (when he uses the diary to chastise an associate). Ah Quin's spelling by sound, his almost stream-of-consciousness style, and his arbitrary capitalization may point to educational roots firmly planted in an oral tradition. (As a side note, learning English via an oral tradition provides an interesting basis of commonality for a number of early American ethnic and immigrant authors, like the writers of slave narratives and Native American autobiographies.) Nevertheless, the fact that a nineteenth-century Chinese immigrant had the skill, time, and dedication to write an extensive diary defies expectations regarding the "laboring masses" who came to the United States to work in the gold mines and on the railroads and were assumed to be uneducated and illiterate in Chinese as well as in English.

As the first-person record of a Chinese life during the age of Chinese exclusion, the diary includes surprisingly little mention of hostile racial relations, but much to the contrary. There are two incidents that could be construed as racially motivated, but Ah Quin doesn't explicitly characterize them as such. On the ship to Alaska, Ah Quin is very seasick and a man (presumably white) seems to think him lazy and throws water on him while he is sleeping. Ah Quin writes, "the first mate named Colby put water in my blanket . . . good many days he think me go sleep and lazy" (June 6, 1877). Another time he is at Black Point in San Francisco with at least one other Chinese man when "many bad boys through [threw] the stone to hurt us, but not hurt us any" (June 2, 1879). It's not clear what, exactly, happens at Black Point or what race the "bad boys" are, but something threatening occurs and Ah Quin, in his typical manner, gives us few details.

A third incident could be construed to be a racially motivated crime— someone breaks into the pawnshop in the front of his house in San Diego and steals about $60 worth of merchandise, then pours oil on the front door the next evening in an act that Ah Quin thinks is attempted arson. Although the burglary and attempted arson might be interpreted as hate crimes, it is equally probable that these transgressions are the result of a large loan Ah Quin received from a fellow Chinese that Ah Quin cannot pay back on demand. On several occasions before the break-in, Ah Quin is threatened with harm if he does not deliver the payment. When he asks a lawyer friend for advice, the friend suggests that Ah Quin pay an installment, which he immediately supplies, but the $100 he pays might not be enough of the $1,000 requested to stave off the threat of harm. Unfortunately, Ah Quin says nothing else about these three incidents after their initial mention, which is in some ways as interesting as if he did. Did Ah Quin experience overt racism during an anti-Chinese period? Under what conditions would he have coded an incident as "racist"? Why does he say so little in the diary about these three acts of violence when he spends so much time recording matters that seem so much more mundane, like the weather or what time he goes to bed? At the very least, the few details he provides for these incidents speak to his priorities and concerns for the diary. Another writer might have made these scenes, and other similar incidents, central to the document itself. For the length of the diary, from Alaska to San Diego, Ah Quin is more interested in using the diary as a forum to record other aspects of his life that he apparently deems more important or more central. As a man often concerned with adaptation, Ah Quin may have selected out racial incidents for his records, or he might not have perceived incidents as racially motivated. However, he was always aware of difference, as demonstrated in the Alaska volumes, when he makes mention of the Russians, Scotch, and Aleuts, and in his constant references to Chinese as "our people" or "our language."

Since the 1875 Page Law effectively banned the immigration of Chinese women (and interracial marriage was illegal), most Chinese lived in a bachelor society. Nonetheless, Ah Quin manages to marry, has twelve children, and actively participates in the rearing of his family. While he is in San Francisco, he attends the wedding of one of his friends and seems to ask another friend to act as a matchmaker for him. The following year, the San Diego paper announces Ah Quin's marriage to a woman he meets at the San Francisco Chinese mission (her origins are unclear—she is either a merchant's daughter or, more likely, a woman rescued from slavery).[9] One might imagine that Ah Quin, as a successful businessman and entrepreneur, would be a staunch patriarch in his house, but he appears more egalitarian, often consulting his wife in business matters. He writes, "[I] talked to my Wife about Charley England restaurant on I st. near 4th and 5th. but she not like take it . . . my Wife very post-on [pissed at] me say I ought not to take business. But I not mind [what] she said, so she is very bad treat me. and made me sorry also. It strike me very bad and hurd me in bosom. I not fell good tonight or not sleep much" (Oct. 7, 1891). To Ah Quin's credit, he makes his wife a partner in some of his business decisions, demonstrating an unusually progressive attitude toward women.

In addition to his unlikely marriage, he has an even more surprising dozen children for whom he serves as an involved father. Ah Quin's skills as a cook and domestic translate easily into help around the house, where he sometimes cooks, mends, and watches at least a few children. It is not unusual for Ah Quin to take a child or two with him when he surveys his businesses (especially his sons, who later run the business) and he regularly escorts children to the dentist, calls the doctor, or takes them to buy socks. On one occasion, he accompanies one of the babies to the Sunday school teacher's house to visit, but the child "makes duty on the floor. I am sorry. we leave" (June 25, 1891). And, remarkably, he helps to deliver at least one baby in the middle of the night. His flock of children must have been a novelty in a San Diego County that had only a few hundred Chinese, so Ah Quin regularly updates the family photo and distributes copies to the numerous women, mostly from Sunday school, who visit them on the Chinese New Year. Perhaps because Chinese wives and families were so uncommon, Ah Quin appreciates Ah Sue and his children more, resisting the stereotype of the Chinese patriarch and head of household who only tends the business and leaves the mundane matters of the home completely to his wife and hired hands. Rather, he is an involved father and progressive husband who consults his wife on business affairs, even if he does not always like what she says.

Finally, Ah Quin demonstrates class mobility and community recognition beyond what might be expected from a working-class immigrant. From his identity as a laborer in the north to his position as a property owner in the south, the improvement in his class standing is reflected in the amount of remittance he occasionally sends home to his mother in China: from $10 in Alaska to $33 and eventually $50 in San Diego. A filial son, despite his commitment to stay in America, he is more ambitious and scholarly than many have imagined nineteenth-century Chinese immigrants to be, and he is a community dignitary (or novelty?) whose noteworthy events surprisingly are published in the local paper, including his marriage, the birth of his son, and his translation of an assaying book. He was so successful that after his tragic death in 1914, his obituary notes that his assets were valued at a remarkable $50,000.

The prolific record of Ah Quin's life sheds new light on the nineteenth-century Chinese immigrant experience because, most notably, it helps to question a number of stereotypes long held about this population, such as their lack of literacy, family life, and class mobility. But the question still remains: how representative is Ah Quin? For now, we can say he is probably fairly unusual, given the length and breadth of his diary alone, but how (a)typical is a question that remains to be answered.

GRAPHE: WRITING WITHIN CONTEXTS

When speaking about Ah Quin's written text, it is important to place it precisely within the nonfiction tradition of which it is an example: the genre of the diary. In a perfect world, the ideal diary would begin at the moment of birth (in utero for psychoanalysts) and end with the recording of the author's death. In other words, it would be a full and complete record of the self for the full duration of the life that is lived. But this is clearly impracticable. In practice, a diary is always an incomplete record of a life, a sporadic, episodic document that is pertinent to some years and not to others. In this sense, Ah Quin's diary is typical. It begins when he is twenty-eight and continues intermittently until he is about fifty-four. In his later years, as he has more children, he writes more sporadically, mostly when he is sick and apparently in convalescence. His diary trickles off, with fewer and fewer entries, before ending uneventfully some twelve years before his death.

As befits the diary, Ah Quin's imagined audience is neither clear nor (likely) consistent. He might be writing to an imagined future self; he might be writing to his missionary teachers; or he might be writing more for the act of writing itself, as if the recording of his life gives it clarity and/or substance. At only one moment in the diary does he address an audience directly. After he is cheated out of a significant amount of money, he writes, "Dear the Childrens hope you all don't do such fool like I do" (Dec. 30, 1891). Although it appears from this quote that his children are his audience, when he begins the diary during the age of exclusion of Chinese women to the United States, he cannot expect to have children. In addition, even though he continues the diary for over twelve years after the birth of his first child, he directly addresses his children only once. In context, this quote shows that his children were probably only a transient or situation-specific audience. To complicate matters, on at least two occasions he shows the diary to white friends who marvel at his achievement. Finally, because Ah Quin's diary remains unpublished, it has not had to satisfy marketplace demands in the same way as similar texts (e.g., the abolitionist agenda of African American slave narratives and the assimilationist agenda of Japanese American internment diaries). The absence of marketplace forces might allow for a degree of flexibility and fluidity not available in published ethnic nonfiction. With these points in mind, who is the audience for Ah Quin's diary? The most comprehensive answer is that the text seems to be directed to different audiences at different times. Generally, Ah Quin may envision an older, wiser version of himself as the most persistent audience. The early volumes, filled as they are with biblical passages, might be directed to missionary teachers or classmates to illustrate devotion; the San Francisco volume may be aimed at other Chinese to demonstrate English mastery; and the later volumes may be pointed to descendants and/or whites to exhibit ingenuity. The fact that there may be multiple imagined audiences is interesting because it infers a text with a degree of transparency and immediacy unusual even among nonfiction.

Viewing a diary as Literature presents an interesting paradox. If the traditional requirements for Literature include a purposeful beginning, climax, and ending, these cannot be achieved in the diary. The proper ending in a diary, for instance, should be a description of the death of the author, which would presumably be considered an important event for the day. But this cannot reasonably be written by the author. Since the diary cannot, by one traditional definition, meet the standards for Literature, we must fathom other criteria through which to read it. We can ask, for instance, about its internal coherence. Does it begin with certain conventions to which it remains faithful? Are there rhetorical devices that enhance the meaning of the text? Does the narrative take as its focus specific themes or issues for which it provides a certain insight? In the case of the Ah Quin diary, the conventions are so consistent from the first entry, including bicultural dates, the weather, the time of eating, waking, sleeping, that speculation arises about the possibility of earlier volumes in which these conventions were developed gradually (chronological gaps suggest the same). Nonetheless, as a specimen, Ah Quin's work follows basic diary conventions, including format, audience, and distinct rhetorical patterns.

Aside from its distinctiveness as a diary, Ah Quin's text also must be examined in terms of its predominant message. Specifically, it begins as a travel narrative, opening on the eve of Ah Quin's move from Santa Barbara to Alaska; it has components of the conversion narrative, with its strong biblical presence and Christian motifs; it can be called the story of a self-made man in the style of Benjamin Franklin or Horatio Alger, given the progression from working class to entrepreneur; and there is even an argument to classify it as a conquest or assimilation narrative.[10] Given these prevailing themes, the Ah Quin diary is all of these and none of these. It draws upon elements in each of these conventions, (un)knowingly grounding itself in a firmly established tradition of American writing, but at the same moment it takes liberties with these conventions in order to achieve its desired ends. Similar to and yet different from established themes in nonfiction writing, Ah Quin's is ultimately a new kind of tale, the story of a man who stands in a cultural hyperspace, attempting to mediate between two sometimes opposed worlds.

As a document by a Chinese American immigrant about the life of Chinese Americans, Ah Quin also writes within the context of an already established ethnic textual tradition. However, his work chronologically predates the Asian American canon, setting up interesting questions of influence. Using a Bloomian analysis of literary history, it is as though the diary represents a father text that appears only after the family is already well underway. What happens when an absent literary father emerges? The relationship between absent father and what would be literary successors must somehow be reconciled. As a first-stage autobiographical work, that is, one that remains in a raw and unpublished form, it differs from second-stage nonfiction, including works by Pardee Lowe and Jade Snow Wong, and third-stage works, like those written by Maxine Hong Kingston, in that it avoids the marketplace pressures of published texts. Yet, the variety of bicultural themes and tensions in Ah Quin's diary anticipates the themes of assimilation, adaptation, and subversion displayed in the Chinese American canon. The fact that the diary appeared nearly thirty years after the genre was born, and shares themes common in the Asian American canon, demonstrates a kind of reverse literary history in which the presence of earlier publications makes way for the importance of this new/old one (and others like it).[11]

Ultimately, we will probably never know what drove Ah Quin to write his diary or what kind of satisfaction he may have received from being able to capture or recover the events of his day. He may have written as a way to pass the time, to practice his English, to rehearse lessons from the Bible, to quantify his acts before the Lord, to guard against becoming obscure, to organize his life, or to feel like he was producing something of meaning or of value—as if the art of writing was a significant act of accomplishment in itself.

According to Steven Kagle, a diary often arises at a moment of tension in the author's life and is used as a way to resolve a change of place or a stage of growth (e.g., puberty). It follows that the resolution of the tension would often bring with it the resolution of the text, reinforcing the diary's episodic nature. Ah Quin's diary begins with travel and, although he moves several times, he lives in San Diego for nearly a dozen years before the diary trickles to an uneventful end. Thus, the diary isn't very useful to resolve the tension and perhaps excitement of traveling to a new environment. However, if we examine the work from a different point of view, from the point of view of living in the midst of racial and cultural hostility, then it makes sense that the conflicts of biculturalism might never be resolved for a first-generation immigrant, and that accepting a persistent sense of cultural double consciousness, whatever its manifestations, might be the only key to peace and satisfaction. Through this lens, Ah Quin can be said to be writing squarely within Kagel's diary tradition. The fact that Ah Quin didn't discard or destroy the volumes of his work over so many years, and that the text was at times a relatively polished document with signs of editing and revising throughout, means that it ultimately wasn't intended to be a private document at all, but one meant to be read. What readers may not have realized is what valuable information about the immigrant experience this and similar work contains for scholars in disciplines ranging from literary studies to sociology, history to anthropology.

NOTES

I am grateful to the Literature and Writing Department at California State University, San Marcos (CSUSM), especially Heather Richardson Hayton and Madeleine Marshall, for their helpful and substantive feedback on an earlier version of this chapter. Thanks also to Kathleen Moore and Christopher Johnson for their endless, insightful conversations with me about Ah Quin; to Murray Lee for introducing me to Ah Quin; and to a CSUSM university professional development grant for support of this project. All quotations from the diary are from the unpublished manuscript, San Diego Historical Society Archives. Of note, as this article goes to press, another volume of the diary has been found and plans are underway to have it join the others in the San Diego archives.

1. For more biographical information about Ah Quin, please see Murray Lee's article, chapter 17 in this volume.

2. See Mathews (1977, 286–87).

3. In Alaska, he only mentions cooking Chinese food when he feels sick, when he makes for himself rice soup with dried oysters.

4. The only version of volume 2 that remains is the beautifully recopied text, so we cannot see what may have been altered from the original. The missing original volume 2, along with the copybooks mentioned in the diary, suggest that other volumes of the diary may also be missing.

5. It is unclear, exactly, to what these whiskers refer. They are called "sea whiskers" and "whiskers."

6. For more on Ah Quin in San Francisco, see Chen (2000).

7. See Gusdorf (1956, 29).

8. See Chen (2000, 106).

9. See Griego (1979), Chen (2000), and M. Lee (chapter 17 in this volume).

10. See Kagle (1979).

11. See my unpublished essay, "In the Absence of the Father: Ah Quin's Arrival in Asian American Literature," on Ah Quin's anxiety of influence.

REFERENCES

Bjorkland, Diane. 1998. *Interpreting the Self: Two Hundred Years of American Autobiography.* Chicago: University of Chicago Press.

Bunkers, Suzanne, and Cynthia A. Huff, eds. 1996. *Inscribing the Daily: Critical Essays on Women's Diaries*. Amherst: University of Massachusetts Press.

Chen, Yong. 2000. *Chinese San Francisco, 1850–1943*. Stanford, Calif.: Stanford University Press.

Conway, Jill Ker. 1998. *When Memory Speaks: Exploring the Art of Autobiography*. New York: Vintage.

Eakin, Paul John, ed. 1991. *American Autobiography: Retrospect and Prospect*. University of Wisconsin Press.

Fox-Genovese, Elizabeth. 1987. "To Write My Self: The Autobiographies of Afro-American Women." In *Feminist Issues in Literary Scholarship*, ed. Shari Benstock, 161–80. Bloomington: Indiana University Press.

Griego, Andrew R. 1979. "Mayor of Chinatown: The Life of Ah Quin, Chinese Merchant and Railroad Builder of San Diego." Master's thesis, San Diego State University.

Gusdorf, Georges. 1956. "Conditions and Limits of Autobiography." In *Autobiography: Essays Theoretical and Critical*, ed. James Olney, 28–48. Princeton, N.J.: Princeton University Press.

Jelinek, Estelle. 1986. *The Tradition of Women's Autobiography: From Antiquity to the Present*. Boston: Twayne.

Kagle, Steven. 1979. *American Diary Literature 1620–1799*. Boston: Twayne.

Kagle, Steven. 1988. *Late Nineteenth-Century American Diary Literature*. Boston: Twayne.

Krupat, Arnold. 1985. *For Those Who Come After: A Study of Native American Autobiography*. Berkeley: University of California Press.

Lejeune, Philippe. 1996. "The 'Journal de Jeune Fille' in Nineteenth-Century France." Trans. Martine Breillac. In *Inscribing the Daily: Critical Essays on Women's Diaries*, ed. Suzanne Bunkers and Cynthia A. Huff, 107–122. Amherst: University of Massachusetts Press.

Mathews, William. 1977. "The Diary: A Neglected Genre." *Sewanee Review* 85, no. 2 (spring): 286–300.

Olney, James, ed. 1980. *Autobiography: Essays Theoretical and Critical*. Princeton, N.J.: Princeton University Press.

Olney, James. 1980. "Autobiography and the Cultural Moment: A Thematic, Historical, and Bibliographical Introduction." In *Autobiography: Essays Theoretical and Critical*, ed. James Olney, 3–27.

Sayre, Robert. 1980. "Autobiography and the Making of America." In *Autobiography: Essays Theoretical and Critical,* ed. James Olney, 146–68. Princeton, N.J.: Princeton University Press.

Smith, Sidonie. 1976. *Where I'm Bound: Patterns of Slavery and Freedom in Black American Autobiography.* Westport, Conn.: Greenwood.

Spengemann, William. 1980. *The Forms of Autobiography: Episodes in the History of a Literary Genre.* New Haven, Conn.: Yale University Press.

Swindells, Julia. ed. 1995. *The Uses of Autobiography.* London: Taylor and Francis.

II

Discrimination and Exclusion across America

4

Exploring New Frontiers in Chinese American History: The Anti-Chinese Riot in Milwaukee, 1889

Victor Jew

For at least a decade now, a handful of scholars have explored uncharted territory in Asian American studies. That terrain has been described as "east of California." Steven Sumida noted in *The Journal of Asian American Studies* that "east of California" is that expanse of Asian America(s) that is different—different from the West Coast, from California, from San Francisco and Los Angeles.

This chapter contributes to the "east of California" project. It examines an instance of Chinese American history that occupies yet another subset of non–West Coast Asian American historiography. This chapter examines an in-betweenness—east of California and west of New York. I will examine an episode of Chinese Exclusion Era history in the "Midwest," a region that defies easy definition, yet is often identified as a space of shared values. The states bordering the Great Lakes (but not all the Great Lakes, at least in 1999) and those stretching to the Plains, or approaching the Rocky Mountains, are often included under the rubric "Midwest." However vague, the "Midwest" needs its Asian American legacies recovered and, as this chapter shows, there are stories to recover from "the heartland."

My story is a forgotten piece of Chinese American history, but to many historians of Chinese America that is a familiar predicament. Much pre–World War II Chinese American and Asian American history is forgotten, "lost" or left unwritten, either due to a lack of primary sources or, in the case of the National Archives, the opposite quandary: an inundation of documentation in the Record Group 85 (Immigration Service) files.

Granted, historians of pre–World War II Chinese America share a common plight. Nevertheless, I suspect that my story is a special case that illustrates especially well the complexities of what is remembered and what is forgotten. That this episode was forgotten is remarkable. That its public record is so sparse is, frankly, amazing.

What occurred in March and May 1889 did not happen in secret, nor did it develop in private, unrecorded moments. What happened in Milwaukee, Wisconsin, that late winter and spring was a large-scale anti-Chinese riot—I suspect the only citywide anti-Chinese pogrom in a major "Midwestern" city. Quite possibly, it was the only mass anti-Chinese instance in the north and east of the Mississippi River. (There was a violent anti-Chinese episode in Waynesboro, Georgia, in the 1880s.)

Witnesses at the time recognized the scale of this disturbance, although they offered ambivalent testimony about its long-term consequences. One Milwaukee newspaper described the window smashing and Chinese hunting as "very like a riot." In nearby Chicago, the *Chicago Tribune* frankly said that Milwaukee had not seen so large an urban disturbance since May 1886—a reference to the Bayview Massacre, the worst civil disturbance in that city's nineteenth-century history.

Nevertheless, this instance of anti-Chinesism on the shores of Lake Michigan was quickly forgotten. Moreover, it remained forgotten for the next one hundred years. Histories of Milwaukee do not mention this episode. Nor are there references to this front-page newspaper event in the voluminous index to the *Milwaukee Sentinel*. Occupying row upon row of card catalog drawers, this index was a bibliographic task compiled in the 1930s under the auspices of the Works Progress Administration. One can find numerous references to other "riots" and disturbances from the 1850s through the 1890s, but not a card on the anti-Chinese riot of 1889. If it is possible to sweep an elephant under a rug, then the forgetting of Wisconsin's anti-Chinese moment is roughly analogous to that feat.[1] This chapter tries to recover the circumstances of the March 1889 pogrom and restore this episode to the status of "fact," to allow it to take its place within a growing body of recovered "facts" about pre–World War II Chinese American history.

To Asian Americanists and nineteenth-century U.S. historians, Chinese-targeted violence on the shores of Lake Michigan is "news." Historians are more familiar with the acts committed in Denver, Seattle, Tacoma, San Francisco, and Rock Springs, Wyoming.[2] From the 1850s to 1908, recorded instances of anti-Chinese violence numbered 153. These outbreaks tolled 143 Chinese murdered and 10,525 displaced from their homes and businesses. The peak years of this violence were the 1880s, the years of the Chinese Exclusion Act (1882) and the onset of its regime of ever harsher amendments.[3] That decade witnessed ninety-one instances of anti-Chinese violence, the years 1885 and 1886 forming a midpoint apex with thirty and forty-three events apiece.[4]

Milwaukee would share the dubious distinction of being one of two sites of anti-Chinese violence to end the decade, the other outbreak occurring in Flagstaff, Arizona. While we can now add the mobbing in "Cream City" to the list of Chinese-targeted pogroms, we also need to note a key difference from other incidents of anti-Chinese violence. Milwaukee's day (and night) of Chinese rage happened because of interracial sex.[5]

Sexuality was one of many anxieties animating Western Chinophobic riots, but it was not the precipitating cause in the Pacific Coast and Rocky Mountain outbursts. While accusations of filth and immorality stalked Chinese settlers, Western riots fed on fears of Chinese labor competition; the Chinese supposedly undercut adult, white, and (primarily) male workers (see Tam, chapter 7 in this volume). By contrast, the Milwaukee incident was sparked by charges of Chinese sexual misbehavior with white females. Cream City flared into its anti-Chinese firestorm because two Chinese men, Hah Ding and Sam Yip Ya, were arrested for allegedly taking sexual liberties with a number of Milwaukee females. Making this situation more explosive was the fact that the females in question were underage (fourteen and younger) and that all of them were white.

In first breaking the story about the alleged multiple sexual assaults, the *Milwaukee Sentinel* greeted its morning readers with this headline: "Chinese Demons. Their Terrible Practices in Milwaukee. Children Enticed into Laundry Dens and then Ruined." Keeping readers salivating for more details, the paper would entice them the following morning with "Chinese Horrors. Twenty Two Children Are Lured into the Dens."[6]

In addition, both the *Sentinel* and the Madison-based *Wisconsin State Journal* circulated hair-raising theories the day after Hah Ding's and Sam Yip Ya's arrests. Both newspapers reported as a verified fact that something much more sinister was at work, something that signified a moral epidemic stretching from Wisconsin to Illinois. The lead paragraphs for both papers' accounts asserted that a "league" or "alliance" of Milwaukee- and Chicago-based Chinamen existed for the sole purpose of transporting white girls from Wisconsin to be brides for Chinese in Chicago. "It is now thought to be proven that a regular traffic was carried on in young girls. . . . An alliance exists between the Celestials in Chicago and their brethren in Milwaukee, whereby half a dozen

Chinamen in Chicago have married white girls from Milwaukee, who have paid money for their wives."[7]

This accusation, so fantastic that even one of the newspapers declared it "well nigh incredible," would later be repudiated by Superintendent Richard Whitehead of the Humane Society, the man who first accused the two Chinese of misdeeds. Nevertheless, the editors at the respectable *Sentinel* thought the charges credible enough that they gave them front-page prominence during the crucial first days of the scandal.

Given the small numbers of Chinese residents in the Midwest and Great Lakes states, one wonders how they could have set off this moral panic, which prefigured the white slavery panic of the Progressive Era. At the beginning of the 1880s, most of the Chinese residents in the United States were in California. That state recorded 75,132 Chinese residents in the tenth census of the United States; the next highest states were Oregon (9,510) and Nevada (5,416). The region that we call "the Midwest" had miniscule numbers (the Wisconsin state census for 1880 did not bother to list Chinese or Oriental nativity). Nevertheless, the agricultural states in this region did experience a demographic trend that signaled the new presence of Chinese. Between the 1870 census and the 1880 census, the following before-and-after population events occurred: Michigan recorded one Chinese resident in 1870; ten years later, it showed twenty-seven. Iowa had three, Ohio counted one, and Illinois listed one in 1870; in 1880 they had thirty-three, one hundred and nine, and two hundred and nine respectively. Three states—Indiana, Minnesota, and Wisconsin—listed no Chinese residents in 1870; ten years later, they registered twenty-nine, twenty-four, and for the Badger State, sixteen Chinese.[8] For a state such as Wisconsin, going from zero to a double-digit figure represented the appearance of not only a countable but a newly visible presence. A "Chinaman" could now be seen and watched within both the imaginary city and on real-world streets and sidewalks. Moreover, these appearances and settlements occurred within the context of a growing and eventually successful nationwide campaign for Chinese laborer exclusion.

By the time of the sex scandal and riot, there were approximately sixty Chinese in Milwaukee; the vast majority were laundrymen.[9] Instead of concentrating within a Chinese ethnic sector, the Milwaukee laundrymen fanned outside the city's central business district to establish Asian hand laundries in numerous wards and neighborhoods. This pattern was similar to that pioneered by Chinese laundry workers in Chicago. In that nearby Great Lakes city, Chinese laundries grew from one in 1872 to nearly two hundred in the

1880s, many of them expanding beyond the city's "loop," or its core business district.[10]

Much like their Chicago countrymen, the Milwaukee Chinese would find themselves the objects of local curiosity and the subjects of newspaper coverage. Cream City newspapermen would outfit the local Chinese with the usual "Chinamen" stereotypes popular in nineteenth-century America. (Interestingly, the *Milwaukee Sentinel* published some stories in the early 1880s that were unusually sympathetic to the city's Asian laundrymen.) Nevertheless, by mid-decade, the laundries and their owners were increasingly portrayed as morally dangerous, and their businesses were depicted as "dens" of opium eating and filth.

In some of these accounts, a new species of trouble began to emerge. Strangely portending the outburst of 1889, the *Milwaukee Sentinel* and the *Daily News* reported a ruckus at Lee Chung's on Grand Avenue in the fall of 1885. While investigating the circumstances of the subsequent commotion (a man named Wah Lee had complained of theft at Chung's laundry) the police detectives found a strange sight within the inner rooms of a "washee" place. Hiding beneath the bed of one of the Chinese was a "little girl" who was white and "quite pretty."[11] Stories of illicit white-Chinese relations started circulating for at least four years prior to March 1889. The 1885 affair would not be the last; indeed, one year before the citywide explosion of 1889, accusations again flew and city officials groused at their inability to stop the coming riot. With a year's worth of frustration building into a slow-burning resentment, the headlines of March 7, 1889, led many Milwaukee men to demand a final solution.

Many Milwaukee men would not sit quietly at home reading those headlines; they would act. For those who wanted to vent their anger, they knew where they could show their manhood. For those who were merely curious, who wanted to catch a glimpse of the "Chinese heathens," they also knew where to go. For both groups and others—the bored, the idle, as well as a large contingent of teenage boys—the place to congregate would be Market Square, outside the old city hall. Inside the old city hall was the Municipal Court, and the two prisoners would face Judge James Mallory for their preliminary hearing.

James Mallory was a familiar figure in politics both in Milwaukee and throughout the state (he was the Democratic candidate for governor in 1877). A judge on the Municipal Court, he would attain yet more notoriety in 1886 because of a more renowned urban disturbance. In May 1886, the city witnessed its bloodiest labor dispute as the Wisconsin state militia fired a deadly volley at an advancing march of workingmen demonstrating for the eight-hour day. Five would be killed and ten wounded in the Bayview Massacre. James Mallory would tend the judicial machinery as the forums of legal order blamed the demonstrators and exonerated the troops who fired upon the unarmed crowd. Mallory's court would arraign nineteen men for "riotous behavior" and a grand jury would return fifty indictments against forty-nine men. That grand jury received a firm bracing from the judge when he told them "[o]ur constitution does not protect any . . . freedom of speech" for what he called the "reckless criminal conduct of anarchists and demagogues."[12]

The Chinese affair would present Judge Mallory with another urban crisis. While not on the scale of the Bayview Massacre, the 1889 Chinese incident would be no less emotional and no less conflagratory. The dry tinder for urban fire began to accumulate early as word spread that Mallory was going to hear the evidence on Friday morning.

Many who arrived at Market Square wanted to witness the court proceedings. The room itself could not accommodate all the onlookers, so Judge Mallory's courtroom soon became a spectacle in itself, as two hundred or more men took nearly every available seat and seemed to occupy every possible standing space. With the overcrowding the men were packed in the immediate chambers and overflowed out the door, through the hall, and down the stairs. Many wished to move forward to get into the already sardined courtroom, but were unable "to advance a foot."[13] When the case of *Wisconsin* v. *Sam Yip Ya* was called, the two hundred or more men in the courtroom surged forward, requiring a number of Milwaukee policemen to keep order.[14]

The proceedings were short. Whatever judgment (and retribution) the men wanted was aborted by an apparent legal stratagem. The attorneys for the accused got a continuance: they said they needed an adequate translator and none was to be found in Wisconsin except for a reputed Chinese scholar and former missionary who lived in Evansville. After an hour and a half of being squeezed into the courtroom, the "very large" and disappointed crowd began to file out the door and down the stairs into the morning air.

Their grumblings would continue. While in the courtroom, many of the male onlookers expressed themselves very audibly; their threats could be heard prominently in the courtroom. With the grant of the continuance, an angry growl arose from the courtroom observers, and in the public square outside the courtroom the inchoate rage soon took a clearer form. "String them up to a lamp post," cried a dozen "determined looking men."

The police did not want to lead the two prisoners into the human hive that was buzzing in the street below; they waited, hoping the crowd would disperse, but the men refused to go home. By the time the police brought the two suspects out the door, the crowd in Market Square had grown to a sizeable number, estimated by three newspapers as being anywhere from two hundred to five hundred "men and boys."

As the two Chinese suspects walked from the old city hall to the county jail, the men in the crowd followed very close, despite a police escort protecting Hah Ding and Sam Yip Ya. Various cries of "lynch them" and "get a rope" accompanied the procession. Described as "surging" toward the jail, the nearly two hundred to five hundred men and boys deliberately crowded up to the two suspects and jammed them until the police had to drive the mob back. With the doors of the jail closed and the two prisoners secured, it appeared that a crisis had been averted. But the week's troubles had only begun. Contrary to expectations, the crowd did not disperse when the prisoners disappeared behind the closed doors of the jail; the men in Market Square gathered "in knots of half a dozen or more" and "freely discussed" the crimes attributed to "the Celestial heathens."

Saturday proved to be a repeat performance of Friday, yet with more danger. Again, the two attorneys argued for a continuance, again it was granted, and once more amassed onlookers went away disgruntled. That morning, a number of Milwaukeeans believed that the city was ripe for some rope, according to the *Daily Review*, and many arrived ready for a lynching. At least one individual seemed to goad this sentiment by his very presence. He was the father of one of the alleged victims, and he brandished a horse pistol.

Even though the mood seemed right, and one man showed off a noose, no lynching occurred. But the newspapers noted that the public display produced its desired effect: the two Chinese were white with fear. They had turned pale and one of the prisoners became a mass of uncoordinated legs and feet—he had to be buoyed along by the arm of a policeman. With the closing of the jail doors, the crisis seemed averted once more. But that was a mirage; it only grew stronger. According to the *Daily Review*, Saturday's mob had grown to three thousand in strength. The next day's Sabbath would provide no respite for rumor and anger. If the two Chinese under police protection could not be strung from a lamppost, then perhaps other Chinese could be taught a lesson.

The scene that greeted Milwaukee police on Monday morning was foreboding. The square was now "black with people." But the police could have rested easy that day; no lynching would occur. The only problem was that the anti-Chinese spirit would grow beyond Market Square to include the entire city. For the next twelve hours, Chinese would be harried out of their places of business and harassed if seen on the streets. This would be Milwaukee's anti-Chinese riot of 1889.

The anti-Chinese riot was born of good intentions. The police thought they could avoid another "wild scene" by sequestering Hah Ding and Sam Yip Ya in the city hall and then breaking up the crowd into smaller groups. Believing this tactic would be most effective in disrupting the lynch mob mentality, the police decided to withdraw their protection of Chinese laundries and concentrate their forces at the site of the previous week's disturbances. There, the police would further suppress the hanging urge by physically breaking up the crowd with constantly moving nightsticks. The result was peace at Market Square, but disorder everywhere else in Milwaukee, for the crowd became like a monstrous being, its mass broken down but quickly reordering into smaller groups to attack Chinese laundries. The police plan both succeeded and failed: it succeeded in diluting the lynch spirit at Market Square, but it failed to dispel the anti-Chinese sentiment and, indeed, sent that spirit roving throughout the city.

This unforeseen result led to the day's stonings and near lynchings of Chinese laundrymen unconnected to the alleged crimes testified to that morning in Judge Mallory's courtroom. Instead of three thousand concentrated outside the jail, groups of one hundred to one thousand would congregate outside a Chinese laundry and launch a hail of rocks and stones to smash windows, storefronts, and doors. In addition, many of these attacks seemed to target more than property. The mobs wanted to do more than stone storefronts; they sought to terrorize the laundrymen inside those besieged locales.

One of the first recorded incidents, perhaps the first to occur in the riot, happened at 618 Chestnut Street. At one o'clock in the afternoon, a group of men moved off Market Square and walked up Chestnut Street. At the 600 block they congregated at a Chinese laundry and smashed its windows. Two Chinese escaped up Winnebago Street. Later, the crowd formed at State and Fourth and smashed the windows of Ring Shane's laundry. The police received reports of other raids: one at Fond du Lac Avenue near Fifteenth Street, another on Walnut Street, others at the corner of Cherry and Twelfth.

The police, still believing that a real lynching of the criminal suspects would occur at the old city hall, placed all their night officers on duty to protect Hah Ding and Sam Yip Ya. Meanwhile, acts of violence against Milwaukee's Chinese population continued through the night. The next morning would find a preliminary assessment: on the south side of the city, all the laundries on Mitchell Street, seven in number, had been attacked and abandoned. The same was true of the west side and outlying districts.

The mobbings made one newspaper call the day's acts "very like a riot." That paper, *The Evening Wisconsin,* seemed to stop short of calling the day's events a full-blown riot. Nevertheless, the deeds in Cream City were dangerous and destructive; they were very much like the violence that drove Chinese out of other locales during the 1880s.

Milwaukee's mobbing was also different from Western "Chinophobic" uprisings. One key difference lay in the accelerated nature of the Wisconsin outrage. What would have taken months in a Western locale in 1885–1886 took only days in Milwaukee. Whereas anti-Chinese violence in Western cities often mobilized over a number of weeks, the Milwaukee agitation took only four days.

Among the issues that played a role was interracial sexuality, which proved a highly volatile accelerant. The far away *San Francisco Examiner,* from a city well-acquainted with anti-Chinese sentiment, noted that enough of the scandal "leaked out" from the preliminary hearing to "bring the [anti-Chinese] feeling to a red glow" that would turn to "white heat," generating an outlook demanding "nothing short of a general exodus of the Chinese."[15]

As stated earlier, this Wisconsin episode has been lost to history and memory,[16] but it did not go unnoticed at the time in Milwaukee or other cities. The "Chinese Horrors" and the "near riot" made regular front-page appearances in the city's four English-language dailies as well as the Polish *Kuryer Polski* and the German papers, *Milwaukee Herold* and *Excelsior.* Regionally, the *Chicago Tribune* and the *Detroit Free Press* carried notices, as did the *San Francisco Examiner* and the *Atlanta Constitution* (both had front-page stories about the riot).[17] Outside Milwaukee, the newspapers described Hah Ding and Sam Yip Ya as "Mongolian wretches" or "Celestial Brutes." They depicted the two Chinese as victimizers and the Milwaukee girls as unwilling victims. Newspapers in neighboring cities (Chicago and Detroit) or far-off locales (San Francisco and Atlanta) turned their attention elsewhere when the disturbances ended. Had they paid closer attention, they might have been surprised by later developments, as were many chagrined Milwaukeeans by the end of the preliminary hearing. For in the course of those proceedings it was revealed that some of the underage females had actually visited Sam Yip Ya and Hah Ding on many occasions for a number of months. Four girls testified that they had gone to the laundries repeatedly, knowing that they would experience intimacies. As one Milwaukee paper noted, the courtroom atmosphere shifted at the hearing of those revelations.[18]

Nevertheless, even after the disclosure of these ramifying details, the two Chinese would remain incarcerated and, two months later, Sam Yip Ya would be convicted on a sexual felony after jury deliberations that lasted only ten minutes. Thereafter the story becomes murky. What became of the girls, their families, the two Chinese laundrymen, and their fellow Chinese Milwaukeeans? We have only a few clues. We learn from an October 1889 news story that more than six months after the initial revelations, all the girls were having problems being readmitted by public or parochial schools. Principals saw the girls as bad schoolyard influences and priests shunned them as moral lepers.[19] What eventually became of them is hard to discover because they ceased being newsworthy once the affair was forgotten. Sam Yip Ya and Hah Ding also faded from view. After their incarcerations—Sam Yip Ya in Waupun State Prison and Hah Ding in the Milwaukee County Jail—their paper trails evaporate. Did they return to Milwaukee? Did they move to Chicago? All they left behind was their brief notoriousness in the spring of 1889. And what of their Chinese neighbors and fellow Asians in Milwaukee? During the riot, many Chinese laundrymen left for other Wisconsin communities such as Oshkosh. Once the hostilities died down, most returned to Cream City and tried to carry on business as usual.

With each passing month and each changing year, the public memory of what occurred in March 1889 became dimmer, the mobbing was assimilated into a record of other urban disturbances, and Milwaukee's historians, not noticing the Chinese in their midst in any event, let slip a social fact that told much about the city's ethnic tensions, its gendered racial history, and its Midwestern Chinese.[20]

What can we learn from the Milwaukee incident of March 1889? How can we use it to map Midwestern Asian American history? Perhaps the most obvious finding, and very important in light of recovering lost Chinese American history, is the simple fact of being there: that there were Chinese living in the Midwest during the Exclusion decades. They settled as early as the 1870s and moved into small communities such as Fond du Lac and Racine (Wisconsin) as well as large cities (Chicago, Detroit, and Milwaukee). They also drew attention. Newspapers noted that a Chinese student attended a public school in Fond du Lac in January 1874, and the first Chinese to arrive in Portage, Wisconsin, in 1879, soon established a laundry (one week after arrival). A year earlier, the first Chinese to arrive in Watertown "caused a sensation" when he walked the streets.[21]

The Milwaukee incident also confirms insights from Mid-Atlantic and "East Coast" Chinese American research. The Chinese in Milwaukee, not unlike the cutlery workers in Beaver Falls, Pennsylvania, or the Chinese of Boston, Massachusetts, had complicated daily relations with non-Chinese, the nature of which needs to be reexamined for its contradictions and subtleties.[22] These Chinese did not have one-dimensional (or sexless) relations with white Bostonians or Milwaukeeans. While certainly not all Chinese were involved in interracial relationships, as were Sam Yip Ya and Hah Ding, much less the illegal liaisons between these two and the underage Milwaukee females, nevertheless it appears that a complicated set of relations marked different dealings with Chinese, depending on age, class, ethnicity, and gender. For example, one group that publicly defended the Chinese were some Milwaukee women who referred to themselves as a group of "prominent and respectable Ladies." These "prominent ladies" of Cream City said that lower-class white girls would often prey upon Chinese laundrymen in that Great Lakes city, badgering them for money and "us[ing] such vulgar language as only suits a woman of the town." The ladies asked, "How can such men be blamed?" and then proceeded to castigate the parents of these girls for allowing them to haunt Chinese laundries "after 9 o'clock at night."[23]

Finally, the Milwaukee incident teaches us that the concept of "Midwest" needs to be understood contingently; we should not read our twentieth-century conceptions of Midwest back into the historical record. One can say that the region began to acquire its connotations of centrality, stability, and "heartland" virtue during the Progressive Era, when journalists and public intellectuals began to extol the area for its purported difference from crowded East Coast cities. We should remember that what we call "Midwest" was often a moving and mobile imaginary: it was actually a receding West. Theodore Dreiser depicted this well when he wrote the following conversation for his eponymous character, "Sister Carrie"

"Are you a born New Yorker?" asked Ames of Carrie.
"Oh, no, I've only been here two years. . . ."
"You're not from the West, are you?"
"Yes, I'm from Wisconsin," [Carrie] answered."[24]

We need to recover the different construals of "place" that particular groups made of their various "Midwestern" locales—places such as Fond du Lac, Watertown, or Milwaukee. We need to see how these construals differed by ethnicity, racialization, gender, and class. Finally, for a more comprehensive Chinese

American history, we need to recover what meanings Chinese pioneers gave to this place we now call middle, but which is still east of California.

NOTES

1. Nevertheless, the *Sentinel,* if not its index, gave front-page coverage to the Chinese-related events. Indeed, the paper seemed to have exclusive access to various on-the-spot witnesses, such as police detectives and the ever-present Superintendent of the Humane Society Richard D. Whitehead.

2. Roger Daniels, ed., *Anti-Chinese Violence in North America* (New York: Arno Press, 1978). This book, a volume in the Asian Experience in North America series, reprinted journal articles from 1929 to 1974 about anti-Chinese pogroms. It includes studies on Chinese-targeted outbreaks in Seattle, Tacoma, Denver, Los Angeles, Humboldt County, and outside the United States in Vancouver and Torreón (Coahuila, Mexico).

3. The 1870s had the next highest number of outbreaks with thirty-three. The 1860s and 1890s had eleven instances apiece, and the front and tail ends of this era—the 1850s and 1900s—had the fewest incidents with five and two respectively. John R. Wunder, "Anti-Chinese Violence in the American West, 1850–1910," in *Law for the Elephant, Law for the Beaver: Essays in the Legal History of the American West,* ed. John McLaren, Hamar Foster, and Chet Orloff (Pasadena, Calif.: Ninth Judicial Circuit Historical Society, 1992), 214, 219.

Professor Wunder has tabulated the figures and frequency of anti-Chinese violence from secondary sources such as Henry Tsai Shih-shan's *The Chinese Experience in America* (1986), Sucheng Chan's *Bitter Melon: Stories from the Last Rural Chinese Town in America* (1987), Elmer Clarence Sandmeyer's *The Anti-Chinese Movement in California* (1939), and Sucheng Chan's *Bittersweet Soil: The Chinese in California Agriculture, 1860–1880* (1986).

4. Wunder, "Anti-Chinese Violence," 220.

5. Sexuality figured in the more infamous case of anti-Chineseism that occurred in Los Angeles in 1871. The Los Angeles Chinese Massacre of October 24, 1871, in which nineteen Chinese men and boys were killed, fifteen by lynching, was said to have started because of a dispute that got out of hand—a dispute over a Chinese woman between two rival Chinese groups.

6. *Milwaukee Sentinel,* 6 March and 7 March 1889.

7. *Wisconsin State Journal,* 7 March 1889.

8. Elmer Clarence Sandmeyer, *The Anti-Chinese Movement in California* (Urbana: University of Illinois Press, 1939, 1991), 21. These figures are taken from table 6

"Chinese in the United States, by States and Territories." Sandmeyer culled these figures from the U.S. Census.

9. This is an anecdotal number drawn from the observers of the March 1889 riot. Their rough sense of the size of Milwaukee's Chinese population was reported in the English-language newspapers. In particular, the Chinese community's self-appointed and press-anointed spokesperson, Sam Ring Kee, gave this approximate figure. *Milwaukee Sentinel,* 2 April 1889.

10. Paul C. P. Siu, *The Chinese Laundryman: A Study in Social Isolation* (New York: New York University Press, 1987), 26.

11. "A Day in the City: Seven Chinamen Locked up by Police, A Young White Girl Found in One of Their Dens," *Milwaukee Sentinel,* 22 September 1885; "Chinamen Acquitted, Convincing the Court That They Had Been Wrongfully Accused of Crime," *Milwaukee Daily Journal,* 22 September 1885.

12. Robert C. Nesbit, *The History of Wisconsin,* Vol. 3, *Urbanization and Industrialization, 1873–1893* (Madison: State Historical Society of Wisconsin, 1985), 406–409 passim.

13. "Hints of Violence: Immense Crowd around the Municipal Courts Today," *Milwaukee Daily Journal,* 8 March 1889.

14. "When the Case of the State against Sam Yip Ja [sic] and Hah Ding was Called, the Crowd Surged Forward until a Number of Policemen Was Required to Keep the Bar Enclosure Clear," *Milwaukee Sentinel,* 9 March 1889; "Hurried to Jail. Chinamen in Danger of Violence from Citizens."

15. "The People up in Arms: Residents of the Cream City Have Had Enough of Chinese," *San Francisco Examiner,* 12 March 1889.

16. No local folklore redacts the stories of Sam Yip Ya and Hah Ding. Milwaukee and southern Wisconsin folktales, so rich in their retellings of other ethnic memories, are silent. One might expect some kind of "survival" among Chinese Milwaukeeans today, some stray injunction, joke, or narrative, but none seem to exist. Many Chinese Milwaukeeans expressed surprise at my recounting of both the anti-Chinese riot and the plight of the two accused laundrymen. The one published ethnography about Milwaukee's Chinese is also mum. Maurine Huang, "Chinese without a Chinatown: Chinese Life in Milwaukee," *Milwaukee History* 14, no. 2 (spring 1991): 2–19.

17. "Wanted to Lynch the Chinamen," *Chicago Tribune,* 12 March 1889; "Rioting at Milwaukee," *Detroit Free Press,* 12 March 1889; "The People up in Arms: Residents of the Cream City Have Had Enough of the Chinese," *San Francisco Examiner,* 12 March 1889; "Mobbing the Chinese: Excitement in Milwaukee Yesterday Afternoon," *Atlanta Constitution,* 12 March 1889.

18. *Milwaukee Daily Journal*, 12 March 1889; *Milwaukee Sentinel*, 13 March 1889.

19. "Barred Them Out: An Outcome of the Recent Chinese Cases," *Milwaukee Sentinel*, 25 October 1889.

20. Bayrd Still, *Milwaukee: The History of a City* (Madison: State Historical Society of Wisconsin, 1948); Gerd Korman, *Industrialization, Immigrants, and Americanizers: The View from Milwaukee, 1866–1921* (Madison: State Historical Society of Wisconsin, 1967).

21. The following references can be found in the *Milwaukee Sentinel* index: "Chinese Student Attends Fond du Lac Public School," 31 January 1874; "Yon Sing Lone Representative in Fond du Lac," 27 March 1874; "First Settlers Arrive in Portage," 15 April 1879; "Establish Laundry in Portage," 22 April 1879; "Laundry to Be Established in Racine," 18 August 1879; "Presence on Streets Causes Sensation in Watertown," 21 August 1878; "To Open Laundry in Watertown," 24 August 1878; "To Open Laundry in Milwaukee," 23 March 1874; "Chan Wong Given License to Sell Teas in Milwaukee," 10 December 1874.

22. K. Scott Wong, "'The Eagle Seeks a Helpless Quarry': Chinatown, the Police, and the Press. The 1903 Boston Chinatown Raid Revisited," *Amerasia Journal* 22, no. 3 (1996), 81–103. Edward J. M. Rhoads, "Asian Pioneers in the Eastern United States: Chinese Cutlery Workers in Beaver Falls, Pennsylvania in the 1870s," *Journal of Asian American Studies* 2, no. 2 (June 1999), 119–55.

23. "The Chinese Case," *Evening Wisconsin*, 18 March 1889.

24. Theodore Dreiser, *Sister Carrie*, the Pennsylvania Edition, historical editors, John C. Berkey and Alice M. Winters; textual editor, James L. W. West III; general editor, Neda M. Westlake (Philadelphia: University of Pennsylvania Press, 1981), 330.

5

Riot in Unionville, Nevada: A Turning Point

Elmer R. Rusco

At eight o'clock on the morning of January 10, 1869, an armed group of about sixty white men, organized as the Anti-Chinese League of Unionville, Nevada, marched down the main street of the camp to Chinatown, accompanied by "music and banners," in a brazen and temporarily successful attempt to expel Chinese men from the town by force. There were no deaths or injuries because the Chinese did not resist, but the mob carried weapons, described as shotguns, rifles, and "other implements of warfare." Reportedly, the thirty-five expelled were all the Chinese men living there at the time. They were put on a wagon and driven twenty-five miles to Mill City, the nearest station on the Central Pacific Railway, and were thus presumably ushered out of the area.[1]

At first glance this does not seem like a significant incident, and Nevada historians have paid little attention to it. At the time, however, the Unionville riot was a very important event to white Nevadans. In fact, it was a turning point in the reaction of Nevadans to the Chinese. This chapter is too short for discussion of all the impacts of the riot; it will treat the incident primarily as the most significant failed attempt during the nineteenth century to protect the legal rights of the Chinese.

WHITE RACISM AND EARLY NEVADA

At its beginning, Nevada was strongly racist. Both territorial law (from 1861 to 1864) and early state law were systematically racist. In 1864 nonwhites (never defined but identified specifically in many statutes as Indians, blacks, and Chinese) were not allowed to vote, hold office, serve on juries or in the militia, attend public schools (except for the unlikely possibility that a school district would create a segregated school), marry a white person, or testify against whites in either civil or criminal cases.[2] It is inconceivable that this complex pattern of racist laws could have been enacted by legislators elected by white males if it had not coincided with the prejudices of the voters.

However, in the late 1860s a local Reconstruction effort was going on in the state, led by a number of leaders of the Union/Republican party. This movement was in sympathy with the antiracist goals of congressional majorities during the Civil War and the Reconstruction of the South. Alexander W. Baldwin, Nevada's only federal judge, played a key role in this effort to repeal Nevada's racist laws. His reaction to the Unionville riot demonstrated his commitment to this antiracist view, at that time a radical and minority position.

UNIONVILLE AND JOHN C. FALL

What became Nevada had long been home for thousands of Native Americans. White settlement was very limited until 1859. But when precious metals were discovered at what became the Comstock mining district in that year, there was an explosion of the white population in that area, followed by similar growth at other Nevada sites where gold or silver was discovered.

Unionville was one of the mining boomtowns that sprang up soon after "the rush to Washoe." It was (and its surviving remnant remains) located slightly more than one hundred miles northeast of Virginia City (figure 5.1). In 1861 Indians led white prospectors to mineral deposits along Buena Vista creek, on the east slope of the Humboldt Range, and a mining camp quickly sprang up along the canyon down which this creek flowed. For two decades, Unionville was the most prosperous mining camp in Humboldt County, although it suffered the ultimate fate of all mining camps when the ore ran out.[3]

Unionville was considerably smaller than the Comstock. Unlike the situation in the better-known camp, the town was dominated from an early date by only one capitalist. John C. Fall had been a successful merchant in Marysville, California, and later in Carson City, Nevada (the future capital of the state and close to the Comstock). In 1862 Fall purchased seventeen mining claims in Unionville, and he acquired fifty-three more in 1864. When the initial surface mining had to be replaced with underground mining, Fall lacked sufficient capital to dominate Unionville without help. Although Fall was a Democrat, business and family ties connected him closely with John H. Kinkead, a Republican territorial treasurer (1861–64) and governor (1879–83) of Nevada.[4] It was reported in late 1865 that Fall had just spent a year in New York City raising capital to develop his claims.

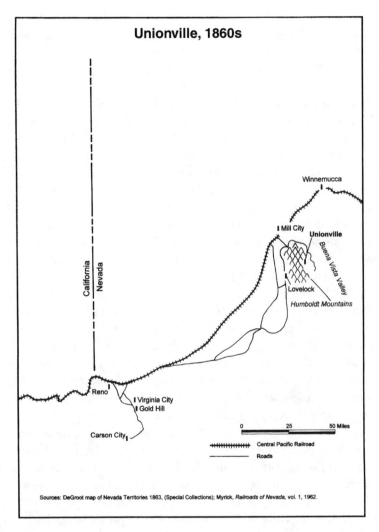

FIGURE 5.1
Map of Unionville, Nevada, and surrounding areas (Copyright © 1997 Karen Laramore.
Reprinted with permission.)

For many years Fall's partner was Daniel W. Temple of Bloomfield, New Jersey.[5] Eventually, Fall and Temple owned the Arizona mine, the richest underground mine in the area, along with the nearby Wheeler (or Henning) mine. They also built the Pioneer Mill, located below the town where the canyon opened out into Buena Vista Valley, and followed this up by purchasing the

Etna Mill and moving it to Unionville. Fall and Co. also operated the largest and most successful general store in Unionville for many years. There is no doubt that Fall was the "richest person in Unionville."[6]

Fall was one of the few white mining moguls who hired Chinese workers, although apparently these immigrants never constituted more than a minority of his employees. There are unsubstantiated reports that he also hired Indian and Hispanic workers. This policy suggests that he was not prejudiced; however, there were basic economic reasons behind it. The Chinese were good workers, more tractable than white workers, and accepted lower wages. While we do not know precisely the wages paid in Unionville, elsewhere in the state at that time Chinese could usually be hired for half the pay of white workers.[7]

Young Chinese men had first come to California in search of sudden wealth after gold was discovered in that state in 1849. They also came over the Sierra Nevada to get rich quick at mining in Nevada, and were engaged in placer mining on what became the Comstock before the discovery of silver in 1859 (see Liu and Valentine, chapters 1 and 2 in this volume, respectively). However, they were effectively barred from filing claims of their own in Nevada.

The first mining claims in Nevada, including those in Unionville, were filed under a form of "squatter law" (first developed in California) followed by local prospectors; there was at the time no federal law governing mining. The first mining regulations adopted in Nevada, in Gold Hill (on the Comstock), contained a provision stating that Chinese could not file mining claims. Later, Chinese exclusion was simply taken for granted.[8]

When Congress in 1866 passed the first federal mining law, it not only retroactively legalized this process but also flatly excluded the Chinese from filing mining claims. Although the law did not specifically refer to the Chinese, it restricted the filing of mining claims to U.S. citizens or those who had filed for citizenship. A federal law, the 1790 Naturalization Law, barred Chinese from becoming citizens because it contained a provision stating that only "free white" persons could become citizens through naturalization. But Chinese could and did acquire mines in the state during the nineteenth century by purchasing claims from whites.[9]

Employment as miners or mill workers was another matter. In Unionville as well as the Comstock, after the initial period, most miners were not prospectors but employees of the mine owners.[10] No law forbade mine owners from hiring nonwhites to work in the mines, but in practice white miners' unions accomplished this result through collective bargaining. Only in the mines at Cortez, owned by Simeon Wenban, and in those owned by John C. Fall in Unionville were Chinese hired in significant numbers.[11]

The January 1869 riot did not persuade Fall to abandon his policy of hiring Chinese, so Chinese returned shortly after the riot. In July 1869, a newspaper correspondent identified only as "Cyclops" reported that white miners were striking against Fall because of an increase in the work day to ten hours. Cyclops alleged that Fall's move was an excuse to hire Chinese workers "whom they can oblige to work as many hours as they please." We know that there were Chinese in the camp again by the fall of 1869.[12]

By the time of the 1870 population census the number of Chinese in Unionville had grown from the thirty-five expelled in January 1869 to fifty-four, and their numbers increased again during the next decade to one hundred and ten. A number of the Chinese were identified in the census as miners or mill workers.

Unionville also differed from the Comstock in that it was a Democratic stronghold, in contrast to the larger camp, which was controlled in most elections before the 1890s by Republicans. The most important newspapers shared the party orientation of their regions. The *Humboldt Register*, published in Unionville from the town's inception in 1863 to October 1869, when it moved to Winnemucca, was strongly Democratic. The *Territorial Enterprise* and *Gold Hill News*, the two most important newspapers on the Comstock for many years, were strongly Republican during the same period.[13]

William J. Forbes, first editor/publisher of the *Register*, supported an attempt in 1863 to expel the Chinese from Unionville. In May of that year the *Register* reported that a meeting of "citizens" had been held April 27 to consider the "propriety of ordering the removal of the Chinese from within the town limits." The outcome of this meeting was the selection of a committee of ten men, "authorized to wait on the Celestials at two o'clock on the following day, and give them notice to remove their habitations within one week, and also to inform them that if such notice was not complied with within the specified time, they would be removed by the citizens." Forbes approved of this decision, remarking that it was desirable to expel the Chinese at an early date because "it would be more trouble to drive them out after they had become more numerous; and, in large or small number, they are a plague to any town." At the same time, Forbes was welcoming white immigrants from California, writing that "There's room and work and pay for all."[14]

No actual expulsion was reported in 1863; Chinese presence in the town was noted four months later. But the *Register* continued its strongly anti-Chinese stance. In 1867 George G. Berry became publisher, and he followed the same policy as Forbes. Berry was also an attorney. On his arrival in Humboldt County in 1862 he studied law with the county's district attorney, P. H. Harris, and he was admitted to the practice of law in April 1863. Berry was popular with the voters and, running as a Democrat, was elected district court judge in 1866. He played an important role in the riot and its aftermath.[15]

An editorial by Berry during the 1868 general election stated clearly his racist views, which he insisted were those of his party and not shared by the Republican leaders of the state. Berry charged that the Radicals favored "the civil and political equality of all men upon a common ground of natural and inalienable rights." Berry firmly rejected this stance, asserting that the *Register* stood for the proposition that "he that is not for the supremacy of the white race is against it." He went on to assert that "The Democratic party maintains that the Declaration of Independence . . . was never intended by its authors to embrace the inferior and savage races, but that it simply related the distinction of cast [sic], founded on birth, blood and divine right then existing in all European countries." Berry asserted that the nation's founding document was simply "an open declaration that in the cradle all Europeans were equal before the law and endowed with the same rights." On the other hand, he charged, the Radical party believed that the Declaration "was intended to embrace literally all human beings of all nations, kindred and tongues, who might fall within the protecting aegis of the Federal Constitution." In another editorial, Berry charged specifically that Republican Senator William Stewart and Representative Thomas Fitch were embracing the Radical theory and that Stewart's reelection that year would give him a chance to bring "both Chinese and nigger suffrage [to] Nevada."[16]

Berry's editorial linked his racist views to another crucial question—the class struggle within the white community. He asserted that a vote for Chinese labor was also a "vote to aid in concentrating the wealth of the nation in the hands of the few until we will have but two classes in the country—the debtor and the creditor, the master and the slave."

Neither Stewart nor Fitch campaigned in 1868 in favor of Reconstruction policies against racism or emphasized the Chinese issue, but both had supported the national Reconstruction program in Congress. Stewart was a leader in the effort to add the Fifteenth Amendment to the federal Constitution to extend the right to vote to African American men, although he was careful to point out that it would not allow Chinese to vote. Stewart even sponsored a successful congressional bill to protect the civil rights of Chinese.[17]

LOCAL RESPONSES TO THE RIOT

Just before the riot took place Judge Berry, in spite of his racist views, spoke out against using violence. He issued a warning through his newspaper that "forcible expulsion and banishment of all the chinese [sic] now in town . . . is not the proper course to take in a matter of such grave concern . . . and could only end in bringing discredit on those who would accomplish a good work, but go about it the wrong way." He went on to assert that attempts to halt Chinese labor in the mines "must be lawfully done by the voice of a majority of the people."[18]

Not only did the Anti-Chinese League ignore Berry's advice, but it forced him to pay a swift and substantial price for having offered it. Two weeks after the riot, Berry announced that he had just learned the previous Wednesday that "the pale rider Death had marked us for its victim." The Humboldt County Working Men's Protective Union temporarily took over the *Register*. Berry soon moved far away from Unionville to Elko, in the northeast corner of the state, where for several years he was one of the publishers of the *Elko Independent*. The *Humboldt Register and Workingman's Advocate*, as the *Register* became known, had a short life and was owned, at different times, by W. S. Bonnifield, a leader of the riot, and J. J Hill, one of the persons indicted as a rioter.[19]

Immediately after the riot, leading Republican newspapers in the state condemned it. The *Carson Appeal*, edited by Republican Henry Mighels, said that "the rights which are invaded in this case are not only those which belong to Mr. Fall, as an American citizen, nor those of the Chinamen thus molested (who are protected not only by law and solemn treaties) but they affect the entire community."[20] Similar sentiments were expressed by the *Territorial Enterprise* and the *Reno Crescent*, also Republican journals.

Attempts by local law enforcement officials to prevent the riot or to charge the rioters failed. Initially, the problem was partly that "the crowd was too large and determined to resist." Democratic sheriff H. N. Thacker was reportedly present when the Chinese were expelled and "notified the party that their acts were unlawful, but did not attempt to summon a posse, as, under the circumstances, he regarded it useless, no preparation having been made to resist the League, as but few supposed they intended to resort to force."[21]

Afterward, Sheriff Thacker and District Attorney P. H. Harris secured some indictments of rioters, but these never came to trial. The rioters made no attempt to conceal their identities; the later federal indictment listed seventeen rioters by name, resorting to John Doe identifications in only two cases.

Newspaper accounts indicate that Harris sought a compromise with state Senator McKaskia S. (commonly referred to as M. S.) Bonnifield, whose nephew
Bill (W. S.) Bonnifield was reportedly the leader of the riot. When this effort
failed, the indictments were dropped. Later, John C. Fall reportedly filed a
complaint against several rioters, but this was dismissed by Justice of the Peace
Anthony T. Buckner when Fall failed to appear to testify at a hearing.[22]

The precise grounds on which rioters could have been prosecuted locally
were not reported, but there is no doubt that under both the common law and
Nevada statutes their actions were illegal. The first action of the first Nevada
territorial legislature in 1861 was to adopt the common law. At that time this
body of law outlawed the crime of assault, for which actual violence was un-
necessary. The common law definition of assault included "an intention, coupled with a present ability, of actual violence against [a person]. . . . When the
injury is actually inflicted, it amounts to a battery." The common law definition of a riot likewise recognized that threats of violence, "calculated to strike
terror into the public mind," were sufficient to constitute a riot. In addition,
the 1861 legislature adopted a Crimes and Punishments Act recognizing the
same principle. Another section of this law also stated that assault included
credible threatened violence.[23]

The state's attorney general lacked the authority to prosecute local crimes,
and there was later some question of the adequacy of state laws to cover situations of this sort, but the criminal law of the state clearly outlawed what happened on January 10.

THE FEDERAL PROSECUTION

The most important legal effort to punish the rioters was a federal indictment
against nineteen individuals, although this too never got to trial. On February
1, 1869 a federal grand jury then sitting in Carson City issued an indictment
against these individuals for "violently and injuriously combin[ing] and con-
federat[ing] together" with unknown others to drive Ah Wee and thirty-four
other subjects of the Chinese emperor from Unionville. The indictment also
charged these nineteen individuals with forcing the Chinese "with strong
hand by force of arms and with multitude of people" to "quit their property
and to cease from carrying on their business" in Unionville.[24]

Although the indictment contained a general statement charging the rioters with "violation of the Laws of Nations" and the "Laws and Constitution"
of the United States plus "the Peace and Dignity of said United States," its
principal charge was that the actions of these individuals had violated the

Burlingame Treaty, which had been concluded the year before by the United States and China.

The indictment was asked for by federal judge Alexander W. Baldwin. According to the *Carson Appeal*, Judge Baldwin had asked the grand jurors at their first meeting to consider the riot as one of three major issues. He told them that "it is notorious, that a short time ago, at the town of Unionville, . . . a number of inoffensive laborers, who had committed no crime, save that of belonging to an unpopular nationality, were by a body of armed men driven from their homes and compelled to quit their avocations." Baldwin specifically cited the Burlingame Treaty as a basis for the indictment, saying that the "violent exclusion" of the Chinese "is in my opinion—so long as the treaty stands unrevoked—an offense against the national sovereignty, of which the nation's Courts have jurisdiction."[25]

Mighels's *Carson Appeal* endorsed this action, saying that it was "something eminently worthy of a judicial officer of [Judge Baldwin's] responsible position and wide spread influence."[26]

Baldwin was one of the Republican leaders of the state who strongly endorsed the efforts of national leaders of his party to end racist laws. In an Independence Day address the previous year, he had stated that the "long and bloody war" brought on by the secession of the southern states had been fundamentally about the abolition of slavery. He declared that the victory of the Union had been "achieved at a cost which nothing could have warranted but the requirement of so sacred a cause."

Moreover, Baldwin linked Reconstruction to the Chinese cause.[27] Along with territorial governor Warren S. Nye, territorial judge John W. North and the state's first attorney general and publisher Mighels, Baldwin genuinely fought against racist laws.[28] However, Judge Baldwin's attempts to secure an end to the general pattern of racist law were futile. He did not act quickly to follow up on the indictment of the Unionville rioters. Not until April 6 did he issue an order to U.S. Marshal Richard V. Dey to arrest eighteen of the persons indicted.

Marshal Dey also moved slowly, and originally arrested only one person. This was Lewis Dunn. But Dunn managed to get lawyers (one of whom was M. S. Bonnifield) to file a writ of habeas corpus before the local state judge, at this time still George Berry. Berry ordered Dunn released, on the grounds that the violation of a treaty did not justify a criminal indictment in federal court and that state courts had jurisdiction over federal prisoners in the case.[29]

Dey did not believe that Judge Berry's order was valid, but "not having the necessary force at hand to resist said order of discharge [he] was compelled to release" Dunn. His next move was to arrest another person named in the indictment, J. J. Hill. Hill was quickly transported to Carson City, out of the jurisdiction of Judge Berry. Attorneys for Hill filed a writ of habeas corpus in the state supreme court, citing the Berry decision. This court quickly ruled that state courts had no jurisdiction over the federal courts.[30]

But Hill never had to face trial, nor did any of the others who had been indicted, and he reportedly spent no time in jail.[31] Hill's principal defense was that the Burlingame Treaty was not yet in effect because it had not yet been ratified by the U.S. Senate. On July 31 Judge Baldwin dismissed the entire indictment on this ground. The judge nevertheless indicated his intention to pursue the matter further; his order dismissing the indictment stated that the treaty was "now in full force and virtue" and referred to the possibility that a future federal grand jury might indict Hill again. For this reason, he released Hill only on condition that he post a $500 bond. However, there was no later indictment and Judge Baldwin was killed in a train wreck in California in November 1869. The failure of this attempt to punish the Unionville rioters marked the last time in the nineteenth century that either civil or criminal cases were filed in the federal court in Nevada to protect Chinese rights.[32]

In later years, the rioters also were rewarded rather than punished by local and state voters. Several were elected to public office. Two members of the Bonnifield family became District Judges in Humboldt County and M. S. Bonnifield was later elevated to the Nevada Supreme Court by the electorate. J. J. Hill was elected to county office several times, while Dunn served as clerk to the county commissioners and Hill was the elected state printer for several terms.[33]

THE STATE LEGISLATURE AND POLITICAL PARTIES
The reader can be pardoned for doubting at this point that the Unionville riot of 1869 was a major event in nineteenth-century Nevada history. However, the riot quickly became a turning point in terms of the reaction of white male Nevadans to another consequence of the riot—an attempt to enact a bill to expand state law to help protect Chinese workers.

The legislature met in early January 1869, and there was an early attempt to pass a law that allegedly would have broadened the coverage of existing antiriot laws and given the governor authority to act under these laws if local authorities did not. However, these measures contained new provisions outlawing the use of force in certain circumstances. John C. Fall and E. F. Dunne, a Republican who had been Humboldt district court judge before George Berry, asked

Governor Henry G. Blasdel to send troops to Unionville. Moreover, Dunne reportedly believed that state law was weak in this area and he "proposed to pass a bill through both houses under suspension of the rules to-morrow, giving him [the governor] the powers required."[34]

There were large Republican majorities in both houses—in the Assembly, thirty-four members of the Union Party compared with five Democrats, and in the Senate fifteen Unionists versus only five Democrats. Support for the bill actually introduced was provided primarily by Union/Republicans, but ultimately no bill was passed at all in response to the riot.[35]

Labor historian Richard Lingenfelter has pointed out that the provisions of the bill could have been used to strike down labor agreements reached on the Comstock after miners' unions had conducted successful strikes against owners. The miners there had won through these means the relatively high wage rate of four dollars a day, and the bill may have been an attempt to undermine labor's successes under cover of a law to protect Chinese workers.[36]

The miners' unions throughout the state reacted strongly against this bill, and eventually submitted a petition vigorously opposing it, reportedly signed by 2,700 voters in Storey County, where both Virginia City and Gold Hill are located. This number represented a major part of the electorate on the Comstock; it is 82 percent of the total Storey County vote for governor in the 1870 general election.[37]

The stated opposition to the bill from the unions was expressed solely in terms of opposition to the Chinese. For example, a resolution signed by the leaders of the Virginia City Miners' Union and the Gold Hill Miners' Union, published about two weeks after the Assembly bill was introduced, stated that "we are determined that side by side with the Chinaman we will not work; nor shall they usurp the places in this State that belong exclusively to the American citizen."[38] This reaction obviously intimidated a number of Union/Republican party members. After initially passing the Assembly, with Union/Republican support, the measure was killed near the end of the session.

Another continuing impact of the Unionville riot was that in the late spring and summer of 1869 there were several statewide meetings to organize a workingman's party as an alternative to both the Republican and Democratic parties. These meetings were attended by delegates from miners' unions in Virginia City, Gold Hill, Humboldt County, and White Pine County, plus three other unions in the state. The *Territorial Enterprise* claimed that the delegates to one meeting represented "three or four thousand members of associations."

While this "party" ended up not nominating candidates for office in 1870, the threat of a labor party had significant effects on the Republicans. After 1869 Republican leaders joined leaders of the Democratic Party in denouncing the Chinese, with very few exceptions (notably Henry Mighels of Carson City).[39]

Moreover, the 1870 election saw the first defeat for the Union/Republican party in the state; a Democratic governor and representative were elected (there was no race for the U.S. Senate that year) and the Democrats nearly won a majority in the Assembly. They failed to win the Senate because only half the Senate seats were up for election that year. It is highly likely that the fact that some Republicans could be charged with being pro-Chinese was the major reason for this reversal of the party's fortunes.

One more impact of the riot was the enactment by legislatures elected in 1870 and subsequent years of numerous laws and resolutions specifically attacking the Chinese, although Native Americans and African Americans were not so targeted.

In short, the attempt to punish the anti-Chinese rioters in Unionville in early 1869 was a turning point in Nevada electoral and legislative history. Ironically, instead of the riots strengthening and accelerating the move toward antiracist legislation, the fact that a major part of the working class was deeply hostile to the Chinese converted most Union/Republican leaders to an anti-Chinese stance and intensified racist sentiments among the electorate.

Although this pattern differed in detail from the development of anti-Chinese sentiment in California in the last forty years of the nineteenth century, it displayed a similar dynamic. Alexander Saxton, in *The Indispensable Enemy,* has described how the white working class in that state was united by what they saw as the threat from competition with Chinese workers.[40]

NOTES

The map in this chapter was drawn by Karen Laramore.

1. *Humboldt Register,* 16 January 1869, 3, and 4 April 1876, 2:1; *Carson Appeal,* 14 January 1869, 2. The incident is discussed briefly in Gary P. BeDunnah, *A History of the Chinese in Nevada, 1855–1904* (master's thesis, University of Nevada, Reno, 1966), 12.

2. Elmer R. Rusco, *Good Time Coming? Black Nevadans in the Nineteenth Century* (Westport, Conn.: Greenwood Press, 1975), 21–41.

3. *Humboldt Register,* 16 May 1863, 2:2; Alan H. Patera, *The Humboldt Range: 19th Century Mining Camps* (Lake Grove, Ore.: Western Places, 1995), 1–5, 17–44; Nell

Murbarger, *Ghosts of the Glory Trail* (Palm Desert, Calif.: Desert Magazine Press, 1956), 8–22.

4. *Winnemucca Silver State,* 14 December 1954, 3:2; *Carson City Silver Age,* 13 July 1861, 4:4, and 20 October 1861, 3:4; Myron F. Angel, *History of Nevada 1881* (Berkeley, Calif.: Howell-North, 1958), 355.

5. Records in the office of the Humboldt County Recorder, Winnemucca; *Gold Hill News,* 21 December 1865, 2:3.

6. Francis Church Lincoln, *Mining Districts and Mineral Resources of Nevada* (Las Vegas: Nevada Publications, 1982), 202–3; Patera, *The Humboldt Range,* 23–25, 35; Frederick Leslie Ransome, *Notes on Some Mining Districts in Humboldt County, Nevada* (Washington, D.C.: Government Printing Office, 1909), 12; Angel, *History of Nevada,* 211.

7. See *Gold Hill News,* 16 January 1869, 2; W. S. Bonnifield, quoted by Doris Cavanagh in *Humboldt Star,* 23 May 1934, 1:4, 4:5–8; *Gold Hill News,* 16 January 1869, 2.

8. For the early treatment of Chinese miners in California, see Robert F. Heizer and Alan F. Almquist, *The Other Californians* (Berkeley: University of California Press, 1971): 254–56; Ping Chui, *Chinese Labor in California, 1850–1880* (Madison: State Historical Society of Wisconsin, 1963): 10–39. Material on the Gold Hill provision is in BeDunnah, *A History of the Chinese:* 5–7.

9. Richard E. Lingenfelter, *The Hardrock Miners* (Berkeley: University of California Press, 1974), 107–8; Bill Ong Hing, *Making and Remaking Asian America through Immigration Policy 1850–1990* (Stanford: Stanford University Press, 1993), 23, 31–33, 36. I am indebted to David Valentine for alerting me to the significance of the citizenship requirement in the 1866 mining law. See chapter 2 in this book.

10. See Lingenfelter, *The Hardrock Miners,* and Mark Wyman, *Hard Rock Epic: Western Miners and the Industrial Revolution, 1860–1910* (Berkeley: University of California Press, 1979).

11. Donald L. Hardesty, *The Archaeology of Mining and Miners: A View from the Silver State,* Special Publication Series, no. 6 (Pleasant Hill, Calif.: Society for Historical Archaeology, 1988), 78, 90; Hubert Howe Bancroft, *History of the Life of Simeon Wenban* (San Francisco: The History Co., 1889).

12. *Elko Independent,* 14 July 1869, 2:2.

13. On the partisan nature of nineteenth-century Nevada papers, see Jake Highton, *Nevada Newspaper Days* (Stockton, Calif.: Heritage West Books, 1990).

14. *Humboldt Register,* 2 May 1863, 4:1.

15. Russell W. McDonald, "Early Courthouses and Lawyers of Humboldt County," *The Humboldt Historian* 1, no. 1 (summer 1978): 9–10.

16. *Humboldt Register,* 19 September 1868, 2; and 31 October 1868, 2.

17. Charles J. McClain, *In Search of Equality: The Chinese Struggle against Discrimination in Nineteenth-Century America* (Berkeley: University of California Press, 1994), 36–40.

18. *Humboldt Register,* 9 January 1869, 3.

19. *Humboldt Register,* 3 February 1869, 3; Richard E. Lingenfelter and Karen Rix Gash, *The Newspapers of Nevada* (Reno: University of Nevada Press, 1984), 249–51.

20. *Carson Appeal,* 14 January 1869, 2.

21. *Carson Appeal,* 14 January 1869, 2; *Humboldt Register,* 17 April 1869, 3.

22. *Humboldt Register,* 23 January 1869, 2.

23. Statutes of Nevada, 1861, chapter 28, section 40.

24. Federal Records Center-San Francisco, Records of the District Court of the United States for the District of Nevada, criminal case no. 407, *U.S. v. W. S. Bonnifield, et. al.*

25. *Carson Appeal,* 17 February 1869, 2.

26. *Carson Appeal,* 17 February 1869, 2. See also *Reno Crescent,* 20 February 1869.

27. *Territorial Enterprise,* 8 July 1868, 3.

28. Rusco, *Good Time Coming?,* 54–55.

29. The decision could not be found in the judicial records for Humboldt County but was printed in full in the *Humboldt Register,* 17 April 1869, 2.

30. Ex parte J. J. Hill on Habeas Corpus, *Opinions,* Supreme Court of Nevada, 1869: 154–60.

31. *Humboldt Register,* 22 May 1869, 2; *Winnemucca Silver State,* 18 September 1878, 2:2. A civil suit for false imprisonment was filed by Lewis Dunn against Judge Baldwin and others connected with the indictment, but the suit was dismissed several months later. *Humboldt Register,* 17 April 1869, 3; 11 December 1869, 2.

32. For Baldwin's death, see *Territorial Enterprise,* 16 November 1869, 2:1–2, 3:1. The records of the U.S. District Court for Nevada were examined in search of such cases. This situation contrasts sharply with the situation in California. See McClain, *In Search of Equality.*

33. I am indebted to Jay Marden of Winnemucca for access to his index to various Humboldt County newspaper articles about the Bonnifield family and to Judy Adams of the Humboldt County Library for repeatedly providing information.

34. *Carson Appeal,* 12 January 1869, 2; *Reno Crescent,* 16 January 1869, 2.

35. *Journals* of the Nevada Assembly and Senate, 1869 session; *Carson Appeal,* 21 January 1869, 2; *Humboldt Register,* 30 January 1869, 2.

36. Lingenfelter, *The Hardrock Miners,* 111–12.

37. *Carson Appeal,* 4 March 1869, 3. This petition could not be found in the state archives.

38. *Territorial Enterprise,* 22 January 1869, 2:6.

39. Material in this section is from an unpublished manuscript by the author, "Race and Culture in a Western State: Chinese and the Law in Nevada."

40. Alexander Saxton, *The Indispensable Enemy: Labor and the Anti-Chinese Movement in California* (Berkeley: University of California Press, 1971).

6

Telling Their Own Stories: Chinese Canadian Biography as a Historical Genre

Nancy S. Lee

In *Beyond Silence: Chinese Canadian Literature in English*, Lien Chao argues that the Chinese in Canada were "silenced" for most of their history because they were barred from participation in mainstream discourse. She writes: "Had the Chinese been given access to mainstream politics, media, religion, and literature, their contributions to Canada, their legends and mythologies would have been incorporated into Canadian culture long before the 1990s."[1]

Social stigmatization, discrimination, and outright persecution plagued Chinese virtually from the moment they arrived in 1858 in British Columbia, Canada's westernmost province, until well into the twentieth century. Mirroring the United States, in 1885 the Canadian government instituted Chinese exclusion laws that severely curtailed Chinese immigration until 1967, when the laws were officially repealed. With the end of the Exclusion Era, the push for demarginalization and cultural acceptance was on. By the early 1990s, the efforts of Chinese Canadians bore fruit and a number of Chinese Canadian biographies and novels based on personal narratives became best-sellers. Among the most notable was Denise Chong's *The Concubine's Children: Portrait of a Family Divided*, a 1994 biography of her family that won several Canadian book awards, was shortlisted for the prestigious Governor General's Literary Award, and became a national bestseller. Chong tells the story of her family's roots in China and their lives in Vancouver's old Chinatown. Her work is a superb example of Chinese Canadian biography as a genre of historical writing. This genre can be considered historiography because it draws its evidence from personal narratives that form an oral history, passed from one generation to the next, in Chinese Canadian families that trace their roots back to the first pioneers from Guangdong Province in China. In this manner,

Chinese Canadian biography captures, in a unique and important way, a history that would otherwise be unfamiliar to the larger society.

A comparison between excerpts from Canadian history textbooks used in British Columbian schools, possibly during the 1970s,[2] and Chong's work will demonstrate that the history of Chinese Canadians has been left out of conventional historiography for most of the nearly 150-year presence of Chinese in Canada. This comparison will show how biographies like *The Concubine's Children* counter this past proclivity by offering a richer and more substantive account of Chinese Canadian history. A component of the analysis will give evidence supporting historian Hayden White's contention that language is not a neutral medium and that the style/form of written language actively constructs the meaning of text in addition to fulfilling its aesthetic function. Therefore, the way a given text is written should be "counted among the other kinds of content (factual, conceptual, and generic) that make up the total content of the discourse as a whole."[3] White's point is critical to my argument that historical narratives constructed out of personal narratives can be considered a form of historiography by virtue of content and by the way they are written. Judged on these two criteria, biographies offer renditions of bygone events as "legitimate" as any found in standard history books. The study of personal narratives like *The Concubine's Children* tells us much about the discrimination Chinese Canadians faced in the early years of their collective history.

Chong reconstructs her maternal grandparents' lives from roughly the 1900s to the 1940s and, in doing so, sheds light on Vancouver's Chinatown and on some of the major events in Canadian history that impacted Chinese immigrants at that time. She portrays her grandparents as everyday people facing ordinary and extraordinary challenges, the latter amplified by prejudice and legalized discrimination. In fact, Chong owes her own existence to the consequences of the Chinese Immigration Act of 1923 for her grandfather Chan Sam's life. Had the Canadian government not imposed the act, her grandfather might never have considered purchasing a concubine (who would eventually bear him a daughter, the author's mother). Chan Sam paid the $500 Head Tax to enter Canada in 1913. Only Chinese were forced to pay the exorbitant tax, which was raised from $50 in 1885 to $500 in 1904 to discourage Chinese from coming. However, this did not deter men like Chan Sam, who were determined to achieve a better life in Canada. Chong's grandmother, May-ying, came in 1924 to be Chan Sam's concubine while his wife waited back in China. The concubine did not pay the Head Tax because Chan Sam secured false papers for her by spending a large sum of money to obtain the birth certificate of a deceased Chinese Canadian woman born in the Vancouver area. Many Chinese desperate to come to Canada resorted to this route, paying exorbitant fees to enter the country as "paper" brides and family members. Thus, Chan Sam's decision to splurge on an "overseas bride" was fueled by personal motives—loneliness and a desire to start a family—and by his distrust of the Canadian government. The 1923 Chinese Immigration Act was intended to halt Chinese immigration permanently; those already in Canada could return to China but were given two years before their reentry status was revoked. Chan Sam was afraid that if he left Canada to visit his wife in China, he might never return— he could not afford to travel frequently between his two homes and he feared the Canadian government could change the laws on reentry without notice, leaving him stranded in Guangdong. Thus, the act forced men like Chan Sam to make the difficult decision whether to go home to China for good or risk decades of separation from loved ones by staying in Canada. The social ramification of the act was to drive a wedge between many Chinese in Canada and their families back in China. This division lasted more than sixty years in Chong's family. Canadian exclusionary policies coincided with World War II and China's Communist Revolution in 1949 to split Chan Sam's family until 1987, when Chong and her mother were reunited with the other half of the family in their ancestral home in Guangdong Province.

Throughout *The Concubine's Children,* Chong details unsparingly the often brutish life many Chinese Canadians of her grandparents' generation led in the Chinese ghetto. Chan Sam and May-ying are portrayed as individuals struggling with the pressures of marginal living created through unjust laws that restricted Chinese in everything from the right to vote to the types of jobs they could hold to the freedom to live where they pleased. These restrictions were tough enough to bear during economically healthy periods but when the Great Depression struck, Chinese like Chan Sam and May-ying were hit hard. It was difficult enough for white men to find work but for Chinese laborers like Chan Sam it was next to impossible: "The Chinese sank like stones to the bottom of the labor pool."[4] Chong's mother, Hing, was born during the Depression. With Chan Sam out of work, May-ying's earnings as a waitress were all the family lived on. This pittance eventually dried up when the restaurant May-ying worked for folded. The Depression was a rough time for Chan Sam and May-ying, but Chong describes worse situations in Chinatown during the 1930s:

> By [1932], destitute Chinese men, most of them elderly, were begging in the streets, gambling on a helping Chinese hand. The first Chinese deaths from star-

vation finally forced the provincial government to show some concern. It funded the Anglican Church Mission's soup kitchen in Chinatown, but it expected a Chinese to be fed at half what it cost to feed a white man on relief. Some destitute Chinese said they'd rather starve than accept relief.[5]

This passage captures not only the horrible conditions in Chinatown during the Depression era but also the animosities that ran deeply between whites and Chinese. Much of this enmity was fueled by ignorance and anti-Chinese hysteria that was augmented after the railroad's completion in 1885. In 1907 a major riot flared when the Asiatic Exclusion League in Vancouver incited attacks against Chinese and Japanese businesses that caused considerable property damage in Chinatown. In the newspapers and in political propaganda, Chinese were cast collectively as the "Yellow Menace" or the "Mongol Horde," threatening to overrun North America and imperil white civilization. Chong details the ugly stereotypes that plagued Chinese in Chan Sam's time, including Chinatowns "as dirty and disease-ridden, as centers of gambling and crime," and Chinese as "shifty-eyed, pigtailed Chinamen" who "smoked opium, lay with Chinese prostitutes, fed on rats and enslaved white girls."[6] Chong counters these calumnious stereotypes with a representation of Chinese based on their actual lived experiences:

> No one saw the contrasting truth, that there were, among the bachelors, a few upstanding families living there. These included the wives and children of the merchant class who could raise the money to pay for the five-hundred-dollar head tax on each family member, who could install them above their ground-floor businesses, and who could afford to send their children back to China for part of their education. Selling out their business was always an option, too, if Canada got unbearably inhospitable, to pay for the family's passage home.[7]

We see from these examples that biographies like *The Concubine's Children* operate on two levels—evidence from the personal history of an individual and evidence from the public history of the individual's society/culture/country as it affected his or her life. Biography's focus on personal narrative can help to shatter stereotypes by demonstrating the unique experiences of the individual and, in doing so, prove by example that no person's life can be pigeonholed into predefined notions based on his/her race, culture, or creed. Simultaneously, there were plenty of circumstances in Chan Sam and May-ying's lives that were similar to the experiences of other Chinese in Vancouver's Chinatown and, by extension, other Chinatowns across

Canada. Many negative consequences of these collective experiences were direct conditions of discrimination and the laws that upheld exclusion of Chinese from mainstream Canadian society in the early decades of the twentieth century.

A biography like Chong's provides a text of the history of Chinese Canadians that reads very differently than that scripted in mainstream literature and history books up until the late 1970s and early 1980s. Until that time, if Canadian history books mentioned Chinese at all it was usually in a passing reference to the transcontinental railway. History texts frequently eulogized and romanticized the construction of the railroad but failed to give recognition to the significant contribution of Chinese laborers. An exploration of passages from three school history textbooks, *Canada: Great Nation of the North* (1968), *The Canadian Experience* (1969), and *The Story of Canada* (1929), will illustrate the tendency of older textbooks to elide the Chinese from Canadian history, either by scripting their presence out altogether or by employing rhetorical tropes that construct a discriminatory subtext of exclusion within the historical narrative. I have identified three such tropes and named them the tropes of *diminution, commodification* and *corroboration*.

The story of the railway is romanticized in this excerpt from *Canada: Great Nation of the North*:

It was the age of railroads that made Canada a nation. Railroads had spanned the United States since 1869. The Canadians were determined that they too could build one to unite their far-flung territories.

The government was so eager to help that it offered to grant a right-of-way 20 miles wide all across the country to speculators if they could build the railway through it.

The right-of-way led through some of the continent's most rugged mountains. So much rock had to be blasted to push through the road of rails that the builders set up a dynamite factory of their own to make the explosives near at hand.

They used river canyons where they could, chopping narrow shelves for the railway into canyon walls. Where mountains were too tall for the road to go over them, the men blasted tunnels through. Deep ravines were crossed with bridges supported by timbers.

Men slaved and sweated; some sickened and died, but the railway pushed on. By the end of the 1880's the long line of "turkey tracks," as settlers called the slender trail of ties and rails, reached the prairie. For a thousand prairie miles the going was easy, across level ground.[8]

The title, *Great Nation of the North*, declares from the outset this narrative's intention to be an anthem to Canada's "Nordic magnificence." The metaphor of northernness is deeply ingrained in the Canadian psyche and speaks of rugged geography, formidable weather, people toughened to snow and ice. The rhetoric of this particular excerpt carries on these romanticizing associations in the way it describes how the railroad passed through "some of the continent's most rugged mountains" and how it describes the quantity of rock that had to be blasted and the deep ravines that had to be crossed. In this manner, the text conflates the romance of the North with the building of the railroad, a predictable development since the transcontinental railway itself became a grand symbol of nationhood. The importance of the railway is evident in the first line of this excerpt, "It was the age of railroads that made Canada a nation." This sentence presents the railway as the symbol of an era that looked to the railroad as both the physical and figurative backbone of a new nation.

This textbook eulogizes the historical importance of the railroad, but nowhere does the text mention the thousands of Chinese who toiled on the Pacific portion of the transcontinental railroad between 1881 and 1885, and the more than six hundred who were killed working the most dangerous assignments, which few white men cared to touch. The fact that the Chinese have been simply left out of this story is the most obvious example of exclusion. But they are also excluded via the trope of *diminution*, which is manifested in the line "Men slaved and sweated; some sickened and died, *but* [my emphasis] the railway pushed on." The word "but" redirects the emphasis in this sentence away from the men who slaved and died to the railway's unhindered progress. The trope turns the text in such a way as to *diminish* the significance of the men against the railway they built. The trope's influence is felt throughout the text—obstacles are "blasted," "carved," "chopped," and "crossed" in the name of pushing the railroad through. All obstacles to the railway's progress—including sick and dying workmen—are "downsized." In this manner the human element in building the railway is reduced by the trope of diminution virtually to the point of exclusion.

The trope of diminution also operates against the Chinese in *The Canadian Experience*. Twenty-six pages are devoted to the "saga" of the great Canadian railway but only one sentence mentions the Chinese: "Three portable dynamite factories produced supplies of this new, powerful explosive to blast a way through the rocks, and coolies brought from China provided cheap labour."[9] The trope in this case diminishes the enormity of the Chinese contribution by abridging four years of toil and suffering down to seven words: "coolies

brought from China provided cheap labour." There is also another exclusionary trope at work here, what I call the trope of *commodification*. This trope operates by syntactic paralleling of the words "coolies brought from China" with
the words "dynamite factories." Pairing the Chinese with dynamite in the same
sentence gives the impression that Chinese were on par with a building commodity. The word "cheap" used in this manner further gives the impression
that Chinese were like discount hardware and, therefore, expendable. The
trope of commodification's effect is that of depersonalization, and this is fur-
thered in the paralleling of the words "produced supplies" with "provided
cheap labour."

In contrast, Chong's treatment of the building of the railroad "reinserts"
the Chinese into the historical event of the building of the railway. Her narrative of the railway, though short, gives details of the iniquities the Chinese endured while laboring on the tracks:

> [D]istaste for the Chinese presence did not deter white contractors who were
> looking for cheap labor to carve out the great transcontinental railways across
> the United States and Canada. Their governments bought their claim that the
> Chinese would work for much less and were more reliable than the available
> white labor, mostly Irish. Though many Chinese, assigned the most dangerous
> jobs, died building the railway, racist resentment sped along the newly built iron
> rails. Whites in the east railed against the inevitable eastward settlement of a
> race they condemned as alien, steeped in moral depravity and degradation.[10]

Chong summarizes in one brief paragraph the racism and perilous working conditions Chinese workers endured on the railroad, the details of which
were ignored by conventional history texts for decades. Our comparison between Chong and the school history textbooks demonstrates how entirely different versions of history can arise out of the same historical evidence, depending on what material is included or left out and how the text is written.

As mentioned above, the Chinese were usually depicted in an openly racist
manner whenever they appeared in mainstream literature. Occasionally, however, there were exceptions to the overt racist depictions, such as our final examples, from a 1929 school textbook called *The Story of Canada*. The text de-
votes half a paragraph to describe the Chinese presence in the gold rush and
their role in the building of the Canadian Pacific Railway (CPR):

> During "the Reign of Richard McBride" agitation against the Orientals in
> British Columbia reached a head. The Chinese had come into Cariboo in the
> Gold Rush, and many thousands had been brought to build the C. P. R. After

some difficulty between the Provincial and Dominion governments a head tax of fifty dollars was placed on Chinese immigrants in 1885. This was later increased to one hundred dollars, and finally to five hundred dollars. In 1923 further immigration of Chinese was forbidden.[11]

Upon first reading, this passage may seem progressive for its time. Events related to the Chinese are reported in greater detail than in our two previous examples, written more than forty years later. However, the dehumanizing power of the earlier described trope of commodification is present in the phrase describing how the Chinese "had been brought" to build the railway, as though they were goods and not people. Further down the page, the Chinese are mentioned in this description of the Japanese and East Indians:

> In 1907 the Japanese began to arrive in large numbers, and there was a great outcry against them. In September of that year riots occurred in Vancouver. "Chinatown" was damaged, but the determined Japanese fought off the assailants. An agreement made in 1908 between the Japanese Government and the Government of Canada regulated the immigration of Japanese into the country. *This agreement has worked well* [my emphasis], and has been renewed and modified so that now only one hundred and fifty Japanese a year are admitted. East Indians began to arrive in 1905, and in 1914 a Japanese steamer, the *Komagata Maru*, brought several hundred to Vancouver. The East Indians were refused admission, and, after considerable difficulty, the vessel steamed away back to the Orient.[12]

What I call the trope of *corroboration* is active in the above paragraph. This trope corroborates the victory of Canada's anti-Oriental policies by associating Chinese exclusion with the successful curtailment of Japanese immigration, which is emphasized by the word "only" in the sentence, "now *only* one hundred and fifty Japanese a year are admitted." The power of the trope's corroborative effect is in the phrase, "this agreement has worked well." This phrase pushes the meaning of the text toward the successful examples of Japanese and East Indian forced exclusion. In this way, the trope is able to embed an anti-Chinese subtext without mentioning Chinese exclusion at all.

Through historical hindsight one can understand why the rhetoric of the 1929 textbook is constructed in this fashion. Until the 1923 Chinese Immigration Act, the Head Tax and subsequent increases did not deter Chinese immigration completely.[13] The 1923 act was enacted in response to the general demand that absolutely no Chinese be permitted to enter the country. Since this textbook was written six years following the new law, one can speculate that perhaps public confidence in the law's effectiveness was still cautionary. Hence the Chinese, and immigration policies affecting them, are linked to the actions taken against the Japanese and East Indians through the trope of corroboration to imply that Canadian exclusionary measures against Orientals are effective and will continue to ward off the threat of the "Yellow Peril."

When we pull the language of the school textbooks apart, we discover that the way in which the texts are written—the type of words chosen, the rhetorical devices used—contributes another layer of meaning to the content of the text. We see that embedded in the text is a subtext that reflects the discriminatory attitudes toward Chinese at the time the textbooks were written. This brings us to one of Hayden White's most significant contentions, his theory that all written narratives, whether fictional or nonfictional, employ the literary devices and rhetorical strategies of telling a story through written language. In other words, White argues that if we focus only on the writing of a text, then the difference between fictional and nonfictional narratives is actually an arbitrary construction because *all* writing—all language—is figurative. In this manner, historical text can be considered an "extended metaphor" because it "does not *reproduce* the events it describes; it tells us in what direction to think about the events and charges our thought about the events with different emotional valences."[14] Furthermore, White maintains that historical writing is dominated by narrative, or storytelling, and that "narrative has always been and continues to be the predominant mode of historical writing."[15] White believes that far from negating the efforts of historians through this claim, "histories gain part of their explanatory effect by their success in making stories out of *mere* chronicles."[16] This point is illuminated by applying one of White's techniques to illustrate the importance of narrative. Let us isolate three important events from Chong's narrative and list them in chronological order:

1. Chan Sam arrives in Vancouver in 1913.
2. The Chinese Immigration Act is instituted in 1923.
3. May-ying arrives in Vancouver in 1924.

These events remain isolated occurrences without a plot structure, subplots, or other narrative mechanisms to construct a story that links the events in a cogent and meaningful way. It can be difficult to remove the "arbitrary line" between nonfictional and fictional writing to see that historical texts are subject to the same literary rules and constructions as a novel. However, White's point that all writing is figurative must not be taken out of context when considering works of history. White is not arguing for *any* piece of literature to be considered historiographical, nor is he in any way implying that historical facts themselves are fictional. Rather, he wants readers of historical texts to remember that historical facts exist but that the written text that conveys these facts must be authored; ergo, the way in which a text is written is never free of the author's own predilections, which are in turn influenced by the social, cultural, and historical contexts in which she exists. The literary devices, plot structure, and other narrative strategies employed in a text can reinforce the "factual, conceptual and generic" content of the work or bury a subtext within the text that covertly influences the direction of understanding, as shown in our textbook examples.

Following White's theories, Chong's biography, and Chinese Canadian biography in general, can be considered a form of historiography because of content *and* form. The content of her work captures a unique history and presents, as Chong says, a "contrasting truth" to standard accounts of Chinese Canadians. The form utilizes the omniscient narrator and dialogue as narrative techniques. In her introduction, Chong identifies these as two literary devices she uses to construct a narrative that is the fairest to the lives of those she characterizes in her story. She implies that the style of writing affects the content of the narrative:

> There are as many different versions of events as there are members of a family. The truth becomes a landscape of many layers in an ever-changing light; the details depend on whose memories illuminate it. . . . Above all, I wanted to be true to the individual lives of the family. It seemed that the most fair and honest way to do that was to tell the story as an omniscient narrator. This involved some necessary interpretation of events and some reconstruction of dialogue. I approached it as one might approach the task of restoring a painting—the original canvas was someone else's. Of course, in the very act of writing a book, I myself bring another shading of truth.[17]

Thus, Chong's "realistic" style of storytelling is achieved paradoxically in an unrealistic way—via necessary interpretation and reconstruction of events and conversation—to create the illusion of realism. The omniscient narrator, for example, is a mechanism that allows Chong to leap between different time periods and disparate locations, tie together subplots, flip in and out of characters' thoughts, and alternate between two stories, that of her grandparents and her mother in Canada and that of her mother's sisters in China. This effect of stylistic realism harks back to the "free indirect style" (*style indirect libre*) as perfected by Flaubert. According to historian Dominick LaCapra, the free indirect style was a radical literary innovation for its time; it was a style that achieved an "indeterminancy of voice . . . in which a use of language may play in two registers—those of the character and the narrator—with the possible modulations of irony and empathy this entails."[18]

Chong uses the omniscient narrator voice to slip in and out of characters' thoughts, such as where the omniscient voice describes May-ying's thoughts when she hears the news that she has been sold as a concubine to a sojourner in Gold Mountain. Her "Auntie" (actually her master) tells May-ying, "'I'm only doing what is best for you. I want you to have *on lock cha fun.*' May-ying heard the echo of these words in her head. Her mother had used these same words of farewell. She had wished her a life of contentment, a life never short of tea or rice. It only reminded May-ying of that tearful parting."[19] Immediately following, the omniscient narrator slips "outside" the thoughts of May-ying to describe the outward expression of anger she felt over this decision: "In a flash of temper, May-ying kicked the table legs. He's only a peasant, she said. Why couldn't Auntie find a boy from a decent family near Canton? She shoved the table top, splashing tea. She repeated that she did not want to go, that she did not want to eat rice from a strange land."[20] The omniscient voice thus modulates between the narrative and the narrated—i.e. the characters—in an unrealistic manner that, paradoxically, heightens the sense of veracity of Chong's narrative. We recall in her introduction that Chong states that to remain true to past events she resorted to reconstructing the past. A better term for the above example is invention, because it was impossible for her to have been there to witness May-ying shoving the table in anger and even more improbable that the author would be privy to May-ying's exact thoughts at that moment. What she knew of her grandmother's story she received from her mother. Even if Chong's grandmother did pass on the details of this story to her daughter, it is still a memory that Chong must reinterpret and reinvent through writing.

A final point on the omniscient narrator technique is that it enables Chong to weave personal narrative together with historical facts. For example, Chong builds up to the moment Chan Sam and May-ying first meet, after May-ying disembarks at the docks in Vancouver in 1924, by taking detours into May-ying's life before coming to Canada and into Chan Sam's first eleven years in Vancouver. May-ying's story focuses mostly on her bad luck having been born female and poor in China in the early 1900s. She was sold twice, first as a servant and then as a concubine. Her story builds up to her arrival in Vancouver, with the omniscient voice narrating in extensive detail her journey from her village in Guangdong to Hong Kong and finally Vancouver:

> After eighteen days at sea, the ship steamed into the port of Vancouver. Mountains and sea seemed to diminish man's efforts at fashioning this young cityscape. Among the wide-eyed disembarking passengers was a tiny girl, who, but for her mature hairstyle, looked too young to have left home. Her birth certificate said she was born in Ladner, British Columbia. The fertile farmland of the Fraser Valley just outside Vancouver was dotted with Chinese laboring in the fields for white farmers.[21]

Many Chinese during the Exclusion Era entered Canada illegally as "paper brides," paper daughters and sons, parents, and siblings. With the government exercising tight restriction on legal avenues of immigration for Chinese, many who wanted to enter Canada resorted to buying the identities of Canadian-born Chinese, as Chan Sam did for May-ying. The asking price was high and there were no guarantees that the false papers would secure entry. But it was a risk those ambitious or desperate enough were willing to take.

Chan Sam's story begins with a flashback from the scene in which he stands at the docks awaiting May-ying. As the omniscient voice of the narrator, Chong has him "remembering" the ordeal that awaited him after landing in Vancouver in 1913:

> [H]e was herded into a dock-side low brick building to spend three months in quarantine behind barred windows and under guard. Despite their protests that they had already stood naked in a line for examination by the white doctor on-board ship, the men were fumigated with sulfur, and so were their belongings. Inside the packed and filthy "pigpen," as the Chinese called it, amid the noise from trains rumbling into the adjacent western terminus of the transcontinental railway, it had been hard for them to keep fast their belief in Gold Mountain's fairy tales, spun from men before them who'd gone to make their fortunes.[22]

Immediately following this paragraph, Chong delves into a piece of history that begins at the Pearl River Delta, from where the majority of the early Chinese immigrant men originated, and continues to the gold rush, to the building of the railway, and back to the personal history of her grandfather, whose father before him had sojourned in Gold Mountain in the nineteenth century. May-ying's and Chan Sam's respective journeys to Canada offer plenty of examples in which the omniscient narrator device effectively weaves the plot's disparate strands together by spanning the parameters of time and geography, of the personal and the historical.

The other literary device Chong relies upon, dialogue, is employed to heighten dramatic moments or at points where the narrative seems better told through the characters' "own" voices. An example of a dramatic scene is when Chan Sam takes May-ying to *dim sum* at a Chinatown teahouse after he picks her up at the docks. At this point May-ying does not know what to make of her new husband: the restaurant owner greets Chan Sam at the door and "May-ying hoped the ebullient greeting hinted well at her husband's status in this new land."[23] But May-ying was soon to learn of her unfortunate fate—she finds out that Chan Sam had farmed her out to the teahouse owner to work off what it cost him to bring her over to Canada. Chong constructs this scene using dialogue:

> At the end of the meal, the owner parted the curtain and stood before them. "Everything taste all right?"
> "Very tasty, very tasty." Chan Sam reached into his trouser pocket and made an elaborate gesture of reaching for money.
> "No, no, put your money away." The owner slid onto the bench across from May-ying and poured a cup of tea for himself.
> Then Chan Sam told her: "*Ah* May-ying, this gentleman is your new boss."[24]

Another example of dialogue used to embellish and heighten the realism of the narrative is where Chong describes May-ying's dreary life as a Chinatown waitress. May-ying and her waitress friends would end a long hard day at their jobs by visiting each other to indulge in cigarettes and gossip:

> Each one had the same litany of complaints: they were hard up and short of money; they were having problems with the men in their lives.
> "The trouble with Chan Sam," May-ying was fond of saying when her turn came, "is that he always has to be Number One." What peeved her most was how difficult it was to make him see anything her way. "Talking to Chan Sam any which way, coming or going, is useless. He doesn't hear what I'm saying. Every time he opens or closes his mouth to me, it's '*Gum Gee!*' or 'Bull-lo-shit!'"
> "How frustrating," others murmured.
> "Such a man could make one sick enough to die," they said—which was what they always said of each other's men.[25]

The above two examples illustrate how dialogue used strategically at key moments of the narrative sustains the reader's interest through dramatic emphasis and the constructed illusion that the reader is right there "hearing" the characters as they verbally interact, expressing their thoughts and feelings directly. Dialogue and the omniscient narrator are two literary devices that work together to create an illusion, as though these events really did happen exactly the way Chong recounts them. The result is a story that has the feel of a documentary—the perspective of the omniscient narrator gives the impression that the reader is watching the lives of the characters as they unfold. The moments of dialogue interspersed with the narration heighten the sensation that we are drawn into the action by the events themselves without any interference from the author. But, in fact, it is the author who has created this sense of objectivity through the strategies and techniques she uses in her writing. As a final note, the power of the omniscient narrator to conjure the feeling of objective realism is heightened by Chong's decision to begin and end in the first person voice, which identifies Chong as the storyteller. This establishes the fact that the characters of her story are her relatives and that, ultimately, it is their stories she strives to tell.

In summary, Chong's reconstruction of her grandparents' story is both a personal history and a recounting of the major events that affected the development of Chinese Canadians' collective history. Most significant of these events were the Exclusion Acts and the ignominious Head Tax, anti-Chinese legislation that directly or indirectly impacted several generations of Chinese Canadians in families like Chong's. *The Concubine's Children* offers a Chinese Canadian version of Canadian history that was virtually ignored in conventional historiography, like school history textbooks. Not until the latter half of the twentieth century, when social and cultural changes created the right conditions for inclusion, did Chinese Canadians finally find a voice in mainstream historical texts. Finally, we must remember that the history explored here belongs to a specific Chinese immigrant group: the early generations of Chinese in North America were nearly exclusively from one geographical area in China, the *Say-Yup* (Four Districts) area of Guangdong Province in southern China. They were also overwhelmingly men. Many Chinese in North America can trace their roots back to the first pioneers from Guangdong, but subsequent waves of Chinese immigrants have come from other areas of China and the world. The telling of the stories of these early Chinese immigrants helps to educate not only the greater society but also other immigrant groups within the Chinese community itself.

NOTES

Developed and excerpted from M.A. thesis, master of arts in liberal arts and sciences, San Diego State University, 1999.

1. Lien Chao, *Beyond Silence: Chinese Canadian Literature in English* (Toronto: Tsar, 1997), 17.

2. The textbooks used here were chosen from the Curriculum Collection at Simon Fraser University, Burnaby, British Columbia. Specific information could not be found at Simon Fraser University or through the British Columbia Ministry of Education regarding the exact period these textbooks were used in the provincial school system. However, that they were in the collection at the university, which was a depository for school texts used in provincial curriculum, indicates they were circulated and used in public schools at some time in the past.

3. Hayden White, *Figural Realism: Studies in the Mimesis Effect* (Baltimore: Johns Hopkins University Press, 1999), 4.

4. Denise Chong, *The Concubine's Children: Portrait of a Family Divided* (originally published in 1994; Toronto: Viking, 1995), 49.

5. Chong, *The Concubine's Children*, 55.

6. Chong, *The Concubine's Children*, 14.

7. Chong, *The Concubine's Children*, 14–15.

8. Jane Werner Watson, *Canada: Giant Nation of the North* (Champaign, Ill.: Garrod, 1968), 92–93.

9. John S. Moir and D. M. C. Farr, *The Canadian Experience* (Toronto: Ryerson, 1969), 289.

10. Chong, *The Concubine's Children*, 12.

11. George M. Wrong and Chester Martin, *The Story of Canada* (Toronto: Ryerson, 1929), 348–49.

12. Wrong, *The Story of Canada*, 349.

13. The 1885 exclusion law that implemented the Head Tax had an immediate and dramatic effect on immigration—the numbers of Chinese immigrating to Canada dropped from thousands in the early 1880s to 212 in 1886. However, the numbers reached over a thousand again by 1890. Edgar Wickberg, ed., *From China to Canada: A History of the Chinese Communities in Canada* (Toronto: McClelland and Stewart in association with the Multiculturalism Directorate and the Department of State, 1982), 59.

14. Hayden White, *Tropics of Discourse: Essays in Cultural Criticism* (Baltimore: Johns Hopkins University Press, 1978), 91.

15. White, *Figural Realism*, 3.

16. White, *Tropics*, 83.

17. Chong, *The Concubine's Children*, xi.

18. Dominick LaCapra, *"Madame Bovary" on Trial* (Ithaca, N.Y.: Cornell University Press, 1982), 137.

19. Chong, *The Concubine's Children*, 8.

20. Chong, *The Concubine's Children*, 8.

21. Chong, *The Concubine's Children*, 10.

22. Chong, *The Concubine's Children*, 11–12.

23. Chong, *The Concubine's Children*, 24.

24. Chong, *The Concubine's Children*, 25.

25. Chong, *The Concubine's Children*, 81.

III

Livelihood in the New World

7

The Recurrent Image of the Coolie: Representations of Chinese American Labor in American Periodicals, 1900–1924

Shirley Sui Ling Tam

Recent studies of stereotyped depictions of Chinese Americans in the mass media have concentrated mainly on newspapers, fiction, and film,[1] while largely ignoring the presence of stereotyped images in periodicals. This chapter examines the portrayal of Chinese Americans in American periodicals during the period 1900 to 1924, in particular their unfavorable representation as laborers in America.[2] Although periodicals did not have the kind of grassroots readership enjoyed by newspapers, with improved technology, more advertising, and lower prices, they reached an expanding middle class and became influential in shaping public opinion in the early twentieth century.[3] In general, magazines propagated prejudicial perceptions of Chinese Americans, and these took root in the minds of readers who had little chance of actual contact with Chinese in America.

A review of periodical articles published from 1900 to 1924 shows Chinese workers almost always described as undesirable and inferior. Anti-Chinese writers were not the only ones who produced shadowy representations of Chinese workmen; many sympathetic contributors employed derogatory images when defending Chinese workers, albeit inadvertently. Many comments about Chinese laborers repeated nineteenth-century stereotypes and did not reflect reality in the early twentieth century. In fact, the whole question of Chinese labor stemmed from a troubling social issue: the conflict between rising unionism and the fear of union militancy. Unflattering and unfair depictions of Chinese workers continued independent of changes in historical circumstances, however, providing evidence of the persistence of racist attitudes.

Supporters of Chinese immigration included intellectuals and diplomats who argued for the acceptance of Chinese workers in America based on studies or close observation of Chinese residents; agricultural capitalists who preferred to import Chinese immigrants for farmwork; and Chinese intellectuals who defended Chinese resident workers against discriminatory charges. Opponents included Americans who favored continued exclusion of Chinese immigration, especially advocates of West Coast trade unions who objected to the entry of foreigners into the American labor pool.

CHINESE WORKERS IN THE NINETEENTH AND TWENTIETH CENTURIES
The debate about Chinese workers was detached from the real situation of Chinese laborers in early twentieth-century America. Because of segregation and restrictive immigration laws, the Chinese no longer served as an alternate source of labor. When the Chinese first came to America after 1850, they took up mining jobs in California.[4] But they also engaged in manufacturing enterprises, and prior to 1870 some became merchants. The large-scale employment of Chinese in the building of the Central Pacific Railroad beginning in 1865, however, played the greatest role in the shift from independent gold mining to toilsome wage labor. The building of the railroad crystallized the image of the Chinese as exploitable workers.[5]

After the completion of the railway, however, Chinese laborers faced fierce opposition from other California workers. With the government's tacit endorsement of Sinophobia following passage of the Chinese Exclusion Act in 1882, anti-Chinese agitation persisted and directly affected Chinese employment. At the same time, Chinese-owned small factories or sweatshops faced an increasingly competitive market with the growth of corporations in California and the influx of products from the East Coast after the completion of the Central Pacific Railroad in 1869.[6] By the turn of the century, manufacturing (mainly sewing) employed less than one-quarter of the Chinese in San Francisco, while nearly two-thirds labored in laundries or as domestic servants, work sought by few whites.[7] To create job opportunities without incurring opposition from trade unions, Chinese residents had to open more ethnic businesses in Chinatowns or increase exports to mainland China. Chinese entrepreneurs, for instance, began to practice Chinese medicine in the ghetto, manufacture junks for sale, or even export seaweed gathered locally.[8] Chinese laborers segregated in the ghetto had little choice but to work for these Chinese-run enterprises. In agriculture, successive exclusion laws cut the number of available workers so substantially that many Chinese farmers abandoned the practice in the 1900s.[9] Agricultural fieldwork now went primarily to Mexicans, who could easily cross the border. Japanese also arrived to fill the labor vacuum until 1924, when they too were barred. As one economic historian has noted, job competition between white and Chinese workers was reduced to a minimum by 1890.[10]

Mob violence forced many Chinese workers to withdraw to Chinatown, where they concentrated in laundry and restaurant businesses.[11] Residential segregation effectively confined the Chinese to their ghettos. In 1892 and 1902, the Chinese Exclusion Act was extended, and in 1904 the Chinese were excluded permanently from immigrating to the United States. Consequently, the Chinese population fell drastically and not until the 1920s did second-generation Chinese Americans experience some population growth. Chinese immigrants posed little threat to local white workers, who had no desire for the kinds of jobs typically performed by Chinese residents. However, both exclusionists and supporters of Chinese immigration continued to write about what the Chinese had supposedly done in the past and not about the lives of Chinese in the first two decades of the twentieth century. Their arguments served to reaffirm the low status of Chinese laborers in America.

Indeed, the persistent appearance in periodicals of Chinese immigrants as "coolies" bore scant resemblance to reality. "Coolie" implied involuntary or slave-like status, a negative and inaccurate representation of Chinese domestic laborers. The term "coolie" originated in India;[12] in China it literally meant "bitter strength" or unskilled laborers, not slave-like bondage.[13] Chinese workers came to North America at their free will through a credit-ticket system that advanced payment for the emigrant laborers.[14] But the popular correlation of Chinese laborers with coolies undermined their image and harmed their status in the American labor market.

CHINESE WORKERS AS SCAPEGOATS FOR UNION SUPPORTERS

The labor situation in California was from the start unfavorable to Chinese workers. The California Constitutional Convention of 1849 included a special provision outlawing slavery: "Neither slavery, nor involuntary servitude, unless for the punishment of crime, shall ever be tolerated in this State."[15] Only "free white males" gained the right to vote.[16] Racial distinctions thus determined policy from the very founding of the state.

Although the trade-union movement did not take solid root in early-twentieth-century America, the Chinese labor issue did energize emerging unionism in California. When Chinese workers first entered the labor market, the union movement was still in its infancy. Dislike for Chinese workers became a unifying force for the young labor movement in California and the slogan "The Chinese Must Go" became a rallying cry among disconnected laborers in the Golden State.[17] Chinese were blamed for the drop in the price of gold in the mid-1860s. At the same time, corporate mining began to replace independent or small-group mining.[18] The dream of free white labor met further frustration in manufacturing industries and agriculture as large corporate businesses began to dominate the market. Small enterprises were also hard-hit by cheap goods imported from the East Coast over the newly completed railroad. Chinese laborers, who suffered as much as American workers, were held responsible for the loss of market competitiveness. In agriculture, corporate farming created a great demand for seasonal labor, a life that appealed to few white workers. Yet many white laborers regarded Chinese migratory farmworkers as agents of large agricultural enterprises and believed that the use of Chinese field workers undermined a fair society based on individual effort.

Early attempts to organize labor in California exploited deep-seated racism, increasingly exaggerating the presence of Chinese laborers as a menace to American workers' survival. Labor historian Alexander Saxton observes that despite the different origins of white American workers, they had one thing in common—they were not Chinese.[19] Beginning in the 1870s the craft unions grew rapidly in California and anti-Chinese slogans quickly became inseparable from the union movement. The Knights of Labor, a national trade union that represented craftsmen and manual laborers, singled out the Chinese for attack.

In the late nineteenth century, the special interests of craft unions overcame the Knights' general appeal, and Knights membership dwindled. The American Federation of Labor (AFL) gradually eclipsed the Knights of Labor, but it followed the Knights' anti-Chinese stand. The AFL—founded in the 1880s by Samuel Gompers, who headed it until his death in 1924—acted on behalf of white, skilled, native-born workers only. It avoided the more extreme means adopted by the Knights, such as strikes, which evoked fear among the middle class and employers who associated the agitation with foreign-born anarchists and socialists. Learning from the failures of the Knights, who had advocated idealistic labor unity and welcomed even unskilled workers and immigrants, the AFL was pragmatic in pressing for special benefits for its native-born craftsmen. In the period 1890 to 1910, the AFL inherited the Knights' Sinophobia as a means to ensure craft domination and exclude noncraft labor from occupational competition. The Chinese easily became scapegoats for the grievances of nonskilled workers seeking higher-paying jobs. The craft unions realized two benefits by decrying the Chinese and pacifying their nonskilled competitors. On one hand they barred the Chinese from entering the skilled trades and pushed them into the manual labor force; on the other hand, the unions kept their doors closed to nonskilled workers while using the anti-Chinese campaign to direct attention to Chinese laborers as the cause of unemployment.

The anti-Chinese movement in California had become a national issue by 1882, when Congress passed the first Exclusion Act against Chinese immigration. Although the Chinese population declined substantially after the series of Exclusion Acts, the AFL never abandoned its strong campaign against Chinese workers. The continuous opposition to Chinese workers by California labor unions in the early twentieth century was primarily symbolic. By this time, the "Chinese question" had little effect at the state level on the increasingly influential unions. The unions, in fact, were particularly successful in pushing for state labor legislation up until 1920.[20]

Politicians also fastened on the Chinese as a convenient means for the attainment of their objectives. The California Workingmen's Party as well as the Democratic and Republican parties manipulated the Chinese labor scare to gain votes from American working-class constituencies. Organized during the depression of 1877, the Workingmen's Party popularized the slogan "Chinese Must Go" as a successful strategy for attracting workers. Similarly, California's Democratic Party invoked color prejudice to win support from both foreign-born and native white laborers. The Republican Party, which sided more with the interests of capitalists and agriculturists, also tried to curry favor among workers by supporting the exclusionist stand against Chinese immigrants. Even the American Socialist Party, purported backer of both skilled and unskilled laborers, in its heyday from 1900 to 1920 yielded to its most right-wing members and took up the AFL's nativist, anti-immigrant policies.[21] Despite the shrinking population of Chinese workers in the early twentieth century, politicians maintained their anti-Chinese rhetoric to retain the support of American exclusionists.

A study of articles published in the periodical press shows that voices on both sides of the labor divide shared condescending perceptions of Chinese workers in California. Most of the essays concerning the Chinese appeared in the early 1900s, probably because the Chinese question was frequently discussed around the time of the passage of the permanent Exclusion Act in 1904. The prejudicial stereotypes reappeared in the 1910s and 1920s, however, without reference to the changing situation of Chinese in America. Periodicals discussing the Chinese labor problem ranged widely, from academic journals, national interest periodicals, and literary publications to regional magazines.

In the *Annals of the American Academy of Political and Social Science*, A. E. Yoell, secretary of the Asiatic Exclusion League of North America in San Francisco, discussed the situation of Chinese laborers.[22] The *Annals* had a tradition of remaining neutral on controversial questions by presenting detailed information to assist the public in taking a position. Yoell's work demonstrated how some Americans despised Chinese workers as inferior and saw them as a threat to white labor by accepting starvation wages and harmful working conditions. Yoell provided data to document the persistent pattern of low wages and long hours among Chinese who worked as seamen, butchers, broom makers, garment workers, laundry workers, cooks, waiters, and domestic helpers in Hawaii and San Francisco. Apparently, Yoell was the only writer who compared the wages and working hours of Chinese and white labor in detail. Although Yoell did not document his sources precisely,[23] his figures impressed readers with the danger posed by low-wage Chinese to American workers. A reader of Yoell's article would learn, for instance, that a Chinese butcher felt satisfied with less than $9 per week for working sixteen hours per day, whereas a white butcher demanded $20 per week for ten hours per day, more than three times the Chinese butcher's rate.[24] The great gap shown in wages and hours vividly likened the Chinese workers to African slaves and created a strong sense of how the Chinese impaired the dignity of white labor.

Besides criticizing how little Chinese laborers expected from employers, some writers resented the strong work ethic and thrifty way of life of the Chinese. They argued that these characteristics were not virtues but, like the starvation wages accepted by Chinese workers, would eventually harm the welfare of American laborers. California senator Julius Kahn, for example, wrote about Chinese laborers in the *Independent*, which became a nonsectarian New York-based publication. He described the Chinese laborer as endowed with "a devil-born capacity for doing more work than he ought."[25] He saw the Chinese as docile machines with feeble mental abilities and interpreted their industriousness in a completely negative sense.[26] Another senator, George C. Perkins, expressed a similar opinion in the *North American Review*, a magazine that promotes the national interest. A successful San Francisco businessman who had been a state senator, governor of California, and then a U.S. senator, Perkins claimed that the Chinese tolerance for a low standard of living would eventually "overwhelm the laborer of any nation having modern civilization."[27] He described Chinese work habits unfavorably as emerging from an old and backward civilization and feared they would eventually undermine "a civilization of a high plane."[28] Like other opponents of Chinese laborers who attacked Chinese forbearance of low wages and long working hours, these writers persuaded readers that Chinese diligence threatened the esteem of American labor.

While some articles downgraded Chinese work habits as undesirable, other essays declared directly that the mere presence of a Chinese labor force was in itself not a blessing to Americans. The availability of Chinese workmen would only enrich employers and consequently exacerbate the unequal distribution of wealth. In diverse magazines such as the *Forum* (a periodical distinguished by two-sided debates), *Outlook* (a weekly for general miscellany), *Harper's Weekly* (a literary publication), and the *Saturday Evening Post* (a literary and family magazine), various writers in the 1900s held the Chinese responsible for the growing gap between business owners and American workers.

A contributor to the *Forum* reminded readers that any increases in production attributable to Chinese workers paled in comparison to the public problem they amplified, namely the sharply skewed distribution of wealth.[29] In Europe, he stated, a portion of labor's profits went toward the purchase of stock in the concern, so that ultimately the workers would have some small voice in the enterprise's direction. Such an improved system would never be possible with an abundant supply of Chinese laborers, because employers would not need to negotiate with white workers. James Phelan, mayor of San Francisco, raised a similar alarm in the *Saturday Evening Post*.[30] Phelan warned readers that the real issue was "not so much the increase of more wealth as the equitable distribution of the great wealth" Americans produced.[31] He argued that labor welfare should rank above economic prosperity, thus offsetting any contribution of Chinese workers. An article in *Outlook* claimed that expanding local commerce through employment of Chinese workers would have adverse effects: cheap Chinese labor meant concentration of capital, whereas high-priced white labor symbolized fairer distribution of wealth.[32] The writer in *Harper's Weekly* reassured readers that the Chinese contribution to local commerce could hardly compare to the immense value of American workingmen to industry.[33] All in all, these writers added fuel to the anti-Chinese discourse, advancing the argument that short-term material benefits generated by Chinese hard labor would in the long run enrich only capitalists and aggravate social inequity.

In the 1910s, Chinese immigration ebbed further following the exclusion laws, and the Chinese role in the local economy remained small; yet essays continued to claim that Chinese laborers could imperil equality of opportunity in America. One labor partisan became furious when the *California Labor Commissioner Report*, published on May 30, 1910, confirmed an agricultural labor shortage. He wrote in the *World Today* (a periodical for study at home) that the report represented only the interests of the agricultural aristocracy.[34] The writer denied the existence of a labor shortage and warned that Californians should not encourage the further centralization of agriculture through an abundant supply of low-cost Chinese workers. The essay illustrated how the fear of an influx of Chinese workingmen had not waned, despite passage of the 1904 Exclusion Act.

The alarm over the potential employment of Chinese workers associated with any claim of a labor shortage revived during World War I. An article in *Sunset*, a regional magazine of the West, warned that America should not follow in the footsteps of its European allies who imported Chinese labor for unskilled work.[35] The writer cautioned readers that Americans had made this mistake before, consequently flooding the country with undesirable coolies for several decades, until the passage of exclusion laws. Periodical writers argued that a need for labor should never justify a return to the importation of Chinese workers. They revived the negative image of Chinese workers whenever employers expressed concerns about finding adequate labor.

In arguing against adding Chinese workers to the California economy, some prolabor writers asserted that cheap Chinese labor might not increase California's wealth significantly because of the Chinese penchant for sending large sums of money home. One keen advocate of prohibitive immigration policies writing in the *Arena*, a periodical noted for its advocacy of social reform and labor unionism, likened the Chinese laborer to "a leech fastening himself upon the vitals of the country, leaving nothing, taking everything."[36] George C. Perkins flatly stated that "none of the earnings of Chinese [in America were] invested here."[37] San Francisco mayor Phelan gave undocumented, quantitative support to this argument by claiming that "since 1868 [the Chinese] exported from the United States $400,000,000 in gold on this account alone."[38] Phelan went so far as to declare that southern slaves were more beneficial to the country because "the slaves worked for a *comfortable* subsistence, and did not drain the soil of its wealth by the exportation of the 'wage fund.'"[39]

Accusing the Chinese of exporting their earnings from America was surely an effective way of discrediting them. Not only were the Chinese responsible for enriching the employers, but they also drained money from the country. Rather than seeing the Chinese as hardworking contributors to the American economy, the periodical writers cast them as parasites.

An essay in the *Arena* perhaps best summarized the attitude of American labor and its supporters toward Chinese workers. The writer argued that it was not fair for the religious journals to accuse the AFL—which advocated Chinese exclusion—of self-interest, because even if the AFL was self-interested, it was "the most commendable selfishness": the desire for "self-protection and the preservation of American ideals."[40] A Pennsylvania congressman, Boies Penrose, writing in the *Independent* in January 1902, proclaimed the labor unions' demands "just."[41]

Supporters of American labor generally depicted Chinese employees as undemanding laborers who toiled unreasonably long hours for shameful wages and thus stimulated the unequal distribution of wealth. Those preoccupied with the "Chinese problem" overlooked irreversible economic trends in California, however. Large-scale enterprises booming along both coasts threatened the independence of American workers. Moreover, restrictive immigration laws had nearly removed the Chinese as a source of cheap labor for growing industries. Labor's lament about the Chinese menace to American workers from 1900 to 1924 did not have an anchor in reality. Corporation owners had already imported other immigrant laborers to fill the gap. Despite the search for a scapegoat, persistent accusations against the Chinese did nothing to solve the problems of American workers in the early twentieth century.

CHINESE WORKERS IN THE EYES OF UNION OPPONENTS

From the 1900s to the 1920s, trade unions in California began to challenge the growing power of big business enterprises and sometimes created the impression of chaos, especially because trade unions, in mobilizing public sentiment, in turn inadvertently encouraged mob violence against Chinese. The general public began to associate Chinese with agitation and believed that the Chinese had somehow caused instability. Concerns about union radicalism also grew. Americans troubled by union militancy began to write articles more in favor of Chinese laborers in order to criticize union aggressiveness. The unions' strategy of denouncing Chinese laborers gradually was turned against them by the opposing camp. But union opponents rarely rectified the coolie stereotype; although supportive of Chinese employment, many still described the Chinese workers condescendingly. In the end, like the pro-exclusionists, the antiunion writers only manipulated the Chinese image to advance their own arguments while leaving the prevailing negative view of Chinese laborers intact.

In the same issue of the *Annals of the American Academy of Political and Social Science* that carried Yoell's article, Mary Roberts Coolidge, a professor of sociology at Stanford and author of *Chinese Immigration,* a book defending Chinese settlers, argued that unions had incorrectly accused the Chinese of usurping jobs from Americans.[42] She explained that during economic depressions agitators and demagogues found a receptive audience among temporarily jobless white workers. The foreign faces of Chinese were readily seen as causing unemployment, although many Chinese were also victims of the recessions. Throughout her essay, Coolidge tried to counter the negative Chinese images asserted by American laborers. She found that widespread unemployment, falling wages, and the decline of small industries in late nineteenth-century California were not caused by competition from Chinese workers but by the arrival of inexpensive products from the East Coast after the completion of the Central Pacific Railway. After the Chinese were excluded from immigration, Coolidge said, labor problems reappeared, meaning that the Chinese did not cause joblessness among white workers, who in any event seldom sought the types of jobs typically occupied by Chinese.

Coolidge was one of the few Americans who defended Chinese immigrants in America by dispelling popular stereotypes about them. She was also highly respected in China, which she later visited. Even so, Coolidge sometimes still positioned Chinese workers below their American counterparts. For instance, she recalled how in the early mining period Chinese chiefly worked the poor-quality and abandoned claims.[43] In the shoe and boot industry, where even in the East only women and children were willing to work, Chinese men took jobs, and earned the same low wages as women employed in eastern factories. In the course of pacifying American labor's anger toward Chinese workers, Coolidge retained the passive, inferior image of Chinese laborers willing to accept the least-appealing sorts of jobs. Coolidge was much more successful in arguing that Chinese immigrants were not a risk to American white laborers than in showing that Chinese workers were as intelligent and capable as Americans. A Chinese workman, in Coolidge's view, was still far from the free white laborer in America.

In a more direct attack on labor-union views, some writers accused trade unions of seeking control of California politics by using Chinese workers as scapegoats. In the *Overland Monthly*, Mrs. E. V. Robbins, a missionary advocate, upbraided Denis Kearney, a politician and leader of white workers in the 1870s, for his anti-Chinese demagoguery.[44] The *Overland Monthly* was a magazine for promoting California. Although Robbins was sympathetic to the fate of Chinese victims of violence, she nevertheless limited her definition of Chinese "fine fellows" to those educated in the Chinese classics but who needed to take up manual work in America. Moreover, she made no attempt to defend Chinese coolies, who did not fall under her category of fine fellows. Consequently, Robbins's article perpetuated the coolie stereotype, despite her disapproval of mob attacks on Chinese workers.

Ho Yow, the imperial consul-general for China in the United States, whose eloquent public addresses sought to persuade Americans to repeal the Chinese exclusion laws, mildly criticized the unions' fear mongering about Chinese workers.[45] Ho mentioned that among the labor unions "a vague notion" existed that, with the Chinese excluded, unionists faced less danger of interference from nonunion workers or scabs when they wielded the strike against their employers. Ho argued that this belief was an unfortunate misunderstanding; he assured Americans that Chinese workers could never occupy the position of American workers. However, Ho's defense of Chinese laborers reasserted their inferior position when he compared the two racial groups. Ho remarked, for instance, that the Chinese could not work as "dexterously as the Americans, or . . . turn out in a given time as much product."[46] Despite Ho's attempt to side with the Chinese immigrants, such disparaging descriptions of Chinese performance breathed life into the old derogatory image of the Chinese workingman.

Hubert Howe Bancroft, the premier historian of California in the early part of the century, displayed contempt for Chinese laborers even as he criticized the radicalism of the unions. In the *North American Review*, Bancroft discredited the notions put forth by the unions regarding the Chinese: that they would steal jobs from white workers, overrun the country, or forever accept low wages.[47] But like many other sympathetic writers, Bancroft assumed the inferiority of Chinese workers, informing readers that the Chinese took only the kinds of jobs that white men disdained. Especially in his conclusion, Bancroft recalled most of the unpleasant Chinese traits enumerated by other Sinophobes. He wrote that by instinct and tradition Chinese workers were exclusive, disliked change, and hated strangers. Bancroft's article fell into the same category as other essays sympathetic to the Chinese; these works mainly served the purpose of discrediting union radicalism or showing that Chinese workers were harmless. The essays, nevertheless, reproduced many of the outdated stereotypes used by union supporters.

Other articles echoed these opinions. Reverend Robert C. Bryant, from Rockford, Illinois, submitted an article to the *Arena* in which he complained about the unjust demands of American workers who tried to exclude Chinese laborers in exchange for special rights and opportunities for themselves.[48] Throughout the essay, Bryant claimed that the trade unions' calls for the permanent exclusion of Chinese labor contradicted the Christian principle of brotherhood, which advocated equal opportunity and rights for all. However, in response to the union charge that Chinese undercut the labor market,

Bryant admitted that the Chinese worked cheaply. He could not deny the unions' grievance that general wage levels would fall. Indeed, Bryant reiterated the image of the low-wage Chinese laborer.

Joaquin Miller also disapproved of the union's ruthless attacks on the Chinese labor force in California. A defender of Chinese immigration, Miller had been a miner for several years in California before pursuing law studies in Oregon. His past experience working side by side with Chinese miners offered him the opportunity to observe the immigrants firsthand. Miller contributed two essays to the *North American Review*, portraying union members in California as unproductive and unjust in their claims.[49] He remarked that real workingmen were silent men in the forests and fields who outnumbered the vocal city laborers as represented by the head of the AFL. Miller also pointed out that union members went on strike at a time when there was plenty of work at the best wage rates offered.

In his defense of the Chinese, however, Miller was less effective. While he could refute the claim that Chinese laborers were filthy because he had observed their daily bathing habits, Miller informed readers that the Chinese culture was unprogressive and detested change. Furthermore, he did not rate Chinese workers highly when he wrote that the "little yellow Cantonese" took up the heaviest, dirtiest work and it did "not hurt them to lean over and hold the head down all day."[50] Miller also repeated the cheap-labor image by writing that Chinese would work "at half or quarter the price."[51]

An essay published in the *Living Age* (a weekly eclectic periodical) warned readers that ever since Denis Kearney had organized the city's workingmen in an attack against Chinese immigrants, San Francisco had been emphatically a trade-union city.[52] But like other sympathetic writers, the contributor did not praise the Chinese laborers; he still thought of them as coolies keeping "all the essentials of slavery."[53] Furthermore, he shared the union supporters' opinion that the Chinese workers led a separate existence and left the country when they had hoarded enough money.

Articles criticizing union radicalism in California generally spoke more favorably of Chinese laborers than did other essays from the same period. The plight of the Chinese workers became an occasion for disclosing unstable conditions caused by union politics. However, little concerted effort went toward dispelling the stereotypes perpetuated by prolabor writers. Chinese workers remained a marginal presence in the labor economy and were still viewed through the lens of the nineteenth-century stereotype: submissive, inferior, parasitic, alien.

CONCLUSION

At first glance, the exclusionists and supporters of Chinese laborers seemed to be discussing the "Chinese problem" in periodicals published between 1900 and 1924. In fact, most participants in the debate manipulated the Chinese image to advance other arguments. These writers either interpreted Chinese virtues negatively to justify exclusion or confirmed derogatory images of Chinese while criticizing the tactics of the unions. In the end, contributors from both camps revived old arguments about Chinese workers, even though economic circumstances had changed. The fact that Chinese workers had been thoroughly excluded from the white labor market and confined to ghetto work or ethnic businesses was rarely mentioned in the periodical literature. Such irrelevant stereotyping showed that racial prejudice, not socioeconomic realities, sustained the unflattering descriptions. Consequently, American periodicals carried the misleading image of the Chinese coolie from the nineteenth century into the early twentieth century. Chinese labor was not the real subject, but instead was a proxy used by some writers to expose their displeasure with union aggressiveness or their dismay at the declining welfare of the American workforce. The persistence of the Chinese question in the popular press reflected the social anxieties spawned by a rapidly changing economy and had little to do with the actual role of Chinese workers in the labor market. This periodical research also supports other recent studies of Chinese American stereotypes in newspapers, fiction, and film by showing how journals and popular magazines, like other mass media, propagated derogatory images of Chinese in America.

NOTES

1. For instance, Jules Becker, "The Course of Exclusion, 1882–1924: San Francisco Coverage of the Chinese and Japanese in the United States" (Ph.D. dissertation, University of California, Berkeley, 1986); William F. Wu, *The Yellow Peril: Chinese Americans in American Fiction 1850–1940* (Hamden, Conn.: Archon Books, 1982); Gina Marchetti, *Romance and the "Yellow Peril": Race, Sex, and Discursive Strategies in Hollywood Fiction* (Berkeley: University of California Press, 1993).

2. Periodicals selected for this study were drawn from the *Readers' Guide to Periodical Literature*, 1900–1904, 1905–1909, 1910–1914, 1915–1918, 1919–1921, 1922–1924; *International Index to Periodicals*, 1907–1915, 1916–1919, 1920–1923; *Cumulative Magazine Subject Index*, 1907–1949; and *Poole Index to Periodical Literature*, 1897–1902, 1902–1907.

3. Frank Luther Mott, *A History of American Magazines, 1885–1905*, vol. 4 (Cambridge, Mass.: Belknap Press, 1957); Doris Marguerite Will Meadows, "Creed of

Caste: Journalism and the Race Question during the Progressive Era, 1900–1914"
(Ph.D. dissertation, New York University, 1984).

4. See David Valentine, chapter 2 in this volume.

5. Sucheng Chan, *This Bittersweet Soil: The Chinese in California Agriculture,*
1860–1910 (Berkeley: University of California Press, 1986), 38.

6. Ping Chiu, *Chinese Labor in California, 1850–1880: An Economic Study*
(Madison: State Historical Society of Wisconsin for the Department of History,
University of Wisconsin, 1963), xi.

7. June Mei, "Socioeconomic Development among the Chinese in San Francisco,
1848–1906," in *Labor Immigration under Capitalism: Asian Workers in the United*
States before World War II, ed. Lucie Cheng and Edna Bonacich (Berkeley: University
of California Press, 1984), 378.

8. See William Bowen, Linda Bentz and Robert Schwemmer, and Dolores K. Young,
see chapters 10, 8, and 9, respectively, in this volume.

9. Chan, *Bittersweet Soil,* 407.

10. Chiu, *Chinese Labor in California,* xii.

11. See Victor Jew and Elmer Rusco, chapters 4 and 5, respectively, in this volume.

12. *The New Encyclopaedia Britannica,* vol. 3 (Chicago: Encyclopaedia Britannica,
1997), 601. The term "coolie" derived from the Hindi word *kuli,* an aboriginal tribal
name, or from the Tamil *kuli,* meaning wages.

13. Kil Young Zo, "Credit Ticket System for the Chinese Emigration into the United
States," *Nanyang University Journal* 8–9 (1974/1975): 138.

14. U.S. Congress, Joint Special Committee to Investigate Chinese Immigration, *Report*
of the Joint Special Committee to Investigate Chinese Immigration, 44th Congress, 2d
session, 1877, S. Rept. 689; Thomas W. Chinn, ed., *A History of the Chinese in California:*
A Syllabus (San Francisco: Chinese Historical Society of America), 15; Persia C.
Campbell, *Chinese Coolie Emigration to Countries within the British Empire* (London:
King and Sons, 1923), 28–29; Zo, "Credit Ticket System," 129–39.

15. Walton Bean, *California* (New York: McGraw Hill, 1973), 130; Robert F. Heizer and
Alan J. Almquist, *The Other Californians: Prejudice and Discrimination under Spain,*
Mexico, and the United States to 1920 (Berkeley: University of California Press, 1971), 94.

16. Bean, *California,* 130.

17. Elmer Clarence Sandmeyer, *The Anti-Chinese Movement in California* (Urbana:
University of Illinois Press, 1939).

18. Paul Ong, "An Ethnic Trade: The Chinese Laundries in Early California," *Journal of Ethnic Studies* 8, no. 4 (1981): 97.

19. Alexander Saxton, *The Indispensable Enemy: Labor and the Anti-Chinese Movement in California* (Berkeley: University of California Press, 1971), chap. 1.

20. Gerald D. Nash, "The Influence of Labor on State Policy, 1860–1920: The Experience of California," *California Historical Society Quarterly* 42, no. 3 (1963): 241–57.

21. Donald Guimary and Jack Masson, "The Exploitation of Chinese Labor in the Alaskan Salmon Industry," *Chinese America: History and Perspectives* (1990): 101.

22. A. E. Yoell, "Oriental vs. American Labor," *Annals of the American Academy of Political and Social Science* 34 (September 1909): 247–56.

23. Yoell merely mentioned the sources of data at the end of the article, without exact documentation for each figure. He stated that his information came from the U.S. Bureau of Labor, correspondence of county officials of California, and files of the Asiatic Exclusion League of San Francisco.

24. Yoell, "Oriental," 249.

25. Julius Kahn, "The Japanese Question from a Californian's Standpoint," *Independent* 62 (3 January 1907): 27.

26. Kahn, "The Japanese Question," 29.

27. George C. Perkins, "Reasons for Continued Exclusion," *North American Review* 183 (July 1906): 20–21.

28. Perkins, "Reasons for Continued Exclusion," 21.

29. Truntun Beale, "Why the Chinese Should Be Excluded," *Forum* 33 (March 1902): 52–58.

30. James Phelan, "The Case against the Chinaman," *Saturday Evening Post* (24 December 1901): 4.

31. Phelan, "The Case against the Chinaman," 4.

32. "Chinese Immigration," *Outlook* 81 (30 December 1905): 1057.

33. "The Chinese Cannot Come," *Harper's Weekly* 46 (4 January 1902): 5.

34. John T. Bramhall, "The Oriental in California: A Problem of Immigration," *World Today* 20 (April 1911): 464–72.

35. Charles G. Hodass, "Our Chinese War: Will the War Draft on Our Labor Open the Door for John Chinaman?" *Sunset* 39 (July 1917): 34, 65–68.

36. Charles F. Holder, "The Dragon in America," *Arena* 32 (August 1904): 117.

37. Perkins, "Reasons for Continued Exclusion," 19.

38. James D. Phelan, "Why the Chinese Should Be Excluded," *North American Review* 173 (July 1901): 670.

39. Phelan, "Why the Chinese Should Be Excluded," 670, italics mine.

40. Helen M. Gougar, "Shall Educated Chinamen Be Welcome to Our Shore?" *Arena* 30 (November 1906): 507.

41. Boies Penrose, "Chinese Exclusion and the Problem of Immigration," *Independent* 54 (2 January 1902): 12–15.

42. Mary Roberts Coolidge, "Chinese Labor Competition on the Pacific Coast," *Annals of the American Academy of Political and Social Science* 34 (September 1909): 340–50.

43. See also David Valentine, chapter 2 in this volume.

44. E. V. Robbins, "Chinese Slave Girls: A Bit of History," *Overland Monthly* 51 (January 1908): 100–02.

45. Ho Yow, "Chinese Exclusion: A Benefit or a Harm?" *North American Review* 173 (September 1901): 318.

46. Yow, "Chinese Exclusion," 318.

47. Hubert Howe Bancroft, "Folly of Chinese Exclusion," *North American Review* 179 (August 1904): 263–68.

48. Robert C. Bryant, "The Problem of Immigration: Chinese Exclusion," *Arena* 27 (March 1902): 260–66.

49. Joaquin Miller, "The Chinese and the Exclusion Act," *North American Review* 173 (December 1901): 782–89; Miller, "The Ruinous Cost of Chinese Exclusion: A Laboring Man to Laboring Men," *North American Review* 186 (November 1907): 422–26.

50. Miller, "The Ruinous Cost of Chinese Exclusion," 423.

51. Miller, "The Ruinous Cost of Chinese Exclusion," 423.

52. Sydney Brooks, "Japan and the United States," *Living Age* 252 (9 February 1907): 323–32.

53. Brooks, "Japan and the United States," 325.

8

The Rise and Fall of the Chinese Fisheries in California

Linda Bentz and Robert Schwemmer

In 1850, when California became a state, it was a land of abundance and opportunity. It was endowed with natural resources such as gold, rich soil, timber, and extremely plentiful fisheries. The news of California's wealth spread internationally and Chinese settlers began to establish fishing camps along the Pacific coast as early as 1853. These pioneers of the commercial fishing industry built Chinese junks to pursue marine resources, establishing a fascinating maritime presence in the West. Fishing activities expanded and by the 1870s fishing villages were found from the California and Oregon border to the southern reaches of Baja California, as well as inland along the Sacramento River Delta. In the nineteenth century, at the height of the commercial fishing industry, Chinese made up one-third of the fishery workers in California.[1]

During the early 1870s, state and federal fishery agencies began to understand that the Pacific coast fisheries needed to be quantified and regulated to avoid overfishing and depletion. They wanted to avoid the fate of the east coast fisheries, which suffered from pollution and overuse. Chinese fishermen were accused of depleting the fisheries along the Pacific coast. Their fishing methods, their vessels, and their lifestyle came under intense scrutiny and ultimately laws were passed to limit fishing operations. This chapter will explore the operations and cultural aspects of the Chinese commercial fishing industry and state and federal restrictions that caused the decline of Chinese fishing activities in nineteenth-century California.

CHINESE FISHING ACTIVITIES IN CALIFORNIA

When Chinese settlers arrived on the Pacific coast in the mid-1850s, they found the California fisheries overflowing with types of marine life that were considered delicacies in China. Shrimp, abalone, shark, and red fish were just a few of the many types of marine resources that were available for harvesting. The earliest recorded Chinese fishing camp was established in 1853 in Monterey.[2] When the fisheries expanded by the 1870s the primary fishing centers included San Francisco (where the shrimp fisheries were located), Monterey (which offered squid, market fisheries, and abalone that was gathered until the mid-1860s), and San Diego (primarily abalone and market fisheries). Smaller fishing villages or camps were scattered along the California coast in areas such as Santa Barbara and the Channel Islands. The marine resources from these centers were sold fresh locally and shipped to Chinese communities all along the west. However, through established markets and marketing networks, the bulk of the resources were dried and exported to China. In many cases, Chinese merchants in Chinatowns handled these transactions.

When Chinese fishermen arrived in California and saw the variety and abundance of fish available they must have realized that they could make a fortune by fishing, processing, and exporting marine products. Many of the fishermen came from fishing regions in China and had the skills to obtain many species of fish and sea creatures that ranged from whales to snapping turtles to abalone. Fishermen used traditional watercraft for transport to the fisheries and for housing while fishing in remote locations. The Chinese fishermen also knew how to process and export these goods to a ready market in China. Through their proficiency, their tenacity, and their use of traditional methods, Chinese fishermen initiated the commercial fishing industry in California.

Yet fishing was a dangerous job and fishermen met with disaster—both physical and financial. The maritime environments along the California coast are unstable at best. Factors such as fog (which reduced visibility), uncharted hazards, prevailing currents, and changing weather patterns all contributed to treacherous conditions. These factors were complicated by the fact that Chinese junks in the nineteenth century were equipped with crude navigational gear. There was no radar to guide vessels through extreme conditions. Chinese fishermen were at the mercy of their skills and the performance of their watercraft. A local Santa Barbara newspaper article spoke of the challenges faced by Chinese fishermen: "Their avocation is full of thrilling adventures, and the hardships that they are compelled to endure, the outside world knows little of."[3]

Financially, fishermen were at risk as well. Fishing equipment was expensive; for example, in 1892 a Chinese junk, the *Acme*, sold for $250.[4] This is a substantial amount of money considering that a man's three-piece suit cost about $8 and a Chinese cook earned $40 per month.[5] Fishing nets and guns could be lost overboard or in a wreck, thereby reducing profits.

Newspaper and journal accounts of the period described Chinese fishermen and the disasters they endured. A Chinese vessel wrecked on Santa Rosa Island in the 1870s. A lone Chinese survivor was found starving on a remote beach by the owner of the island. The survivor went to work at the owner's ranch and was employed there for many years.[6] In 1884 another junk wrecked while fishing, as recounted in a Santa Barbara newspaper: "It has not been quite a year ago that a junk in the vicinity of Anacapa Island was allowed to run a reef and sunk, the party being rescued by the sloop-Ocean King. The business is rapidly growing and is destined at no distant day to be one of some magnitude."[7]

The ship was at thirty-five tons register and was built for fishing, hunting, and gathering abalone and shells in and around the Channel Islands. The vessel was anchored near the island when a gale sprang up and the ship drifted upon a reef and struck a rock. The ship was a total loss. Fortunately, another ship saved the crew of the junk, which consisted of eight men from Santa Barbara.[8] Another incident that occurred on a Chinese junk was recounted in a newspaper in Santa Barbara: "one of the hunters on the Chinese Junk had the misfortune to shoot himself. The ball entering the arm at the elbow and coming out at the shoulder."[9]

A tragic event occurred in March 1900 on San Nicolas Island off the coast of southern California. Three Chinese fishermen were dropped off on the island to harvest abalone with supplies to sustain them for a few months. While the fishermen were away from their camp, some sailors who were catching crawfish near the island raided the Chinese camp and stole their supply of rice and fifteen hundred pounds of abalone meat. The Chinese fishermen were left helpless and without provisions. Their employer in Santa Barbara attempted to hire a schooner to retrieve the men and the remaining abalone, but was unable to find a vessel. During the fishermen's prolonged stay on San Nicolas, one of the men died. The remaining two men were ultimately rescued from the island just as they were becoming alarmingly weak.[10]

Why would the fishermen risk so much? Several factors must be considered. Chinese settlers had few economic options and limited fields of employment, and fishing could be extremely lucrative. Yes, the hazards could be economically costly, but the risks had to be weighed against the potential for profits. Chinese fishermen must have known that conditions were right for success, with an abundance of fish, skilled fishermen, and established trade networks to China. It appears that the risk was worth taking.

CULTURAL TRADITIONS OF CHINESE FISHERMEN IN CALIFORNIA

The fishermen who came to California from China displayed great skills and rarely deviated from cultural practices. Several cultural practices can be seen in Chinese fishing operations, such as the organization of fishing companies, use of gear exported from China, and the use of vessels designed after watercraft used in China for centuries.

Fishing companies were organized in keeping with tradition. Fishermen structured their activities under at least three organizational patterns: first, the owner-operator; second, the owner-lessor and lessee-operator; and third, the owner-employer. These patterns were probably all partnerships. Ownership was based on who held the assets of the company, such as camp structures, vessels and gear, and processing equipment. Since the land was usually leased, the camp property was not considered an asset.

The owner-operator pattern was perhaps the most common pattern in the early shrimp fishery. In this type of organization the number of men required to perform the job formed a partnership. They found a fishing area, built a camp and vessels, obtained gear, and began their fishing and processing activities. As Peter Schultz describes this arrangement: "Each boat was apparently run by an independent partnership, which included a man on shore to prepare the boiling vat for the crew's return. Each group had its own pier, its own nets and processing equipment, and its own drying fields, storage sheds and living quarters."[11]

The structure of this partnership could vary based on capital equipment. One partner might own the vessel, while other partners could own the capital materials. Profits were split by giving the owner of the vessel a share, then expenses would be deducted. The remainder would be split equally among the rest of the partners.

Partnerships were terminated near the time of the Chinese Harvest Festival. During this season, income from the previous year would be distributed and all debts paid. At this time fishermen were free to join other companies, or remain in their current partnership for another year. This time of year coincides with the end of the peak shrimp-fishing season during the months of June, July, and August, when assets were the highest.[12] This time of year held particular symbolism and significance. In China, farmers and people not involved in fishing considered this autumn celebration to be the Moon Festival. It is the time to give thanks for all that is bountiful. For fishermen, the moon also holds great importance because it governs the waters and the tides.

A second type of organizational pattern was found in Santa Barbara and San Diego. This was known as the owner-lessor and lessee-operator pattern.

This form was common in the later years of Chinese fishing activities. In this scenario, the owners were usually Chinese merchants with businesses in Chinatown. They leased the camps, vessels, and gear to operators. These were fishermen who formed a partnership.

When the operators had a junk load of fish, they returned to the merchant and sold their catch at a fixed price. The members of the partnership divided the money between themselves based on shares. An example of this process occurred in Santa Barbara: "Sing Chung, a prosperous merchant here . . . had a number of men and boats fishing and gathering abalone shells and 'sea mosses' from San Diego to our islands."[13]

In the final organizational pattern, the owner-employer model, the owner of a vessel would find the Chinese crews and pay wages.[14] Rogers and Brothers of Santa Barbara displayed this type of pattern:

> Parties of Chinese fishermen were on the various Channel Islands most of the year. Messers. Rogers and Bros. of this city sent out today for San Miguel, a party of five men for abalone, seal skins and oil. The number of abalone to be obtained by such a party is impossible to estimate. Low tide being the only time when they can be gathered and the lower the tide, the more are exposed to view.[15]

The gear used by Chinese fishermen was extremely efficient. Several types of apparatus were used, including bag nets, troll lines, pry bars, and traps. The bag net was brought from China and used in the shrimp fisheries in the San Francisco Bay area. Robert A. Nash described the nets used in the shrimp fisheries:

> These nets . . .from China, were made of a very strong grass fiber with a mesh of $3\frac{1}{2}$ at the mouth gradually diminishing to $\frac{1}{2}$ inch or less at the narrow end. . . . The nets were set in rows utilizing stakes common to two nets between nets. In this way broad areas were covered so that any swimming animals that moved with the tidal currents were likely to be taken.[16]

Contemporary observers found this use of the bag net to be interesting, especially the "very peculiar and amusing" practice of shouting and pounding the side of the vessel and throwing a pole into the water at such an angle that it would return to the fisherman's hands. These methods would frighten the fish into the bag net.[17]

The Chinese adherence to traditional practices is best displayed by fishermen's use of traditional watercraft. Junks in China have traditionally been used for many purposes, such as fishing, transportation of cargo, and ferrying. G. R. G. Worcester, in his classic work, *The Junks and Sampans of the Yangtze*, claims that sea-going junks from North China were among the oldest known ships and date back perhaps thousands of years.[18]

Chinese shipwrights built and used traditional watercraft at several locations along the Pacific Coast. Junks built in California during the nineteenth century possessed construction characteristics unique to Chinese watercraft. Contrary to Euro-American–built vessels, where interior frames dictate the shape of the outer hull, the junk's outer planking was bent to create the shape and fastened to bulkheads. The outer hull of a junk was flush and built with two-inch, rough-cut California redwood planking. The carvel design or flush planking was not unique in itself, but the Chinese method of fastening the planking to the bulkheads was new. The planks were edge-fastened with black iron-cut nails, whereas Euro-American fasteners were driven through the outer surface of the planks. Chinese shipwrights then applied a material called chunam to the planking and other seams to make them watertight. Chunam (chu'nam) is a mixture of lime paste mixed with oil and other organic fibers such as grass, animal hair, or bamboo. Most California junks' exteriors were then treated with t'ung oil, rather than by applying paint (see figure 8.1).

Junks were steered with a rudder located in the stern, or rear, of the vessel. The rudder, when lowered, extended below the vessel's bottom and could be raised completely out of the water to prevent damage in shallow water or when anchored. The solid bulkheads served as interior walls dividing the vessel into at least three compartments, providing areas for living quarters and space devoted to storing the fish cargoes. Toward the front of the junk and located on deck was a typical Chinese windlass used to raise the anchor.

The use of native redwood represents the most obvious departure from traditional junk-building techniques. This change in materials may have caused changes in vessel design. For example, redwood was used in practically all features of the junks, including frame, keel, planks, floor, and bulkheads. In China at least three different types of wood could be used in junk construction.[19] Redwood was a good choice of wood for California junks because it was amply available in California during the nineteenth and early twentieth centuries. Some of the advantages of this wood material were that it could be easily obtained in wide and long dimensions, it was cost efficient, and it was resistant to rot.

In addition to revealing the use of redwood as a construction material, research suggests that junks were not built from plans; rather, they were built

FIGURE 8.1
Single-masted junk, the *Quock See Wo*, which worked in shrimp fisheries in the San Francisco Bay area

from traditional Chinese methods and under the specifications of the owners. The experience of the builder dictated the size and general arrangement of the vessel.

It appears that junks were designed according to their intended use, distance to the fishery, and target catch. These aspects also dictated the number of vessels working in each fishery. Robert A. Nash, author of "The Chinese Shrimp Fishery in California," estimated that there were approximately eighty-nine vessels (junks and sampans) working the shrimp fisheries at the peak of operations, around 1885. He calculated the average life span of a Chinese junk in the San Francisco area at 12.7 years.[20] Before 1885, Norman B. Scofield of California Fish and Game has stated that there were more than fifty vessels in the shrimp fisheries.

The junks of San Francisco were shrimpers and the distance to the fishing grounds was short, so only one sail was required. Although this was the typical design after about the 1890s, the shrimp fisheries utilized sampans during the early days of the shrimp fisheries. The sampan was a smaller craft than the junk, constructed without decks, and was propelled by sail, oar, or poles. The average length of a sampan was twenty-one feet and the capacity rarely exceeded ten net tons. Two-masted junks were also used for carrying cargo to the market in San Francisco.

The junks of San Diego and Santa Barbara traveled longer distances and required multiple masts. Junks found in these areas were larger because they were required to travel great distances into Baja California and to the Channel Islands, respectively, to obtain abalone. Chinese fishermen would travel in ocean-going junks from San Diego as far south as Bahia de Tortugas, a passage of approximately four hundred miles.

Their reliance on traditional skills can be attributed to several factors. Shipwrights in China had successfully built fishing craft in the Chinese tradition for centuries. The Chinese junk design, with the shallow draft and open work space, was well suited for the shrimp fisheries and for the transportation of marine resources. Finally, many of the fishing villages were isolated and, overall, Chinese settlers kept to themselves, so an open exchange of ideas was extremely limited.

DECLINE OF THE FISHERIES
Through their traditional methods and clannishness, Chinese fishermen in California thrived. Yet during the 1880s, as their success grew, the host communities began to believe that Chinese fishermen prospered at the expense of

all others. Chinese fishermen were accused of depleting the California fisheries. All along the coast, fishermen and their junks were closely scrutinized while legislation was passed to control and limit Chinese fishing activities. Further opposition came as Chinese settlers along the southern coast of California were suspected of using their junks to smuggle immigrants and opium from Baja and the Channel Islands. Chinese fishermen suffered at the hands of state and federal agencies.

The motivation to restrict and eliminate Chinese fishermen from the Pacific Coast fisheries germinated in the anti-Chinese sentiment that gripped the nation during the late nineteenth century. Contributing factors to this movement included the general depression that was prevailing in the east and had reached the West Coast; California was suffering from a decline of mining returns and, nationally, stocks were crashing. In 1873 San Francisco was feeling the effects of a severe economic depression. Small local industries that had enjoyed a temporary boom during the Civil War were decimated at the war's end, when products from the East flooded the West Coast. The completion of the transcontinental railroad (1869) added to the downturn in the economy because it made possible the transportation of even more goods. To many people, it appeared that only the Chinese fishermen were prospering during this difficult time. Hostilities toward the Chinese reached a fever pitch.

The restriction upon Chinese fishing began with investigation and regulation. The first restriction placed upon Chinese fishermen occurred in 1860, when a license fee of $4 was levied and enforced among Chinese fishermen. The license fee was repealed in 1864. During the 1870s Chinese fishermen began to be attacked from several fronts. The U.S. Commission of Fish and Fisheries began to investigate the Chinese fisheries. The commission had originally been established as part of the Smithsonian Institution and, although the federal government recognized that the regulation of the fisheries should be left up to the states, the Fish Commission's mandate was to gather information and study the cause and decline of coastal fisheries in the United States. In 1879 and 1880 David Starr Jordan surveyed the Pacific Coast fisheries in conjunction with the tenth census. The conclusion of the survey was that the quantity of fish was being "constantly and rapidly diminished by Chinamen with their fine-meshed nets."[21]

There is no primary source material extant that explains why the Chinese fishermen used these fine-mesh nets. Scholars have proposed that Chinese fishermen used the nets in China in the shrimp fisheries, so it was natural that fishermen continued their use in California.[22] These men kept to traditional practices, partly because many fishing villages were isolated. Overall, Chinese settlers kept to themselves, so an open exchange of ideas with Euro-Americans was extremely limited.[23]

The visit by the Fish Commission to San Diego added to the problems that the Chinese fishermen were experiencing. By 1879 the Chinese had been harvesting abalone along the rocky shores of San Diego, the coastal islands, and Baja, California, for about fifteen years. Abalone was becoming harder to find, so Chinese fishermen ventured into Mexican waters in search of abalone. The Mexican government became concerned about the depletion of their fisheries and in 1879 they required a $60 annual license fee on each Chinese junk. If fishermen avoided the fee, they faced imprisonment and their junks and cargo could be seized.[24]

Junks in San Diego were limited by their foreign status. They were considered alien vessels, therefore they were not registered in the United States, and traveled under a permit from the U.S. customs house. The reporting process in San Diego was as follows:

They carry no papers except an alien certificate, which insures to the crew permission to land upon their return to the city. In addition to the Chinese names, the junks are numbered by the customs officers, and are known to them by their numbers only. The junks return as seldom as possible, but if they have occasion to visit San Diego, with or without cargo, they report at once to the customhouse and pay tonnage tax of 83 cents per ton; $1.50 for entering, 67 cents for survey, and 20 cents for a certificate. It is currently reported that, to avoid payment of these customs dues, the junks often transfer their cargoes of abalone shells, meats, etc., to small boats that come out to sea, off San Diego, for this purpose, and to bring supplies.[25]

In addition to the fishermen's other troubles, the U.S. government took action against the Chinese. The passage of the Scott Act in 1888 and the Geary Act of 1892 denied the entry of Chinese laborers into the country and created increased risk to Chinese fishermen who traveled into Mexican waters and returned to San Diego. Fear of deportation or the desire to move operations to Baja caused some Chinese merchants to sell their vessels to Euro-Americans in 1892. Chinese fishing activities in and around San Diego experienced a severe decline.

Fishermen in northern California faced similar discrimination. N. B. Scofield, who was a protégé of David Starr Jordan, joined the California State

Board of Fish Commissioners. This commission was established in 1870 to "provide for the restoration and preservation of fish in the waters of this State."[26] Scofield wrote several reports that accused Chinese shrimp fishermen of catching large numbers of smelt in their nets. Smelt was the principal food of young salmon descending the Sacramento River. Due to these reports, in 1898 the Board of Fish Commissioners recommended to the California state legislature that shrimp fishing be prohibited between the months of May and October. These months coincided with prime shrimp fishing season.

The Chinese challenged the constitutionality of the law and the legislature repealed the closed season in 1905. Yet much damage had been done to the Chinese fishermen. Due to the Exclusion Act and state laws restricting the taking of shrimp during certain months, the number of vessels began to decline. While reviewing the effects of the closed season, the Board of Fish Commissioners stated that there were fifty vessels engaged in the shrimp fishery in 1885 and only twenty-eight to thirty-two remaining in 1904. In another attempt to end the Chinese fishing industry, the legislature enacted a much more damaging law by prohibiting the exportation of dried shrimp and shells from the state. This action sealed the fate of the Chinese shrimp industry in California.[27] Sadly, this and the various other restrictions placed on its activities contributed to the decline of the Chinese fishing industry in California.

Laws and regulations placed upon Chinese fishermen were harsh and based in the racism of the time. Most members of the U.S. Commission of Fish and Fisheries and the State Board of Fish Commissioners were not scientists. They did not have the expertise to understand biological processes that affected the fisheries, such as climatic changes, pollution, and shifts in predator/prey populations. Climatic changes can drastically affect the types and amount of fish in a given region. For example, fish populations have been altered during El Niño events. El Niños are an extreme weather condition caused by a temporary change in the water temperature of the Pacific Ocean around the equator. They occur irregularly about every three to seven years. El Niño has caused droughts in Africa, Australia, and Brazil and flooding in California and South America. Moreover, tropical species of fish (unexpectedly) became available on the west coast of the United States.[28]

DISCUSSION

Chinese fishermen in California commanded the sea and the waterways for more than forty years and pioneered the commercial fishing industry. Their accomplishments can be attributed to many factors, such as a ready market in

China, skilled labor, entrepreneurial merchants, and interactions with various Euro-American community members.

The market in China consisted of millions of people who depended upon fish as their major source of animal protein. It is no wonder that fish take on great importance in a country where the coastline is immense and waterways and lakes are abundant. It appears that the abundant fisheries in California were perfectly suited for the Chinese table. Chinese fishermen in California harvested practically any marine resource that could be obtained in an efficient manner. A large variety of fish and marine resources were exported to China, including abalone, squid, barracuda, mullet, sheepshead, squid, rock fish, halibut, flounder, anchovies, cod, skates, salmon, sturgeon, sea slugs, sea turtles, sea urchins, algae, seaweed, whale bones (ground into fertilizer), genitals of male sea lions, and shark fin, which was considered a delicacy.

An indication of the amount of marine resources that were exported can be found in customs documents. Although the amount of fish caught in California waters varies from year to year, the yield from 1888 is a good example of the yields of the California fisheries. That year the fisheries off Monterey exported $13,620 of squid, $78,576 of abalone meat and shells, and $78,576 of shrimp and prawns.[29] In 1892, shrimp alone was exported to eight points of entry in China: Ichang, Kinkiang, Ningpo, Foochow, Tamsui, Tainan, Swatow, and Chungking.[30]

For over a century Chinese settlers have been described as unskilled workers who received little compensation for their hard labor. However, the knowledge and expertise of the fishermen resulted in a lucrative livelihood. Current research suggests that Chinese settlers arrived in the United States with knowledge of the fishing profession and shipbuilding. They had the intention to make their livelihood on the sea.

Scholars of Asian American studies have debated this issue for years and proposed that fishermen were out-of-work railroad or mine workers. However, Sandy Lydon, author of *Chinese Gold: The Chinese in the Monterey Bay Region*, suggests that the Chinese fishermen who worked the waters off of California obtained their skills in China. Through his extensive work with the Chinese of Monterey, he learned that men who decided to migrate to the United States were trained in a skill. For example, if they came from a fishing region, they were trained to fish.[31]

Further evidence of Chinese fishermen arriving in California as skilled laborers can be found in census records. The census reveals that the residents of Point San Pedro, a shrimp fishing village on San Pablo Bay in northern California, emigrated from the areas of Guangdong Province where shrimp fishing was a common livelihood.[32] The ability to process marine resources also required expertise: "with their vast experience drying fish in China, the fishermen knew which fish could be dried without cleaning, which could be dried by hanging rather than spreading on racks, and how long to leave them in the open air before bundling them for shipment."[33] Chinese junks built along the Pacific Coast were products of skilled craftsmen as well. Little is known about Chinese shipwrights, and questions remain, such as how was the skill of the master carpenter passed down, and did the shipbuilders remain at one location or travel to different communities to build ships? Perhaps the answers to these questions will be uncovered as more information becomes available.

Current research suggests that Chinese entrepreneurs were involved in the Pacific Coast fisheries. Many entrepreneurs engaged in the fishing industry were merchants. Merchants were among the earliest Chinese immigrants to the United States and enjoyed an elevated status within Chinese communities. For instance, Sing Chung, a local merchant in Santa Barbara, owned six junks by 1885 and had crews working the Channel Islands as well as other fisheries in Southern California. Sing Chung was well respected among members of the host community. Several articles ran in Santa Barbara newspapers describing the activities and wealth of the Sing Chung Company and a local notable, District Attorney C. A. Storke, spoke favorably of Sing Chung in 1898:

> I have known him for fifteen and more years. He is a prominent Chinese merchant in the city of Santa Barbara, and has been largely interested in speculation in Santa Barbara, he has rented lands, farmed large areas through his agents and has conducted business in a wholesale manner. He is considered good for all that he contracts. He is considered one of the most reliable Chinese residents in the city of Santa Barbara.[34]

Verification of Storke's statement can be found in land lease records. In 1889 Sing Chung and two partners leased land for the purpose of brick making.[35] In 1890 Sing Chung leased land from Kate M. Bell at the Dos Pueblos Ranch in the Goleta Valley. One of his neighbors was Alex More, the owner of Santa Rosa Island.[36] This information is curious, because Sing Chung's junks were known to frequent Santa Rosa Island. No record has been found of Sing Chung after 1898.

Fortunes were to be made in San Diego as well. Another successful businessman was Quong Sow Kee, a merchant in San Diego's Chinese community. His death notice, posted in the *San Diego Union* on September 1, 1887, stated that he was one of the "wealthiest Chinese merchants with an estate worth over one-half million dollars." He owned the *Sun Yun Lee,* a three-masted vessel measuring fifty two feet in length with a net tonnage of 13.88. Another San Diego local notable, Ah Quin, the legendary mayor of Chinatown, was reported to have been involved in the abalone trade as well.

Chinese settlers in California have been portrayed as clannish men who lived in bachelor societies and rarely communicated with the host communities. However, there is evidence that Chinese fishermen interacted with Euro-Americans in San Francisco and in San Diego. In San Francisco, a local landowner named Richard Bullis assisted Chinese fishermen in the shrimp fishery:

> Anti-Chinese discrimination was rampant in the 1870s and the Chinese fishermen used Bullis as their contact and "front" with the San Francisco market. Californians did not approve of Chinese skippers of vessels of any size so it was Bullis who took the shrimp to 'Frisco and it was he who brought back from Redwood City the 900 cords of wood China camp used each season. . . .[37]

Additional evidence of interactions with Euro-Americans can be found in San Diego's Chinese community. Chinese settlers have long been accused of buying goods exclusively from Chinese merchants. In San Diego, Chinese fishermen traded rice and supplies with local Euro-Americans and also purchased lumber for their vessels and houses from Euro-American merchants. Moreover, negotiations were made with Pacific Mail Steamship agents to transport fishery products to Chinese distributors in San Francisco.

CONCLUSIONS

During the nineteenth century, Chinese fishermen could board their junks and sail the open seas when marine resources were at their most abundant. They could sail away from the mainland, where hostility and intolerance was the order of the day. During the early days of the Chinese fishing industry, Chinese fishermen were able to pursue marine resources unchallenged. The fish, shrimp, and abalone were there for the taking. Sadly, all this changed when an ungrateful state passed restrictive laws that pushed the Chinese from the fisheries. Chinese junks vanished from the ports and oceans of the Pacific Coast and all that is left are sparse collections of photographs and recorded accounts. Revelations of the contributions made by Chinese fishermen are just beginning to unfold and further research is required to provide a more complete picture of the fishing industry. With every new document, photograph, and oral history, these brave Chinese pioneers' important legacy will be recovered.

NOTES

1. Arthur F. McEvoy, *The Fisherman's Problem* (Cambridge: Cambridge University Press, 1986), 76.

2. Sandy Lydon, *Chinese Gold: The Chinese in the Monterey Bay Region* (Capitola, Calif.: Capitola Book Company, 1985), 32.

3. *Daily Independent* (Santa Barbara), 22 June 1885.

4. Bill of Sale from Wo Sing, Medical Practitioner of the City of San Diego, to Mrs. Mary Augusta Chase for a price of $250. From unsorted documents of the San Diego Port Registry (National Archives, Washington, D.C.).

5. Margaret Jennings, "The Chinese in Ventura County," *Ventura County Historical Society Quarterly* 29, no. 3 (1984), 6; and Immigration File of Gin Gain number 1002, National Archives and Records Administration-Pacific Region, San Bruno, California, Chinese Exclusion Acts Case Files, 1894–1965, Record Group 85.

6. K (the author signed her name as simply "K"; scholars believe the author to be Martinette Kinsell), "Shearing Time on Santa Rosa Island," *Overland Monthly* 21, series 2 (May 1893): 495.

7. *Daily Independent* (Santa Barbara), 5 June 1885.

8. *Daily Independent* (Santa Barbara), 31 July 1884.

9. *Daily Independent* (Santa Barbara), 25 June 1885.

10. *Morning Press* (Santa Barbara), 27 March 1900.

11. Peter D. Schultz, "Excavation of a Brickwork Feature at a Nineteenth-Century Chinese Shrimp Camp on San Francisco Bay," *Northwest Anthropological Research Notes* 22, no. 1 (1988): 121.

12. Jennie Quok Lim, interview, 23 August 1970; Robert A. Nash, "The Chinese Shrimp Fishery in California" (Ph.D. dissertation, Geography Department, University of California, Los Angeles, 1973), 162.

13. "Olden Days," *Santa Barbara News Press,* 30 November 1975.

14. Nash, "The Chinese Shrimp Fishery," 58.

15. *Daily Independent* (Santa Barbara), 27 October 1883.

16. Nash, "The Chinese Shrimp Fishery," 239.

17. Robert F. Walsh, "Chinese and the Fisheries," *The Californian,* 4, no. 6 (1893): 835–36.

18. G. R. G. Worcester, *The Junks and Sampans of the Yangtze* (Annapolis, Md.: Naval Institute Press, 1971), 7.

19. John C. Muir, "One Old Junk Is Everyone's Treasure: The Excavation, Analysis, and Interpretation of a Chinese Shrimp Junk at China Camp State Park" (master's thesis, California State University, Sonoma, 1999), 135.

20. Nash, "The Chinese Shrimp Fishery," 257; Norman B. Scofield, "Shrimp Fisheries of California," *California Fish and Game* 5 (1919): 9.

21. *San Diego Union*, 14 January 1880. For more information regarding the U.S. Fish and Fisheries Commission and their position with regard to Chinese fishermen, see McEvoy, *The Fisherman's Problem*, 93–119.

22. Personal communication with Patrick Smith, January 9, 2001.

23. Muir, "One Old Junk Is Everyone's Treasure," 132.

24. *Salinas Weekly Index*, 30 October 1884.

25. J. W. Collins, "The Fishing Vessels and Boats of the Pacific Coast," U.S. Fish Commission, *Bulletin of the United States Fish Commission* 10 (1890): 32.

26. McEvoy, *The Fisherman's Problem*, 101.

27. Nash, "The Chinese Shrimp Fishery," 135–36.

28. U.S. Department of Commerce National Oceanic and Atmospheric Administration website: www.elnino.noaa.gov.

29. Phillip L. Weaver, "Salt Water Fisheries of the Pacific Coast," *Overland Monthly* 20, second series (1892): 162.

30. Walsh, "Chinese and the Fisheries," 837.

31. E-mail communication with Sandy Lydon, April 15, 1998.

32. Nash, "The Chinese Shrimp Fishery," 186.

33. Lydon, *Chinese Gold*, 36.

34. Immigration file of Ye Yin Li, 1898, Chinese Exclusion Acts Case Files, Record Group 85, National Archives Federal Records Center, Laguna Niguel, California.

35. Santa Barbara County Book of Land Leases, Book C, 242.

36. Santa Barbara County Book of Land Leases, Book C, 541.

37. Richard Dillon, "China Camp," in *Cathay in Eldorado: The Chinese in California* (San Francisco: Book of the Month Club, 1972).

9

The Seaweed Gatherers on the Central Coast of California

Dolores K. Young

On July 15, 1876, an ad appeared in the local paper in the city of San Luis Obispo that began: "Opposition to Chinese. Patronize White Industry. . . ."[1] In an effort to assist a Euro-American woman, a Mrs. Sutherland, to establish a laundry shop and win over customers from existing Chinese laundries, the paper's editor wrote the following note in the same issue: "We hope all American people who believe in the encouragement of white enterprise in opposition to coolie labor will see to it that Mrs. Sutherland receives a patronage that will make permanent in our midst this long needed enterprise."[2] The laundry ad, together with the editor's note, demonstrated the widespread anti-Chinese movement espoused by the various labor unions of the day, who either believed erroneously that Chinese labor was the cause of unemployment or simply chose to use the Chinese as a scapegoat for workers' grievances. Eventually, the anti-Chinese strategy was also adopted by the political parties, particularly the Workingmen's Party, formed in 1877, whose popular rallying cry was, the "Chinese Must Go"[3]

North of San Luis Obispo, in Monterey County, due to severe labor shortages in the 1870s, Chinese workers were hired to build the Southern Pacific Railroad, yet they were exploited. With low pay and long hours, they were given the most dangerous assignments, which were rejected by white workers. Many were killed by tunnel fires and explosions and quite a few were maimed.[4] Along the coast in Monterey County in the 1880s, Chinese fishermen faced incoming, hostile Italian and Portuguese fishermen, who invaded their fishing ground attempting to drive them out. To avoid confrontation, the beleaguered Chinese fishermen took to night fishing, and restricted their catch to a kind of fish unwanted by the hostile fishermen. So the Chinese fished in lantern-lit boats at night, while the Euro-American fishermen slept.[5]

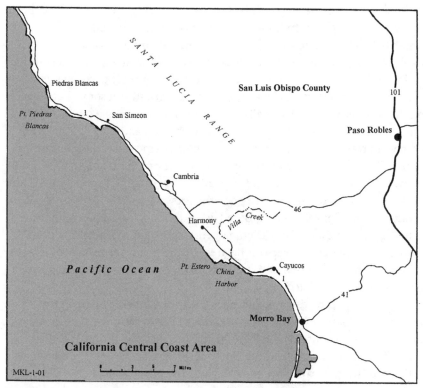

FIGURE 9.1
Map showing location of seaweed industry, Central Coast of California, 1870–1970
(Copyright © Murray K. Lee. Reprinted with permission.)

It was believed that some of the dislocated fishermen who sought a means of livelihood in the midst of anti-Chinese mania drifted south and crossed the Monterey-San Luis Obispo county line. They arrived at the towns of San Simeon, Cambria, and Cayucos on the coast of San Luis Obispo County, sometimes known as the Central Coast of California (figure 9.1). There, on the rocks of the Pacific Ocean, they discovered *Ulva*, a particular kind of seaweed that grew only in this region of California. Thus began the tiny seaweed industry in the Central Coast, which lasted from about 1870 to 1970.

To this small group of immigrants, credit must be given for originating *Ulva* cultivation in California. *Ulva* gathering was unheard of hitherto. Neither the American Indians, nor the European settlers, nor the Yankee explorers from the eastern states had ever grown the crop. It is conjectured that the

Chinese growers associated the plant with a seaweed in their native land. From knowledge brought from home or from sheer ingenuity and by trial and error, they had learned to turn a hitherto useless weed into a valuable and profitable product that they were able to sell to a domestic market in San Francisco and a foreign market in China. By doing so, they were able to survive and even prosper in difficult times. Unlike their compatriots, the toilsome wage earners on the Southern Pacific Railroad, they escaped the inhumane treatment by the railroad bosses because they were their own bosses, and they enjoyed a life of peace and tranquility. And unlike the night fishermen in the north, competition with Euro-Americans was out of the question: the art of seaweed growing was unknown to others, and they alone possessed the special knowledge of marketing the product. Since both the growers and the consumers of the product were Chinese, they aroused little jealousy or hostility in the surrounding community. They even gained respect and friendship among the early Euro-American settlers in the area. In the turbulent history of Chinese immigration, this enclave of *Ulva* growers on the Central Coast appeared to be an oasis of racial harmony.

This chapter provides a preliminary study of Chinese seaweed growers on the Central Coast of California from about 1870 to 1970. Given the shortage of information about this small group and their unique profession, this study was primarily based on personal interviews with many local residents who claimed to have first-person knowledge of the growers or their children. By and large, the informants were enthusiastic in providing lively descriptions and useful information about two topics: (1) the operation of seaweed gathering as a business and (2) the lifestyle of the seaweed gatherers.

THE SEAWEED BUSINESS

In the late 1860s, the Chinese immigrants came to the north coast of San Luis Obispo County, sometimes referred to as the Central Coast of California. They came quietly and unobtrusively, perhaps uncertain of their fate in a new land. Here were rich ranch land and farmland settled by newcomers from the eastern states and European immigrants, primarily Swiss Italians and later-arriving English and Germans. Ranch land reached all the way to the ocean. The Chinese immigrants needed a place on the water's edge. In the early days, when land laws were vague, a few settlers had come to California to own land as squatters. So the ranch owners leased a plot of land to the Chinese immigrants for a rent of one dollar a year, a mere token fee to ensure that the squatter's right would not be exercised. The Chinese could not be happier, as all they wanted was a place to work without harassment. From the start, it was a happy arrangement and the interracial relationship was a cordial one.

The heartened immigrants set to make a home for themselves on the shores of the sea. They gathered driftwood and built cabins to house themselves. *Ulva*, the seaweed of choice, grew abundantly on the rocks along the shore, scattered over a wide area, in some places stretching a mile on each side of a grower's cabin. Often one grower's cabin was as much as five miles away from another. The grower's life was a lonely one. It was particularly harsh for the women, who spoke little English and could hardly communicate with infrequent Euro-American visitors on the ranch.

There is little information regarding the annual production of seaweeds from 1870 to 1940; however, there exists a single record that shows that the shipment of a "Chinese Product" from San Simeon Bay in 1869 was worth $3,000.[6] It is possible that the shipping clerk was uncertain of the nomenclature of the unfamiliar commodity and that was a shipment of *Ulva;* Cambria's local historian, Geneva Hamilton, called the "Chinese product" seaweed.[7] This shipment also happened to include butter, tallow, cheese, hide, and other items, and it was listed with a total worth of $62,000. If this shipment was representative, then one might surmise that 5 percent of the goods produced in the county and shipped from San Simeon might be attributed to the effort of about twenty Chinese immigrant families. At smaller landing piers, such as those in Avila or Cayucos, seaweeds were certainly transported, but no shipping records were kept for the county's exports at the time. No record was taken when seaweeds were transported by rail or by truck, either. In a high-production year, such as 1869, the 5 percent figure might even be low.

From the Monterey-San Luis Obispo county line south to Villa Creek near Cayucos, the coastline stretches more than one hundred miles. This is a rugged shore with steep hills and precipitous mountains. The rocks and boulders along the shore, constantly washed by a rush of fresh sea water and warmed by the year-round sunshine proved to be an ideal place for seaweeds (figure 9.2). Of the many kinds of seaweed, the Chinese were interested in only one, a dark green, leafy plant that the Chinese immigrants called "Zitoy," but other local residents called *"Ulva"* or "sea lettuce." While the Chinese growers mainly cultivated *Ulva*, some might have grown an additional variety, a dark brown plant called Kelp. This plant grew elsewhere in California, but *Ulva* flourished only on the Central Coast.

FIGURE 9.2
Shook Hing gathering seaweeds in 1970 (Copyright © Dolores K. Young. Reprinted
with permission.)

Since *Ulva* already grew wild on the rocks, the growers' job was to gather it,
so the name "seaweed gatherer" was quite appropriate. In the beginning, the
growers had to identify the rocks on which *Ulva* had already taken root. Then,
numerous kinds of undesirable seaweed were burned away by a kerosene torch
or smothered with hot ash; *Ulva* alone was induced to grow. It took about four
months for the plant to mature, and when it reached eighteen to twenty-four
inches in height and had large, wavy leaves, it was ready to be picked. The leaves

were picked by hand and meticulously washed to rid them of sand (since *Ulva* that contained sand would be rejected at the marketplace). After washing, the leaves were carried up the bluff to higher ground. To do this, the grower placed the wet leaves into baskets that were attached to each end of a shoulder pole. Experienced growers could jump over slippery rocks and climb the bluff, seemingly with little effort, even with a heavy load. Ranch workers nearby marveled and admired the agility and energy of the workers, especially the women, who participated equally in this family business. After harvesting, seaweed leaves had to be carefully dried in preparation for export. To dry them, the leaves were spread on the ground and shaped into two-foot squares (figure 9.3). As the

FIGURE 9.3
George Lum and his wife and children drying seaweeds, late 1960s (Copyright © Dolores K. Young. Reprinted with permission.)

leaves dried, they tended to cling together, making it easier to turn them over. Drying took weeks, since thorough drying was necessary to prevent spoilage. Finally, the two-foot squares were stacked and baled into burlap bags, until each bag weighed about a hundred pounds. Only then was the seaweed ready for shipping. In the nineteenth century, bales of seaweeds were taken by horse-drawn carts to the landing piers at San Simeon and Avila Beach, where they were then hauled to schooners headed for San Francisco. Later, toward the end of the century, when the Southern Pacific Railroad linked San Francisco to San Luis Obispo, the seaweeds were transported by train. In the early twentieth century, seaweeds were moved by truck or even by Greyhound bus to urban areas.

Ulva was eventually exported to China from San Francisco. Kelp, the brown variety, was similarly cultivated and possibly exported to China; however, it was never a major product for Chinese immigrants on the Central Coast. Both seaweeds were considered a choice food in China, but *Ulva*, in particular, was a great delicacy.

During World War II, the coastline in the western states was cordoned off for military purposes and the seaweed gatherers were forced to abandon their trade. Many joined the war effort. After the war, some returned to work, among them Long Hop Wo,[8] George Lum[9] and How Wong.[10] However, with the Communist takeover of China and the resulting cessation of trade with the United States, the more important overseas seaweed market disappeared. After the retirement in the late 1960s of George Lum, who worked for thirty-five years at the Sibley Ranch in Cambria, the seaweed business in the Central Coast was carried on for a while by a lone gatherer, How Wong. He had inherited the business from his uncle who, with his fellow pickers, began the work in the late 1860s. When How Wong died in 1975 at the age of eighty, after farming the plant for sixty-five years, the history of one hundred years of seaweed gathering on the Central Coast ended (figure 9.4).

The *Ulva* seaweed is said to be rich in essential minerals and vitamins. The Chinese long championed its value both as food and as medicine. Very likely, Chinese immigrants introduced uses of *Ulva* to the residents who lived in Cambria, Cayucos, and San Simeon. They, in turn, developed different ways to consume it, including as a salad condiment and as a snack. Hamilton wrote:

> Mrs. Storni spoke highly of sea lettuce [*Ulva*] as a food which her family and others of Cambria enjoyed by toasting in the oven until crisp, then eating as a condiment, soup additive or ingredient with other combined foods. The fresh

leaves were sometimes added to salads. Others of the community recall that the weed was used extensively as a food supplement in early days when drought caused a scarcity of other foods.[11]

Ulva still lies on the slippery rocks on the beaches of the Central Coast, but no one harvests or exports it anymore. Today, advanced technology has allowed for large-scale production of seaweeds in Japan and China, and the efficiency and savings have rendered the seaweed gatherers, like so many other workers, obsolete.

FIGURE 9.4
How Wong, seaweed farmer for sixty-five years, in 1970 (Copyright © Dolores K. Young. Reprinted with permission.)

LIFESTYLE

The life of a seaweed picker was full of drudgery, for water had to be carried to the cabin from a well, often miles away near the ranch owner's quarters. In the evenings all seaweed work and housework had to be performed under a flickering candlelight, for electricity did not come to the ocean's edge until the late twentieth century. Children had to walk miles to a rural school, often a one-room school house with a lone teacher. Loneliness often besieged the seaweed gatherers. The nearest fellow picker lived four or five miles away along the coast. While men had infrequent dealings with ranch workers or villagers, women had fewer opportunities for social contact. Often, solitude reduced them to a state of near insanity and they eagerly awaited the time when the harvest was over and they could go to San Francisco for some relief. Generally, they all lived and worked in isolation from dawn to dark, listening only to the rhythmic ocean roar.

The desire to meet and to socialize among themselves eventually led to the establishment of a center in the town of Cambria, located between San Simeon and Cayucos. The center was a club where the celebration of Chinese New Year took place, and where unmarried men came on nonworking days. Some men lived at the club for a period of time. It was a place to socialize or, in some cases, to smoke opium or gamble. The center also served as a place where local residents met seaweed growers; as friendships were formed and as the seaweed growers earned the respect and the trust of the townspeople, they could, for instance, go to a store to purchase goods without paying cash, because they had established an account with the store owner.

During the Chinese New Year's celebration, the center was decorated in ribbons and flags. A long table would be set up upon which food (a roast piglet, perhaps, among other things), would be displayed. Not only the Chinese but also the townspeople celebrated, for they were invited to join the merrymaking and to partake in the New Year's feast. Outside the center, on Main Street and Bridge Street (the town's main thoroughfares), firecrackers exploded, lanterns glowed, and drums beat, transforming the sleepy cow town of Cambria into a bustling square of holiday activity.

Extreme isolation may have encouraged gregariousness and social activity. Almost all the interviewees had the impression that seaweed farmers were by no means shy and reserved, like hermits. Rather they easily made friends in town and on the ranches. For instance, Lee Qui,[12] who lived alone, was active in community activities and made many friends, among them Constable Roy Genardini. Asked if Lee Qui encountered prejudice in the community, the interviewee responded, "With Roy defending him, no one dared to harass him." Lee Qui also liked children, particularly those on the ranch of his ranch owner, Caroline Filipponi. The children loved to watch Lee light the kerosene torch and set the rocks on fire. When the flame shot sky-high, the children leaped for joy. Long Hop Wo was always helpful at the Hearst Ranch, particularly when George Hearst threw an "all invited, all you can eat" steak party. How Wong had many friends in Cayucos, like John Alexander and Rita Soto. John, a ranch owner and neighbor, always exchanged gifts with Wong on Christmas Eve. How liked to drop in at Rita's kitchen (Rita was also a neighbor) to chat with her. If on that day she happened to have gone down to the beach and caught a few abalones, she would ask How to stay for lunch, for she cooked delicious abalone dishes.

The seaweed growers were generous by nature, in spite of the fact that they were very thrifty. Coming back from a vacation in San Francisco, they often showered their Euro-American friends with gifts. For adults, they brought a set of china with elegant engravings, a pretty tea pot, or an embroidered painting. For children, they gave the much-remembered soft Chinese candies. For everybody, they offered roast duck and pressed dry plums. Their generosity won the hearts of the town's citizens, young and old.

Even though they were often generous toward friends, the seaweed gatherers allowed themselves little luxury. One interviewee remembered that burlap bags were treasured, and some gatherers saved them rather than export them away with the seaweed. Bill Martony, How Wong's young friend, often took How and his wife grocery shopping. Martony described how carefully How and his wife selected each item, choosing only those of good quality and lowest in price. When How Wong's car broke down on a mountain trail, he carefully examined the problem and learned to fix it himself, instead of taking it to an auto shop. In the end, he became a good mechanic. How Wong was not the only frugal one. All growers regarded frugality as a supreme virtue. Handy and self-reliant, they built their cabins themselves from driftwood gathered on the ocean shore. Their cabins still stand today, a testimony to their skill as craftsmen. So self-reliant were they, that they had very few expenses. Rent was nearly free, as was the well water (and, of course, they had no electrical bills). They usually kept a small garden, where they grew some vegetables. The seaweed people, being southern Chinese, loved fish, and fish was readily available from the ocean. Among the few necessary provisions they regularly purchased was their staple of rice. They appeared to have made good money (although their per capita income is unknown).

During the Depression years, when unemployment was rampant, the overseas seaweed market was unaffected and the seaweed folks worked steadily through the difficult time. When they came to town, gentle in demeanor and seemingly with no lack of cash, they were considered by the locals as "smart business men,"[13] and not as laborers.

The life of the growers' children was a happy one. They went to various elementary schools scattered around the county. For instance, Harding Jung[14] went to Washington School, close to his cabin home on the Hearst Ranch. The brothers Kee Jim and Bill Jim went to Harmony School,[15] the closest to their south Cambria home. All of George Lum's five children[16] either went to Cambria Grammar School or to Santa Rosa School, both located in Cambria. For high school, all attended Coast-Union High in Cambria. They excelled scholastically and many were good in sports. School yearbook pictures show them sturdily built and robust looking, possibly due to their participating in the physical toil of seaweed work (figure 9.5). Some were also good in music, and played instruments. Their many achievements are documented in the yearbooks of Coast-Union High.[17]

It was well known that the seaweed gatherers took their children's education seriously. The parents made sure the children did their school work at the cabin every night. A good example is the Jim family, as described by a childhood friend. Kee and Bill were brothers who were notably talented in music. Bill played trumpet and Kee played clarinet in the school band. Asked if the instruments were expensive and if the father bought them, the informant said, "Oh, yes, they were expensive, but the father would do anything for the children's education." He then related that since the cabin had no electricity, the father spent an enormous amount of money to purchase batteries to install an electric light so that the children could do homework at night in the cabin.

Many interviewees remembered Lillian Dennis,[18] the lone teacher at the Washington Elementary School in Piedras Blancas. Lillian was an energetic, imaginative, and kindhearted lady. Like a pioneer, she came to California at the turn of the century looking for a better life. The shortage of teachers led her to take courses at a teacher's training college in San Jose. After graduation, she taught at many schools along the California coast, including Washington School and Coast-Union High. Lillian taught her students real things. Her biology class was conducted either on a mountain slope or at the Pacific shore. One of her outstanding pupils was Harding Jung, upon whom she heaped praises. Touched by Lillian's devotion to their children, the seaweed gatherers themselves instilled in the younger generation a love toward America. Thus

FIGURE 9.5
George Lum's grandchildren on the seaweed farm, late 1960s (Copyright © Dolores K. Young. Reprinted with permission.)

Harding's father, Long Hop Wo, named his son after the sitting president at the White House, Warren Harding.

The ranch owners wanted the seaweed gatherers on their premises, not only because they served as an additional watchful eye for trespassers on their vast territory, but also because they added activity to an otherwise dull ranch life. In gratitude for the use of the ranch land and water, it was customary for the seaweed gatherers to throw a huge outdoor party for all workers on the ranch, owners as well as ranch hands, following the harvest. The seaweed gatherers would show off their culinary skills and then retreat to San Francisco for a short vacation. Another way gatherers often honored ranch owners was to name one of their children after the owner. The warm relationship shared by owners and seaweed gatherers was confirmed by Hamilton, the local historian. In her words, "these Chinese, who for the most part were smart business men [were] well liked by the community. Their numerous children attended local schools and oft ranked among the top students scholastically. . . . The older residents of Cambria recall with pleasure their childhood associations with [the] Chinese."[19]

Among the many stories involving relationships between seaweed gatherers and residents, there was one that was unique and interesting. How Wong, the last seaweed gatherer, continued to work long after his fellow gatherers retired and left the area. His cabin was located two miles north of Cayucos, at the mouth of Villa Creek. Unlike other gatherers, he was the owner of his cabin and the surrounding plot of land, because he had inherited it from his uncle, who in the 1860s came to the coast as a squatter and exercised his squatter's right.[20] How was drawn to the ocean, the clean air, and the folks in Cayucos. He loved his abode, where he, the sojourner-turned-owner, sank his roots. Some time in the late 1950s, after the death of his first wife, he went to China to marry Shook Hing. When they returned, Shook Hing reportedly burst into tears when she saw the humble cabin that was to be her home. She thought she had married a rich man from America. During the first days of her stay in the simple dwelling, she could be seen shaking her head and muttering to herself, "Old man no good." One can surmise that How Wong, being very proud of his ownership of the cabin and the adjoining small piece of real estate, might have bragged while in China. As years went by, Shook Hing proved herself to be a real help to How. Aside from her daily chores in the kitchen, she also walked miles, carrying water from the nearest well to her cabin almost daily, and assisted in seaweed work.

In 1971, while sitting on a rock for a rest, How Wong met Bill Martony, a twenty-three-year-old Vietnam veteran. Before long, Wong offered a job to Bill to help him pick seaweed. Soon Bill's girlfriend, Bernadette, was hired (they soon married) and for the next two years, How Wong, Shook Hing, Bill, and Bernadette were inseparable. Wong called Bill his "number one son," especially because his own grown children rarely visited him in Cayucos. Bernadette remembered Shook Hing's loneliness. She was always excited when Bernadette invited her along to visit Bernadette's mother. Before Bernadette's car hit the curb, Shook Hing was already pounding on the car window, eager to jump out to meet a rare living soul. When loneliness became unbearable, she went to San Francisco for a few days, but she always returned with renewed energy. The locals liked her, as Hamilton remarked: "Though . . . Mrs. Wong speaks little English, she is a willing helper and a gracious hostess to infrequent guests."[21]

Wong died in 1975 and years later Bill purchased the entire ranch on which Wong's cabin was built. Bill would gladly give interviews and tours of the land, happy to show where Wong slept, ate, and read his newspapers, and fondly remembering the four of them enjoying a delicious meal cooked by Shook Hing, which she prepared without the benefit of electricity, running water, or a refrigerator. How Wong was not forgotten by his community, for near a quiet cove called China Harbor, west of Cayucos and on the top of a hill, there is a bronze plaque on which is written,

China Harbor has seen the likes of the Chumash and Spanish explorers, Swiss/Italian dairy farmers, rum runners and cattle ranchers. During prohibition, the secluded harbor was a drop-off point for liquor smugglers. China Harbor is reported to have received its name from the Chinese immigrants, who were smuggled ashore here from as early as the 1870's. These immigrants worked the mines, railroads, ranches and settled along the coast between Cayucos and San Simeon as seaweed farmers. The last of these seaweed farmers, How Wong resided immediately south of China Harbor and farmed the sea until about 1975. (figure 9.6)

These few words sum up the true history of the region, commemorating the seaweed folks as well. But history books in libraries and in schools, distorted by discrimination, often omitted the Chinese presence and contribution. Unfortunately, the plaque is located on private ground and is inaccessible to the public.

SIGNIFICANCE

On the northern coast of San Luis Obispo County from the 1870s to 1920s, when the anti-Chinese mania swept over California, a small group of Chinese seaweed gatherers lived in harmony with the local Euro-American settlers and enjoyed a life without racial hatred. These Euro-American settlers had arrived in the pioneering days of the 1860s (the town of Cambria was founded in 1866) and had become involved in a variety of activities, including raising livestock, growing crops, dairy farming, and working in small-scale mining and lumber industries. Often business owners themselves were the workers in their own enterprises. No large industries existed here and no

FIGURE 9.6
How Wong's cabin (The cove on the right is known as China Harbor, where on a bluff is placed the bronze plaque commemorating the early settlers.) (Copyright © Dolores K. Young. Reprinted with permission.)

organized labor movement took hold here. The Workingmen's Party would find it difficult to recruit a member here. San Simeon, Cambria, and Cayucos were frontier towns bustling with activity, high hopes, and good will.

Left alone to pursue their own destinies in a milieu without discrimination, the seaweed gatherers exhibited a lifestyle that completely contradicted the stereotype of the Chinese character in the nineteenth and twentieth centuries. For instance, according to one stereotype, the Chinese by nature liked to live in crowded, dingy quarters (witness the Chinatowns). But the seaweed growers lived and worked for one hundred years on the shores of the Pacific Ocean, a clean, large, open space. George Lum and Long Hop Wo stayed on as long as they could, not because they needed to work, but because they loved the ocean. How Wong, who rarely visited San Francisco, still jumped on the slippery rocks at age eighty. The love of nature is a universal human trait, and the Chinese seaweed gatherers were no exception.

Another stereotype was that the Chinese had no desire to be assimilated into the American culture. Rather they were "enslaved"[22] to their traditional culture. Accordingly, they were merely sojourners, not good citizens, returning to their homeland as soon as enough wealth was accumulated, thereby contributing little to the growing American economy. The seaweed gatherers did not fit this image at all. They frequently associated with the townspeople, enjoying their friendship. Moreover, they embraced American culture through their children, encouraging them to excel even in sports and music, which the traditional Chinese school often neglected. When their children did well in the local schools, they sensed a profound pride and in turn they developed a loyalty toward America. They also contributed to the American economy. One interviewee asserted that all the seaweed gatherers bought war bonds during World War II. Another intimated that How Wong owned common stocks of American companies. Furthermore, none of the seaweed gatherers returned to China after their retirement. To be sure, they sank their roots deeply into the American soil. How Wong was immensely proud of his camp on the seashore. He loved to brag about his cabin to the point of being absurd (Shook Hing definitely thought so). How Wong was fortunate that his uncle in the late 1860s exercised his squatter's right and took possession of the cabin and the surrounding, tiny piece of land, and that How Wong inherited it all. It made all the difference for him for he felt that he was truly an American. He rarely left town to visit San Francisco. Had the Chinese been permitted to own land, all the seaweed gatherers would have purchased land. It was the discriminatory laws that prevented the seaweed growers from staying on and becoming permanent settlers in the region.

In the anti-Chinese era, entrepreneurship was never ascribed to the Chinese character. Rather the stereotype depicted a large crowd of people acting in unison, devoid of individuality. For instance, one writer described the railroad workers as "Celestials swarming on a giant ant-hill."[23] The Chinese were likened to ants. Considering their ingenuity in identifying a plant that no one had cultivated before, and the decision to grow this plant to make a living for themselves and their families in the anti-Chinese era when jobs were scarce, the seaweed gatherers were truly entrepreneurs. By taking this bold enterprise, they became their own masters, never to be exploited by the railroad barons or agricultural capitalists. They had also escaped the wrath of labor unions and their members, who imagined that the Chinese had stolen their jobs. In the end, they had indeed found their gold in the form of a weed in Gold Mountain.

Today, seaweed gathering is a thing of the past and gone are the old community of pioneers and their way of life. The Central Coast has become a tourists' haunt. Travelers from all over the world come to gaze upon the rocks where the incoming waves of the Pacific Ocean break into a white mist. *Ulva* leaves still lie there. But no one will gather them and no one knows the important role they played in the history of Chinese immigration.

NOTES

1. *San Luis Obispo Tribune,* 15 July 1876, 5.

2. *San Luis Obispo Tribune,* 15 July 1876, 5.

3. Patricia Mary Ochs, *A History of Chinese Labor in San Luis Obispo County* (San Luis Obispo, Calif.: San Luis Obispo County Historical Society, 1970), 42.

4. Sandy Lydon, *Chinese Gold: The Chinese in the Monterey Bay Region* (Capitola, Calif.: Capitola Book Company, 1985), 79–111.

5. Lydon, *Chinese Gold,* 55–56.

6. Myron Angel, *History of San Luis Obispo County* (Oakland, Calif.: Thompson and West, 1883; reprint, Fresno, Calif.: Valley Publishers, 1979), 331.

7. Geneva Hamilton, *Where the Highway Ends* (San Luis Obispo, Calif.: Padre Productions, 1974), 90.

8. Robert Evans, schoolmate of seaweed gatherers' children, interview by the author, Paso Robles, Calif., 1995.

9. Victor Wong, son of seaweed gatherer George Lum, interview by the author, tape recording, La Jolla, Calif., 2000.

10. John Alexander, ranch owner and landlord of seaweed gatherer How Wong, interview by the author, tape recording, Cayucos, Calif., 1995; Bill and Bernadette Martony, friends of seaweed gatherer How Wong, interview by the author, tape recording, Cayucos, Calif., 1998; Rita Soto, friend of seaweed gatherer How Wong, interview by the author, tape recording, Cayucos, Calif., 1997.

11. Hamilton, *Where the Highway Ends,* 89.

12. Caroline Filipponi, interview by the author, San Luis Obispo, California, 1995.

13. Hamilton, *Where the Highway Ends,* 86.

14. Evans interview.

15. Fred Storni, schoolmate of seaweed gatherers' children, interview by the author, tape recording, San Luis Obispo, Calif., 1998.

16. Wong interview.

17. Coast-Union High School of Cambria, Calif., Yearbooks, 1910–1936.

18. Jim Soto, schoolmate of seaweed gatherers' children, interviewed by the author, Cambria, Calif., 1999.

19. Hamilton, *Where the Highway Ends*, 86.

20. Hamilton, *Where the Highway Ends*, 90.

21. Hamilton, *Where the Highway Ends*, 89.

22. Stuart Creighton Miller, *The Unwelcome Immigrant: The American Image of Chinese 1785–1882* (Berkeley: University of California Press, 1967), vii.

23. John H. Williams, *A Great and Shining Road* (New York: Random House, 1988), 100.

REFERENCES

Chan, Sucheng. 1986. *The Bittersweet Soil: The Chinese in California Agriculture, 1860–1910.* Berkeley: University of California Press.

Chinn, Thomas W. 1969. *A History of the Chinese in California.* San Francisco: Chinese Historical Society of America.

Gillenkirk, Jeff, and James Motlow. 1987. *Bitter Melon: Stories from the Last Rural Chinese Town in America.* Seattle: University of Washington Press.

Hamilton, Geneva. 1974. *Where the Highway Ends.* San Luis Obispo, Calif.: Padre.

Krieger, Daniel E. 1988. *San Luis Obispo County: Looking Backward into the Middle Kingdom.* Northridge, Calif.: Windsor.

Lydon, Sandy. 1985. *Chinese Gold.* Capitola, Calif.: Capitola Book Company.

Takaki, Ronald. 1989. *Strangers from a Different Shore.* Boston: Little, Brown.

Williams, John H. 1988. *A Great and Shining Road.* New York: Random House.

Wilson, Neill C., and Frank J. Taylor. 1952. *Southern Pacific.* New York: McGraw Hill.

Wong, H. K. 1987. *Gold Mountain Men.* San Francisco: Bechtel.

10

The Five Eras of Chinese Medicine in California

William M. Bowen

In the face of labor and immigration discrimination, the Chinese medicine industry in California has been a remarkable success story and made a unique contribution among the Chinese industries that developed in this state. The success of Chinese medicine can be seen in its longevity, its effectiveness, and its cross-cultural appeal among both patients and practitioners. Although there have been other important Chinese industries, such as seaweed gathering, abalone harvesting, and junk fishing, they did not have the same impact and eventually died out.

Chinese medicine came in with the very first Chinese immigrant workers and has flourished in varying degrees through five different definable eras over 150 years. The criteria used to define these eras include whom Chinese medicine catered to or was utilized by, the types of medicine practiced, the location of the doctors' practices in and outside of Chinatowns, and the racial and gender backgrounds of the practitioners. Now, at the opening of the new millennium, Chinese medicine is a widely used and accepted form of alternative medicine.

The first era, or the "Early Period," of Chinese medicine in California can be dated from 1848 to 1870. During the early part of this first period the concepts, practices, and pharmacopoeia of Chinese medicine were introduced in California by immigrant Chinese workers who used it for self-treatment. The latter part of the first era was marked by the entrance of self-, family-, and professionally trained Chinese doctors who came to the California frontier to practice medicine on Chinese patients. Some of these physicians were self-taught in China, others developed their skills after they arrived in the United States. Still others, such as Dr. Woh of Los Angeles, were heir to a lineage of family physicians, while others, such as Dr. Hong Soi, also of Los Angeles, trained in the hospitals and medical schools of China.

The second era, or the "Heyday," of Chinese medicine in California, 1871 to 1912, was defined by a pronounced and spreading influence, as Chinese medicine reached near or equal footing with Western medicine. During this era, word of Chinese medicine and Chinese herbal doctors spread throughout the labor camps, mines, ranches, railroads, and cities, reaching non-Chinese, who in turn sought out the doctors. By the 1880s, Euro-Americans and Hispanics, especially adult women of these two ethnic groups, had joined Chinese in using Chinese medicine. Chinese doctors opened practices focusing on pulse diagnosis and herbal medicine in Euro-American business districts in many of the major cities of California, while high-profile Chinese grocery and herb stores were established in Chinatowns and sold Chinese herbs to both Chinese and non-Chinese clientele.

During the third era, or the "Period of Decline," 1913 to 1930, Chinese medicine suffered increased persecution under the growing power of the Western legal and medical establishment. Chinese doctors were pushed out of Euro-American neighborhoods and back into Chinatowns; there they assumed a low profile and directed their services principally toward Chinese.

The fourth era, or "Holding Period," 1931 to 1970, saw Chinese medicine serve Chinese in Chinatowns almost exclusively, except for the rare practitioner who went public in the Euro-American world and was usually severely persecuted for it. Even in Chinatown, up to at least 1950, Chinese medicine was in low gear because the supplies of Chinese herbs being shipped from China to the United States had been cut back due to the Japanese invasion of mainland China and World War II.

The year 1971, following the opening of China during the Nixon administration, marked the start of the fifth period, the period of "Gradual Acceptance" of Chinese medicine in California. Chinese medicine began a comeback, with a new focus on acupuncture and with Chinese herbs playing a supporting role. Doctors of Chinese medicine began to treat many new diseases they had not attended to in historic times. More and more, Euro-Americans entered the profession, and they began to dominate it; female practitioners of Chinese medicine became more conspicuous than men. Chinese medical offices, operated by both Chinese and non-Chinese, opened once again in Euro-American business districts. During the 1980s, Chinese medicine struggled hard for acceptance as a bona fide health discipline. In the 1990s, Chinese medicine continued to evolve to become a distinct health-care profession and a key compo-

nent in alternative medicine, which has grown to rival Western scientific medicine in terms of patient draw and patient spending.[1] As California moves further into the twenty-first century, it seems obvious that Chinese medicine will
continue to spread and even interpenetrate the Western medical establishment,
especially in the treatment of pain conditions.

EARLY CHINESE IMMIGRANT WORKERS

Many Chinese immigrants packed traditional Chinese herbal remedies in
their luggage for their shipboard journey to America. In 1964, the Chinese
Historical Society of America examined three subbasements filled with personal luggage belonging to Chinese pioneers who had left the luggage for safe-
keeping at the turn of the century at the Son Loy Company of Grant Avenue
in San Francisco. Almost all of the luggage contained some Chinese herbs or
medicine, suggesting that Chinese immigrants considered their traditional
medicines to be critical personal items for their voyage to America.[2]

Stewart Culin, writing in 1887, suggested that the taking of traditional
medicine was a very important, popular, and even indispensable aspect of the
daily life of the early Chinese working in America.[3] The archaeology of the
early West supports this claim. Chinese medicinal vials have been found at a
Paiute Indian site in the Mono Basin. The Paiute apparently obtained the vials
through trade with Chinese workers. Similar Chinese medicinal vials had also
been found at Chinese sites, including Weaverville and Riverside, again pointing out the importance of traditional medicine to Chinese workers overseas.[4]

Chinese companies that employed Chinese immigrants imported traditional Chinese medicines and supplied them to their workers. A. W. Loomis
notes, "scarcely an invoice of goods can go to the trader in the most distant
mining settlements, or to the [Chinese healers] who follow the camps of the
railroad workers, but medicines will occupy a prominent place in it."[5]

Chinese workers probably also gathered indigenous local plants that were
similar to those found in China for use as food and medicine, especially in the
railroad and mining camps located in rugged natural settings. Many medicinal and food herbs used in China, such as bindweed (Convolvulus arvensis),
cocklebur (Xanthium strumarium), cattail (Typha spp.), pine (Pinus spp.), and
willow (Salix spp.) are found in modern-day California and were also present
at the time of the Chinese immigrant workers.[6]

The Chinese immigrants gathered native species of animals for their own
personal use or for shipment back to China. Two articles in the Sacramento
Daily Bee mention the collection of a local species of reptile by Chinese work-

ers for use as medicine.[7] W. A. Rogers, in an article in the *Harper's Weekly*, described how this same species was an ingredient in a Chinese prescription he purchased in Chinatown in San Francisco.[8] A reporter covering a story on Chinatown in 1891 mentioned how one individual housed native species of animals, ready for use as medicine, in the basement of his Chinese herb store.[9] Even in recent years, several species of plants and animals indigenous to America have been found in Chinese herb and grocery stores, suggesting a continuous interest in local varieties of traditional Chinese medicines by overseas Chinese.

CHINESE HERB GROCERY STORES

Chinese communities or Chinatowns developed in California as a result of Chinese banding together to collectively face the anti-Chinese sentiment and discriminatory legislation of the 1870s–1880s. San Francisco Chinatown, for example, grew from three thousand residents in 1853 to thirty thousand by 1895.[10] The presence of large numbers of people in Chinatowns made Chinese grocery stores feasible enterprises for entrepreneurial-minded Chinese. The Sanborn map of Riverside, California, for instance, listed several Chinese grocery stores in operation by 1883.[11] Chinese medicines were available in these Chinese grocery stores as part of the regular stock in trade and were quite popular, first with Chinese and then later with non-Chinese.

It was not long before the Chinese established stores and import networks specializing solely in Chinese herbs. Loomis, writing in 1869, noted a dozen or more such herbal establishments in San Francisco and pronounced that "every town in the country where there are Chinese has its medicine store." Loomis went on to note that "the Chinese of our cities are constantly taking medicines."[12] J. W. Ames, writing in 1875, described a Chinese herb store, located at the corner of Dupont and Jackson streets in San Francisco, and its many, varied, and exotic medicines.[13] Likewise, J. H. Bates in 1897 described the remedies available in Chinese herb stores in San Francisco.[14] W. A. Rogers stated in 1899 that the Chinese herb stores had well over three thousand remedies from which to choose.[15]

San Francisco was not the only city in California with Chinese herb stores. The 1913 International Chinese Business Directory of the World listed twenty-two herb and drug companies in Los Angeles. One of these herb stores, Wing On Tong, in Chinatown, remains in operation to this day, suggesting the ongoing importance of such stores to the Chinese community.

By the latter part of the 1880s, Euro-Americans and Hispanics began to consult the Chinese physicians and herbalists and to buy Chinese medications in the highly visible Chinese herb and grocery stores.[16] Many of those who ended up at the Chinese herbalist had wandered from one Western doctor to another to no avail. The end of the line was the Chinese herbalist.

Chinese herbs were also available to Euro-Americans and Hispanics through mail order. Indeed, some Chinese herbalists developed a booming mail-order business. In an 1899 *Los Angeles Times* article, Dr. T. Foo Yuen said, "we send our medicines to every state in the Union and to the Dominion of Canada." Dr. Chuck Sal of O'Farrel Street in San Francisco, circa 1912, invited potential patients to mail-in for a symptom sheet, which they could fill out at home and send back to him. He would then return, for a fee, a prescription of Chinese herbs.

THE EARLY CHINESE DOCTORS (1848–1912)

The Chinese immigrant physicians dispersed throughout the Pacific coastal region. William Tisdale pointed out in 1899 that there were "many Chinese physicians in San Francisco and other cities of the Pacific Coast."[17] Without question, Chinese doctors made a vital contribution to the health care of the western frontier, treating a wide range of patients, both Chinese and non-Chinese. They cured patients whom Western medicine had viewed as hopeless. In terms of income, social standing, and political influence, Chinese doctors attained a stature greater in America than they ever could have in their homeland, where only a handful of elite scholar/physicians ever had access to the higher circles of society.[18]

Most of the Chinese physicians eventually oriented their practice toward Euro-American and Hispanic patients exclusively because it was much more profitable than just treating Chinese. The Chinese doctors advertised in English or, like Dr. Ah Poo Ji Tong of Los Angeles, in English and Spanish, in the major newspapers of the day. They printed business cards in English; located their practices outside of Chinatown in respectable, centrally oriented business areas such as Horton Plaza in San Diego, where Dr. Low Luke practiced; and decorated their offices with tasteful Western-style furnishings. Some had English-speaking business managers. Others, such as Dr. Guarding Liu of Los Angeles who had a large patronage of Hispanic patients, would even hire a "Mexican girl" who could read and write Spanish to serve as a translator, secretary, and nurse, thus improving their ability to reach out to the Hispanic community.[19]

Often, well-to-do Euro-Americans and Hispanics paid high prices to see the more well-known Chinese doctors such as Drs. Foo and Wing in Los Angeles or Li Po-Tai in San Francisco (figure 10.1). Many of the patients of the Chinese doctors were respectable lawyers, journalists, bankers, business people, and even Western physicians, demonstrating that the Chinese medical treatments were not merely "snake oil" chicanery and legerdemain, but something that

FOO AND WING HERB CO.

(INCORPORATION.)

DR. LI WING	DR. T. FOO YUEN
Secretary and Treasurer.	President.
Son of the late Dr. Li Po Tai, of San Francisco.	Ex-official Physician to the Emperor of China.

Dr. T. Foo Yuen desires to announce that he has formed a co-partnership with Dr. Li Wing recently of San Francisco, a son of the celebrated Chinese physician, the late Dr. Li Po Tai, who practiced his profession in the city of San Francisco for nearly half a century.

Dr. Foo has had no connection for nearly a year with the Flowery Kingdom Herb Remedy Company, but has been in business by himself for that period. He has made the present very desirable arrangement with Dr. Li Wing for the reason that his practice has grown too large for him to give it proper attention alone, and because he desires to devote a portion of his time and energies in establishing an Oriental College of Medicine, and in teaching and illustrating the principles underlying the Chinese system of medicine, for the benefit of the American people. His remarkable record, particularly during the past year, in the cure of various diseases by the use of his purely vegetable herbal remedies is at once a guarantee of his capacity for performing this work of instruction and a prophecy of its success.

Dr. Li Wing, the new member of the firm, was trained in the science and practice of Oriental medicine by his father, Li Po Tai, and was also a student at the great Imperial Medical College at Pekin. He has a certificate to this effect from the Acting Chinese Consul-General at San Francisco, and has also papers from Judge Rosenbaum, a well-known attorney of that city, and from others attesting his attainments and experience. He is a worthy successor to his celebrated father, and is unquestionably destined to a very notable career in his chosen profession. Taken together, Drs. Foo and Wing are by far the most learned, scientific and talented Oriental physicians in America, and the most thoroughly representative of all that is best in the Oriental system of medicine.

Persons desiring information, for themselves or their friends, upon the Oriental system of medicine should write for descriptive literature, such as Dr. Foo's New Gift Book, of 125 pages, which contains a great deal of very valuable information and is sent free on request. Or you may investigate this system for yourself, free of charge. You will be surprised at the favorable impression which you will receive from the winning personality of these physicians, and from the manifest breadth and scope of their information and skill. Diagnoses by the pulse and opinions are given free in all cases. Write to the doctors. or call at No. 929 South Broadway, Los Angeles. Electric cars pass the door. Telephone West 142.

Dr. T. Foo Yuen and Dr. Li Wing.

FIGURE 10.1
Well-known Chinese doctors in 1897, Drs. Wing and Yuen (From *Land of Sunshine*, May 1897.)

could impress and benefit a wide range of successful and intelligent people of the American West.[20] For example, Dr. Tong Po Chy in 1893 cured S. J. Houghton, superintendent of the mines in San Francisco, of tuberculosis in seven weeks time.

Chinese medicine has been successful cross-culturally because it has catered to the needs of Chinese, Hispanic, and Euro-American patients, building a unique cross-cultural bridge during many moments of racial anxiety and hostility. Chinese medicine has even offered employment to non-Chinese, as during the late nineteenth and early twentieth centuries, when Euro-American men were employed as office managers and Hispanic women as office girls. Students and practitioners of Chinese medicine continue to come from a variety of races and ethnic backgrounds. This multiracial mix of patients and practitioners has surely helped to promote better racial understanding and tolerance.

Western patients often preferred a Chinese doctor because he was often more skilled or knowledgeable than his Western counterparts or because the Chinese herbs he prescribed were more effective than Western-style medications. For certain ailments, such as venereal disease, blood poisoning, and the flu, Chinese treatments were definitely superior to Western treatments.[21] As one Western doctor remarked to Tisdale in 1899, "I am sorry to think that these degraded heathens can do things with their herbs which our own doctors . . . cannot do."[22] Modern scientific studies have backed up the value of Chinese herbs; rigorous testing has demonstrated that some Chinese herbs are indeed effective.[23]

The surgery that was practiced by Western doctors was feared because of poor anesthetics and the chance of infection.[24] Hence, anxious patients welcomed the nonsurgical alternatives the Chinese doctors offered. Dr. Wah Hing of Sacramento said he "could treat appendicitis without the knife" and Dr. Mar Chung of Bakersfield said he could "cure all chronic diseases of men and women without operations." In one of Dr. Wong's patient testimonials, a G. Myer stated, "Three years ago I had what common doctors call a tumor. I had been cut and slashed by them for three weeks. Two weeks later the tumor had grown as large as a pint bowl. I took three doses of Dr. Wong's medicine; the tumor disappeared without the use of a knife and without my suffering."

The natural herbal medicines of the Chinese doctors, which were basically without side effects, were viewed as welcome alternatives to the often harsh Western chemical drugs in use around the turn of the century. With many of the Western drugs, such as mercury or laudanum, the cure could be worse than the illness. In contrast, Dr. Hong Soi of Los Angeles claimed that he "did not use opium or poisonous drugs." Likewise, Dr. Low Luke of San Diego said he "used no poison drugs."

Dr. Wong Him, Dr. Wong, and Dr. Kwong, like many other Chinese doctors, had hundreds of patient testimonials on file in their offices in Los Angeles (figure 10.2). Their testimonials are by no means unique. At Dr. Fong Wan's trial before the Federal Trade Commission in 1940, over two hundred patients testified to the miraculous relief provided by his Chinese healing remedies.[25] Chinese medicine has been successful medically because it has presented a viable alternative to the surgery and harsh chemical drugs of Western medicine, relying first in the late nineteenth and early twentieth centuries on pulse diagnosis and natural herb remedies, and then later on acupuncture, massage, traditional exercise, and herbology.

Often, Euro-American patients went to the Chinese doctor for the treatment of impotence or sexually transmitted diseases because the Chinese doctors did not subscribe to the Victorian moralism of the day. In addition, the Chinese doctors offered more confidentiality for the Euro-American or Hispanic patient, because they usually did not speak English or Spanish well and were members of a different social circle. Hence, the chance of the doctor breaking confidence through a slip of the tongue was greatly reduced.[26]

Euro-American women often found that they were much better treated by the Chinese doctors than Western physicians. They may have been less subject to gender bias from Chinese doctors and more sensitively treated. Perhaps the sensitive, nonintrusive approach of Chinese medicine is why so many women have entered the field today. When the visual images of the Chinese doctor found in the early newspaper advertisements are compared with comparable images of the Western doctor, the Chinese doctor appears much more sensitive, boyish, clean-shaven, and "feminine" than the stern, forbidding, bearded, and "masculine" Western doctor (figure 10.3).[27] From 60 to 70 percent of the Chinese doctors' patients were women, suggesting that in addition to their better bedside manner, the doctors had developed more or better women's treatment regimes.[28]

Its framework of noninvasive, sympathetic, and receptive doctor-patient relations has also contributed to the success of Chinese medicine. This framework has provided more confidentiality in private matters, such as sexually transmitted disease and other embarrassing illnesses, and been more sympathetic to gender concerns, especially in the treatment of women. Finally, Chinese medicine has recognized illnesses, such as candida albicans, Epstein-Barr disease, and premenstrual syndrome, often denied or ignored by Western counterparts.

As implied above, the Chinese doctors often advertised their services in the Euro-American newspapers of the day. Over fifty different advertisements

DR. KWONG,

The well known Chinese Doctor, who has made himself famous by his wonderful cures of CHRONIC DISEASES.

Read the following testimonials:

I was an invalid for 21 years and doctored a great deal without any benefit. Some American doctors here claimed I had a tumor, which must result in having an operation performed. I quit them and went to Dr. Kwong, who cured me sound and well in six weeks' time.
MRS. HANNAH CHEESEBROUGH,
829 San Pedro street, Los Angeles.

I was treated by American doctors for four years for stomach trouble, indigestion and dyspepsia, but got no relief. Dr. Kwong cured me in two months' time.
WALTER REED,
P. O. Box 630, Los Angeles.

Los Angeles, Cal., March 18, 1891.—This is to certify that Dr. Kwong cured me of a very stubborn case of catarrh which troubled me for five years. J. G. DeLONG,
420 South Main Street.

Los Angeles, Cal., August 22, 1890.—My lungs were troubling me for two years; I coughed a great deal and my friends became alarmed and advised me to try Dr. Kwong's treatment. I did so and was completely cured in nine weeks. MISS E. P. CALER,
824 South Broadway.

DR. KWONG'S Office and Residence
311 SOUTH BROADWAY, - - - LOS ANGELES, CAL.

FIGURE 10.2
Advertisement with a sample of patient testimonials, 1892 (From *Los Angeles Times*, November 6, 1892.)

Dr. Wong

Cures hundreds of people by his Vegetable Compound. He eliminates all the poison from the system. He has cured many a hopeless case, and he can cure you. Seventeen years in city.

PULSE DIAGNOSIS

Office and Sanitarium,
713 South Main St.

FIGURE 10.3
Advertisement with an image of a caring and sensitive doctor, 1899 (From *Los Angeles Times*, March 2, 1899.)

from 1871 to 1912 have been discovered. These advertisements contain a great deal of valuable information about Chinese medicine and Chinese doctors. When the terms used in the advertisements for illnesses that the doctors said they could treat are examined collectively, the most frequently listed include rheumatism, lung and stomach complaints, tumors, consumption, blood disorders, asthma, and irritation of the mucus membranes (figure 10.4).

The advertisements show that the Chinese doctors practiced pulse diagnosis and herbal therapy exclusively. There is absolutely no mention of acupuncture or any other Chinese medical technique. In addition, all the Chinese doctors were males; there were no female practitioners, as in modern times.

In regard to their legal status, William Tisdale remarked that the Chinese doctors were not recognized by the law.[29] In Los Angeles and other cities of California, Chinese doctors were arrested and sometimes fined for the practice of illegal medicine. However, some doctors made powerful friends who offered them immunity from prosecution, as with Dr. Li Po-Tai, who befriended Senator Leland Stanford and Governor Hopkins. In contrast, in Stockton in 1888, Dr. Low Fook Wan was arrested for practicing medicine without a license and placed in an insane asylum.

Newspaper articles railed against the Chinese doctors. The *San Francisco Call* once stated that "the large increase of Chinese medical practitioners in this

DR. JIM YEN,

THE GREATEST of PHYSICIANS and SURGEONS,
319½ SOUTH SPRING-st,
OFFICE: NO. 4 WILSON'S COURT.
Los Angeles, Cal.
Dr. Jim Yen is a graduate of the medical
schools and universities of Canton, having
received his diplomas therefrom, and has
practiced extensively in all the hospitals of
Hong Kong. He treats and cures consumption, rheumatism, asthma, catarrh, paraly-
sis, and all diseases. Persons are invited
to call and consult him.
Testimonial to the Public.
For the last sixteen years I have found
nothing but temporary relief from terrible
headaches and pains in my back. Feeling
was destroyed in the back of my head.
Hearing of Dr. Jim Yen's wonderful herb
remedy cures I tried his remedy. The result was a perfect cure, therefore I heartily
recommend him to all sufferers. Yours re-
spectfully, MRS. J. W. McINTOSH. 319½
South Spring st. No. 6 Wilson's Court, January 18, 1893.

FIGURE 10.4
Advertisement that lists ailments treatable by Chinese medicine, 1893 (From *Los An-geles Times*, January 27, 1893.)

city has had the effect of withdrawing a number of Celestials from the less lu-crative business of washing the dirty linen of Americans."[30] Obviously, the *Call* believed most Chinese doctors were quacks out to make a quick dollar at the expense of hapless patients. In truth, while some might have fit this descrip-tion, the evidence suggests that Chinese doctors certainly did not as a rule.

The *Chicago Times* on January 11, 1881, published an article, with a similar skeptical tone, entitled "Chinese Quack Doctors" that stated, "San Francisco is cursed with a gang of Celestial Quacks, who, under the guise of doctors, do a thriving business, both for themselves and the undertaker." The article went on to state that the doctors were "shrewd adventurers, who see in the credulity of our afflicted peoples the opportunity to grow rich. One of the most successful of these impostors was a fisherman, who some white speculators set up in business."[31] The attitude of these articles, along with the legal prosecution of Chinese doctors, is a theme seen repeatedly in the history of Chinese medicine in California. It is a general reflection of an overall view of the Chinese in California seen in the persecution of and discrimination against a people who were in reality making an important contribution to the welfare and development of the state.

One of the most famous and successful of the early Chinese doctors was Li Po-Tai of San Francisco. Although William Tisdale in 1899 called Li Po-Tai the first of the Chinese doctors to come to the United States, Henry Harris said in 1932 that he was reputed to have been a barber back in his Chinese homeland.[32] This disagreement over the qualifications, abilities, and motivations of Chinese doctors is a predominant theme. Some said the Chinese doctors were quacks preying upon sick patients; others extolled their virtues. Overall, the evidence suggests that the Chinese doctors did much more good than harm and were by and large ethical in their dealings with their patients and the public. Thus, the lion's share of critical and skeptical remarks seem to be motivated by discriminatory attitudes toward exotic races and cultures.

Whatever Li Po-Tai's occupation was in China, he was a successful practitioner who came to San Francisco during the early days of the gold rush and lived there for forty to fifty years, until his death in 1893, when he was succeeded by Tong Po Chy. Li Po-Tai's son, Li Wing, also a doctor, received training at the Imperial College of Medicine in Peking. Li Wing opened his practice in Los Angeles with T. Foo Yuen. In his heyday, Li Po-Tai made upwards of $75,000 a year. Between 150 and 300 patients, coming from all parts of the United States, consulted him daily.[33] He soon became one of the richest men in San Francisco. Li Po-Tai advertised in English and practiced exclusively among Euro-Americans.[34] Although Samuel Williams in 1875 called him the "quack high priest of charlatans . . . who played on the credulity of the public," thousands of patients said that his herbal remedies had cured them, after all other means had failed.[35] Williams quotes Li Po-Tai as making the following commentary on the Chinese in America: "You can no more expel him than you can the rats . . . [since] he does not mind persecution; I am not sure that it does not agree with him."[36] The quote indicates Li Po-Tai's stoic awareness of the resilience of Chinese in the face of persecution. Even more resilient, he is one example of a Chinese doctor who was well respected and sought after even in an age of discrimination and exclusion.

THE THIRD AND FOURTH ERAS (1913–1970)

Chinese doctors in America practiced openly and on near equal footing with Western-style physicians until the 1920s–1930s, when increased persecution and pressure from Western authorities forced most of their businesses to close down.[37] From the late 1930s through the war years it was difficult to get shipments of Chinese herbs from mainland China, so their prescription was cut back. In general, from the 1930s to the 1970s Chinese medicine, especially that directed toward non-Chinese, lay fallow except for the practices of rare individuals, such as Fong Wan of Oakland in the 1930s, Guarding Liu of Los Angeles in the 1940s, and Thomas Wing, also of Los Angeles, who practiced from 1947 to 1952.

While Gor Yun Leong estimated there to be one hundred Chinese doctors in San Francisco in 1936 and Guarding Liu mentions, in a 1948 pamphlet, that there were one hundred and twenty Chinese herbal doctors in California, forty of whom were in Los Angeles, the doctors they referred to must have had a limited amounts of Chinese herbs with which to work. They must also have restricted their treatments to Chinese in Chinatowns, provided very low-profile treatment of Euro-Americans and Hispanics, or dispensed Chinese medicine under some other credential, otherwise they would have been subject to merciless persecution.[38]

Fong Wan's son, Richard, heir to his practice in Oakland, claimed that his father was the only Chinese doctor who fought back against the persecution. Indeed, Fong Wan, who became a multimillionaire with two medical practices and several restaurants, was arrested and acquitted twenty times during his career for false advertising and practicing medicine without a license.[39]

The only other route to stay in business was demonstrated by Dr. Thomas Wing, who was able to publicly advertise and endure in Los Angeles, because he dispensed his Chinese herbs under the auspices of a doctor of chiropractic license.[40]

THE MODERN, "GRADUAL ACCEPTANCE" PERIOD (1971–PRESENT)

In the 1970s, Chinese medicine started to make a comeback in California. Since then, it has grown considerably in stature and importance. In a basic shift, Chinese medicine has moved from a focus on herbal therapy to a focus on acupuncture. Indeed, many modern practitioners rely almost exclusively on acupuncture. When the public now thinks of Chinese medicine, their first thoughts are usually of acupuncture, not Chinese herbs. By 1988, there were over three thousand state-licensed acupuncturists practicing in California.[41] As of 2000, Chinese medicine has become a key component in alternative or complementary medicine.

As Chinese medicine has grown in importance in California, the public view of it has begun to change. For instance, an examination of thirty-seven articles about Chinese medicine that appeared in the *San Diego Union* newspaper during 1972–1991 revealed that articles representing Chinese medicine in a favorable light were about equal in number with those focused on something wrong with it, indicating a lessening of a persecutory public attitude.[42]

Chinese doctors are no longer persecuted as they once were. Probably the last Chinese doctor to suffer persecution in San Diego was Dr. Tomson Liang, who was a part-time acupuncture doctor and part-time engineer at Hughes Aircraft. In 1974, an injunction was brought against Liang by the State Board of Medical Examiners, who contended that he had been practicing medicine without a license. The persecution of Liang continued a long history of discrimination against Chinese doctors and Chinese medicine.[43] It was only in the late 1980s and in the 1990s, when many Euro-Americans became doctors of Chinese medicine, that the persecution stopped, suggesting that at least some of the persecution was racially or culturally motivated.

In historic times, all the doctors of Chinese medicine in California were Chinese males. In the modern period, there has been a great deal of change in the ethnicity and gender of practitioners.[44] Over the period 1988–1990 in San Diego, the overall percentage of Chinese practitioners of Chinese medicine dropped slightly, while the percentage of Euro-American practitioners increased slightly. By these dates more Euro-Americans than Asians were practicing acupuncture in San Diego. There was a slight increase in "Other Oriental" practitioners, such as Koreans, but their overall percentage remained nearly the same over the two-year period.

In terms of gender, the percentage of Chinese and Euro-American male practitioners dropped slightly, while the percentage of female Chinese and Euro-American practitioners rose slightly. These figures reflected a growing female presence in the discipline. In some sense, Chinese medicine may be becoming, like nursing, more of a woman's field. Ten years later, in 1999, in San Diego there had been only a slight increase in the overall number of acupuncturists but a significant increase in the percentage of female practitioners and a significant decrease in percentage of Chinese practitioners, showing the continuation of two trends.

It is not known if any type of licensing was required of Chinese doctors in historic times. Tisdale remarked that in 1899 a Chinese doctor could practice virtually without hindrance, but he does not mention licensing. Periodically, some of the doctors were arrested for practicing without a license, but they were usually acquitted by the courts. In the modern period, acupuncturists must complete training in an approved school for two or three years to sit for the test to be a licensed acupuncturist. For another year of training, they can receive the title of OMD, or oriental medical doctor.

When the acupuncture license first became available in California in about 1980, many acupuncturists already possessed other degrees and training. Theirs was a career shift. From 1988 to 1990, the percentage of other degrees possessed by acupuncturists dropped, pointing to a trend in which acupuncture was becoming a distinct degree profession, with individuals coming fresh into the field.

In the historic medical advertising of Chinese doctors, the most common complaints listed were rheumatism, lung and stomach complaints, tumors, consumption, blood disorders, asthma, and irritation of the mucus membranes. During 1988–1990, the most commonly listed terms in Chinese medical advertisements were stop smoking, sinus, allergies, weight loss, arthritis, headache, pain, backache, sports injuries, sciatica, and insomnia.[45] Over the two-year period from 1988 to 1990, there were some changes in the term frequencies. There was a rise in the number of listings of sinus/allergies, pain, arthritis, backache, athletic/sports injuries, and stress/stress reduction terms. There was a drop in the total number of smoking, weight loss, sciatica, and insomnia terms and a trend toward more treatment of pain conditions.

Of all the terms, only arthritis and asthma were mentioned in both historic and modern advertising. If historic continuity is taken as evidence, this may show that these two complaints can be helped by Chinese medicine. The entrance of so many new medical complaints to the field of treatment shows that Chinese medicine has been adapted to address many different types of problems over the course of time. However, some acupuncturists might be faulted for thinking that Chinese medicine or acupuncture will help or cure any condition.

The medical language used in Chinese medicine has also changed over time. Commonly, Western scientific language has slipped into the traditional discourse of Chinese medicine, as in the use of terms such as "depression" or "hormones." To a lesser extent, there is also incorporation of a "New Age" discourse, exemplified by terms such as "balance" or "attune," reflecting the trend for Chinese medicine to speak to and serve the alternative or counterculture community.[46]

Some new themes have emerged in modern Chinese medical advertising.[47] The first theme is that acupuncture is a good career. In historic times there were no colleges of Chinese medicine in California, although in the 1890s Drs. Foo and Wing mentioned they wanted to open one. Secondly, a significant number of advertisements are oriented toward the treatment of pain, which parallels an increased acceptance by the Western scientific establishment of acupuncture as valuable for lessening pain. Thirdly, many advertisements are directed toward the treatment of diseases not recognized by Western medicine, such as premenstrual syndrome and candida albicans. In contrast, in historic times, Chinese doctors treated the same diseases as their Western counterparts.

In modern times, it appears that many patients visit doctors of Chinese medicine for the same reasons patients did in historic times: Western medicine has not helped them, or they desire a more natural, less harsh treatment, or they are drawn by the possibility of an improved patient-physician relationship with the Chinese medical health provider. One study showed that patients saw the acupuncturist as more empathetic, sensitive, competent, caring, and open, while less authoritarian, sexist, paternalistic, and condescending than Western doctors.[48]

Today in San Diego the majority of the patients of Chinese medicine are women, usually thirty years old and up, which also was the case in historic times. What is new is that the acupuncturists think that about 50 percent of their female cases have psychological problems as the chief underlying cause of their distress. Psychological causation or psychological conditions, except perhaps "nervousness," were not an issue in historic times. The acceptance of, naming, and treatment of distinct psychological conditions is, then, a new development in Chinese medicine in California.[49] By 1988, practitioners, especially non-Chinese, were using lay counseling as part of their Chinese medical therapy and counseling had become a required course at acupuncture colleges.

CONCLUSION

Chinese medicine has been one of the most successful of the Chinese industries that developed in the state of California. For the past 150 years, through five different eras, Chinese medicine has served the needs of Chinese, Euro-Americans, and Hispanics, adapting to changing circumstances. The evidence suggests that doctors of Chinese medicine have done much more good than harm and the skeptical remarks and criticisms that have been directed at them and their profession have often been motivated by discriminatory attitudes toward exotic races and cultures. Interestingly enough, in recent times the criticisms of Chinese medicine have diminished in proportion to the number of Euro-Americans that have entered the discipline!

In the face of discrimination and persecution, doctors of Chinese medicine have endured and even prospered. Chinese medicine made rich men out of many Chinese practitioners, defying the stereotype of the unskilled and unsuccessful Chinese worker who was a burden to the labor force. Many Chinese doctors rose to a much higher station in the new land than they ever could have in China. Their success has helped to debunk negative cultural and racial stereotypes and has helped to facilitate tolerance and understanding.

The popularity and success of Chinese medicine and its eventual evolution to mainstream status has validated the cultural knowledge of Chinese, who were once excluded precisely because of their "exotic" or "foreign" ways. Even as the stereotype of "ancient Chinese wisdom" worked against or exoticized Chinese immigrant laborers, it has been part of the appeal of Chinese medicine, especially for the many desperate patients who were looking for something different from the Western system that had brought them little relief from their health concerns. Now Chinese medicine is fast becoming an essential aspect of our culture, helping to demonstrate the lasting value and significance of the Chinese presence in America.

NOTES

1. David Eisenberg et al., "Unconventional Medicine in the United States," *New England Journal of Medicine*, 320, no. 4 (1993): 246–52.

2. Thomas W. Chinn, ed., *A History of the Chinese in California: A Syllabus* (San Francisco: Chinese Historical Society of America, 1969), 78.

3. Stewart Culin, "Chinese Drug Stores in America," *American Journal of Pharmacy* 59 (1887): 596.

4. Brooke S. Akrush, *The Precontact and Postcontact Archaeology of the Mono Basin Paiute: An Examination of Cultural Continuity and Change* (Ph.D. dissertation, Department of Anthropology, University of California, Riverside, 1989), 157.

5. A. W. Loomis, "Medical Art in the Chinese Quarter," *Overland Monthly* 2 (June 1869): 496.

6. F. Porter Smith and G. A. Stuart, *Chinese Medicinal Herbs* (San Francisco: Georgetown Press, 1973).

7. *Sacramento Daily Bee*, 22 October and 1 November 1869.

8. W. A. Rogers, "A Chinese Prescription," *Harper's Weekly* 43 (1899): 1239.

9. Gwen Kinkead, "A Reporter at Large, Chinatown," *New Yorker* 67, nos. 17 and 18 (10 and 17 June 10); *Asian Week*, 4 March 1988, 1, 4; *Escondido Times Advocate*, 2 March 1988, A9.

10. Henry G. Schwartz, ed., *Chinese Medicine on the Golden Mountain: An Interpretive Guide* (Seattle: Wing Luke Memorial Museum, 1984), 8, 16; Judith Liu, "Birds of Passage: Chinese Occupations in San Diego, 1870–1900" (San Diego:

Chinese Historical Society of Greater San Diego & Baja California, 1989), 2; Henry Harris, *California's Medical Story* (San Francisco: Stacey, 1932); J. Dyer Ball, *Things Chinese* (Shanghai: Kelly and Walsh, 1925).

11. Harry Lawton quoted in Margie Akin, "Chinese Ceramics at Agua Mansa," unpublished manuscript, on file at the Department of Anthropology, University of California, Riverside (1988), 2.

12. Loomis, "Medical Art in the Chinese Quarter," 496.

13. J. W. Ames, "A Day in Chinatown," *Lippincott's Magazine* 16 (October 1875): 495–502.

14. J. H. Bates, *Notes of a Tour in Mexico and California* (New York: Burr Printing House, 1897), 123.

15. Rogers, "A Chinese Prescription," 1239.

16. Chinn, *A History of the Chinese in California*, 78.

17. William M. Tisdale, "Chinese Physicians in California," *Lippincott's Magazine* 63 (March 1899): 411–16.

18. Jessica Ching-Yi Kao, "Alternative Health Care Practitioners in a Chinese American Community: A Preliminary Report of Findings," unpublished paper, University of California, Riverside, Tomas Rivera Library (1981); Paul D. Buell and Christopher Muench, "Chinese Medical Recipes from Frontier Seattle," *Annals of the Chinese Historical Society of the Pacific Northwest* (1984): 101.

19. Guarding Liu, *Inside Los Angeles Chinatown* (privately printed, 1948), 204.

20. Tisdale, "Chinese Physicians in California," 412–13.

21. Schwartz, *Chinese Medicine*, 43–45.

22. Tisdale, "Chinese Physicians in California," 412–13.

23. James Bensoussan et al., "Chinese Herbal Medicine for Irritable Bowel Syndrome," *Journal of the American Medical Association* 280, no. 18 (1998): 1586.

24. Schwartz, *Chinese Medicine*, 68.

25. Robin Bishop and Nissi Wang, "Fong Wan, King of the Herbalists," *Gateways: Exploring New Horizons in Chinese Medicine* (spring 1989): 1.

26. Christopher Muench, "Chinese Medicine in America: A Study in Adaption," *Caduceus: A Museum Quarterly for the Health Sciences* 4, no. 1 (spring 1988): 16.

27. William M. Bowen, "Early Chinese Medicine in Southern California," *Gum Saan Journal* 17, no. 1 (June 1994): 5–6.

28. Muench, "Chinese Medicine in America," 14–15.

29. Tisdale, "Chinese Physicians in California," 415.

30. Reported in the Marysville *Daily Appeal,* 29 March 1865.

31. "Bancroft Scrapbooks Chinese Clippings," vol. 9, 415–16 (1981), University of California, Berkeley, Bancroft Library.

32. Tisdale, "Chinese Physicians in California," 412. See also Henry Harris, *California's Medical Story* (San Francisco: Stacey, 1932), 272.

33. Tisdale, "Chinese Physicians in California," 415.

34. Ames, "A Day in Chinatown," 501.

35. Samuel Williams, *City of the Golden Gate: A Description of San Francisco* (San Francisco: Book Club of California, 1875), 21. See also Tisdale, "Chinese Physicians in California," 415.

36. Williams, *City of the Golden Gate,* 35–44.

37. Bishop and Wang, "Fong Wan, King of the Herbalists," 1, 4.

38. Gor Yun Leong, *Chinatown Inside Out* (New York: Barrows Mussey, 1936); Guarding Liu, *Inside Los Angeles Chinatown,* 201; Schwartz, *Chinese Medicine,* 76.

39. Bishop and Wang, "Fong Wan, King of the Herbalists," 1.

40. Thomas W. Wing, *Regain Health Naturally* (privately printed, 1947).

41. Richard Yeh, "The Training and Practice of Traditional Chinese Medicine in California" (paper presented at the Fifth International Conference on the History of Science in China, University of California, San Diego, 1988).

42. William M. Bowen, *The Americanization of Chinese Medicine* (Ann Arbor, Mich.: UMI Dissertation Services, 1993), 95–137.

43. Bowen, *The Americanization of Chinese Medicine,* 95–137.

44. Bowen, *The Americanization of Chinese Medicine,* 138–97.

45. Bowen, *The Americanization of Chinese Medicine,* 138–97.

46. Bowen, *The Americanization of Chinese Medicine,* 325–50.

47. Bowen, *The Americanization of Chinese Medicine,* 394–436.

48. Bowen, *The Americanization of Chinese Medicine,* 138–97.

49. Bowen, *The Americanization of Chinese Medicine,* 512–42.

IV

Influences: From Old World to New World

11

The Chinese Empire Reform Association (Baohuanghui) and the 1905 Anti-American Boycott: The Power of a Voluntary Association

Jane Leung Larson

When Chinese citizens staged a nationwide boycott against American goods in 1905, they hoped to end the U.S. exclusion policy. Although they failed in this goal, they accomplished something far greater. In the view of some scholars, the 1905 boycott marked the beginning of mass politics and modern nationalism in China, prefiguring the republican revolution of 1911 and the May 4 movement of 1919.[1] For the first time, a broad spectrum of Chinese, from the educated elite to illiterate laborers, joined in a common cause, as citizens rather than subjects, to express a political opinion independent of their government. Voluntary associations, such as chambers of commerce, study societies, and even women's organizations, were the engines of the protest, although few had ever before undertaken political action. Equally important were the newspapers that provided not only news of the boycott but its ideological underpinnings and a lively forum for discussion of strategy. Perhaps most crucial for the boycott's rapid development into a mass movement was the contribution of Chinese organizations outside China that provided the impetus for the boycott and substantial organizational and propaganda resources. This chapter reveals new information on the key role of one powerful and sophisticated overseas Chinese organization (the Chinese Empire Reform Association or Baohuanghui 保皇会) in the early and most important stages of planning and publicizing the boycott, and it argues that the association's organizational strengths magnified the political impact of the boycott.

It is a long-standing question how the call to boycott could have galvanized such a rapid and widespread response from people with so little experience of political participation. The boycott has been described as a decentralized, atomized, and even chaotic movement carried out by a variety of organizations with no national coordination or strong leadership.[2] An important clue to the boycott's ultimate success as a social movement may be found in the crucial role of the highly organized Baohuanghui, which provided much of the boycott's initial inspiration, strategy, ideological support, financial backing, propaganda, and information channels, and some of its key personnel.

The boycott was the product of its extraordinary times. The last decade of China's last dynasty, 1900–1911, spawned what some historians have argued was China's most vibrant civil society,[3] marked by the emergence of Western-style voluntary organizations and an independent press.[4] In 1900, the Qing Dynasty court was reeling from the shock of the destruction of Beijing by Western forces retaliating for the Boxer Rebellion. Realizing that the dynasty's only chance for survival was systemic reform, the court began to modernize the country's education, military, and industry to gradually bring about a constitutional monarchy. Chinese citizens were encouraged to organize literary and commercial associations, found schools with modern curricula, publish newspapers and journals, establish societies to teach about constitutional government, and (in 1909) elect provincial assemblies.

As recently as 1898, the Qing government had violently opposed these same reforms. During the Hundred Days of Reform, from June to September 1898, Cantonese philosopher and teacher Kang Youwei 康有为 and the young Qing Emperor Guangxu 光绪 proposed sweeping reforms to establish a constitutional monarchy. The Hundred Days of Reform were ended abruptly by the emperor's powerful aunt, Empress Dowager Ci Xi, who feared the dynasty would be weakened by such changes. She imprisoned the emperor, executed some of the reformers, and sent others, like Kang, into years of exile.

Kang joined the hundreds of thousands of Chinese living overseas who saw more clearly than their compatriots back home how poorly China measured up to countries like Japan. Kang and others (most notably Sun Yatsen) used their relative political freedom abroad to organize reform and revolutionary groups to challenge the Qing. In 1899, Kang founded the Chinese Empire Reform Association, or Protect the Emperor Society (Baohuanghui), in Victoria, British Columbia. The Baohuanghui was to become the largest and possibly the most influential overseas Chinese organization that has ever existed, with chapters throughout the world and a broad reach into China. When compared to the revolutionary organizations founded by Sun, the Baohuanghui was not only far larger but its organizational structure was stronger and more diversified. In fact, one of the Baohuanghui's most unusual characteristics, its extensive network of commercial ventures, foreshadowed an important, non-Leninist activity that has distinguished both the Guomindang and the post-Mao Chinese Communist Party.[5]

The charter of the Los Angeles chapter described the Baohuanghui's goals: "This association aims to save China and must conform to the principle that each of the 400,000,000 Chinese try to do his best in his duty to his country in order to achieve the reforms proclaimed by His Majesty in the year of Wu Xu (1898) [the Hundred Days of Reform]. The purpose of this association is to establish a constitutional government. After this government is established, we will form a large political party to do everything possible to maintain the constitution and be loyal to China."[6] While the Baohuanghui never evolved into a true political party, it was a voluntary association with many modern features, such as bylaws and a dues-paying membership, directed toward explicitly political goals.

New access to the Baohuanghui's internal workings comes from a large collection of primary documents published in China in 1997, the correspondence of a Los Angeles Baohuanghui leader, Tom Leung 譚良 (Tan Zhangxiao 譚张孝), who had close and frequent contact with Kang Youwei and many other association leaders and members all over the world during the Baohuanghui's most active period, the decade beginning in 1899.[7] While most of the materials in the collection are personal letters to Tom Leung from other members, there are many that were obviously circulated widely, being printed, mimeographed, or hand-copied letters sent by individuals or chapters. Charters and drafts of official documents were also distributed to members for their comments. Of special relevance for this chapter, Kang spent much of 1905 with Tom Leung in the United States, and thus the collection includes letters written to Kang himself concerning Baohuanghui involvement in the boycott.

Kang Youwei was Baohuanghui president. His most famous follower, Liang Qichao 梁启超, was vice-president and many of the Baohuanghui's chapters were led by Kang's former students, like Tom Leung, who had attended Kang's Guangzhou school, Thatched Hut among Ten Thousand Trees, where students had first learned about Kang's radical interpretation of Confucianism as a doctrine of reform. Although Kang spent fifteen years in exile and was always on the move, he used the telegraph, printing press, international mail, and grassroots visits to keep in contact with members. However, the organization's success arose less from its strong leader than from its network of branch chapters whose members initiated (and coordinated) so many activities.

Kang himself encouraged the development of the early chapters. His first letter to Tom, dated December 7, 1899, tells how he arrived in Hong Kong from Canada only to find out that Tom had already left Hong Kong for the United States. "People there [in the United States] have been longing for one of us to be there just like yearning for rain during a drought. Now that you are in the U.S., you can follow my orders to dispatch letters to all cities to encourage them to organize a branch association if they do not have one. Please keep me informed of the situation in all cities."[8]

The organization quickly attracted a broad following among overseas Chinese. In its first year, 1899, there were five chapters, all in North America—Victoria, Boston, Seattle, Portland, and San Francisco—but Liang Qichao claimed that there were already ten thousand members.[9] The Baohuanghui grew rapidly using modern political organizing techniques, such as sending respected and well-spoken notables to communities to make speeches, join local organizations, form association chapters, and then pass on the leadership to local leaders.[10] By 1903, when Liang came to the United States for the first time, he listed fifty local chapters and six regional headquarters, with San Francisco hosting the national headquarters. Elsewhere in North America, there were twelve chapters in Canada, headed by the Vancouver office, and nine chapters in Mexico, with Torreón serving as the headquarters. Moreover, Liang reports that more than half to almost all the resident Chinese were association members in the cities of Vancouver, Victoria, and New Westminster, British Columbia.[11] By May 1905, Tom Leung reports there were "160-plus association branches stretching from Southeast Asia and Australia to America and Japan."[12] Kang put the total number of members in 1906 at seventy thousand.[13]

All of the Baohuanghui activities were meant to teach members how to be citizens of a modern society, to build their confidence as individuals and as a nation, and to learn skills, such as banking, that not only would be useful to a modernizing China but would make money for their political cause. The association established newspapers, publishing and translation companies, schools, and military training academies. Its business arm, the Hong Kong-based Commercial Corporation, was meant to raise money for Baohuanghui causes as well as give Chinese a measure of economic control over their destinies. The result was an international conglomerate, largely funded by shares bought by members, involving land speculation; banks in New York, Mexico, and Hong Kong; mines in Guangxi; streetcar lines in Panama and Mexico; even a restaurant in Chicago. Members also raised funds to bring several hundred Chinese students to Japan, the United States, and Europe. They supported a variety of political activities in China, including a series of uprisings and assassination attempts at the turn of the century meant to topple the empress dowager and her conservative court.

Baohuanghui influence spread far beyond its actual membership, through the intellectual authority of its two primary spokesmen, Kang and Liang, and through its use of a new medium, the modern newspaper. The Baohuanghui owned widely read newspapers in Hong Kong, Singapore, Japan, the United States, Canada, the Philippines, Siam, Java, Hawaii, and China.[14] The reform papers attracted a core of dedicated journalists who used the new technique of investigative reporting to cover the political ferment of the times, reaching a broad audience of readers and spurring on the political activists whose protests were being covered.[15] Moreover, the journalists often became activists themselves, creating the news as they were reporting it, as we shall see below.

The Baohuanghui was open to "any patriotic Chinese . . . regardless of surname, native place, sex or religion" (Los Angeles charter). Even active opposition by Qing government representatives abroad during the association's first few years did little to inhibit membership growth.[16] Of great appeal to all Chinese Americans, especially the laborers, who were most threatened by the exclusion policy, was the Baohuanghui's increasingly aggressive role fighting this policy. Liang Qichao reported in 1903 that, in towns where Chinese received the worst treatment from the Americans, he found the most committed Baohuanghui members.[17]

Ironically, according to L. Eve Armentrout Ma, in spite of the exclusion laws and other forms of discrimination, Chinese in the Americas had greater political freedom than those in other parts of the world, especially in Japan, Southeast Asia, and China, where the activities of organizations were restricted or suppressed.[18] But, the isolation and discrimination suffered by Chinese in the United States turned their attention back to China, where the potential for political change must have never seemed greater. Thus, the Baohuanghui, while taking some action in the United States to influence American immigration policy, was to concentrate most of its efforts and money on supporting the 1905–1906 boycott of American goods in China.

The immigration of Chinese to the United States was the subject of three treaties between the two countries, beginning in 1868 with the Burlingame Treaty, which was initiated by the United States to *encourage* the economically useful migration of Chinese laborers to take part in the California gold rush and the building of the railroads. However, by the 1870s a depression and the completion of the railroads created a spate of anti-Chinese legislation in the West. Thus, in 1880, a weak China was pressured to sign a new treaty allowing the United States to enact legislation restricting Chinese laborers. This opened the way for the first Chinese Exclusion Act, passed in 1882, which suspended immigration of Chinese laborers to the United States for ten years. The act became increasingly restrictive with further legislation in 1888, 1892, 1893, 1894, 1898, and 1902. Enraged but powerless, the Qing government signed the 1894 Gresham-Yang Treaty, which excluded all Chinese except for a few exempt categories, such as officials and merchants. When this treaty expired in 1904, the Chinese government refused to renew it and asked to negotiate a less onerous agreement.

In February 1905, treaty negotiations in Washington had stalled, following the exchange between August 1904 and January 1905 of a series of "dueling drafts" of the new treaty written by the Chinese and the American governments, each of which was promptly rejected in turn by Liang Cheng, the Chinese minister to the United States, or by the U.S. Department of Commerce and Labor. The American side wanted to continue to exclude all Chinese laborers as well as many merchants and students, and introduce new registration of nonlaborers admitted to the United States. The Chinese government, using the argument of reciprocity, agreed to return to the American policy of excluding only laborers, with the condition that the Chinese could bar American laborers from entering China. Furthermore, the Chinese argued that the United States should treat Chinese equally with other Asians and suggested that Chinese laborers be admitted on the same basis as other Asians to the Philippines and Hawaii. The Chinese side also demanded better treatment of the "exempt classes" of Chinese by immigration officials.[19] In May 1905, activists in China, urged on by Kang and Baohuanghui leaders, stepped directly into the diplomatic impasse and dramatically changed the dynamic of this international confrontation.

It is significant that Kang was in the United States during the most intense period of the boycott's planning and implementation, for it highlights the role of the Baohuanghui in the movement. Kang had finally arrived in the United States in February 1905, after years of being refused entry, thwarted by the combined efforts of Qing officials in the United States and the Exclusion Act, which required that he obtain a section 6 certificate from the Chinese government certifying that he was not a laborer, an impossibility given his status as an enemy of the Chinese state.

From March to May, Kang Youwei stayed in Los Angeles in a house rented for him by Tom Leung in Westlake Park, which he described in a poem: "Day after day I walked around, leaning on my cane, and roamed the islands across the wooden bridge. All over the slopes, flowers flourished, and the meadows served as a carpet for me and my books."[20] While his stay allowed him to "forget the worries of one in exile," Kang kept active with Baohuanghui projects, from the Western Military Academy (a Baohuanghui training program for Chinese cadets) to meeting with potential shareholders for the recently formed Commercial Corporation.

While in Los Angeles, Kang sent a telegram to followers in Shanghai, Hong Kong (Baohuanghui headquarters), and Yokohama (where Liang Qichao was). It read:

> The United States has extended the exclusion treaty, but Minister Liang has refused to sign it. Now the U.S. government has sent an envoy to Beijing [U.S. Minister William Rockhill], to ask the Foreign Ministry to sign the agreement. He left ten days ago. This concerns the livelihood of the Chinese people, especially the Cantonese, because they earn tens of millions of dollars here every year. If we are able to get rid of the treaty, it could greatly increase our annual income. Chinese people's lives are impoverished. If the laborers are completely cut off from working in the United States, then the situation inside China will certainly turn into great disorder. Now, all the cities have sent telegrams to the Foreign Ministry to urge them to fight against the treaty. But the Foreign Ministry is cowardly and, if frightened by the United States, will sign it. This is a matter of life or death for our Chinese. I hope you can organize a rally and urge everyone to send telegrams to our government and to provincial governors, appealing for help. At the same time, we should use newspapers to inspire people's enthusiasm. We may succeed in remedying this situation. Save all your expenses to send to us later for reimbursement; please don't be stingy with small expenses. The Chinese in America will continue to give financial support.[21]

In his telegram, Kang did not mention a boycott, but the idea had been floated years before by a Baohuanghui activist. The blueprint for a boycott of American goods to protest Chinese exclusion is widely credited to one of Kang's students, Chen Jiyan 陈继俨 [22] the editor of the association's Hawaii newspaper, New China Daily (Xin zhongguo ribao 新中国日报).[23] His editorials were reprinted in other reform newspapers, and he also came to San Francisco in 1903 to promote the idea among merchants and the Chinese Six Companies.[24]

No action was taken until 1905, when association leaders found themselves with sufficient organizational resources, including a large Chinese American membership and Baohuanghui-funded newspapers and publishing houses in China. The motivation was largely nationalistic, the exclusion policy being seen as just one more example of a foreign country bullying a weak China. In the words of Liang Qichao, writing after the boycott had been organized, "Chinese people's hatred and anger due to the bitterness caused by the Exclusion Act did not just begin today, nor is it limited to only a portion of our people. Since this act brings disgrace to our country and hurts business, it does only damage and brings no benefit. . . . Now, taking advantage of the opportunity to change the treaty, the Chinese are compelled by their shared hatred of this act to plan a way to deal with it. This is a patriotic development for the Chinese people."[25]

After receiving Kang's telegram in late April or early May 1905, Liang Qichao wrote that "I have had constant and urgent communications with Shanghai and Hong Kong by letter and telegram to discuss how to handle this problem." Although he calls for pressure on the Beijing government to maintain its stand against the Americans, he says "we should be aware that if the power of citizens does not provide a backup force, the government still might timidly bungle matters." Chen Jiyan's Honolulu editorials had taken as a model a Japanese boycott against the French, who were giving assistance to Russia's Baltic Fleet during the Russo-Japanese War. Liang asks,

> Why doesn't China think about applying the same methods to encourage our comrades in the commercial world to protest against the United States? Some of us may be afraid that Chinese are just like loose sand that can't easily be gathered together. I and others think we should try. Anyway, no matter whether we succeed or not, there will be benefit and no harm. The question is: in which city should we begin? In fact, Shanghai and Hong Kong are the essential cities, especially Shanghai, which is situated at the mouth of the Yangzi River. It is the number one commercial city in China. So, it has the greatest power to do things.
>
> Shi Bao (Eastern Times 時報), a newspaper published by our party [in Shanghai], now sells 10,000 copies a day. Government officials all over the country read this paper every day. The opinions it expresses have the most power. Thus, I had the paper publish the telegram from President Kang, and every day write articles to explain and criticize, as well as to describe in detail the importance of this matter. At the same time, we should go to each businessman to make contact and drum up support. Owing to the emperor's order, people in all provinces are now setting up chambers of commerce 商會. Though they may exist in name only and not in reality, they still can be used to our advantage in

organizing this project. So, we want to begin with the Chamber of Commerce in Shanghai. We also think that this matter is closest to Guangdong people and, thus, they should be the first group to make proposals. This can make it easier for us to succeed.

We learn this from a lengthy June 7, 1905, letter written by Liang to update members on the boycott's progress and including the text of the telegram and many other documents relating to the boycott. Liang says, "If we hadn't got the telegram from President Kang, then people in China wouldn't have known the truth."[26]

Shi Bao had been established the year before, in 1904, when Kang sent Liang undercover from Japan into Shanghai to found the paper along with two other reformers who also had been living in Japan, Di Baoxian 狄葆賢 and Luo Xiaogao 羅孝高. Di had a long and distinguished history as a reformer and had been allied with Kang as early as 1895. He also had experience in Shanghai as a Baohuanghui organizer of several military operations to overthrow the empress dowager during the Boxer Rebellion.[27] In 1905, *Shi Bao* was supported by the Baohuanghui, and the newspaper should be seen as representing Baohuanghui political views.[28] A letter written to Kang from two *Shi Bao* staff members, Gao De 高德 and Gao Shan 高山 (possibly aliases for Di Baoxian and Luo Xiaogao), promoted *Shi Bao* as worthy of more funds for expansion, saying the paper "will be the vanguard of our party when we succeed and rule China."[29]

In fact, it was *Shi Bao* that spearheaded the boycott in China, after receiving Kang's telegram.[30] On June 22, Gao De and Gao Shan reported to Kang:

Last month we received your telegram and learned that the American minister tried to force us to renew the treaty. We immediately began to use *every ounce* of our strength to deal with this. First, we talked secretly with two of the most respected and influential people in Shanghai and decided to boycott American products. Then we sent people to seek help. We recruited more than twenty powerful people. The most important helpers are Yang Jingqing 杨京卿 and Daotai Zeng Shaoqing 曾少卿. All are members of the Chamber of Commerce.[31]

Zeng, a wealthy merchant from Fujian, would later head the Shanghai Chamber of Commerce, one of the newly established associations that the Qing government had encouraged to promote its reforms. A member of the new class of merchant-gentry (shenshang 绅商), Zeng had purchased an imperial title, *daotai* 道台 (intendant of a circuit, that is, a superintendent of a district), and he would become the official leader of the boycott.

On May 10, the Shanghai Chamber of Commerce held a meeting in the guild hall of the Guangdong Association that was attended by as many as several thousand. After hearing the boycott leaders read an article by Liang Qichao entitled "The Story of the Exclusion of Chinese Laborers," they formulated the outlines of a boycott:

1. Don't buy any American merchandise.
2. Chinese merchandise must not be exported to the United States.
3. Workers must not unload American merchandise arriving in port.
4. All Chinese employees employed by American firms, including compradors, secretaries, interpreters, and waiters, must quit their jobs.
5. Send these resolutions by telegram to the Foreign Ministry in Beijing, the Board of Trade, the governors and governors-general of all provinces, and the imperial envoy of China in Washington, D.C., and recommend to them that the treaty be abolished.
6. Inform the American Chamber of Commerce in Shanghai of our resolutions and ask them to transmit them to the U.S. consulate in Shanghai, to pass on to the U.S. government.
7. Send these resolutions by telegram to all cities in China, asking them to gather people together to discuss and carry out the resolutions and enhance our momentum and strength.[32]

Following the meeting, Liang reports that the resolutions were sent to thirty cities around China and twenty-one replied, saying they would carry them out. In Shanghai, schools and religious groups made resolutions that "all students who are studying in schools operated by Americans should leave them," and "all people who have joined American churches should leave them and join English or German churches." A second general meeting on May 16 in Shanghai reaffirmed the decision to boycott, but postponed the start until August 1, by which time it was hoped that the American government would back down.

While the Shanghai Chamber of Commerce led the boycott efforts, *Shi Bao* continued to organize on other fronts, sending people to Beijing to persuade Qing officials not to give in to American pressure, cabling other newspapers to ask for their help, and reporting on all boycott activities that were not "confidential or cannot be made public." *Shi Bao* also began to turn down advertisements from Americans, adding that, in doing so, we may lose several hundred dollars a month, but we have to do it for our country. When the boycott is put into practice, we will distribute more fliers and publish a survey of American goods. We also have to send more people to inland provinces to lobby in hopes that [the boycott] will arouse the whole country. This requires a considerable amount of money. . . . The comrades overseas are all enthusiastic about this matter. If you can immediately send the money you have raised, we can start to make the necessary arrangements.[33]

What triggered Kang's urgent telegram to his followers in Shanghai, Japan, and Hong Kong? Before Kang left Los Angeles in mid-May, he learned of an unusual event that took place in Tom Leung's home—the arrest of a Qing official who was also an open supporter of Kang's. The official, Vice Commissioner Wong Kai Kah (Huang Kaijia) 黃 开 甲, probably met Tom Leung through Tom's brother-in-law, Huang Qiaokai 黃 翘 开, who was part of the Chinese delegation to the 1904 St. Louis Louisiana Purchase Exposition.[34] Wong headed the delegation, no doubt appointed because he was an eloquent English speaker from Guangzhou who at age thirteen in 1872 had gone to study in the United States with the Chinese Educational Mission and then had returned in 1881 to work in Shanghai as a translator and secretary to officials and diplomats.[35] Back in the United States, Wong was shocked to find that Chinese who came to work on or participate in the St. Louis exposition, laborers and merchants alike, had to travel under sixty-one special rules that did not apply to participants from other countries. Wong Kai Kah wrote an article in the January 1904 *North American Review* condemning the exclusion policy and describing the Chinese merchants' reaction to the sixty-one rules: "Every merchant in whom there was incited a desire to participate in the Fair, who made preparations, at expense of time and money, and who changed his determination upon the publication of these rules, will not bear a kindly sentiment towards the United States in his business dealings; he, no doubt, from personal grievances, either real or fancied, will become an agitator, where otherwise he might have remained passive." Wong further suggests that retaliation, such as a boycott, was possible.[36]

After the fair closed in December 1904, Wong Kai Kah, probably accompanied by Tom's nephew, came to Los Angeles, where he stayed with Tom Leung for several months.[37] For a Qing official, Wong was extraordinarily supportive of the Baohuanghui cause, no doubt in part because of his American education and the influence of Yung Wing, who had organized the Chinese Educational Mission and was a prominent follower of Kang's. The *Los Angeles Times* reports that Wong gave the welcoming speech at the banquet for Kang Youwei when he arrived in Los Angeles in March 1905, "voic[ing] in sturdy terms the devotion of the Chinese people to the Emperor and His Excellency Kang Yu-wei, whom he hoped to see in power with the Emperor restored to his pre-rogatives."[38] On March 21, immigration officials staged a nighttime raid at Tom Leung's home, wrongly thinking Wong's papers had expired, and Wong, not one to take such an injustice lightly, filed a formal complaint of harass-ment with the U.S. State Department. A June 7, 1905, *Los Angeles Times* story on this incident began, "It has just transpired that the arrest of a Chinaman in Los Angeles was the direct means of bringing about the threat of a boycott of all American goods in China—the problem that the President is laboring with." The article claimed that after the arrest, Wong "straightway sent over an edict [to China] and put the grand kibosh on American goods therein. This was the beginning of the boycott." We have no confirmation that Wong sent such an edict or had any direct role in setting off the boycott, though he had extensive contacts in Shanghai, where the boycott started, and had actually re-turned to China (and Shanghai) during the time that the boycott was being planned. We also know that Wong landed on American shores again on Au-gust 15, as China's representative to the Portsmouth Peace Conference con-cluding the Russo-Japanese War. He made this statement to the press upon ar-rival in San Francisco: "I want it to be understood that there is not an official in China who has anything to do with the boycott, and as a last word I will say that it is the earnest desire of my government to have the most friendly rela-tions with the United States."[39]

Given the circumstances described above, it is plausible that Wong Kai Kah had some role in inspiring the boycott or provoking Kang to take action. He may also have served as a conduit of communication between the United States and China for boycott activists and sympathizers, including Qing gov-ernment officials. But, it was certainly not he alone who mobilized China's first national mass movement. The Tom Leung documents show how rapidly the activists escalated their protests, with only a few days ellapsing between the receipt of Kang's telegram, their sending telegrams to the Foreign Ministry in Beijing, and the decision to organize a national boycott against the United States.

The Chinese were feeling confident after seeing the reaction of the Ameri-can minister, William Rockhill, upon arriving in Shanghai on May 20. In a let-ter to Kang from Mai Menghua 麦猛华 one of Kang's former students who was in Shanghai working with *Shi Bao*, this reaction is described:

It happened that the American minister had just arrived in Shanghai and was greatly shocked upon learning of the situation. He immediately requested a meeting with the board of directors [of the Chamber of Commerce] and tried to convince them [that the treaty does not intend to prevent Chinese people from entering the work force]. . . . The board of directors was firm in attitude. The American minister could not do anything about it, only saying the treaty was misunderstood . . . . Judging from his words and attitude, I think he was afraid. Our foreign ministry has promised us a vigorous fight. The American minister has been intimidated. . . . It is evident the hard line is the only way in foreign affairs. When we advance, they retreat. . . .[40]

Shi Bao played such a key role in advocating for the boycott that Gao De and Gao Shan report, "as a result, the American minister has often found fault with *Shi Bao*."[41] Rockhill saw the significance of this rapidly developing press, and wrote President Theodore Roosevelt in July, saying, "There is now coming into existence in China a public opinion and a native press, both crude and usually misinformed, but nevertheless it is a public opinion and the [Chinese] Government knows it and recognizes that it must be counted with. This public opinion and press are at least developing a national spirit in China."[42]

In the United States, the opinions of Chinese Americans were for the first time heeded by politicians. The Baohuanghui was only one of many Chinese American organizations that supported the boycott, but it wielded the greatest influence on American politics. Kang Youwei had left Los Angeles in May 1905 with a small entourage (including Tom Leung) on a seven-month journey around the United States to meet Baohuanghui members and learn about American society. He also used his excellent reputation with Americans to great advantage by explaining the Chinese position on the exclusion policy. For example, in St. Louis, he made a speech before the American Baptist Missionary Union Convention, which then passed a resolution calling for the easing of the exclusion acts.[43] This group, like many other American church and academic organizations, saw the exclusion policy as threatening their interests in China, which included a substantial missionary presence and American-run high schools and colleges (with twenty thousand students in 1905).[44]

Kang would also meet twice with President Roosevelt in June concerning the boycott and exclusion policy. Roosevelt was seeking to temper the Baohuanghui demands for a complete end to the exclusion policy, while Kang wanted to impress upon Roosevelt the harshness and unfairness of both the laws and their enforcement, which as applied by the Immigration Bureau went

far beyond the law in their restrictions on Chinese immigration. While Roosevelt was indeed sympathetic to Kang's presentation of the Chinese case, he
was only able to issue executive orders in hopes of alleviating the poor treatment of the exempt classes of Chinese who had to undergo detention upon
entry to the United States. According to McKee, "Roosevelt lacked the authority to dissolve the Association or to make enough concessions to conciliate it;
he could only keep channels of communication open and hope for a more favorable turn of events later."[45]

Kang wrote a twenty-six-page typed letter to Roosevelt on January 30,
1906, when the effects of the boycott were being felt and the U.S. Congress was
debating the issue. Although some scholars have suggested that the Baohuanghui, given the scholar/gentry background of its leaders and the critical
role of merchants in the boycott, did not object in principle to the U.S. exclusion of laborers,[46] this letter indicates quite the opposite:

> Is there any innate or inherent difference between a laborer and a student, or a
> merchant? Some, having been students or merchants at one time, on becoming
> poor, perform manual labor for a livelihood.
>
> In your schools and colleges are countless students who acquire their educa-
> tion by all sorts of manual labor. But if a poor Chinese student works in like
> manner through school or college, he is incarcerated and sent back to China. Is
> there any justice in that? Whether true or not, it looks as though the dignity of
> labor is but a cant phrase and that while the rich are courted, the poor are de-
> ported.[47]

Another new phenomenon was the willingness of Chinese Americans to
put their money and their energy where their hearts were. A united front organization was formed: the General Society of Chinese Residing in the United
States for the Opposing of the Exclusion Treaty. Its goal was to collect a dollar
from each Chinese person in the United States (about 100,000). By the end of
1905 about $15,000 had been collected.[48] Kang mentions a United Defense As-
sociation (Lianweihui, 联卫会), which had local chapters and raised thousands of dollars to help with the boycott organizing costs in China and with
supporting those who lost their jobs by participating in the action.[49] The
Shanghai boycott organizers made it clear that while they would hold a protest
rally, distribute fliers, and send telegrams to government officials, "we are not
able to raise funds in Shanghai. We expect support from the United States.
Without financial support, we cannot mobilize the public. . . . We hope you
can raise funds in America."[50] Tom Leung raised $200 for the movement in

China, which he sent directly to the Baohuanghui in Hong Kong for forwarding to Guangzhou.[51]

However, treaty negotiations between the United States and China failed, and the boycott started on July 20 in Shanghai.[52] Kuang Shoumin 鄺壽民 who headed the Commercial Corporation in Hong Kong, told how the movement had shaken Guangdong Province, saying that "the sale of American goods has been stopped." However, "people in Hong Kong, being restricted by British law, could not meet openly," but used the commercial guilds to disguise their activities. However, after more organizing, Kuang exults, "People in Hong Kong gradually dare to talk about the movement. This is the beginning of civil rights in China!"[53]

The boycott lasted at least until May 1906 and extended to Fujian and Guangdong in the south, to Tianjin and Beijing in the north, and to the central Yangzi valley as far as Chongqing,[54] but the Shanghai area and Guangdong Province were the most actively involved. The economic impact on U.S.-China trade was considerable and extended past the boycott's end, as reported in 1908 by U.S. Secretary of Commerce and Labor Oscar Straus, who said that American exports to China in 1905 were $57 million and had fallen to $26 million in 1907.[55] Standard Oil, a company with a tremendous stake in the China trade and which had lobbied the U.S. government for modification of the exclusion laws, reported that it sold ninety thousand cases of oil a month in Guangzhou before May 1905, and only nineteen thousand cases a month in November of that year.[56]

By October 1906, the Qing government saw no hope of negotiating a nondiscriminatory treaty acceptable to its people and refused to renew the Gresham-Yang treaty.[57] President Roosevelt, pressured by the boycott as well as by heavy lobbying by business, missionary, and academic interests and growing public opposition to exclusion on the basis of race, attempted to get Congress to pass legislation in 1906 to liberalize the policy. However, Congress would not act, and Roosevelt had to be content with making administrative improvements.[58] He also took positive steps to appease Chinese students, who had been so heavily involved in the boycott, by using Boxer indemnity funds for scholarships to encourage them to come to the United States rather than go to Japan or Europe.[59]

The boycott was new ground for citizen action by Chinese, overseas and in China, both in their relationship with their own as well as with a foreign government. Nongovernmental organizations and individual citizens took independent stands, backing up the negotiations of the rather weak Chinese government with the weight of strongly expressed public opinion. The most powerful statement to the U.S. government was the boycott itself, which was an economic challenge that the Qing government could never have organized itself. This separate role for "civil society" allowed the Qing government to dissociate itself from the boycott when the U.S. government began to apply pressure.[60] Even more significant, perhaps, Chinese were now communicating directly with foreign governments and organizations, with no obstruction from their own government, Kang's meeting with Roosevelt being the most striking example. But this happened in China as well. In Shanghai, for example, Liang Qichao tells how the Chamber of Commerce met on May 20 with the American minister William Rockhill, who told the businessmen that the Chinese minister to the United States, Liang Cheng, had no objections to the treaty extension; on May 23, Minister Liang telegraphed the organizers directly and informed them otherwise.[61] The American consul in Shanghai, James Davidson, submitted lengthy articles to *Shi Bao* explaining the American point of view on Chinese exclusion, which were published along with *Shi Bao*'s rebuttals and then reprinted with the rebuttals as open letters to Baohuanghui members around the world.[62]

As the Chinese planned and carried out the 1905 boycott, they were transforming China's political arena.[63] Guanhua Wang describes how telegrams were used for the first time to coordinate and mobilize a popular movement not only across China but between China and foreign countries. The boycott popularized a whole new vocabulary and writing style that brought political ideas to a much broader audience than in the past. New propaganda media were developed, including newspapers, novels, posters, and protest songs. Public speaking became a popular way to attract boycott participants, and all kinds of persons went on speaking tours, including women and students.

Wang tells how the newly politicized merchant-gentry and intellectuals led the boycott, with the merchants for the first time in the center of action. The merchant organizations were joined by a variety of associations actively involved in the boycott, and Wang says that "it is no coincidence that the movement was most active in regions where voluntary asssociations were most numerous."[64] Yet he finds even organizations of the same type, such as chambers of commerce, lacked established horizontal communication or administrative channels across locales, and thus operated quite independently in planning boycott activities, without much organizational coordination or national leadership. Overlaying the decentralized boycott activities was the powerful organizational influence of the Baohuanghui, which controlled certain key media (*Shi Bao* in Shanghai as well as newspapers in Guangzhou, Beijing, Tianjin, and

Hankou)[65] and had great suasive power over reform-oriented organizations, such as the Shanghai Chamber of Commerce, that were critical to the decision to boycott. This helps explain why in the initial stages of the boycott there was so much agreement in boycott messages and actions taken throughout the nation.

As the boycott developed, the Baohuanghui role became diffuse as more and more voices were heard. By the time all boycott actions ceased, a year after they began, many boycott leaders found themselves in positions of influence, particularly in the constitutionalist movement that began around this time. The boycott's general leader, Zeng Shaoqing, was active in a national group calling for the convening of a parliament, and Chen Jiyan, the Honolulu editor, took over the newspaper of Guangzhou's self-government association in 1907.[66] The Baohuanghui even moved some of its political activities to China. In 1907, the Political Culture Association (Zhengwenshe, 政聞社 founded by Liang Qichao in Japan) was inaugurated in Shanghai, using some of its merchant contacts from the boycott, and then spread rapidly throughout the country. Its purpose was to hasten the initiation of a constitutional government and to guarantee that citizens had rights and responsibilities in the new system. Even though the Zhengwenshe was suppressed by the Qing government in August 1908, its ideas were taken up by other groups. Mass action continued to be led by the Baohuanghui, which in 1908 staged another boycott, this time of Japanese products (the *Tatsu Maru* affair), again with much support from overseas members.[67]

By 1908, the power of the voluntary association had vivid meaning for many Chinese, brought about in part through the Baohuanghui and its many organizational arms. The experience of "civil society" was now a reality for Chinese who had participated in or supported the 1905 and 1908 boycotts, both in China and abroad. These boycotts created the template for succeeding popular movements and heightened the expectations for change whose disappointment would ultimately topple the Qing in 1911.

NOTES

1. Sin-kiong Wong, "The Genesis of Popular Movements in Modern China: A Study of the Anti-American Boycott of 1905–06" (Ph.D. dissertation, Indiana University, 1995); Akira Iriye, "Public Opinion and Foreign Policy: The Case of Late Ch'ing China," in *Approaches to Modern Chinese History*, ed. Albert Feuerwerker, Rhoads Murphey, and Mary C. Wright (Berkeley: University of California Press, 1967), 226; Edward J. M. Rhoads, "Nationalism and Xenophobia in Kwangtung (1905–1906): The Canton Anti-American Boycott and the Lienchow Anti-Missionary Uprising," *Papers on China* 16 (1962): 154; Guanhua Wang, *In Search of*

Justice: The 1905–1906 Chinese Anti-American Boycott (Cambridge: Harvard University Asia Center, 2001).

2. Margaret Field, "The Chinese Boycott of 1905," *Papers on China* 11 (1957).

3. Those "institutions and social groups intermediary between the state and private life" that are "able to influence (though not dominate) the state." Peter Zarrow, "Liang Qichao and the Notion of Civil Society in Republican China," in *Imagining the People: Chinese Intellectuals and the Concept of Citizenship, 1890–1920*, ed. Joshua A. Fogel and Peter G. Zarrow (Armonk, N.Y.: Sharpe, 1997), 232, 235.

4. Mary Backus Rankin, "Some Observations on a Chinese Public Sphere," *Modern China* 19, no. 2 (April 1993): 173–74; Joshua A. Fogel and Peter G. Zarrow, ed., *Imagining the People: Chinese Intellectuals and the Concept of Citizenship, 1890–1920* (Armonk, N.Y.: Sharpe, 1997); Wm. Theodore DeBary, *Asian Values and Human Rights: A Confucian Communitarian Perspective*, (Cambridge, Mass.: Harvard University Press, 1998), 116–17; Mary Clabaugh Wright, "Introduction: The Rising Tide of Change," in *China in Revolution: The First Phase, 1900–1913*, ed. Mary Clabaugh Wright (New Haven, Conn.: Yale University Press, 1968), 1–63; Iriye, "Public Opinion and Foreign Policy," 223. Joan Judge, *Print and Politics: "Shibao" and the Culture of Reform in Late Qing China* (Stanford: Stanford University Press, 1996) emphasizes the unique role of the late Qing press in helping create a demand for the institution of a civil society.

5. It is regrettable that the Baohuanghui has been so little studied by scholars in either the United States or China. Two excellent sources of information on the activities of the organization in the United States and Canada are L. Eve Armentrout Ma, *Revolutionaries, Monarchists, and Chinatowns: Chinese Politics in the Americas and the 1911 Revolution* (Honolulu: University of Hawaii Press, 1990) and Robert Leo Worden, "Chinese Reformer in Exile: The North American Phase of the Travels of K'ang Yu-wei, 1899–1909" (Ph.D. dissertation, Georgetown University, Washington, D.C., 1972).

6. "Luoshengjili Baohuanghui Zhangcheng" 罗省技利保皇会章程 (Los Angeles Baohuanghui Charter), in *Kang Youwei yu Baohuang Hui-Tan Liang Zai Meiguo Suocang Ziliao Huibian* 康有为与保皇会—谭良在美国所藏资料汇编 (Kang Youwei and the Baohuang Hui: a compilation of materials collected by Tom Leung in the United States), ed. Fang Zhiqin 方志钦 (Tianjin: Tianjin Guji Chubanshe [Tianjin Ancient Books Publishing House], 1997), 384 (#111, November 1903). The numbers in the citations refer to the document number on the original documents that can be found in the University of California, Los Angeles (UCLA), East Asian Library collection.

7. Fang, *Kang Youwei yu Baohuang Hui*. Tan Zhangxiao 谭张孝 , known in the United States as Tom Leung 谭良 , a student of Kang's in the 1890s, was not in the top tier of

association leaders under Kang (such as Kang's most famous disciples, Liang Qichao, Xu Qin , Liang 徐勤 Qitian or Ou 梁启田 Jujia), but 欧榘甲 was certainly in the second tier as a leader of the Los Angeles Baohuanghui in the early 1900s. Tom Leung came from Gum Jook (Ganzhu), Sun 甘竹 Duck (Shunde) 顺德 county, Guangdong Province. Tom first came to the United States in 1899 to assist his cousin, Tan Fuyuan 谭富圆 , an herbalist in Los Angeles, and later began his own business, the T. Leung Herb Co. He was my grandfather.

8. "Kang Youwei zhi Tan Zhangxiao Shu" 康有为致谭张孝书 (Letter from Kang Youwei to Tan Zhangxiao), in *Kang Youwei yu Baohuang Hui*, 25 (#502, December 7, 1899).

9. Jung-pang Lo, *K'ang Yu-wei: A Biography and a Symposium* (Tucson: University of Arizona Press, 1967), 258.

10. Ma, *Revolutionaries, Monarchists, and Chinatowns*, 161.

11. Worden, "Chinese Reformer in Exile," 77.

12. Tan Zhangxiao 谭张孝 (Tom Leung), "Jinggao Gebu Tongzhi Shu" 敬告各埠同志书 (Notice to comrades of all cities), in Fang, *Kang Youwei yu Baohuang Hui*, 223 (#579, May 1, 1905).

13. Worden, "Chinese Reformer in Exile," 78.

14. This refers specifically to newspapers during 1904–1909, Lo, *K'ang Yu-wei*, 270.

15. Joan Judge, "Publicists and Populists: Including the Common People in the Late Qing New Citizen Ideal," in Fogel and Zarrow, *Imagining the People*, 165–82.

16. Ma, *Revolutionaries, Monarchists, and Chinatowns*, 159.

17. Ma, *Revolutionaries, Monarchists, and Chinatowns*, 93.

18. Ma, *Revolutionaries, Monarchists, and Chinatown*, 2–3.

19. Delber L. McKee, *Chinese Exclusion versus the Open Door Policy, 1900–1906: Clashes over China Policy in the Roosevelt Era* (Detroit: Wayne State University Press, 1977), 100–102.

20. Kang Youwei, "Zhuisi Luosheng Xihu Gu Zhai" 追思羅生西湖故宅 (Poem, recalling my old home at Westlake in Los Angeles), in Fang, *Kang Youwei yu Baohuang Hui*, 90 (#350, September 18–24, 1905).

21. "Liang Qichao zhi Gebu Liewei Tongzhi Yixiong Shu" 梁启超致各埠列位同志义兄书 (Letter from Liang Qichao to all comrades in all cities), in Fang, *Kang Youwei yu Baohuang Hui*, 113 (#578, June 7, 1905). Rockhill apparently left for China on April 13

(Chang Tsun-wu, *Agitation against the Sino-American Exclusion Treaty* 中美工约风潮 [Taipei: Central Research Institute, 1965], 32), so this telegram may have been sent around April 23.

22. Also known as Chen Yikan 陳儀侃.

23. Chang, *Agitation against the Sino-American Exclusion Treaty*, 27–28.

24. McKee, *Chinese Exclusion versus the Open Door Policy,* 110; Iriye, "Public Opinion and Foreign Policy," 224; Ma, *Revolutionaries, Monarchists, and Chinatowns,* 93.

25. Letter from Liang Qichao to all comrades in all cities, in Fang, *Kang Youwei yu Baohuang Hui,* 122 (#578, June 7, 1905).

26. Letter from Liang Qichao to all comrades in all cities, in Fang, *Kang Youwei yu Baohuang Hui,* 113–28 (#578, June 7, 1905).

27. Judge, *Print and Politics,* 27, 32, 253.

28. Later on, by 1907, the paper's demands for funds were beyond Baohuanghui's capacities, and its editorial stance was also increasingly independent. Judge, *Print and Politics,* 48–53.

29. "Gao De Gao Shan zhi Kang Youwei Shu" 高德高山致康有为书 (Letter from Gao De and Gao Shan to Kang Youwei), in Fang, *Kang Youwei yu Baohuang Hui,* 321–22 (#183, June 22, 1905).

30. Letter from Liang Qichao to all comrades in all cities, in Fang, *Kang Youwei yu Baohuang Hui,* 113 (#578, June 7, 1905).

31. Letter from Gao De and Gao Shan to Kang Youwei, in Fang, *Kang Youwei yu Baohuang Hui,* 321.

32. Letter from Liang Qichao to all comrades in all cities, in Fang, *Kang Youwei yu Baohuang Hui,* 114–15 (#578, June 7, 1905).

33. Letter from Gao De and Gao Shan to Kang Youwei, in Fang, *Kang Youwei yu Baohuang Hui,* 322.

34. Huang Qijun 黄启俊 to Tom Leung, circa fall 1904, Tom Leung papers at UCLA East Asian Library, #267. According to Huang Qijun, his son Huang Qiaokai (also known as Chuda 处达 or Wong Chetat) was hired to procure Chinese products for the fair and got this position because the son was a friend of Wong Kai Kah.

35. Thomas E. LaFargue, *China's First Hundred* (Pullman: State College of Washington, 1942), 123.

36. Wong Kai Kah, "A Menace to America's Oriental Trade," *North American Review* 178 (January 1904): 424.

37. Eugene Anschel, *Homer Lea, Sun Yat-Sen and the Chinese Revolution* (New York: Praeger, 1984), 45.

38. *Los Angeles Times,* 19 March 1905.

39. "Hawaii Bred Boycott; Report Brought in with Imperial Trade Commissioner," *New York Tribune,* 16 August 1905. Wong remained in the United States until October 1905. This and other biographical information is found in LaFargue, *China's First Hundred,* and Anschel, *Homer Lea, Sun Yat-Sen and the Chinese Revolution.*

40. "Mai Menghua zhi Kang Youwei Shu" 麦孟华致康有为书 (Letter from Mai Menghua to Kang Youwei), in Fang, *Kang Youwei yu Baohuang Hui,* 318–20 (#184, June 1, 1905).

41. Letter from Gao De and Gao Shan to Kang Youwei, in Fang, *Kang Youwei yu Baohuang Hui,* 322 (#183, 6/22/1905).

42. Iriye, "Public Opinion and Foreign Policy," 228.

43. Worden, "Chinese Reformer in Exile," 265.

44. McKee, *Chinese Exclusion versus the Open Door Policy,* 194.

45. McKee, *Chinese Exclusion versus the Open Door Policy,* 132.

46. Adam McKeown, "Conceptualizing Chinese Diasporas, 1842 to 1949," *Journal of Asian Studies* 58, no. 2 (1999): 325; Ma, *Revolutionaries, Monarchists, and Chinatowns,* 114.

47. Letter of K'ang Yu-wei to Theodore Roosevelt, January 30, 1906, in Worden, "Chinese Reformer in Exile," 304. Both Kang and his Chinese American followers were willing to negotiate on the issue of the exclusion of laborers, as demonstrated by Kang's acknowledgment in this letter that given the political impossibility of a repeal of exclusion, "any relaxation of the severities of the present law would be welcome" (Worden, 302). Immigration Bureau inspector John Endicott Gardner also reports that from August 1905 meetings with San Francisco Baohuanghui leaders that they would accept the exclusion of laborers if "higher classes of Chinese" were allowed easier entry. Delber L. McKee, "The Chinese Boycott of 1905–1906 Reconsidered: The Role of Chinese Americans," *Pacific Historical Review* 55 (May 1986): 184–85.

48. Shih-shan Henry Tsai, *China and the Overseas Chinese in the United States, 1868–1911* (Fayetteville: University of Arkansas Press, 1983), 114.

49. "Ju Jinyue Chuandan—Lü Mei Huaren Lai Gao" 拒禁约传单—旅美华人来稿 (Leaflet opposing the Exclusion Treaty—manuscript from Chinese living in America), in Fang, *Kang Youwei yu Baohuang Hui,* 381 (#577, June 1905).

50. "Leaflet opposing the Exclusion Treaty," in Fang, *Kang Youwei yu Baohuang Hui*, 383 (#577, June 1905).

51. "Kuang Shoumin zhi Tan Zhangxiao Shu" 邝寿民致谭张孝书 (Letter from Kuang Shoumin to Tan Zhangxiao), in Fang, *Kang Youwei yu Baohuang Hui*, 156 (#189, August 10, 1905).

52. McKee, *Chinese Exclusion versus the Open Door Policy*, 120.

53. Letter from Kuang Shoumin to Tan Zhangxiao, in Fang, *Kang Youwei yu Baohuang Hui*, 156 (#189, August 10, 1905).

54. McKee, *Chinese Exclusion versus the Open Door Policy*; Field, "The Chinese Boycott of 1905," 63–98.

55. Lucy E. Salyer, "*Laws Harsh as Tigers*": *Chinese Immigration and the Shaping of Modern Immigration Law* (Chapel Hill: University of North Carolina Press, 1995), 167.

56. Standard Oil was an important organizing member of the American Asiatic Association, which promoted the Open Door Policy and called for the liberalization of exclusion laws on the basis that exclusion hurt U.S.-China relations and thus trade. McKee, *Chinese Exclusion versus the Open Door Policy*, 16; Tsai, *China and the Overseas Chinese in the United States*, 123.

57. McKee, *Chinese Exclusion versus the Open Door Policy*, 204.

58. McKee, *Chinese Exclusion versus the Open Door Policy*, 205–9.

59. McKee, *Chinese Exclusion versus the Open Door Policy*, 193–97.

60. Eventually American pressure became too great and the Qing issued its first edict against the boycott on August 31, 1905, and over time made moves to enforce it.

61. Letter from Liang Qichao to all comrades in all cities, in Fang, *Kang Youwei yu Baohuang Hui*, 116 (#578, June 7, 1905).

62. Letter from Liang Qichao to all comrades in all cities, in Fang, *Kang Youwei yu Baohuang Hui*, 120–26 (#578, June 7, 1905).

63. Wang, *In Search of Justice*.

64. Wang, *In Search of Justice*, 9, 166–69.

65. Lo, *K'ang Yu-wei*, 270.

66. Iriye, "Public Opinion and Foreign Policy," 226.

67. Ma, *Revolutionaries, Monarchists, and Chinatowns*, 126–27; Iriye, "Public Opinion and Foreign Policy," 226–28.

12

Between Two Worlds: The Zhigongtang and Chinese American Funerary Rituals

Sue Fawn Chung

When Chinese left their homeland for America, they did not know what the future held. Some realistically knew that there was a good chance that they would die either during their passage to Gold Mountain or after they arrived.[1] If this happened either kinsmen, people from their own village or district, or strangers might bury them. However, for many Chinese immigrants and their descendants, a fraternal organization such as the Zhigongtang (or Chee Kung Tong) often directed funerary rituals regardless of place of birth or family name of the deceased.

This is a study of the Zhigongtang's funerary practices between the 1850s and 1920s, when the leaders of the organization incorporated more American rituals. This acculturation effort contradicts late nineteenth-century stereotypes of the "unassimilable" Chinese. For example, in 1879 several Republicans cited the "strangeness" of the Chinese as a reason for passing immigration restrictions. Representative Addison McClure (R-OH) said that the Chinese were "Alien in manners, servile in labor, pagan in religion, [and] . . . fundamentally un-American," while Senator George Edmunds (R-VT) asserted that there was "no common ground of assimilation."[2] Consequently, Congress passed the 1882 Chinese Exclusion Act and its later supplements and never acknowledged Chinese efforts at acculturation. The mixture of Chinese and American funeral rituals was one realm of adaptation in one of life's most important rituals—funerals and burials—as the Chinese lived between two worlds in life and in death.

Chinese immigrants frequently faced hostility and potentially life-threatening situations. As turn-of-the-twentieth-century records from the Bureau of Immigration[3] demonstrate and Haiming Liu has shown in chapter

1 in this volume, Chinese usually migrated to a new location with kinsmen or where they knew someone, or knew someone who knew someone. As they pondered the question of death and funerals as strangers in a strange land, they had few choices. They could be cremated, a practice that had been popular in the Song Dynasty (960–1279) but was used in only a few Guangdong districts by the late Qing Dynasty (1644–1911), or they could be buried.[4] In 1854 a Euro-American traveler in the California Mother Lode district observed a small group of Chinese cremating their dead and a larger group that buried the dead in graves.[5] District associations, family associations, and organizations like the Zhigongtang handled funerals, cremations, and burials through a "death benefits" program and often purchased land for cemeteries.[6] Wealthier Chinese, especially those with wives and family in China, often opted for exhumation and reburial in China, where relations could revere their spirits in accordance to practices established by the neo-Confucianist Zhu Xi (1130–1200).[7] Most, however, remained buried in the United States.

Those who worked in rural areas not dominated by a district or family association or where none were present had to seek alternative organizations to handle their funeral and burial. Their options were few, so many chose to join Zhigongtang, which had no birthplace or family name requirements to provide a proper funerals and burials. Because it was, and still is, a secret society, there is little information about the activities and members of the organization. But when one of its leaders died, the funeral usually was noted, sometimes in great detail, in the local American newspaper. Although the newspaper articles are full of inaccuracies and biases, they reveal some of the basic customs and hint at some of the important traditional beliefs, while describing what American practices had been added. The individual's orientation as a sojourner (one who planned to return to China) or immigrant (one who planned to remain in the United States) sometimes also is seen. Most of the men whose funerals were described in these newspapers elected to remain buried in the United States and thus were truly immigrants. One of the reasons for this was the nature of the Zhigongtang.

HONGMEN ZHIGONGTANG, OR CHINESE FREE MASONS

The Zhigongtang ("Active Justice Society"), a secret society, traced its origins to the Hongmen of Guangdong Province and the Tiandihui of Fujian Province in southeastern China.[8] Established in 1674, the Zhigongtang was an anti-Manchu organization whose members vowed to end the Manchu Qing

Dynasty and reestablish Chinese leadership. The southern Chinese acknowledged the spirit of the first emperor of the Ming Dynasty (1368–1644), Hongwu, as their leader and referred to themselves as Hongmen. Recent studies by Chinese, Japanese, and Western scholars have detailed its history to some extent, but little work has been done on the organization in the United States.[9]

During and after the anti-Manchu Taiping Rebellion (1850–1864), some of the Taiping supporters fled overseas and started anti-Manchu secret societies in overseas Chinese communities, thus creating an international network. Those societies in the United States were linked to the Hongmen Zhigongtang, but often took other, local names because of different goals or ideals. However, all used the Zhigongtang's thirty-six oaths and twenty-one regulations (see appendix A) as their guiding rules and vowed the restoration of Chinese leadership in China.

In 1853 Taiping Rebellion supporter and immigrant from Taishan, Guangdong Province, Luo Yi (*Low Yet)[10] established the first Chinese American organization in San Francisco, probably as a branch of the Hongmen.[11] On January 4, 1854, the San Francisco *Herald* noted that there were 159 members of the Hongmen, many of whom were wealthy merchants and influential men in Chinatown. On the next day the newspaper reported that the recorder's court had confiscated silk banners, documents, and other artifacts from the organization in order to determine its goals and purpose. After translating the thirty-six oaths, the recorder discovered that the Hongmen was a secret brotherhood sworn to overthrow the Manchu government and restore Chinese rule. Although the organization was outlawed in China, the recorder noted that this had no bearing upon its status in the United States and equated it with the Masonic and Odd Fellows' fraternities, a comparison the Zhigongtang leaders later used to increase their prestige in the Euro-American community. By linking their international organization with that of the influential Masonic Order, Zhigongtang leaders established connections with famous American leaders like George Washington and projected the "mystique of patriotism and power."[12] Even though Euro-American Masons later denied any connection between the two organizations, the Zhigongtang still had a degree of respect from the Euro-American community as a Masonic organization, and the leaders used the connection to their political and economic advantage.

The secret society grew rapidly. By February 8, 1855, the *Herald* noted that the Hongmen had eight hundred members in San Francisco and three to four thousand in California, and had a treasury of over $150,000. By 1874 the Hongmentang also was called the Zhigongtang, or Chinese Free Mason Society. The branches were linked to the Triads, a secret society that originated in southeastern China. From the 1870s to the 1890s almost every major Chinese American community had a branch of the Zhigongtang. There was a major division in the organization around 1879–1882 and the Binggongtang, the Second Independent Order of Chinese Free Masons in America, separated from the Zhigongtang. The Binggongtang organization attracted members involved in prostitution, gambling, and opium sales rather than politics (figure 12.1).

At the turn of the twentieth century, the Zhigongtang expanded as popular opposition to the ruling Manchus grew. Between 1893 and 1912 the Zhigongtang federation of North America included thirty-one affiliates (see appendix B), including the Anping kongsuo, Ruiduan tang, Guoan huiguan (Ket On Society, Hawaii), and Baoantang, which supported the radical reformers Kang Youwei and Liang Qizhao (see Larson, chapter 11 in this volume).[13] This organization differed from the Baohuanghui (literally, "Society for the Protection of the Emperor," but often translated "Chinese Empire Reform Association"), which favored monarchy over a republic as advocated by *Sun Yat-sen. According to historian Stewart Culin, two-thirds of all Chinese in the United States around the turn of the twentieth century belonged to the Zhigongtang.[14] The Reno *Nevada State Journal,* on October 14, 1911, estimated that "90% of the Chinese in this country are members of the Free Masons." Although both figures probably were exaggerations, undoubtedly their numbers were large and the Zhigongtang lodges reflected wealth and prestige.

The organization had sufficient funding to allow for the construction of impressive local lodges. Many, like those in Monterey, California, and Tuscarora, Nevada, were built in the 1870s and 1880s and had the same architectural plan: a wooden two-story building. The first floor had recreational, lodging, and cooking facilities and served as a boarding house for travelers and as a social center. The second floor featured the meeting center, with an elaborate altar, silk banners, statues of Guan Gong (the god of war) and other deities, and hand-carved teak or rosewood furniture.[15] The altar justified the organization's tax-free religious status, so Euro-Americans often called the building a "joss house" (either from the incense burned there or from the Portuguese word "dios" for god) or temple. The Zhigongtang built in Los Angeles' Chinatown at 313 Apablasa in 1900 was a two-story brick building with more insurance coverage than any other Chinatown structure: $2,000 for the exterior and $2,000 for the interior.[16] This was an impressive sum of money

Secret Societies
1800s–1920s:

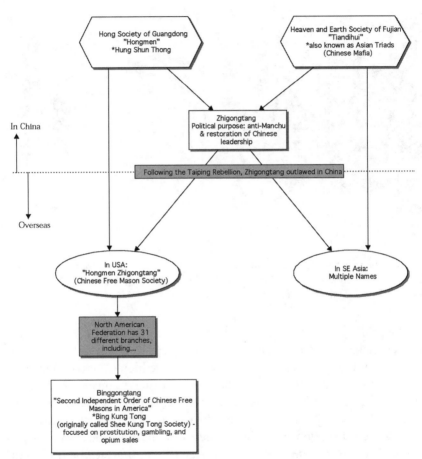

FIGURE 12.1

Chart of secret societies in China and overseas, 1800s–1920s (Copyright © Susie Lan Cassel and Christopher D. Johnson. Reprinted with permission.)

in those days. The San Diego lodge also housed the Chinese Consolidated Benevolent Association, because it was built in 1911, when the functions of the two organizations merged. Zhigongtang lodges often served as the Chinese American community's social center because of their spaciousness and attractive decorations.

FIGURE 12.2
1860s Chinese funeral: Zhigongtang members in the funeral procession walk past the Zhigongtang headquarters in Dutch Flat, California (Copyright © Louise Melton Collection, Golden Drift Historical Society. Reprinted with permission.)

The primary attractions of this secret brotherhood were: (1) community protection in an often hostile environment; (2) creation of an artificial family (family was a major feature of traditional Chinese life); (3) establishment of basic rules of conduct among members; (4) labor recruitment and "employment agency"; (5) economic assistance through a rotating credit system or some similar type of mutual economic benefit; (6) recreational activities, including the celebration of traditional festivals and entertainment, such as gambling, meals, and musical performances; (7) housing facilities for travelers; and most important of all, (8) proper funerals paid through a "death insurance fee" that was part of the annual dues (see figure 12.2).

Since ancient times the Chinese have been concerned with funerary rituals. Only one of the thirty-six oaths required as a part of Zhigongtang membership specifically dealt with funerary rites. The twenty-third oath stated, "Everyone should wear mourning for his parents or relative for three years. During this period he should not behave improperly. Those who break this law will be sentenced to die at Shao Yang Mountain" (see appendix A). The regulation could not be followed strictly in the American West, so as with other practices, the leaders made modifications and simply advised proper mourning behavior for at least three months.

AFTER DEATH: TRADITIONAL CHINESE BELIEFS

The Chinese believe in an afterworld and a connection between the present generation and past ones. In accordance with the dictates of Confucian filial piety and ancestor reverence, the obligations of the living to provide proper burial extends beyond the grave to the spirit world. In return, the spirits serve descendants positively. For those who neglect their proper funerary duties, there is malevolent retribution. The basic idea is that

> a living man had two souls: the *hun,* an emanation of the *yang* (the light, active principle) which gives man his intelligence or spark of life—this spark is sometimes referred to as his *qi* or "breath"—and which after death ascends to the heavens as his *shen;* and the earthier or more material *po,* derived from *yin* (the dark, passive principle) which simply animates the body and which, after the death of the individual, returns to the earth as his *gui.*[17]

Therefore the living had to appease the *shen* and *gui* of the deceased.

Many funerary rituals date back to neolithic times. Minute details for dressing the corpse, putting food and treasure into the mouth, and preparing accompanying items, to name a few, could be found in the *Yili* (Book of Etiquette and Ceremonies) from the Zhou Dynasty (1122–256 B.C.).[18] Although the traditions changed through time and had local variations, some major features were common to all Chinese funerary rituals. Funerals regularly involved wailing, placing food and drink before a symbol of the deceased, wearing white mourning garments, notifying friends and relatives of the death, and visiting relatives of the deceased to express condolences. Specialists or family members prepared the body and dressed it in the deceased's finest clothes. Sometimes the body was wrapped in a white or black shroud. The corpse was placed in a thick coffin. The procession to the graveyard was a major public ceremony. Music was an important part of the funeral. Loud noise and scattered paper with holes scared off any evil spirits that might follow the procession.[19] Mourners carried banners and lanterns.

A geomancer determined the propitious location of the grave. He stood at the front of the coffin at the cemetery and called out three times, "May this family have high officials, wealth, and many sons!" Then he threw a handful of grains or seeds (for plentiful crops and food), coins (for wealth), and nails (for male offspring, since the Chinese word for nails and males are homo-phones).[20] Food, usually roast pork and chicken, and drink were offered so that the deceased had sustenance in the afterworld. In some regions funerary paper money and drawings of objects were burned so the smoke could carry these things to the spirit world. In southern China the body was wedged tightly into the coffin to prevent movement. Then the coffin was buried about eighteen inches beneath the ground.[21] The rites, described in several publica-tions in the late Qing Dynasty, became commonly known among funerary "experts" in the Chinese American community.

MODIFICATIONS OF TRADITIONAL CHINESE FUNERALS

As leaders of an organization that upheld Chinese traditions, Zhigongtang leaders transplanted traditional rituals in the American frontier, but they had to make some modifications. One major change was that members of their fraternal organization, instead of nuclear family members, assumed the fu-nerary duties (figure 12.3). Another was the use of American morticians in the preparation and transportation of the deceased. Also, when Chinese musi-cians could not be found in sufficient numbers to make up a front and rear group, an American band was hired and American songs were played. Because of the shortage of Chinese women and female family members, professional Chinese female mourners were employed to weep and wail. At the graveside, Zhigongtang members, instead of extended family members, bowed to the de-ceased and performed other rituals. In many cases the graveside food offerings had to be protected from potential theft by non-Chinese community mem-bers. By the early twentieth century Christian ministers and church choirs also participated in some funerals. These adaptations can be seen in a series of American newspaper descriptions of Zhigongtang funerals.

On December 16, 1875, the *Dutch Flat Forum* (California) described a Zhigongtang funeral in which Chinese traditional candles were placed at the foot of the open coffin along with offerings of food, tea, and whiskey. The members of the procession knelt two at a time at the foot of the coffin, poured liquid from a cup onto the ground, rose, stepped backwards, and retired. Once all of the members had done this, the coffin was put into the ground and the personal effects of the deceased were burned in a hole dug for that purpose. The coffin was closed, the grave marker set in place, and the grave filled with dirt. In keeping with Zhigongtang rites, a rooster was brought forth, his comb was cut, and the blood was used to write some words. Funeral guests, whether Chinese or not, received a piece of candy, or at some funerals, gold dust or

FIGURE 12.3
1880s: Later Chinese funeral processions were more elaborate, partly because the Zhigongtang members were wealthier and the Chinese population was larger (Copyright © Louise Melton Collection, Golden Drift Historical Society. Reprinted with permission.)

coins to be used to buy something sweet to take the bitterness of death away. In this 1875 funeral there were no family members, only men in the brotherhood.

The *Virginia City Chronicle* (Nevada), December 7, 1878, detailed the funeral of Zhigongtang leader *Won Look, which demonstrated the continuation of tradition and the adaptations that were necessary: Won Look, "a Tartar of high standing and a member of the Masonic fraternity, died after a prolonged illness.... [He] requested that his obsequies should be conducted on the American plan." The reporter described Won Look's $75 rosewood coffin in the "joss house" that was surrounded by flowers to represent immortality, confectionery to symbolize the good things in life, and candles to help guide him into the afterworld. During the funeral procession, an American brass band playing the "Dead March from Saul" led the way. The driver of the hearse was Euro-American and seated beside him was a Chinese man who scattered on the road slips of paper four inches long all during the procession. Behind the hearse were fifty Chinese who wore red-and-blue cotton sashes, the colors of the Zhigongtang. Hired female mourners, a yellow omnibus with Chinese musicians, and finally, an express wagon with graveside foods followed. At the cemetery, incense sticks were lit. Friends took one last look at Won Look before his coffin was lowered into the ground and the food was placed by the grave. A guard watched over the grave as the mourners left, but when he left, about twenty Paiutes went to the grave and began to eat the chicken, pork, and other foodstuffs. When the Chinese heard about this, they rushed to the cemetery to drive off the Paiutes and a bloody fifteen-minute battle ensued. From this and other experiences, Chinese Americans modified the ritual and well into the 1930s either left token amounts of food or took some action to prevent the Native Americans, young children, and poorer members of the Euro-American community from eating the food.

Won Look's funerary rituals were not unlike fellow Zhigongtang leader *Chin Quong Wee of Riverside, California, whose funeral was detailed in the *Riverside Daily Press*, March 18, 1889.[22] According to the lengthy article, the deceased's brother and nephew acted as the chief mourners and about five hundred people attended the ceremony. In accordance with Chinese customs, under an awning in front of his residence were two tables: one table with a roasted pig and dressed but uncooked lamb; the other with cakes, oranges, fruits, nuts, confectionery, and other foodstuffs. The corpse was shrouded in black crepe up to his shoulders and coins were placed in his mouth and ears. A Chinese priest conducted a lengthy ceremony, then the Zhigongtang members and relatives lined up in two rows and bowed to the deceased. Then they offered libations by pouring liquor from a cup onto the ground. The eight pallbearers, all Zhigongtang members, wore white with bands of white around their foreheads. They had bare feet. The decorations on the coffin and on Chin Quong Wee's horse were red and white, part of the organization's colors. An American band led the funeral procession; the American undertaker drove the hearse. Mourners followed, some scattering white paper on the road and others carrying banners and lanterns. A crowd of Euro-Americans brought up the rear.

At the cemetery, the Chinese priest conducted another ceremony. Roast pork, roast chicken, two bowls of rice, and some wine were placed at the head of the grave to be used by the deceased in the afterworld. The fragrance of incense filled the air. After the coffin was lowered into the ground, the Zhigongtang members threw in rosettes of red and white ribbon. Clothing and per-

sonal effects of the departed were burned near the grave. Mourners were offered bread, butter, cigarettes, and whiskey. Finally the guests were invited to a
funerary banquet at a Chinese restaurant for the close of the rituals. With the
exception of the Zhigongtang decorations (which could not be displayed in
public in China because of the organization's anti-government stance), the
American band and undertaker, the graveside refreshments, and the Euro-
American spectators, Chin Quong Wee's funeral was in keeping with centuries-old southern Chinese funerary rituals.

GREATER ACCULTURATION BY THE EARLY TWENTIETH CENTURY

A close examination of the funeral of Zhigongtang leader *Low Hee Sing
(1852–1921) of Winnemucca, Humboldt County, Nevada, demonstrates a
greater acculturation of Chinese American funerals. Several events had an impact upon the Zhigongtang funerary rituals around the turn of the twentieth
century. In 1882 Congress passed the Chinese Exclusion Act, the first discriminatory act excluding a specific racial or national group from a country that
prided itself as a nation of immigrants.[23] Chinese laborers could no longer enter the United States. Between 1880 and 1900 there was a drastic decline in the
Chinese American population, which meant that there were fewer people
from which the Zhigongtang could recruit members and build a reserve treasury for increasing funerary expenses. In 1892 Congress redefined the exempt
classes and excluded Chinese physicians and priests. Chinese Americans
found themselves with a shrinking, predominantly male population without
the benefit of physical and spiritual healers. At the same time, the 1911 revolutionary movement was underway, and it eventually fulfilled one of the political goals of the Zhigongtang. Although there is no documentation, the
Zhigongtang probably grew in membership briefly because of the revolutionary movement. Leaders of the revolutionary movement came from Guangdong and recruited heavily among overseas Chinese. The main problem for
Zhigongtang leaders was who and what form of Chinese government to support. Some Zhigongtang leaders felt that Sun Yat-sen was too radical, while
others believed in his American-inspired ideals. Between 1912 and 1916 dissatisfaction with the presidency of Yuan Shikai, who succeeded Sun in March
1912, led to conflict within the Zhigongtang nationally and internationally.
This led to a decline in membership and community prestige.

At the same time Chinese Americans like Low Hee Sing became more
Americanized. As a Zhigongtang leader and prosperous merchant selling
goods to the Chinese and Euro-American community, Low became familiar

with American customs while maintaining ties to China. In 1880 he married and then left his wife behind in China when he emigrated to the United States. Separated families were common among Chinese Americans, especially because the 1875 Page Law effectively discouraged the immigration of Chinese women.[24] In 1882 Low settled in Winnemucca and opened Quong On Lung on Baud and Fifth streets near the two-story Zhigongtang lodge that had been built in 1878. After the lodge burned down, he contributed to the reconstruction of the building in 1902. The new lodge, situated high on the hillside, was an impressive two-story brick building with a long staircase and elaborate decorations and furniture.[25] From the front porch there was a panoramic view of Chinatown. In 1954 the building was razed and on the site a Euro-American Masonic Lodge was built.

The Low clan was very active in the Zhigongtang. *Low Wei Hoy and *Low Young, who both died in 1908, had been active members of the organization prior to Low Hee Sing's presidency. After Low Hee Sing, another relative, *Low Wing, headed the organization. Low Hee Sing became internationally famous when, on behalf of the Winnemucca lodge, he donated $3,500 to Sun for his revolutionary cause when Sun visited Winnemucca in 1911.[26] This represented the largest single donation of the $300,000 that Sun was able to raise during this tour.

Low was familiar with American customs and probably adopted the Christian faith. Low Hee Sing raised a young relative named Lester Low (or Lowe, b. 1901), who died of natural causes in 1917.[27] Low gave the young boy a Methodist Episcopal Church burial that was attended by a large crowd, including Lester Low's classmates and teachers. Three of Lester's pallbearers were Euro-Americans and three were Chinese Americans. All six were Lester's close friends. The transition to primarily American funerary rites seemed fitting for the younger generation. This experience probably led the elder Low to decide upon what he wanted for his own funeral.

The funeral of Low Hee Sing, who died of tuberculosis,[28] was a mixture of Chinese and American rituals. Low's relative, Low Wing, made the arrangements, probably in accordance with Low Hee Sing's wishes. The *Humboldt Star*, August 3, 1921, described Low Hee Sing's Christian and Chinese funerary rituals in an article titled, "Funeral of Prominent Chinaman Held Yesterday." Reverend J. H. Westervelt of the Methodist Episcopal Church officiated both at the chapel and the graveside, Carlson Undertaking handled the arrangements, a Christian choir sang hymns, and both Chinese Americans and Euro-Americans attended the services and funeral because of Low's pop-

ularity in the community. Chinese funerary rituals began with the proces-
sional. The Chinese "master of ceremonies" headed the funeral procession.
Chinese banners representing Low's affiliations preceded the two flag bearers,
one of whom carried the American flag while the other the Chinese Republic's flag. Notably, the American flag was carried higher than the Chinese flag.
From the hearse, papers with holes were scattered along the way. The pallbearers were all Chinese American friends. The *Silver State,* August 2, 1921,
observed that "A quantity of flowers arranged in different designs were carried
in a car in which appeared the only Chinese lady present." Whether she was
his former wife or Lester's mother or a mistress was unknown. At the Chinese
cemetery by the river the food and sweetmeats were placed on the grave and
the sacred papers burned. No mention was made of a Chinese band or the traditional music played at the gravesite to frighten away evil spirits. The master
of ceremonies was either a Chinese priest or a person with knowledge of Chinese funerary traditions. Like many other Zhigongtang leaders, Low Hee Sing
did not contribute to the exhumation fund and remained buried in Winnemucca.[29] For him, the United States was his home and final resting place.

    Thus as exemplified by Low Hee Sing's funeral, a Zhigongtang leader made
the transition from promoting the preservation of Chinese traditions and
concern for China's future to the acceptance of a combination of Chinese and
American rituals for one of life's most important events: death. Chinese
Americans adopted some practices out of necessity in the late nineteenth century, but by the early twentieth century, they purposefully combined Chinese
and American traditions. The absence of immediate family members, who
usually handled funerary arrangements, and the dearth of Chinese priests, because of the 1892 act, contributed to the transition.[30] Euro-American funerary homes and Christian ministers also had to be willing to participate in the
funerary rites and allow the combination of Chinese and American rites. Although there are no records to substantiate this, it would not be surprising if
Low Hee Sing had been a member of the Methodist Episcopal Church. By the
early twentieth century many Chinese Americans in other Nevada communities had become Christians. If Low had become Christian, this would explain
why the minister and choir were willing to participate in his funeral service.

    The Zhigongtang funerary practices are just one indication of the increas-
ing acculturation of Chinese Americans between the 1850s and 1920s. Men
who held a degree of power and prestige in both the Chinese American and
Euro-American communities headed the Zhigongtang during this period.
Although little is known about the other activities of this secret society, the

funeral practices were noted in local newspapers. The publicity given to the funerals of Zhigongtang leaders makes it possible to show that, despite the American popular images of the "foreign" Chinese who could not assimilate into American society, Zhigongtang leaders and members adopted some important aspects of American funerary practices. In 1875 the Dutch Flat funeral was rooted in Chinese tradition, but by the 1878 Virginia City funeral and by the 1889 Riverside funeral several American features were included, most notably the use of American morticians and American bands, and the presence of American spectators. By 1917, the transition was complete and American rituals played a major role in the 1917 and 1921 funerals. Because a Christian minister officiated and church members participated, the later funerals demonstrate that some of the barriers to acculturation had been dropped. It was now possible to blend American and Chinese funerary rites.

NOTES

1. For descriptions of deaths at sea, see the *Cuban Commission Report, A Hidden History of the Chinese in Cuba* (1876; reprint, Baltimore: Johns Hopkins University, 1903); and Robert L. Irick, *Ch'ing Policy toward the Coolie Trade, 1847–1878* (San Francisco: Chinese Materials Center, 1982), chapter 1.

2. Quoted in Andrew Gyory, *Closing the Gate: Race, Politics, and the Chinese Exclusion Act* (Chapel Hill: University of North Carolina Press, 1998), 5.

3. See "Applications for Duplicate Certificate of Residence," Immigration and Naturalization Service (formerly Bureau of Immigration), RG 85, National Archives and Records Administration, Washington, D.C. I surveyed several thousand files that are the basis for a future study on the 1905 Special Chinese Census.

4. Timothy Brook, "Funerary Ritual and the Building of Lineages in Late Imperial China," *Harvard Journal of Asiatic Studies* 49, no. 2 (December 1989): 465–500, analyzes several districts, including which groups cremated and which did not.

5. Stephen Williams, "The Chinese in the California Mines: 1848–1860" (master's thesis, Stanford University, 1930), 42–44.

6. The most detailed coverage of exhumation is found in Linda Sun Crowder's forthcoming doctoral dissertation in anthropology for the University of Hawaii, Manoa, expected in 2002.

7. Chu Hsi [Zhu Xi], *Chu Hsi's Family Rituals: A Twelfth Century Chinese Manual for the Performance of Cappings, Weddings, Funerals, and Ancestral Rites*, trans., ed., Patricia Buckley Ebrey (Princeton, N.J.: Princeton University Press, 1991). Chapter 4 is on funeral rituals.

8. The history and historiography of the organizations have been discussed in Dian H. Murray, in collaboration with Qin Baoqi, *The Origins of the Tiandihui: The Chinese Triads in Legend and History* (Stanford, Calif.: Stanford University Press, 1994); David Ownby, *Brotherhoods and Secret Societies in Early and Mid-Qing China: The Formation of a Tradition* (Stanford, Calif.: Stanford University Press, 1996); and David Ownby and Mary Somers Heidhues, eds., *"Secret Societies" Reconsidered: Perspectives on the Social History of Modern South China and Southeast Asia* (Armonk, N.Y.: Sharpe, 1993). The information from these excellent studies need not be repeated here.

9. Recent studies include Sasaki Masaya, *Shinmatsu no himitsu kessha: zempen, Tenchikai no seiritsu* (Secret societies in the late Qing period: the founding of the Tiandihui) (Tokyo: Kindai Chugoku Kenkyu Iinkai, 1967); Zhou Yumin and Shao Yong, *Zhongguo banghuishi* (The history of Chinese secret societies) (Shanghai: Shanghai renmin chubanshe, 1993); Zhuang Jifa, *Qingdai Tiandihui yuanliukao* (Studies on the origin of the Qing dynasty's Heaven and Earth Society) (Taibei: Guoli gugong bowuyuan, 1981); Him Mark Lai, *Cong huaqiao dao huaren* (From Overseas Chinese to Chinese American) (Hong Kong: Joint Publishing, 1992); L. Eve Armentrout Ma, *Revolutionaries, Monarchists, and Chinatowns: Chinese Politics in the Americas and the 1911 Revolution* (Honolulu: University of Hawaii Press, 1990) and "Short Biography of Mr. Taam Wu, Head of the Chee Kung Tong," *Annals of the Chinese Historical Society of the Pacific Northwest* 2 (1984): 159–64; Douglas W. Lee, "Political Development in Chinese America, 1850–1911" (Ph.D. dissertation, University of California, Santa Barbara, 1979) and "Sacred Cows and Paper Tigers: Politics in Chinese America, 1880–1900," *Annals of the Chinese Historical Society of the Pacific Northwest* 3 (1985–1986): 86–103; Ch'ing-hwang Yen, *The Overseas Chinese and the 1911 Revolution* (New York: Oxford University Press, 1976); and Florence C. Lister and Robert H. Lister, *The Chinese of Early Tucson: Historic Archaeology from the Tucson Urban Renewal Project* (Tucson: University of Arizona Press, 1989).

10. Pinyin romanization of Chinese names is given whenever possible. Cantonese romanizations are preceded with an asterisk.

11. San Francisco *Herald*, 4 January 1854; and San Francisco *Post*, 18 July 1879.

12. Paul Rich and Guillermo De Los Reyes, "Freemasonry and Popular Culture: Creating Mystiques of Patriotism and Power," *Popular Culture Review* 9:1 (February 1998), 59–80; and Allen E. Roberts, *George Washington: Master Mason* (Richmond, Va.: Macoy, 1976), 164.

13. Armentrout Ma, *Revolutionaries*, appendix B. The names of the organizations were Anliangtang, Anpingkongsuo, Anyitang, Baoantang, Baoliangshe, Baoliangtang, Baoshantang, Bingantang, Binggontang, Cuishengtang, Dunmutang, Guoan huiguan, Hean huiguan, Heshengtang, Huating shanfang, Jingongtang, Jinlan yusuo,

Qinyitang, Qunxiantang, Ruiduantang, Songshi shanfang, Xi'anshe, Xieshantang, Xieshengtang, Xieyingtang, Yangwen zhengwusi, Yiyingtang, Zhaoyitang, Zhigongtang, Zhuliangtang, Zhulin shanfang, Zhunyingtang, and Zuyingtang. According to the *Kiu Kwong Pao,* June 20, 1972, and the Chinese Times, June 18, 1970, both of San Francisco, the Binggongtang was founded in 1878 and celebrated its ninety-second anniversary on June 15, 1970. I am indebted to Him Mark Lai for his assistance on the early history of the Zhigongtang.

14. Stewart Culin, The I-Hing or "Patriotic Rising" (1890; reprint, San Francisco: R. and E. Research Associates, 1970). See also, Gustave Schlegel, Thian Ti Hwui, the Hung-League or Heaven-Earth League (1866; reprint, New York: AMS, 1974); J. S. M. Ward and W. G. Stirling, The Hung Society or the Society of Heaven and Earth (London: Baskerville, 1925).

15. This observation is based upon photographs of the buildings, both constructed in the 1870s, a description published in the Tucson Arizona Daily Star, 22 February 1935, photographs of the Tuscarora Zhigongtang interior when it was moved to Las Vegas (Nevada State Museum and Historical Society photograph collection, Las Vegas, Chinese file), and Lister and Lister, The Chinese of Early Tucson. Lister and Lister uncovered numerous artifacts from Tucson's Zhigongtang headquarters.

16. Report regarding the fire of October 10, 1901, by the Fire Department of the City of Los Angeles. This was the most expensive building in Los Angeles' Chinatown at that time.

17. Albert E. Dien, "Chinese Beliefs in the Afterworld," in The Quest for Eternity: Chinese Ceramic Sculptures from the People's Republic of China, ed. Los Angeles County Museum of Art et al. (San Francisco: Chronicle Books, 1987), 5–12; Michael Lowe, Chinese Ideas of Life and Death: Faith, Myth and Reason in the Han Period (202 B.C.–A.D. 220) (London: Allen and Unwin, 1982). See also, Timothy Brook, "Funerary Ritual and the Building of Lineages in Late Imperial China," 465–500.

18. Dien, "Chinese Beliefs in the Afterworld," and Robert L. Thorp, "The Qin and Han Imperial Tombs and the Development of Mortuary Architecture," in The Quest for Eternity, 1–15; David N. Keightley, "The Quest for Eternity in Ancient China: The Dead, Their Gifts, Their Names," in Ancient Mortuary Traditions of China: Papers on Chinese Ceramic Funerary Sculptures, ed. George Kuwayama (Honolulu: University of Hawaii Press for the Far Eastern Art Council and the Los Angeles County Museum of Art, 1991), 12–25. The most extensive interpretive commentary on Chinese funeral rites can be found in J. J. M. de Groot, The Religious System of China, vol. 1 (Leyden, Netherlands: Brill, 1892).

19. Patricia Buckley Ebrey, Confucianism and Family Rituals in Imperial China: A Social History of Writing about Rites (Princeton, N.J.: Princeton University Press, 1991), 4.

20. Emily M. Ahern, *The Cult of the Dead in a Chinese Village* (Stanford, Calif.: Stanford University Press, 1973), 179. Different localities in southern China have different funerary customs, but Euro-American scholars have not always recognized this.

21. James L. Watson, "The Structure of Chinese Funerary Rites: Elementary Forms, Ritual Sequence, and the Primacy of Performance" and "Funeral Specialists in Cantonese Society: Pollution, Performance, and Social Hierarchy," in *Death Ritual in Late Imperial and Modern China*, ed. James L. Watson and Evelyn S. Rawski (Berkeley: University of California Press, 1988), 15–17 and 124.

22. I am indebted to Paul Chace for bringing this article to my attention.

23. For more information on the 1882 Chinese Exclusion Act, see Andrew Gyory, *Closing the Gate;* Shirley Hune, "The Issue of Chinese Immigration in the Federal Government, 1875–1882" (Ph.D. dissertation, George Washington University, 1979) and "Politics of Chinese Exclusion: Legislative-Executive Conflict, 1876–1882," *Amerasia Journal* 9, no. 1 (1982): 5–27; and Lucy Salyer, *"Laws Harsh as Tigers": Chinese Immigration and the Shaping of Modern Immigration Law* (Chapel Hill: University of North Carolina Press, 1995).

24. George Anthony Peffer, "Forbidden Families: Emigration Experiences of Chinese Women under the Page Law, 1875–1882," *Journal of American Ethnic History* 6 (fall 1986): 28–46, and *If They Don't Bring Their Women Here: Chinese Female Immigration before Exclusion* (Urbana: University of Illinois Press, 1999); and Sucheng Chan, "The Exclusion of Chinese Women, 1870–1943," in *Entry Denied: Exclusion and the Chinese Community in America, 1882–1943*, ed. Sucheng Chan (Philadelphia: Temple University Press, 1991), 94–196.

25. Thomas W. Chinn, *Bridging the Pacific: San Francisco Chinatown and Its People* (San Francisco: Chinese Historical Society of America, 1989), 102–105; James R. Chew, "My Boyhood Days in Winnemucca from 1901–1910," typewritten manuscript in the Nevada State Museum, Carson City, Nevada; oral interviews with Euro-American residents, including Arthur English, who remembered going to Quong On Lung to buy things, especially firecrackers for the Fourth of July (interview conducted in March 1999). See also, Beth Amity Au, "Home Means Nevada: The Chinese in Winnemucca, Nevada, 1870–1950, a Narrative History" (master's thesis, University of California, Los Angeles, 1993); Winnemucca *Silver State*, 22 August 1878, 25 June 1885, 11 February 1899, 31 January 1881, and 11 December 1902; *Reno Evening Gazette*, 28 June 1954, which describes the joss house.

26. The Reno *Evening Gazette*, 6 October 1911, and Reno *Nevada State Journal*, 14 October 1911, describe Sun Yat-sen's fundraising trip through North America. The Republic of China was established on October 10, 1911, and Nevada newspapers supported its creation.

27. The Winnemucca *Humboldt Star,* 23 and 26 February 1917, covers the story of Lester Low and Low Hee Sing. Lester's mother lived in Lovelock and sent her son to work for Low Hee Sing in his store while Lester was in school.

28. Humboldt County Recorder's Office, Deaths, Book 4 (January 1920 to December 1930), 38.

29. This statement is based on a random sampling correlating the names of Zhigongtang leaders in Nevada with the records showing exhumations for reburial in San Francisco or China. None of the Zhigongtang leaders, many of whom had the wealth to pay the expenses, were exhumed. A sample of funeral home records for Reno, Washoe County, showed the same trend.

30. This act, *U.S. Statutes at Large* 27 (1892): 25, extended Chinese exclusion for ten years and required Chinese to have a certification of identification and certificate of residence.

APPENDIX A: ZHIGONGTANG HISTORY, OATHS, AND REGULATIONS

The Zhigongtang, translated "Active Justice Society," was established in 1674 in China, probably as a branch of the Hongmen (Hong sect) of Guangdong and Tiandihui (Heaven and Earth Society) of Fujian-Jiangxi, and was the most politically inspired of these secret societies. Branches existed in many overseas Chinese communities. Around 1854, the organization established a headquarters in San Francisco and by the 1880s had more than three hundred members. There was no centralized organization, and several splinter groups, most notably the Binggongtang, became separate from the political Zhigongtang.

Each Zhigongtang branch had silk banners with the history of the organization, the thirty-six oaths, and twenty-one regulations, which were memorized and recited by the members at meetings.[1] The exact wording differed slightly according to the location and local conditions outside of China. The recitation took place at the main altar, which often had a picture of Wan Tixi (also known as Wan Yulong, the founder of the society), Guanyin (goddess of mercy), Tudi (the earth official), Guan Yu (also known as Guandi or Guan Gong, god of war and justice), or other important figures.

The member vowed to teach to others what the founders transmitted to them. They recalled the sworn brotherhood in the Peach Garden of Liu Bei, Guan Yu, and Zhang Fei of the Three Kingdoms (ca. 220 A.D.), who vowed loyalty, faithfulness, benevolence, justice, filial piety, and obedience to each other and their country. In the same manner, the members made the same six pledges and vowed to help and care for each other as brothers with all of their strength and determination.

Remembering that their country had been occupied by the Manchus (1644–1911), they swore to take revenge for the 128 monks killed by the Qing imperial army at Fujian's Shaolin Temple in 1641 and for the last Ming heir apparent, who was killed by the Manchu agents while fleeing to Burma. They vowed to reestablish Chinese rule in China. Despite the fact that they came from different families, they acknowledged their common fate of helping each other, whether rich or poor, and pledged to follow the thirty-six oaths and twenty-one regulations of the organization until their deaths.

Each of the thirty-six oaths included punishments if the oath was broken. The oaths involved relationships among the brothers, including the vow not to take rewards from outside of the brotherhood; not to be an informant to the Manchus; to respect and protect the female relatives of a member; not to be jealous of a brother's wealth; to share one's wealth with brothers; not to steal from a brother; to assist brothers in time of trouble and while they are in transit; to do one's duties and be loyal to each other; not to make trouble, act against, or fight with brothers; to live in harmony with brothers; and to obey the organization's rules, which must be kept a secret from outsiders and non-member relatives.

One oath (often noted as #23) required members to regard the parents and family of a brother as if they were their own and, in the same spirit, to mourn brothers, parents, and relatives for three years, an old Confucian practice. Those who broke this oath were sentenced to die at Shaoyang Mountain.

The twenty-one regulations also included punishments if the rules were broken. The regulations stressed loyalty to the emperor and to their family; the maintenance of secrecy of the organization; proper behavior toward people in general as well as brothers; mutual aid, benevolence, and loyalty among members; and other codes of conduct, such as prohibiting the kidnapping of children, stealing, insulting elders, making trouble, and not being brave in times of war.

Note

1. Translations of the oaths and regulations can be found in Gustave Schlegel, *Thian ti Hwui: The Hung League* (Batavia: Lange, 1866), 139; J. S. M. Ward and W. G. Stirling, *The Hung Society or the Society of Heaven and Earth*, vol. 1 (London: Baskerville, 1925), 169–70; Jean Chesneaux, *Secret Societies in China in the 19th and 20th Centuries*, trans. Gillian Nettle (Ann Arbor: University of Michigan Press, 1971), 22–27; Florence C. Lister and Robert H. Lister, *The Chinese of Early Tucson* (Tucson: University of Arizona Press, 1989), appendix A; and numerous other works on the organization.

APPENDIX B

Hongmen (Triad) organizations existed in most overseas Chinese communities. Between 1893 and 1912, the North American organizations in the Zhigongtang federation were

Anliangtang (An-liang t'ang)　安良堂

Anpingkongsuo (An-p'ing kung-so)　安平公所

Anyitang (An-i t'ang)　安益堂

Baoantang (Pao-an t'ang)　保安堂

Baoliangshe (Pao-liang she)　保良社

Baoliangtang (Pao-liang t'ang)　保良堂
(Hawaii)

Baoshantang (Pao-shan t'ang)　保善堂

Bingantang (Ping-an t'ang)　秉安堂

Binggongtang (Ping-kung t'ang)　秉公堂

Cuishengtang (Ts'ui-sheng t'ang)　卒英堂

Dunmutang (Tun-mu t'ang)　敦睦堂

Guoan huiguan (Kuo-an hui-kuan)　國安會館
(Ket On Society, Hawaii)

Hean huiguan (Ho-an hui-kuan)　和安會館
(Hawaii)

Heshengtang (Ho-sheng t'ang)　合勝堂

Huating shanfang (Hua-t'ing shan-fang)　華亭山房

Jingongtang (Chin-kung t'ang)　進公堂

Jinlan yusuo (Chin-lan yu-so)　金蘭寓所

Qinyitang (Ch'in-i t'ang)　親義堂

Qunxiantang (Ch'un-hsien t'ang)　群賢堂

Ruiduantang (Jui-tuan t'ang)　瑞端堂

Songshishanfang (Sung-shih shan-fang)　松石山房

Xianshe (Hsi-an she)　西安社

Xieshantang (Hsieh-sheng t'ang)　協善堂

Xieshengtang (Hsieh-sheng t'ang)　協勝堂

Xieyingtang (Hsieh-ying t'ang)　協英堂

Yangwen zhengwusi (Yang-wen cheng-wu szu)　洋文政務司

Yiyingtang (I-ying t'ang)　儀英堂

Zhaoyitang (Chao-i t'ang)　昭義堂

Zhigongtang (Chih-kung t'ang)　致公堂
　(Chinese Free Masons)

Zhuliangtang (Chu-liang t'ang)　聚良堂

Zhulin shanfang (Chu-lin shan-fang)　竹林山房

Zhunyingtang (Chun-ying t'ang)　俊英堂

Zuyingtang (Tsu-ying t'ang)　萃勝堂

13

Family and Culture in the Control of the Delinquent Chinese Boy in America

Sheldon X. Zhang

DELINQUENCY IN THE CHINESE AMERICAN COMMUNITY

In the late 1960s and early 1970s, reports about Chinatown gangs and related youth violence began to appear in newspapers in San Francisco and New York City.[1] These youth gangs, made up of poorly educated immigrants with few marketable skills, were terrorizing merchants and residents with their extortion schemes and street fights. The general public did not think much of these youth problems, since they were confined within an ethnic enclave, and attributed most of them to the cultural maladjustment of new immigrants from the Old World to the New World.[2] However, events took a drastic turn from this benign image when calculated murders and senseless massacres erupted in several major urban Chinese communities in the late 1970s and early 1980s. The first incident occurred in San Francisco in 1977, when three heavily armed Chinese gang members walked into the Golden Dragon Restaurant and opened fire on customers, killing five and wounding eleven; none of the victims were members of a rival gang.[3] In New York, on Christmas Eve in 1982, three masked gunmen randomly shot customers inside a Chinatown bar.[4] Similar gang-related, violent incidents broke out in Los Angeles, Houston, Boston, Chicago, Vancouver, and Toronto.[5] Today, Chinatown gangs have gained nationwide notoriety and most of what the public knows about Chinese delinquents comes from sporadic and often sensationalized media reports.

Despite the fact that Chinatown gangs have attracted much attention nationwide, aided by such Hollywood portrayals as *The Year of the Dragon* and *China Girl*, the number of Chinese delinquents under official control (i.e., incarcerated or on probation) is small compared to that of other major ethnic groups. For instance, according to the latest population statistics from the California state government, in 1999 the estimated population of Los Angeles County was more than 9 million, of which slightly more than 1 million were classified as Asian and Pacific Islanders.[6] There were twenty-four thousand juveniles currently under probation supervision in Los Angeles County, of which only ninety-four (or 0.4 percent) were Chinese youths, despite the rapid sprawl of the Chinese community in southern California.[7]

Crime and delinquency in the Chinese community have largely been "invisible" due to the barriers of language, culture, and residential isolation. A review of the mainstream literature illustrates this point. For the past fourteen years (1986–1999), there were fewer than ten entries on subjects that had anything to do with crime and Chinese in *Sociological Abstracts,* the most widely used reference source for social scientists. Because of racial discrimination and the restrictive immigration policies against Chinese nationals between 1882 and 1964, there were few Chinese youths in the United States, and most were reported to be law-abiding and hardworking students.[8] Accordingly, social researchers began to wonder why Chinese American communities had such low delinquency rates.[9] In fact, the "model minority" image[10] and the stories of successful Chinese immigrants in science and academics[11] have continued until today and often obscure the stories of many maladjusted immigrant youngsters whose opportunities in life do not extend beyond the edges of urban impoverished neighborhoods or whose substandard academic performances drive them to seek comfort among gangs and delinquent peers.

The repeal of the Chinese Exclusion Act in 1943 and passage of the War Brides Act in 1946 allowed Chinese immigration to the United States to resume. More recently, two historical events have greatly increased the number of Chinese youths entering the United States. First, after the fall of Saigon in 1975, tens of thousands of Southeast Asian refugees, many of whom were of Chinese descent, were allowed entry into the United States.[12] Second, in 1978, the U.S. government established diplomatic relations with mainland China, opening up formal immigration channels to the vast population. The increase of the Chinese youth population in the United States has also brought with it various social problems, particularly youth gangs in many major urban Chinese communities.

DEFINING THE CHINESE CULTURE

Chinese are often treated as a homogeneous group and lumped together for analytical purposes. Although it may be like splitting hairs to differentiate the subgroups among Chinese, it should be acknowledged that much diversity exists in terms of language, cuisine, and customs. These differences arise from such elements as history, geographical origin, area of settlement, time and circumstances of entry into the United States, and level of acculturation.

Chinese Americans can be broadly divided into two groups: those who were born and raised in the United States and those who immigrated to the United States. The U.S.-born Chinese are generally considered more culturally homogeneous than first-generation Chinese because of the former's assimilation to the host society. The most obvious source of cultural difference is the place where one spends most of one's childhood. This geocultural imprint at an early age sets a cultural orientation that prompts one to identify oneself not only as a Chinese, but as a Chinese from a specific region. They are Cantonese, Fujianese, Shanghainese, or Chinese from the Philippines, Hong Kong, Malaysia, or Vietnam. They speak different languages, eat different foods, and worship different gods. These patterned differences in customs, languages, and lifestyles obviously bear consequences on social behavior that are worth exploring, and oversimplification will occur if these groups of Chinese are treated as a homogeneous cultural entity.

At the same time, the subject of juvenile delinquency in the Chinese community does not easily afford the luxury of appreciating fine cultural nuances, because of the small number of youths who are in trouble with the law. Political and cultural sensitivity, therefore, may have to give way to empirical pragmatism. This chapter deals with this issue by identifying what may be considered common cultural norms and beliefs that mark the behavioral boundaries of this ethnic group called Chinese. The purpose here is not to engage in a detailed discussion of what constitutes Chinese culture, rather it is to capture commonly shared cultural expectations that serve as the hallmark of social control in the Chinese culture and therefore make it possible to systematically examine how delinquency is handled in a Chinese family.

Confucianism, Hierarchy, and the Face-Saving Mentality

From the Confucian perspective, social order is established through the maintenance of a hierarchically arranged social structure, where roles are clearly ascribed to each individual and adhered to within the family and community. Rituals and protocols guiding social interactions are well defined and reinforced through a myriad of highly developed feelings of obligation, most of which are hierarchical in nature. The family and community supersede the individual. Respect and reverence for authority are learned from an early age amid the rituals and customs of the patriarchal culture. Rules of conduct are formalized in members' roles to a greater extent than in most other cultures.[13]

An individual's behavior not only reflects one's adherence to these rules, but also the family and kinship network to which one belongs. Unlike Western culture, which emphasizes self-sufficiency and mastery of one's own destiny, Chinese culture views individuals as products of their relationship to the family, especially to their parents.[14]

Social control is accomplished through the teaching of "face" at a young age. Social and legal transgressions are considered a disgrace to one's parents and to the family and detrimental to one's social standing within the community.[15] Shame (or losing face) is most often used to reinforce the adherence to shared social expectations and norms of acceptable behavior, because the consequence of a transgression will be the withdrawal of the family's confidence and support. In a culture in which interdependence is important, the actual or threatened renouncement by others, especially one's own parents, raises the existential anxiety of being truly left alone to face the world. In contrast, formal social control in Western culture relies mostly on rational and systematic application of codified rules that are based on Judeo-Christian ethics.

Family and Kinship Patterns

Many Chinese scholars have argued that there are no "typical Chinese families," just as there are no typical American families. They argue that the variations within a culture are as wide as between cultures.[16] The structure and style of family and kinship patterns largely reflect the level of acculturation, exposure to the mainstream culture, and life circumstances in the host society. Wong argues that the Chinese American family is best viewed as a product of the interaction between structural factors (i.e., restrictive immigration policies and racism) and cultural factors (i.e., Confucian ethics). Because these factors are constantly changing, the Chinese American family is also undergoing constant change and adaptation to the changing social environment.[17]

However, in contrast to other ethnic groups in the United States, such as Euro-Americans, there are a few identifiable patterns of Chinese family relations, at least among first-generation immigrants (among whom most juvenile delinquents are concentrated). Multiple generations living under one roof is a common phenomenon. Members of a family network tend to be blood/marriage related and remain stable over time, with clear hierarchical arrangements. Divorces and remarriages are less common among Chinese Americans than among other ethnic groups, thus frequent exit from and entry by relatives is rare. These family and kinship patterns in Chinese culture bear direct consequence on how delinquent youths are perceived and handled.

PARENTS AND THE CONTROL OF DELINQUENT CHILDREN

There is no known literature on how Chinese parents respond to their delinquent children. In the mainstream criminology literature, parents are either thought to contribute to the development of delinquency because of their own personal problems or are considered incapable of handling their own children because of a lack of knowledge and skills.[18] Considering the central role of parents in the Chinese family, it is safe to say that any systematic study of juvenile delinquency in the Chinese community requires an understanding of how parents respond to their delinquent children, which is the main purpose of the present study.

This study is placed within the conceptual framework of family stress theory, which focuses on the coping process of a family experiencing a stressful event. Coping is a process in which the family, to prevent crisis, uses its internal and external resources to reduce the impact of a particular stressor and the possible pileup of other stressors.[19] It is a process in which the family tries to meet unusual demands caused by changes in the living environment when a routine response is not available.[20] Because a child's legal transgression invokes social stigmatization or disgrace, one can expect it to exert emotional stress on the family system.

Family scientists have devoted much attention to family problems as precursors to juvenile delinquency. Marital disruption and conflict, parental inadequacies, and inconsistency in parenting have been viewed as causal to children's conduct problems. But rarely examined is the subject of parental subjective experiences of and behavioral responses to their children's delinquency. This study takes this approach to exploring how the Chinese family and its patriarchal culture manages and controls its wayward youngsters. There are two questions in this study. First, how do Chinese parents perceive and explain their child's arrest and subsequent sanction? The purpose here is to examine distinctive cultural styles in the interpretation of the child's transgression. Second, how do Chinese parents deal with their child once the child is found guilty and placed under court-ordered supervision? This study assumes that a child's arrest and subsequent probation produces stress on the family system as a result of court-ordered activities and associated social stigmatization, real or imagined. To alleviate the perceived stress, parents attempt to neutralize its impact or minimize the likelihood of its recurrence, or both. It is in the course of coping that this study intends to explore how Chinese parents apply their inherited values and traditions from the Old World to manage and control their delinquent children in the New World.

RESEARCH METHODS

In-depth interviews with open-ended questions were conducted with twenty-eight Chinese parents whose sons were placed on probation for the first time in the Los Angeles County Probation Department. Through a set of screening criteria, the study selected a group of parents whose experiences with the justice system were as similar as possible. Female Chinese delinquents are rare in comparison to their male counterparts, and therefore were excluded from the sampling process. Furthermore, the complex sociocultural constructs surrounding the differential treatment of female delinquents in the Chinese culture may also confound the analysis of the treatment of male offenders. It is very likely that parental response to the child's delinquency varies along gender lines, a subject beyond the scope of this study.

The study selected parents whose children were (1) male, (2) on probation for the first time, (3) from the same supervision program, and (4) placed on probation within the same approximate period of time. Due to budgetary constraints, sampling was limited to five area offices of the Los Angeles County Probation Department that supervised the most Chinese youth offenders in Los Angeles County. A total of twenty-eight parents were interviewed in mutually agreed upon locations. A nominal fee was paid to the respondents for their participation. Except for one mother, who was born and raised in the United States, all parents were new immigrants.

PERCEPTIONS OF THE INCIDENT

Crisis Event

This study found that the arrest and subsequent probation related to the incident were overwhelmingly perceived as emotionally upsetting events, so much so that most respondents reported that the family went through a crisis. The response patterns were clearly one-sided, with respondents emphasizing how the arrests ruined their otherwise peaceful lives and how the court-ordered probation activities broke up daily routines and became the focal concern of the families. It became apparent during the interviews that few of these parents had any prior experience with the justice system. Most parents never anticipated that any member of their family would get into trouble with the law. To most of these respondents, the worst situation they could ever imagine with the police was getting a traffic ticket. After learning her son had been arrested for possessing a weapon, a thirty-four-year-old mother who lived on the money from her part-time job in a restaurant and from a welfare subsidy felt her world was caving in: "The police called me. I was so scared. I dropped my work and went to the police station at once. I was so shaky that I didn't think I could drive. It was the first time in my life that I was in contact with the police. I was crying that day. I got out a vacuum cleaner pole and threatened to hit [minor's name] if he got in trouble again."

Most parents reported that after hearing about the arrest, they could no longer concentrate on what they were doing and had to drop everything to attend to the legal matters. Because of the magnitude of the incidents and the agencies involved (the police and court), many parents were shaken up badly and became preoccupied with the legal matters. For instance, parents reported that they would spend most of their nonworking time making sure their son followed the rules (e.g., attended mandatory counseling classes, paid restitution, and did community service). Even when parents were working, they could not stop worrying about their delinquent children and feared possible relapses. After his son was arrested for burglary, a father who worked in construction and raised his son as a single parent said,

I was very shocked when I heard of his arrest. Now I have worries and worries. I have taken him to psychological counselor as recommended by the police. His probation has made my life a lot more difficult. Now I devote all my free time to him. I have changed my work hours to be with him more. We have also moved to change his environment. I will move again, closer to my work, so that I can bring him to my work. I want to increase the time he spends with me.

In summary, these parents were ill-prepared for events of this nature and their centuries-old traditions only exacerbated their emotional upheaval. They were shocked because their child was trampling the rules of the authority. For these immigrant parents who were struggling to survive in the new country, having to divert time and attention to deal with the justice system (of which few had any prior knowledge) was simply overwhelming. For many of these parents, it was more than a stressful event—it was a crisis.

On the interpretation of the incident event, the majority of the parents were quick to accept the offense as charged by the police, perhaps another culturally typical behavior. In comparison, other ethnic groups, such as Euro-Americans or African Americans, are more likely to utilize available legal resources to their advantage and presume their children to be innocent until proven guilty. After all, the American justice system is permeated with procedures and legal counsels to ensure that the rights of the accused are protected and that due process is carried out. It was rare for Chinese parents to deny any wrongdoing on behalf of their children, to blame someone else, or to accuse the police for arresting the wrong person. When probed about possible causes of their children's transgression, Chinese parents, in general, sought internal explanations, such as poor parenting, lack of supervision, and overindulgence. Their cultural baggage appeared to turn them inward and render them incapable of mastering the many standard answers that were indeed quite fashionable in the mainstream culture—to blame the government, the society, the justice system, racial discrimination, and anything but themselves.

In fact, when prompted with questions on these external sociolegal factors, many parents found it odd that the interviewer would suggest that government or the police might have caused their children to get in trouble. At most, these parents were able to link their children's troubles with the law to the bad friends they were keeping. As one Chinese mother put it, "I don't know why you ask me that the government or police have anything to do with my son's bad behavior. They care enough to help me. They order me to come and I have to come (to court). He (delinquent minor) deserves probation. He should do his time. I don't know much about this country and its law. Whatever they tell me to do, I will do it."

In short, to most respondents, it was neither customary nor culturally acceptable in their home countries to blame the government or the authorities for their child's misconduct. This was in contrast to the mainstream culture, in which delinquency is often explained and studied in the context of such factors as poverty, lack of job opportunities, racism/white oppression, and decayed ghetto areas.

Feelings of Embarrassment and Self-Blaming
Feelings of embarrassment and disgrace were common emotional reactions among the respondents, many of whom questioned themselves as competent parents. They asked repeatedly what could have gone wrong in their parenting that led their child astray. The majority of the parents felt responsible for their child's behavior and blamed themselves for having failed in their efforts to steer their child in the right direction. Many mothers broke into tears during interviews and described how embarrassed they felt after receiving the phone call from the police. To many, the memory of the incident (i.e., having to face the police and a probation officer) was nightmarish enough to bring up feelings of shame and disgrace for the rest of their lives. A forty-two-year-old new immigrant mother who was working as a waitress said,

> I feel so ashamed by my son's behavior [burglary]. I have to go to court to sit with other criminals. I had never thought that I would one day go to the crim-

inal court to face the judge. Others will only blame me for being a bad parent. I have always been trying to ask my son to have self-respect and feel a sense of self-worth. I never dare to discuss my son's arrest with anyone else. It is such a shameful thing. There is a saying in Chinese—one should never get involved with the court as long as one lives, just as one must avoid the hell when he passes on. I must have done something wrong in my previous life and now I am being punished.

Another mother, who was working as an acupuncture assistant, felt so embarrassed about her son's arrest for auto theft that she could not muster enough courage to go to the police station to pick him up. She noted,

It was a big shock to me when [minor's name] was arrested. It was a big disgrace to this family. I had to bring his brother with me to the police station. Even his brother didn't want to go. He blamed [minor's name] for losing the family's face [i.e., tarnishing the family reputation] and complained that we parents didn't do a good job. I felt awful. Our family is very old-fashioned and we have been teaching our children to always have "face" [i.e., be upright and honorable] regardless what they do in their lives.

In sum, it was hard not to notice the intense feelings of embarrassment among the respondents, perhaps another typical cultural response. Most parents felt they had lost their "face" (i.e., been disgraced) for their children's transgressions. Such a display of parental reactions to delinquent youngsters is absent from the mainstream criminology literature. On the other hand, in the mainstream culture, which emphasizes individuality and independence, it is a common assumption that one is responsible for one's own behavior. Euro-American or African American parents may feel disappointed about their delinquent youngsters, but rarely do they feel responsible for the children's behavior. In traditional Chinese culture, however, it is almost irresponsible for parents not to draw such a connection.

Acculturation and Education: From Enmeshment to Differentiation

In a few isolated cases the native-born and college-educated (in the United States) parents were less inclined to feel personally responsible for their children's transgressions. Instead, they were able to find causes in the larger society as contributing to their children's downfall, such as the lack of job opportunities and structured activities for their children, the bad influence of gangs in the neighborhood, the media, and the urban environment. Such was the case for an engineer and his wife (both college educated in the United States) who placed much of the blame on the gang members with whom their son was socializing: "His problem started when he was transferred from Downey to Alhambra High. He was really out of control. Government should really control gangs at school. Right now there is not control at all. I don't think parents are responsible for their children's wrongdoings. He chose his way. As a parent, I can't choose his friends."

While shocked to hear about her son's arrest for vandalism, another college-educated mother, born and raised in the United States, seemed able to differentiate herself from the incident and remained coolheaded about the situation,

> I am not a hyper person. Do you have any proof of his guilt? . . . After he was transferred to a public school at tenth grade, he has been exposed to all types of kids and became curious. He met different people. [Minor's name] is a bold child and likes to take risks. And also there is the bad influence of violent movies. Now I keep telling [minor's name] "you have to be responsible for yourself." His psychologist said he was looking for excitement.

The less-educated and new immigrant parents, on the other hand, were only able to acknowledge those bad friends as a part of the problem that got their sons in trouble with the law. Few would place the blame on larger social factors.

Court-ordered parenting classes also appeared to have an effect in enabling parents to avoid self-blaming and emotional enmeshment with their children. After attending the court-ordered parenting classes, a Chinese father said,

> We were devastated at first. It [delinquency] was not acceptable in this family. Now we know better from the court-ordered parenting classes. We have a support group to call on each other for help. We didn't know how to deal with [minor's name], but now we know how to cope with him. We have little confidence in whether he will get in trouble again. We try to provide him with as many tools as possible, but we can't make choices for him. There is no way to choose friends for him. Parents just don't have enough control over the influence from the environment. We feel powerless. In Hong Kong, we spank our kids; but in this country we can't spank him.

While few in number, these cases appear to point to an effect of acculturation on parental perception of and response to their delinquent children. The more acculturated, the more likely a Chinese parent will think like a mainstream American who is able to externalize family and personal problems and find culturally acceptable causes to exonerate themselves. New immigrants, however, are less likely to do so. Such differences in perception bear consequences on coping behavior and determine the extent to which parents are willing to invest time and effort to help their children.

Role Reversal and Breakdown of Family Hierarchy

When discussing what might have gone wrong, most parents shared the same complaint—a lack of parental control over their children. Many parents noted that they felt powerless in front of their children because they were busy making ends meet and had little time or little knowledge of how their children were doing at school or with whom they were socializing. Instead, their children were often thrust into playing the adult roles, such as doing the family banking, filling out paper work for the Department of Motorized Vehicles, or interacting with social service agencies. Parental control was thus significantly weakened. The family hierarchy that traditionally maintains the stability of many immigrant Chinese families was no longer viable. These youngsters made their own decisions and socialized with whomever they chose. In short, they were no longer looking up to their parents for guidance, protection, or even financial welfare. A Chinese mother from Hong Kong complained that she often felt out of control over her son, "The school counselor said he [minor] was in control of me. That's why. I have no control over him. If we were still in Hong Kong, things would never be like this. I would hit him. He is tired of my talking to him. I told him to appreciate the environment. He is very lucky to be in this country. I am angry. I don't know how to teach him."

After her son was arrested for burglary, a forty-five-year-old mother said that she had seen it coming because her son was wanted by the police for probation violations.

> I wanted the police to arrest him and put him away because I couldn't control him. He was driving me and his two sisters crazy. We used to drive around every night looking for him. I am a bad parent and can't fulfill my responsibility. I have tried everything. I can't control him. I am frustrated, angry, and sad. He is out running everyday. I don't know where he sleeps and how he eats his meals. All parents love their children. But I often wonder why I even gave birth to him.

Because of their limited knowledge of the host society, schools, and justice system, these parents were no longer able to occupy their traditional hierarchical positions by providing guidance and protection, or imposing discipline. Role reversal is likely to become an important conceptual issue in explaining the causes of delinquency in the immigrant Chinese community. If the traditional Chinese family is to function effectively as a social control mechanism, parental authority and capabilities are crucial elements in the scheme. Unfortunately, when the role is reversed and children are pushed to assume parental responsibilities, adult-like behaviors (namely delinquent behaviors) often ensue.

CONTROLLING THE DELINQUENT CHINESE BOY

To explore how Chinese parents control their delinquent children, this study examined two specific aspects of their coping behavior, namely, efforts to reduce the level of perceived stress and social stigma, and to prevent possible recurrence of the incident (i.e., recidivism): (1) parental shaming, a culturally based practice aimed at inducing embarrassment and guilt in the youngster, and (2) use of social support in supervising the delinquent youngster.

Based on Braithwaite's theory of reintegrative shaming, crime is best controlled in societies where there is a strong sense of familism and communitarianism.[21] There is a clear sense of boundaries with regard to appropriate behaviors, and violation of community standards is controlled through a continued process of shaming and reintegration. Braithwaite believes that such shaming is more effective in controlling delinquency than are formal institutional sanctions.

This study explores two aspects of the shaming practice—parental shaming and communitarian shaming. Parental shaming is a common cultural practice in which parents use verbal and facial expressions as well as physical means to display their disapproval over a child's transgression, with the aim to induce shame and guilt in that youngster. Communitarian shaming involves sharing the negative information of the minor's transgression with one's relatives or immediate social circle, thus making the youngster aware of his delinquent status.

Although parental shaming has often been discussed in academic colloquiums on informal social control in Asian cultures, few published studies have examined the specific practices that induce feelings of shame or guilt. Through unstructured, open-ended questions, Chinese parents in this study were found to be more inclined to use verbal shaming than nonverbal or physical actions to express their disapproval of their delinquent child's behaviors. Very few parents used physical means (i.e., corporeal punishment) to express their feelings, although many of them said that they would like to exercise their parental authority in a corporeal way, but feared child protective service agencies.

As for communitarian shaming, few parents shared the negative stories about their delinquent child with relatives or members of the immediate social circle. Most parents felt disgraced by their sons' behavior and the last thing they wanted to do was to further embarrass themselves by sharing the news with their neighbors or relatives. As one Chinese mother put it, "We have never had this happen to us before. It is shameful enough for us to deal with the court. We dare not to tell our friends or relatives about our son's problem with the police. Every time I come to the court or probation office, I will feel sick. My heart just feels empty. I can never feel at ease."

In sum, this study found that shaming was an idiosyncratic parenting behavior and thus elusive to systematic empirical exploration. Shame and guilt, as conceptualized in much of Western culture, are mostly portrayed as something detrimental to one's self-esteem and growth, and parents and teachers alike are advised to avoid practices that may trigger feelings of shame and guilt. However, in the context of the Chinese culture, shaming (at least verbally) was a common practice among the respondents in reply to their children's legal transgressions.

Supervision and Building Alliance with Probation Officers

All parents reported a significant increase in their time and effort in the supervision of their delinquent sons. Although not by choice, probation was the only government agency that respondents regularly called upon in their efforts to keep their children on track. Most Chinese parents indicated that they welcomed the structure and strict rules imposed by the court. They were even grateful that probation officers spent time with their children and worked with parents to impose the court order. Parents who previously felt powerless in front of their wayward child now were able to call on the probation officer to intervene. In fact, several parents often threatened to call the probation officer whenever they believed their child was getting out of control. This leverage provided by the justice system appeared to restore the culturally sanctioned hierarchy and empower these parents to resume their traditional role.

Still, many parents experienced increased stress as a result of their diverted time and effort in the supervision of their children in accordance with court orders. As ordered by the juvenile court, these parents had to assist their children in paying restitution, in driving them to see their probation officer, in accompanying them to attend tutoring and counseling classes, and in helping them complete community service. After her son was adjudicated for assault and carrying a weapon, a mother said his probation had added more stress to her already stressful job working as a waitress in a restaurant: "I am spending more time watching him now. I have more worries. I have to make sure he comes home on time each day. I talk to him more and tell him not to stay out late. We have to do a lot more things with him now. We gave him a pager to track him. Now I know where he is because I page him all the time. He has to report to me all the time. When he goes out, he has to get permission. Otherwise, he can't leave the house. I think he has learned a lesson." Another mother, whose son was arrested on grand theft auto, said, "I am very worried he might be in trouble again. There are too many distractions in his life now. This is a very confusing age for him. Psychological counseling is not helping me; it only gives me headaches. I have to go everywhere [minor's name] goes. I feel so tired most of the times. Each month we have to see his probation officer once. For the whole month my heart feels heavy."

Although most parents complained of the stress and worries they experienced while supervising their children, all respondents reported significantly improved family relationships because of the increased interactions between parents and the delinquent children. These parents believed that their delinquent children would turn around because of the improved interactions. Much of published literature in criminology appears to support their belief in that a good relationship between parents and their youngsters often serves as a strong deterrence to delinquency. As a Chinese father put it, "We grew closer. As parents, we talk to him a lot about his day or his activities at school. Actually we channel all of our energy into his life. We have nothing else in our mind but his well-being. I am taking him to school every morning, making sure he is there. His mother calls him at school everyday to check up on him. Right now I don't want him to socialize with anyone, especially his gang friends."

A Chinese mother, who had just gone through a divorce, felt her relationship with her delinquent son was never better than after he was placed on probation:

> Probation is good. More disciplines and structure in his life. I welcome all court orders. Now we do everything together. I am taking [minor's name] with me to everywhere. We are together more often. I don't drink anymore. When [minor's name] was arrested, I felt that I had failed on everything, my marriage first, now my family. I was very hurt. I was never a drinker. But right after the incident, I drank to pass out, to forget about everything. Now I am happy. I see [minor's name] every day at home.

In sum, more parent-child activities, although time demanding, were observed among most respondents. The significant increase in family involvement resulted from two factors: (1) court-ordered activities and (2) parents' feelings of guilt for not having paid much attention to their children previously. Respondents in general relied on themselves to supervise their delinquent children. But many also resorted to the supervision services provided by the Probation Department. Besides probation and the court-ordered parenting classes, Chinese parents sought little external assistance (e.g., formal social agencies, such as social work, individual counseling, support groups, and schools). Several factors could contribute to this failure to utilize formal social services. Unlike other socially disadvantaged ethnic groups, such as African Americans, these Chinese immigrant parents lacked the proper knowledge of the resources available in their communities. Their limited language ability and restricted social network further hampered their efforts to seek formal social services and utilize them to their advantage. Additionally, there is also a lack of cultural support and tradition for the use of public resources for private or personal problems. In the countries where these immigrant parents came from, social services similar to those in the United States are basically nonexistent.

DISCUSSION

While the small sample size in this study may imply methodological limitations, it was a result of several factors—the restrictive screening criteria for interview inclusion (e.g., male and first-time offenders on formal probation), limited funding, and the relatively small delinquent population. But while the sample was small, responses from the interviewed parents were surprisingly consistent, and thus generated findings that can serve as building blocks for theory construction to guide future empirical studies on Chinese delinquents. These findings may also encourage justice policies that strengthen parental roles and exert effective control over wayward youngsters in the Chinese American communities.

This study yielded several significant findings. First, the subject matter was relatively new and rarely studied. With the rapid increase of the Chinese population in the United States, juvenile delinquency among Chinese communities has become a recognized social problem that requires systematic examination. Building a body of knowledge thus becomes an important task among the few scholars who share this interest. In a culture heavy on tradition and hierarchy, parental perceptions and response to delinquent children are crucial to effective policies in the prevention and control of wayward youngsters among Chinese communities.

Second, while many Chinese studies scholars take culture as a given and examine its position within the host society, this study attempted to delineate
the major themes from which variables can be derived and measured for the
analysis of the interactions between culture and social control. For instance,
to operationalize Braithwaite's theory of reintegrative shaming, this study explored the use of several measures to examine how parents induce the feelings
of shame and guilt among their delinquent children. However, the challenge
still remains to convert some of the key concepts of Braithwaite's theory into
empirical questions, let alone to prescribe workable social policies. For instance, this study failed to produce evidence of meaningful participation of
parents in communitarian shaming.

Third, through this exploratory study, methodological problems were uncovered during interviews with Chinese respondents. Most of them had little
or no prior experience with this type of interview. Many parents had little formal education and were mostly preoccupied with making enough money to
get by. Extra explanations were needed, hence the interviews were significantly
lengthened, increasing the possibility for noise in data collection.

It is hoped that this study will bring about more systematic inquiry into the
causes of delinquency among Chinese immigrant youth, and into the interplay of Chinese cultural norms and customs with those of the larger society as
they are related to the rise of delinquency. It is also hoped that this study will
influence future studies in their gathering of empirical data and providing of
helpful guidance in prescribing effective social control policies.

This study sought to contribute to the scarce knowledge of how Chinese
parents apply their cultural heritage in their social control function. Such
knowledge will help policy makers understand the tremendous challenges
that confront new immigrants in their transition from their traditional way of
living and raising youngsters to learning to do the same in the New World. It
will also promote policies that strengthen the traditional family structure
(rather than replace it with sometimes less-effective social institutions, such as
the court and social service agencies) to effectively manage and control the
most active and troublesome members of a fast-growing population.

This study also called for more research on how Chinese immigrant families survive in a host society where the legal, educational, and social systems
are not conducive to the maintenance of a traditional family structure, and
weakens effective control over troublesome youth. As the Chinese population
increases rapidly in the United States, juvenile delinquents will inevitably
draw more public attention, thus requiring social research into effective social

control policies. However, the real challenge is to design social interventions or policies that accommodate cultural idiosyncrasies, such as strengthening the parental role and the hierarchical structure through the use of shame and guilt, since the "face mentality" will forever remain a key element in the informal social control of wayward youngsters among Chinese immigrants.

NOTES

This study was supported in part by the National Science Foundation (SBR-9300919) and the Los Angeles County Probation Department. The author is solely responsible for the opinions expressed in this article. An earlier version of this chapter was presented at the Sixth Chinese-American Conference in San Diego, California.

1. Charles Howe, "The Growth of Gangs in Chinatown," *San Francisco Chronicle,* 7 July 1972, sec. 1; Rose Pak, "Chinatown Gangs: Ex-Member Talks," *San Francisco Chronicle,* 6 July 1972, 1; Ron Chernow, "Chinatown, Their Chinatown: The Truth behind the Façade," *New York Magazine,* 11 June 1973, 39–45.

2. Ko-Lin Chin, *Chinatown Gangs: Extortion, Enterprise, and Ethnicity* (New York: Oxford University, 1996), 7.

3. Lynn Ludlow, "Golden Dragon Massacre: Pain Still Felt a Decade Later," *San Francisco Examiner,* 10 May 1987, B1.

4. Ralph Blumenthal, "Gunmen Firing Wildly Kill 3 in Chinatown Bar," *New York Times,* 24 December 1982, A1.

5. Michael Daly, "The War for Chinatown," *New York Magazine,* 14 February 1983, 31–38; James Dubro, *Dragons of Crime: Inside the Asian Underworld* (Markham, Ont.: Octopus, 1992).

6. The population statistics were provided by the Demographic Unit of the California Department of Finance. All Asians and Pacific Islanders are customarily lumped into one category, the same way the census data are recorded at the U.S. Census Bureau.

7. Statistical information was made available by the Program Evaluation and Services Office, Los Angeles County Probation Department. This information is good as of April 30, 1999.

8. Chin, *Chinatown Gangs,* 6.

9. Richard Sollenberger, "Chinese-American Child-Rearing Practices and Juvenile Delinquency," *Journal of Social Psychology* 74 (1968): 13–23.

10. Harry H. L. Kitano, *Race Relations*, 5th ed. (Upper Saddle River, N.J.: Prentice Hall, 1997); Chun, Ki-Taek, "The Myth of Chinese American Success and Its Educational Ramifications," in *American Mosaic: Selected Readings on America's Multicultural Heritage*, ed. Y. I. Song and E. C. Kim (Englewood Cliffs, N.J.: Prentice Hall, 1993).

11. E. McGrath, "Confucian Work Ethic," *Time*, 28 March 1983, 52.

12. Diego Vigil and Steve Yun, "Vietnamese Youth Gangs in Southern California," in *Gangs in America*, ed. C. Ronald Huff (Newbury Park, Calif.: Sage, 1990).

13. S. P. Shon and D. D. Ja, "Chinese Families," in *Ethnicity and Family Therapy*, ed. M. McGoldrick, J. K. Pearce, and J. Giordano (New York: Guilford, 1982).

14. Morrison G. Wong, "The Chinese American Family," in *Ethnic Families in America: Patterns and Variations*, ed. C. H. Mindel, R. W. Habenstein, and R. Wright Jr. (New York: Elsevier, 1988), 230–57.

15. H. C. Hu, "The Chinese Concepts of Face," in *Personal Character and Cultural Milieu*, ed. D. G. Haring (Syracuse, N.Y.: Syracuse University Press, 1975).

16. Kitano, *Race Relations*, 232.

17. Morrison G. Wong, "Chinese Americans," in *Asian Americans: Contemporary Trends and Issues*, ed. Pyong Gap Min (Thousand Oaks, Calif.: Sage, 1995), 71.

18. Sheldon X. Zhang, "Measuring Shaming in an Ethnic Context," *British Journal of Criminology* 35, no. 2 (1995): 248–62.

19. H. McCubbin and J. Patterson, "The Family Stress Process: The Double ABCX Model of Adjustment and Adaptation," in *Social Stress and the Family: Advances and Developments in Family Stress Theory and Research*, ed. H. McCubbin, M. Sussman, and J. Patterson (New York: Haworth, 1983); D. H. Olson and H. I. McCubbin, *Families: What Makes Them Work* (Beverly Hills, Calif.: Sage, 1983).

20. R. S. Lazarus, "Cognitive and Coping Processes in Emotion," in *Stress and Coping*, ed. A. Monat and R. S. Lazarus (New York: Columbia University Press, 1977).

21. John Braithwaite, *Crime, Shame and Reintegration* (Cambridge: Cambridge University Press, 1989), 5–9.

REFERENCES

Barth, Gunther. 1964. *Bitter Strength: A History of Chinese in the United States*. Cambridge, Mass.: Harvard University Press.

Blumenthal, Ralph. 1982. "Gunmen Firing Wildly Kill 3 in Chinatown Bar." *New York Times,* 24 December, A1.

Braithwaite, John. 1989. *Crime, Shame and Reintegration.* Cambridge: Cambridge University Press.

Cernkovich, S. A., and P. C. Giordano. 1987. "Family Relationships and Delinquency." *Criminology* 25: 295–321.

Chernow, Ron. 1973. "Chinatown, Their Chinatown: The Truth behind the Façade." *New York Magazine,* 11 June: 39–45.

Chin, Ko-Lin. 1996. *Chinatown Gangs: Extortion, Enterprise, and Ethnicity.* New York: Oxford University Press.

———. 1996. "Gang Violence in Chinatown." In *Gangs in America,* ed. C. R. Huff. 2d ed. Thousand Oaks, Calif.: Sage.

Chun, Ki-Taek. 1993. "The Myth of Chinese American Success and Its Educational Ramifications." In *American Mosaic: Selected Readings on America's Multicultural Heritage,* ed. Y. I. Song and E. C. Kim. Englewood Cliffs, N.J.: Prentice Hall.

Daly, Michael. 1983. "The War for Chinatown." *New York Magazine,* 14 February, 31–38.

Dillon, Richard H. 1962. *The Hatchet Men: The Story of the Tong Wars in San Francisco's Chinatown.* New York: Coward-McCann.

Dubro, James. 1992. *Dragons of Crime: Inside the Asian Underworld.* Markham, Ont.: Octopus.

Gove, W. R., and R. C. Crutchfield. 1982. "The Family and Juvenile Delinquency." *Sociological Quarterly* 23: 301–19.

Howe, Charles. 1972. "The Growth of Gangs in Chinatown." *San Francisco Chronicle,* 7 July, sec. 1.

Hu, H. C. 1956. "The Chinese Concepts of Face." In *Personal Character and Cultural Milieu,* ed. D. G. Haring. 3d ed. Syracuse, N.Y.: Syracuse University Press.

Kelly, Robert J., Ko-Lin Chin, and Jeffrey A. Fagan. 1993. "The Dragon Breathes Fire: Chinese Organized Crime in New York City." *Crime, Law and Social Change* 19, no. 3: 245–69.

Kitano, Harry H. L. 1997. *Race Relations.* 5th ed. Upper Saddle River, N.J.: Prentice Hall.

Lazarus, R. S. 1977. "Cognitive and Coping Processes in Emotion." In *Stress and Coping,* ed. A. Monat and R. S. Lazarus. New York: Columbia University Press.

Lee, C. Y. 1974. *Days of the Tong Wars*. New York: Ballantine.

Liu, Poi-chi, and Mei-kuo Hua Ch'iao Shih. 1981. *A History of the Chinese in the United States of America II*. Taipei: Li Min.

Ludlow, Lynn. 1987. "Golden Dragon Massacre: Pain Still Felt a Decade Later." *San Francisco Examiner*, 10 May, B1.

Martin, Mildred Crowl. 1977. *Chinatown's Angry Angel*. Palo Alto, Calif.: Pacific Books.

McCubbin, H., and J. Patterson. 1983. "The Family Stress Process: The Double ABCX Model of Adjustment and Adaptation." In *Social Stress and the Family: Advances and Developments in Family Stress Theory and Research*, ed. H. McCubbin, M. Sussman, and J. Patterson. New York: Haworth.

McGrath, E. 1983. "Confucian Work Ethic." *Time*, 28 March, 52.

Miller, Stuart Creighton. 1960. *The Unwelcome Immigrant: The American Image of the Chinese, 1785–1881*. Berkeley: University of California Press.

Olson, D. H., and H. I. McCubbin. 1983. *Families: What Makes Them Work*. Beverly Hills, Calif.: Sage.

Pak, Rose. 1972. "Chinatown Gangs: Ex-Member Talks." *San Francisco Chronicle*, 6 July, 1.

Saxton, Alexander. 1971. *The Indispensable Enemy: Labor and the Anti-Chinese Movement in California*. Berkeley: University of California Press.

Seward, George F. 1970. *Chinese Immigration: Its Social and Economical Aspects*. 1881. New York: Arno.

Shon, S. P., and D. D. Ja. 1982. "Chinese Families." In *Ethnicity and Family Therapy*, ed. M. McGoldrick, J. K. Pearce, and J. Giordano. New York: Guilford.

Sollenberger, Richard. 1968. "Chinese-American Child-Rearing Practices and Juvenile Delinquency." *Journal of Social Psychology* 74: 13–23.

Tong, B. 1971. "The Ghetto of the Mind: Notes on the Historical Psychology of Chinese America." *Amerasia Journal* 1, no. 3: 1–31.

Vigil, Diego, and Steve Yun. 1990. "Vietnamese Youth Gangs in Southern California." In *Gangs in America*, ed. C. Ronald Huff. Newbury Park, Calif.: Sage.

Weiss, M. 1977. "The Research Experience in a Chinese American Community." *Journal of Social Issues* 33, no. 4: 120–32.

Wong, B. 1976. "Social Stratification, Adaptive Strategies and the Chinese Community of New York." *Urban Life* 5, no. 1: 33–52.

Wong, Morrison G. 1988. "The Chinese American Family." In *Ethnic Families in America: Patterns and Variations,* ed. Charles H. Mindel, Robert W. Habenstein, and Roosevelt Wright Jr. (New York: Elsevier): 230–57.

———. 1995. "Chinese Americans." In *Asian Americans: Contemporary Trends and Issues,* ed. Pyong Gap Min. Thousand Oaks, Calif.: Sage.

Zhang, Sheldon X. 1995. "Measuring Shaming in an Ethnic Context." *British Journal of Criminology* 35, no. 2: 248–62.

Zhou, Min. 1992. *Chinatown: The Socioeconomic Potential of an Urban Enclave.* Philadelphia: Temple University Press.

14

Unbound Feet: A Metaphor for the Transformation of the Chinese Immigrant Female in Chinese American Literature

Bonnie Khaw-Posthuma

In the pivotal chapter of *The Woman Warrior*, Maxine Hong Kingston recounts the story of Fa Mu Lan, a Chinese woman warrior extolled for her bravery and filial piety. As a Chinese American woman, Kingston's own battle mirrors Fa Mu Lan's: she too struggles with a Chinese patriarchal society that denigrates girls as "maggots" and "slaves." Critics have commented on the inner conflict embodied in the young narrator (Maxine), who negotiates the tensions between her Chinese and Chinese American identities through "silencing"—or the absence of spoken language.[1] Maxine's mother echoes their cultural doctrine of female passivity in the line "a ready tongue is an evil,"[2] thus pressuring her daughter to be mute in America—a place where freedom of speech is a fundamental value. Critics, while analyzing this metaphor of silence, neglect to address another equally important one: the image of the Chinese woman's bound feet.

Traditional Chinese society implemented bound feet as a way to control a female, a means to keep her sexuality[3] and identity contained. A popular saying demonstrates this: "Why must the foot be bound? To prevent barbarous running around."[4] In the second chapter of *The Woman Warrior*, Kingston states, "Even now China *wraps double binds around my feet*."[5] This image of the woman's bound feet is a powerful *physical* and *symbolic* representation of her oppression by her culture. Furthermore, the Chinese female was told her place was by the "hearth" or in the home. The Chinese woman's *physical* being and *social* identity were controlled by her patriarchy. Like her Victorian counterpart, the Chinese woman lived by the adage "suffer and be still." She could not protest against the binding of her feet, otherwise she would be considered a "bad" or disobedient female.

"Communal-centered"[6] Chinese culture in the late nineteenth and early twentieth centuries dictated the individual's position and role within both the family and larger community. This rigid hierarchical system placed women on the bottom rung of the socioeconomic ladder, where they endured both societal and familial control: their larger village and clan governed the family, who in turn governed the women. In addition, women were also "governed by men."[7] Chinese women of this time remained hopelessly entrapped in a cycle of subjugation and abuse. The allied forces of her community and family converged in the literal and symbolic representation of the Chinese woman's bound feet; the female's permanently crippled and deformed feet underscored the fact that her duty remained to the "hearth," or home, and that she must literally be kept from "wandering" outside her given sphere.

What then happened to the dynamics of the Chinese family—and correspondingly, the role of the Chinese woman—when she came to individualistic America? Miller states, "[t]he western concept of individualism threatens the Confucian family, wherein ultimate value resides for the traditional Chinese and which rests on unquestioning obedience to those above you in the hierarchy,"[8] with women assuming the lowest position in this power structure. The Chinese female's struggle between the dictates of these two opposing cultures was especially crucial during the pivotal years of the late nineteenth and early twentieth centuries, when discriminatory laws and practices against Chinese immigrants in the United States reached their peak. Due to social and economic conditions in the United States, the Chinese American woman achieved a freedom and power unknown in her native China—as signified by the symbolic, and sometimes literal, "unbinding" of her feet. Ultimately, these Chinese wives and mothers served as cultural preservers and "beacon[s] against the forces of . . . cultural change outside the home."[9] The literature of Chinese American authors Maxine Hong Kingston, Jade Snow Wong, Amy Tan, Ruthanne McCunn, and Pang-Mei Chang illustrates this evolution.

In order to understand the relevance of the image of women's footbinding in Chinese American literature, one must first understand how this practice came into effect in China and its intimate connection to China's patriarchal tradition. There are several theories on the origin of women's footbinding in China, which attribute them to times ranging from the twelfth century B.C. to the ninth century A.D.[10] The most probable origin of footbinding is during the Southern dynastic rule of sovereign poet Li Yu, who reigned from 961 to 975 A.D.: "A favored palace concubine named Lovely Maiden . . . was a slender-waisted beauty and a gifted dancer. He [Li Yu] had a six-foot high lotus constructed for her out of gold. . . . Lovely Maiden was ordered to bind her feet with white silk cloth to make the tips look like the points of a moon sickle. She then danced in the center of the lotus, whirling about like a rising cloud."[11]

The term "golden lotus," given to the special apparatus on which the palace dancers walked and danced, later became the euphonious term for bound feet.[12] Twelfth-century writer Chang Pang-chi revealed that by his day (circa 1130) footbinding, which arose from the desire to achieve an artistic effect among palace dancers, "slowly set the fashion for the rest of the Chinese world."[13] So what began as an artistic or creative tool later evolved into a symbol of fashion and beauty, and finally into its ultimate manifestation—an instrument for the oppression and control of women. By the late nineteenth and early twentieth centuries, over 80 percent of women in China had their feet bound.[14]

The bound-footed female's life was impaired physically, socially, and sexually. Physically, she was deformed from having her big toe bent backward and the bones in her feet broken. She often relied on other family members or a servant to walk. Pang-Mei Chang's heroine Yu-i, in *Bound Feet and Western Dress*, typifies one such Chinese girl's misery: "Bound feet take years of wrapping. The toe bones have to be broken slowly, carefully. Even after a young girl's feet are perfectly formed, she has to keep them wrapped so they will stay in shape."[15]

This practice not only controlled a female's physical identity, it also controlled her social and sexual being. "It was so inconvenient for the bound-footed to get about," writes Levy, "that her chances for indulging sexually as did the Chinese male were greatly lessened. Footbinding proved to be a significant and lasting development in a nation whose outlook on feminine morality became increasingly stringent."[16] Sexually speaking, the size of her feet determined the woman's desirability as a sex object. Ratings were even given to the different sizes of women's feet: three-inch ones represented the highest grade and were termed "golden lotus," while four-inch ones were called "silver lotus."[17] After subjecting the female to the inhumane torture of bound feet, her culture further controlled the way this embodiment of feminine sexuality was used: Chinese culture viewed a woman's diminutive feet as a sign of her beauty and desirability, so she was not permitted to display them openly. John Byron explains, "bound feet were a symbol of forbidden pleasure . . . [and] the fact they were almost always concealed from men meant that miniature feet were the one part of a woman's body that was inaccessible."[18] Thus the patriarchy kept both her identity and sensuality "under wraps," so to speak. Clearly, the objectification of this female body part suggests that the traditional Chinese female was treated as a sexual commodity and plaything rather than as a human being.

Ruthanne Lum McCunn's *Thousand Pieces of Gold* delineates the lowly position of one such Chinese woman (Lalu), whom male-dominated society treats as chattel. Lalu is sold as a slave in China and later as a prostitute in America in the late nineteenth century. Her mother originally binds her feet in China, forcing her to perform the household chores while tottering painfully on four-inch feet. McCunn describes the painstaking process of footbinding: "every day for two years, her mother had wound long white bandages around each foot in ever tightening bands, twisting her toes under her feet and forcing them back until her feet had become two dainty arcs."[19] This passage underscores the significance Lalu's culture attaches to bound and diminutive feet. In the Chinese community, until the early twentieth century, a woman's small feet converted her into a commodity; tiny feet meant she conformed to the ideal in female beauty and therefore made her more "marketable" as a potential wife. Families looking for daughters-in-law considered first the girl's bound feet, then her face, for "[t]he face was merely an inherited quality; feet . . . were an indication of toil, skill, and ability."[20] Miniature feet also implied she was "demure" and "yielding,"[21] therefore guaranteeing she would make the perfect subservient and filial Chinese wife. This evidence plainly indicates the enormous pressure placed on the young Chinese girl to conform and submit to the torture of footbinding; footbinding ensured both her family and prospective in-laws that she was *both* an obedient daughter and an obedient daughter-in-law.

However, due to the family's desperate economic situation, Lalu's mother eventually unbinds her feet, so that she may work in the fields. This act of unbinding a female's feet signals disaster in Lalu's culture—for it means she will become more "masculine" and thus less suitable for marriage. In a parallel scene from Chang's *Bound Feet and Western Dress*, the protagonist, Yu-i, also has her feet unbound.

Yu-i's amah (grandmother) laments the loss of diminutive feet in both Yu-i and her other granddaughters: "my amah worried for our future. Who would marry us with big feet? We were *bu san, bu si*, neither three nor four [foot size of three or four inches]. We could not work in the fields all day long and do the chores of a man. But neither could we just sit still and stay quiet like ladies in the female quarters."[22] The line Yu-i's amah utters, "Who would marry us with big feet," echoes that spoken by Lalu's mother in *Thousand Pieces of Gold* after her feet are unbound, "Now who will marry you?" Both Lalu and Yu-i become devalued in the eyes of their families and society because their "natural" feet transform them into damaged goods and unmarketable marriage material.

"Natural" or "bare" feet connote coarseness and ill manners and automatically connect a woman to the peasant or laboring class.[23]

Other twentieth-century Chinese American writers depict through the bound-foot symbol the woman's struggle in traditional China to fulfill not only the Confucian dictate of filial piety, but familism. Familism refers to the placement of the family's needs and desires over one's own (Webster's 1989). In Amy Tan's *The Kitchen God's Wife*, the main character, Winnie, must demonstrate her loyalty as a daughter by submitting to an arranged marriage. As a woman in early twentieth-century China, she has no individual choice, as is seen when Winnie describes the differences between Chinese and American society to her American-raised daughter: "[i]n China you were always responsible to somebody else; not like here in the United States—freedom, independence, individual thinking."[24] When Winnie protests against the injustices and hardships society inflicts on her as a female, her family threatens her with mysterious stories of her disgraced and *un*bound-footed mother, who became a "beggar."[25] Winnie describes her: "My mother was not like the Chinese girls Americans always imagine, the kind who walk around with tiny bound feet. . . . My mother was a modern girl. . . . When my mother was eight years old, her feet were already unbound, and some say that's why she ran wild."[26] Sadly, unbound feet implied other derogatory meanings besides "coarseness" and "ill manners"—as shown earlier in the cases of Lalu and Yu-i. Big feet also pointed to wildness and uncontrollable sexuality in a female. Therefore, Winnie must fulfill her role as a dutiful daughter and marry the man her family chooses for her or experience the same humiliation and ostracization her mother did. Although what happened to her mother is never made clear, the family's injunction to her is observe filial duty and maintain the family honor or suffer grave consequences.

In direct contrast to the male- and familism-centered structure in China, American society focuses more on the individual. These basic values of freedom and equality inherent in American society, compounded by the dire social and economic conditions Chinese immigrants faced at the turn of the twentieth century, resulted in the dramatic transformation of the Chinese woman's roles as wife and mother. Adding a further complication, rigid and discriminatory U.S. immigration laws—aimed specifically at Chinese—led to a scarcity of Chinese women, and the dearth of females dramatically altered the way Chinese males viewed and treated them. The Chinese Exclusion Laws of 1882 to 1902 suspended immigration of Chinese laborers,[27] the "first time in American history that a specific group of people [was] excluded on the basis of race and class."[28] This Exclusion Act severely controlled the number of

Chinese women able to enter the United States, so that throughout the nineteenth century Chinese women "never exceed[ed] the 5,000 mark or 7 percent of the total Chinese population."[29] As a result, "most Chinese men, because of their low socioeconomic status, c[ould not] afford a concubine or mistress, much less a wife. Thus having a wife [wa]s a status to be jealously guarded."[30] Accordingly, Chinese men seemed to follow the rule of "supply and demand"—the fewer available Chinese women, the more valuable women became and the less strict were men's requirements for marriage, including whether women's feet were bound.

In America, as in China, these Chinese wives still fulfilled their traditional duties in the home, but now because of difficult social and economic conditions they were free to "wander" outside the household sphere. The Chinese American woman achieved a freedom unknown in her native China—as represented through the symbolic, at times literal, "unbinding" of her feet. Furthermore, her role in the home itself changed, so that the "family [while still] a site of oppression for Chinese women . . . was also a source of empowerment."[31] Chinese American wives not only ran the household and raised the children, they served as "beacon[s] against the forces and temptations of cultural changes outside the home";[32] they were indeed the preservers of Chinese family values. Yet this struggle to unbind their feet, and correspondingly free their identities, turned into a long and difficult one, for Chinese American females contended with *both* the prevailing ideology of Chinese immigrant males and the racism of the larger American culture. For example, during the turn of the last century Americans denigrated both Chinese male and female immigrants: they stereotyped the former as "coolies" and the latter as "potential prostitutes."[33] Notably, immigration officials deemed only bound-footed women as safe and acceptable. They considered these women to belong to the upper class or gentry, and assumed they would therefore take their proper place in the home. One official explained: "There has never come to this port, I believe, a bound footed woman who was found to be of an immoral character, this condition of affairs being due, it is stated, to the fact that such women . . . are necessarily confined to their homes and seldom frequent the city districts."[34] This passage reveals an insidious combination of racism and sexism acting together: the Chinese immigrant female must keep in her "proper" place due to her sex *and* her race. Not surprisingly, a powerful link united the misogynous ideology of American patriarchal society to that of Chinese patriarchal society, as evidenced clearly in the way both attempted to subjugate the Chinese woman through applying the literal and symbolic image of bound feet. Recall, for example, the traditional Chinese saying exalting bound feet as a way to "prevent [her] barbarous running around." Male-dominated societies of both China and America believed bound feet ensured the Chinese female remained in her given place—the home—and both defined a "good" woman as one who submitted, thus equating subservience with morality.

In spite of these numerous hurdles, the Chinese bound-footed woman of the late nineteenth and early twentieth centuries symbolically unbound her feet in the United States, "reshape[d] gender roles and change[d] [her] circumstance for the better."[35] The twentieth-century novels of Chinese American writers attest to this fact in their portrayal of strong Chinese American mothers and wives, as seen in Jade Snow Wong's *Fifth Chinese Daughter*. Wong demonstrates the energy of her China-born, bound-footed mother. Wong's mother epitomizes Chinese immigrant females who transform into the real binding force holding their families together—serving as "beacons against the forces and temptations of cultural change outside the home."[36] Jade's father himself gradually realizes the practical and economic need for the evolution of the Chinese woman's role in America. Before Jade's mother and siblings join him in the United States, the father writes to his wife, explaining his changed views. He states, "Do not bind our daughter's feet. Here in America is an entirely different set of standards, which does not require that women sway helplessly on little feet to qualify for good matches as well-born women do not have to work. Here in Gold Mountain, the people, even women, have equal dignity and rights of their own."[37] Notably, here the character employs the image of bound feet to proclaim his rejection of the values and beliefs of his old traditional world, China, in favor of his new modern world, America. According to him, the size of a Chinese woman's feet no longer determines her future happiness and position in society. This revelation is even more striking because it originates from an emblem of traditional Chinese patriarchy: Jade's father. Furthermore, he acknowledges the importance of the Chinese immigrant wife in supporting the family: "Unlike the Old-World [traditional Chinese] custom of staying at home, [Jade's] father believed that according to New-World [American] Christian ideals women had a right to improve the economic status of their family."[38] Wong's mother epitomizes other Chinese American immigrant wives of the last century who transformed into "indispensable partners to their husbands in their struggle for economic survival,"[39] as she aids in the running of the family's garment factory.

Similar to Jade Snow Wong's mother in *Fifth Chinese Daughter*, the narrator's mother in Maxine Hong Kingston's *The Woman Warrior* personifies a Chinese female immigrant who transforms her role and position in her family once in America. Initially, like Wong's mother, Kingston's mother represents one of the "stay-at-home" wives left behind in China; these women's duty remained that of "keeping warm the hearth fire while their adventurous husband[s] gallop[ed] elsewhere for sexual and economic gratification."[40] Eventually, however, Kingston's mother rejects the role of passive and self-sacrificing "at-home" wife. Instead of assuming the position of the typical daughter-in-law in serving the needs of her new "mother," Brave Orchid utilizes the money her sojourner husband sends home to China to pay her way through midwife school. Sledge explains that for a small percentage of women, like Brave Orchid, their husbands' departure allowed them to assume "total family governance"; moreover, "there arose a strong tradition of womanly self-sufficiency and aggressiveness among Cantonese. Kingston shows the persistence of that tradition among those few Chinese women, like her mother."[41] The mother rejects the status of woman—as wife and slave—and transforms her role from one of victim to one of self-empowerer. Moreover, rather than submitting to the central belief in familism, she places her needs above those of her family in achieving her dream of a medical degree.

When Brave Orchid enters America during the early twentieth century, she reconfigures her identity within the Chinese patriarchy and modifies her role to fit her new home. Once an esteemed midwife in China, she now must perform menial labor in the family-run laundry business and perform migrant farmwork. Chinese immigrant women of this time, "handicapped further by gender, worked primarily in garment and food-processing factories for low piece rate wages"[42] and other low-level subsistence jobs. In addition to raising children, Maxine's mother works tirelessly outside the home in a country she denigrates as a "terrible ghost [foreigner] country, where a human being works her life away."[43] Judy Yung quotes another early twentieth-century Chinese immigrant woman, Margaret Leong Lowe, who recounts similar experiences: "I worked about six days a week. Sometimes I bring home work . . . I be mother, I be father. I had to make money and take care of children."[44] The narrator's mother in *The Woman Warrior,* though not a widow like Mrs. Lowe, demonstrates the complex roles of many early twentieth-century Chinese American females: they assumed the dual responsibilities of husband and wife as they both preserved family unity and Chinese cultural values within the home and worked outside the home to earn money for their family's survival.

In *The Woman Warrior* and *China Men,* Maxine's mother transforms into the guardian of the tenets of Chinese patriarchal culture, as evidenced both by her reactions to the "outside" American culture and by her treatment of family members like her husband and children. While Brave Orchid works diligently to provide financial support for her family, she continually goads her husband into resuming his given role as breadwinner. She tells her children, "it's a wife's job to scold her husband into working."[45] By American standards, Brave Orchid's scolding may seem hateful and malicious, yet by Chinese standards she succeeds in her role as dutiful wife and mother; she "shames" the husband into doing the right thing and thus maintains the code of familism, in which the family's needs come before anyone else's, even the father's. Furthermore, as Sledge explains, "Rage at his wife and children forces him [Maxine's father] out of his humiliating lethargy back into the world of work; he courageously resumes his former role in the face of the majority culture which would . . . demean him."[46]

Similarly, just as she did with her husband, Brave Orchid attempts to teach her daughters the doctrine of familism when she tries to instill the idea that the role of a Chinese female is one of subservience. In *The Woman Warrior*, Maxine's mother tells her she will grow up to be a wife and slave and recounts the tragic story of the family's "no name" aunt, who disgraced the family through adultery and became a "ghost" or outcast. Brave Orchid offers the aunt's story as a "puberty cautionary tale."[47] She states, "Now that you have started to menstruate, what happened to her could happen to you. Don't humiliate us. You wouldn't like to be forgotten as if you had never been born. The villagers are watchful."[48] Maxine's mother cleverly enforces the Chinese ideologies of both familism and female submission. The young narrator not only must conform to her role in the family and society but she must repress her sexuality and identity in order to assume her lowly position as a young, unmarried female.

Paradoxically, Maxine's mother, while acting as an "agent of the patriarchy,"[49] also represents a "potentially subversive model of how 'women simply reject some of men's social constructions . . . and adapt others to fit their own understanding of women's capabilities.'"[50] On the one hand, the mother denigrates women as wives and slaves, while on the other, Brave Orchid exemplifies a Chinese woman's strength and independence by her successes in China as a village doctor and ghost fighter and later in America as the family breadwinner and preserver of cultural values. In the United States, she bestows upon her daughter the major ability she still has available: "one power she has left to bequeath her daughter [is] the power to talk-story."[51] The older Maxine recalls the chant of Fa Mu Lan her mother gave her as a child: "I had forgotten this chant that was once mine, given me by my mother. . . . She said I would grow up a wife and slave, but she taught me the song of the warrior woman, Fa Mu Lan. I would have to grow up a warrior woman."[52] The mother's retelling of the story signifies a crucial part of the novel, for the famed female heroine represents a direct parallel to Brave Orchid herself: both have *un*bound feet, are rebels, and serve as role models for Maxine. Fa Mu Lan went against the norms of her culture in assuming the role of a male warrior, while Brave Orchid defied convention in turning herself into a scholar. Maxine notes the impact of Fa Mu Lan's tale on her life when she compares her life of repression and constant disappointment to the heroine's: "Marriage and childbirth strengthen the swordswoman, who is not a maid like Joan of Arc. Do the women's work; then do more work.... Then I get bitter: no one supports me.... Even now China wraps double binds around my feet."[53] Even though the narrator's feet are not literally bound, her identity is bound and constricted as she tries to fulfill the competing needs of her Chinese heritage, her mother's wishes, and her own desires.

Ultimately for Brave Orchid and other Chinese American women, the journey toward individual identity and equality involves ongoing struggle and difficulty, as shown in the symbol of the female's bound feet in the closing pages of *The Woman Warrior*. Maxine returns once more to the image of diminutive feet. She recalls the story of how her frightened mother and grandmother hid from bandits who raided the theater they attended in China. Significantly, the grandmother possessed tiny feet and could "run no f[u]rther on bound feet";[54] in contrast, the mother possessed "natural-sized" feet and more easily escaped the danger. The grandmother's condition brings the reader back to the tragic plight of Chinese women in the late nineteenth and early twentieth centuries, whose feet and identities were physically and metaphorically bound by their patriarchal culture; they could not "wander" outside their given sphere, the hearth or home. In contrast, the narrator's mother, Brave Orchid, represents the first generation of Chinese women in America whose traditional roles change as their feet and identities are unbound. Maxine herself embodies the second-generation Chinese female, who continuously grows and evolves—a change that began with her first-generation bound-footed mother. But for Maxine Hong Kingston and other Chinese American women, this journey toward self-fulfillment and equality remains a difficult one, as she depicts via the metaphor of silence: "The throat pain always returns, though, unless I tell what I really think."[55] Before, her mother's injunction of the Chinese proverb "A ready tongue is an evil" had controlled her life, transforming her into a mute. Now, she will loosen her tongue and symbolically free her identity, just as her bound-footed Chinese American female predecessors unbound their feet and "wandered" outside their traditional sphere and concomitantly into a new world.

NOTES

1. King-kok Cheung (1988) and Linda Morante (1987) analyze the significance of the narrator Maxine's muteness in *The Woman Warrior*.

2. Kingston (1975, 164).

3. For the purposes of this chapter I use the term "traditional" to refer specifically to late nineteenth- and early twentieth-century Chinese society and focus on the condition of this first-generation Chinese *American* woman during these crucial years. Correspondingly, the situation of the Chinese male sojourner changes in response to both the transformation of the Chinese female and the social conditions in the United States. This essay is an excerpt from my dissertation, which also details the image of men's "bound feet" and the struggles of Chinese male immigrants in the United States.

4. Levy (1966, 41).

5. Kingston (1975, 48), emphasis mine.

6. Chun-Hoon (1971, 60).

7. Aelia Davin, quoted in Miller (1983, 15).

8. Miller (1983, 15).

9. Yung (1995, 46).

10. Levy (1966, 37, 39).

11. Levy (1966, 39).

12. Levy (1966, 39).

13. Levy (1966, 40).

14. Levy (1966, 46).

15. Chang (1996, 21).

16. Levy (1966, 46).

17. Beurdeley (1969, 193).

18. Byron (1987, 66).

19. McCunn (1981, 26).

20. Jicai (1994, 36).

21. Levy (1966, 182).

22. Chang (1996, 23).

23. Levy (1966, 111).

24. Tan (1991, 132).

25. Tan (1991, 132–33).

26. Tan (1991, 100).

27. Chan (1991, 193–94).

28. Yung (1995, 22).

29. Yung (1995, 24).

30. Yung (1995, 7).

31. Yung (1995, 46).

32. Yung (1995, 46).

33. Yung (1995, 24).

34. Quoted in Yung (1995, 25).

35. Yung (1995, 105).

36. Yung (1995, 46).

37. Wong (1945, 72).

38. Wong (1945, 5).

39. Yung (1995, 77).

40. Wang (1985, 25).

41. Sledge (1980, 10).

42. Yung (1995, 88).

43. Kingston (1975, 104).

44. Yung (1995, 90–91).

45. Kingston (1977, 247).

46. Sledge (1980, 10).

47. Miller (1983, 19).

48. Kingston (1975, 5).

49. Miller (1983, 23).

50. Miller (1983, 23).

51. Miller (1983, 24).

52. Kingston (1975, 20).

53. Kingston (1975, 48).

54. Kingston (1975, 207).

55. Kingston (1975, 205).

REFERENCES

Beurdeley, Michel, ed. 1969. *The Clouds and the Rain: The Art of Love in China.* London: Hammond, Hammond and Company.

Byron, John. 1987. *Portrait of a Chinese Paradise: Erotica and Sexual Customs of the Late Qing Period.* London: Quartet.

Chan, Sucheng. 1991. *Asian Americans: An Interpretive History.* New York: Twayne.

Chang, Pang-Mei Natasha. 1996. *Bound Feet and Western Dress.* New York: Doubleday.

Cheung, King-Kok. 1988. Don't Tell: Imposed Silences in *The Color Purple* and *The Woman Warrior. PMLA* 103, no. 1: 162–74.

Chun-Hoon, Lowell. 1971. Jade Snow Wong and the Fate of Chinese-American Identity. *Amerasia Journal* 1 (March): 52–63.

Donnelly, Mabel Collins. 1986. *The American Victorian Woman: The Myth and the Reality.* Foreword by Carol C. Nadelson. New York: Greenwood.

Hsiao, Ruth Y. 1992. Facing the Incurable: Patriarchy in Eat a Bowl of Tea. In *Reading the Literatures of Asian America.* Philadelphia: Temple University Press.

Hsu, Francis L. K. 1953. *Americans and Chinese: Two Ways of Life.* New York: Henry Schuman.

———. 1971. *The Challenge of the American Dream: The Chinese in the United States.* Belmont, Calif.: Wadsworth.

Jicai, Feng. 1994. *The Three-Inch Golden Lotus.* Translated by David Wakefield. Honolulu: University of Hawaii Press.

Kingston, Maxine Hong. 1975. *The Woman Warrior.* New York: Vintage.

———. 1977. *China Men*. New York: Vintage.

Komenaka, April R. 1988. Autobiography As a Sociolinguistic Construct. *International Journal of the Sociology of Language* 69 (fall): 105–18.

Levy, Howard S. 1966. *Chinese Footbinding: The History of a Curious Exotic Custom*. New York: Walton Rawls.

Ling, Amy. 1990. *Between Worlds: Women Writers of Chinese Ancestry*. New York: Pergamon Press.

Lowe, Pardee. 1944. *Father and Glorious Descendant*. Boston: Little, Brown.

McCunn, Ruthanne Lum. 1981. *Thousand Pieces of Gold*. Boston: Beacon.

Miller, Margaret. 1983. Threads of Identity in Maxine Hong Kingston's *Woman Warrior*. *Biography* 6, no. 1: 13–33.

Morante, Linda. 1987. From Silence to Song: The Triumph of Maxine Hong Kingston. *Frontiers: A Journal of Women Studies* 9, no. 2: 78–82.

Pye, Lucian. 1984. *China: An Introduction*. Boston: Little, Brown.

———. 1992. *The Spirit of Chinese Politics*. Cambridge, Mass.: Harvard University Press.

Sledge, Linda Ching. 1980. Maxine Hong Kingston's *China Men*: The Family Historian As Epic Poet. *MELUS* 7, no. 4: 3–22.

Smith, Arthur H. 1899. *Village Life in China: A Study in Sociology*. New York: Fleming H. Revell.

Tan, Amy. 1989. *The Joy Luck Club*. New York: Ballantine.

———. 1991. *The Kitchen God's Wife*. New York: Vintage.

Wang, Veronica. 1985. Reality and Fantasy: The Chinese-American Woman's Quest for Identity. *MELUS* 12, no. 3: 23–31.

Webster's Encyclopedic Unabridged Dictionary of the English Language. 1989. Familism. New York: Portland House.

Wong, Jade Snow. 1945. *Fifth Chinese Daughter*. New York: Harper and Brothers.

Yang, C. K. 1959. *Chinese Communist Society: The Family and the Village*. Cambridge, Mass.: MIT Press.

Yung, Judy. 1995. *Unbound Feet: A Social History of Chinese Women in San Francisco*. Berkeley: University of California Press.

15

Nationalism, Orientalism, and an Unequal Treatise of Ethnography: The Making of *The Good Earth*

Zhiwei Xiao

In recent years, the Chinese government has voiced its unhappiness over a number of American films. While *Kundun* (1997) and *Seven Years in Tibet* (1997) irritated the Chinese because of their pro-Tibet stance, *Red Corner* (1998) angered Beijing because of its criticism of the Chinese legal system. But these were not the first times that the Chinese government has protested against foreign films for representing China negatively. It would be wrong, too, to assume that only the Communists are sensitive to images of China in the foreign media. This chapter will discuss Chinese involvement in the production of the film *The Good Earth* during the 1930s. The objective of this study is to provide a historical perspective on the recent Chinese reaction to American films critical of China and to examine some of the complex issues involved in cross-cultural representation. The events this chapter presents suggest that the Old World (China) was not just a passive object of the New World's gaze. On the contrary, China played an active role in shaping the way it was represented by the New World. While much has been said about American screen images of China and the Chinese people,[1] few have studied how the Chinese responded to this kind of representation. This study is an attempt to redress that imbalance.

THE MAKING OF *THE GOOD EARTH:* THE CHINESE CONNECTION

The film *The Good Earth* was based on Pearl Buck's award-winning novel bearing the same title. It is a story about a Chinese farming family and its struggles in early twentieth-century China. The film begins with a simple farmer named Wang Lung (Paul Muni) marrying a kitchen slave, O-lan (Luise Rainer), in an arranged marriage. Through incredible labor and luck, the couple make their little farm into a success, allowing Wang to buy more land and to prosper. When famine sets in, the family moves to the south as refugees. By a touch of fate, O-lan finds a bag of jewels amid the chaos of revolution. The fortune allows the family to return to the north, and Wang becomes the wealthiest landowner in the province. Riches corrupt the simple farmer, who takes in a tea dancer (Tilly Losch) as a concubine. Calamity occurs when their land is invaded by swarms of locusts. But led by Wang's oldest son (Keye Luke), the villagers beat off the locusts. Tranquility is restored, but O-lan, who has been ill for some time, dies just after her son's wedding ceremony. Wang finally comes to realize that it was she who had kept the family together and was responsible for his success. He stands weeping next to a peach tree his wife had planted and cries out her name, saying, "O-Lan, you are the earth!"

Pearl Buck's novel marched through the bestseller lists in the United States and remained there for almost two years following its 1931 publication. It was also translated into a number of languages and sold well overseas. After film producer Irving Thalberg saw a Broadway play based on this novel in 1933, he decided to make it into an epic film. MGM paid $50,000 to purchase the movie rights, the largest fee Hollywood had paid for movie rights to a book at that time.[2] The film was released in 1937 and immediately became a cinema sensation. American critics hailed it as "Hollywood's first honest approach to the Chinese people."[3] Muni and Rainer's portrayals of the Chinese characters were described as "simple, tender, earthy and amazingly real."[4] The film received seven nominations for Academy Awards and won the Oscars for best actress and best cinematography in 1937. Even forty years later, some still consider it one of the twenty best films in American film history.[5]

This critical acclaim is particularly striking in view of the fact that the production of the film was hindered by a series of difficulties from the very beginning. First, George Hill, the studio-appointed director of this film, committed suicide shortly after the project began. Then, Hill's replacement, Victor Fleming, fell ill and had to be hospitalized before the film was completed. However, the studio was determined to move forward and brought in Sidney Franklin to finish the film.

Apart from those internal problems, MGM was also forced to deal with the Chinese authorities because of the film's subject matter. The Chinese government first learned of MGM's decision to film Pearl Buck's novel through its diplomats in the United States. News reports about the production of this film attracted a great deal of public interest due to the popularity of the novel. In China, Pearl Buck's novel was first translated in 1932 and serialized in *Dongfang zazhi* (Eastern Mercury). Between 1933 and 1949, eight different Chinese translations were published. But it would be a mistake to equate the book's marketability with genuine appreciation. Many people bought the book out of curiosity. They wanted to find out how China was represented by a foreign writer. In fact, some of the harshest criticism leveled against the book came from the translators themselves. For instance, Wu Lifu, the English professor who first translated the book into Chinese, wrote in his introduction that Buck's novel is governed by "human instincts, where robbery plays a crucial role," and that the male characters desire nothing but land, while the female characters display absolute obedience. He noted that intertwined in these stories are the frequent droughts and famine, the ignorance of the peasants, male greed and miserliness, female humility, and the threat of soldiers, robbers, Communists, and countless other disasters. Wu then raised a serious rhetorical question: "But is this the true China? In writing all this does the author not have some sense of white supremacy and propose saving China through invading it?"[6]

Many Chinese government officials shared this critical view of the novel. In an internal document, the members of the National Film Censorship Committee expressed their view of the novel and requested that the government prevent MGM from filming it. The importance of this document warrants its full citation:

A request to prohibit MGM from filming *The Good Earth*, February 2, 1934.

According to reports in *Diansheng Daily* and *Movie Times* of January 11 last year, MGM intends to come to China to film *The Good Earth*. The film script is based on Pearl Buck's novel, in which the Chinese characters, be they peasants, merchants, soldiers or women, are all greedy and hypocritical. There is no one character decent enough to represent the Chinese. The book has been translated into many languages. If it is filmed and distributed throughout the world, it will bring enormous injury to Chinese dignity, a violation stipulated in the Film Censorship Statute. For the purpose of enforcing the statute and protecting our national dignity, this committee requests the ministries of Interior and Education to issue orders to the police departments all over the country to enforce the Regulations Concerning Foreigners Filming in China. We notified all film studios last February that any film or film script based on *The Good Earth* must be submitted for censorship. Anyone who refuses to do so would be severely penalized and denied future requests for censorial approval. Last December we also asked MGM to submit its script for censorship. On January 26 of 1934, we received a letter from the deputy general consul in Los Angeles informing us that a crew of MGM's technicians led by Li Minshi was on its way to China for background footage and asking us to provide aid. We suppose if they have begun background shooting, the film must be near its completion. And if the film is based on the book, it will be too injurious to Chinese dignity to be granted permission for filming in China. Our diplomats should file protest and stop the film from being shown. If the film differs significantly from the novel, it should not use the same title, lest it will further the publicity of the novel and result in more people reading the book and perpetuating bad impressions of China in the minds of many peoples in the world. So long as the film's title and contents differ from the novel, we will grant permission to the studio to film in China, provided they would follow the Regulations Concerning Foreigners Filming in China. The issue concerns national dignity and deserves the utmost attention. This committee resolves to submit its opinion on the matter along with its past decisions with regard to filming *The Good Earth* in China.[7]

There are several observations to be made here. First, the initial Chinese hostility toward the film project was derived from resentment toward the novel. Second, Chinese critics disliked the novel because it failed to provide a balanced picture of China and focused only on the perceived backwardness of the country. Third, the government was divided on how to respond to the film project. While the film censors were hostile toward the production of the film, the diplomats seemed to be more sympathetic and supportive, having approved a visit by an MGM crew for background filming in China. Finally, the report also suggests the astounding lack of coordination between the different branches of the government. Apparently, the National Film Censorship Committee (NFCC) learned about the film production from the news media, and was not officially informed by a government agency until late January 1934. In contrast, the Chinese diplomats first became aware of MGM's decision to film Pearl Buck's novel in early 1933. In fact, it was the Chinese vice consul in Los Angeles who took up the matter with the studio officials, asking that a certain part of the book be omitted in the film version.[8] Apparently, the NFCC was not informed of these developments.

When MGM realized that the Chinese government took a strong interest in the production, and that the filming of this project required cooperation from the Chinese authorities, the studio sought approval from the Chinese Embassy in Washington D.C. The Chinese diplomats then consulted with officials in the ministries of Interior, Education, and Propaganda.[9] Before the studio secured permission to film in China from the NFCC, which was authorized to issue or withhold such permits, MGM sent a production team to China in December 1933 to film background footage. Apparently, MGM hoped that its crew would receive approval from the Chinese officials while in China.

Initially, MGM's application for permission to film in China was turned down.[10] Given the Chinese censors' position stated in the document cited earlier, this decision should come as no surprise. Both the studio and Hill, the director and head of the filming team, were unaware of the controversy surrounding Buck's novel in China.[11] Neither did they know that a year before their arrival, the city government of Greater Shanghai had stopped a local motion picture company from filming Pearl Buck's novel. The explanation given by the Shanghai authorities was, "the plot (of the novel) wrongly presents Chinese life to the world and is viewed as disgraceful to the country."[12]

However, Chinese officials were divided about the film production. Some of them proposed cooperation with American filmmakers because MGM seemed determined to make the picture, and if the company could not film it in China, it probably would go elsewhere for location shooting. In that case, the Chinese government would have absolutely no control over how the film would be made. According to the logic of this argument, giving American filmmakers the opportunity to see the real China might cure them of their misconceptions about China, which were based on visits to Chinatowns in the United States. Hopefully, that would result in a film less derogatory toward China. Furthermore, by cooperating with MGM, Chinese officials could exert some influence on the production and thus provide a safeguard against misrepresentation.[13]

Partly persuaded by these arguments and partly because of Chiang Kai-shek's personal intervention, the Nationalist government eventually granted permission to the MGM film crew.[14] Rumor has it that Hill managed to work his way to Madam Chiang, whose American education and more receptive view of Pearl Buck's novel made her an advocate for cooperation with MGM.[15] At any rate, once the Chinese government approved the project, it did everything within its capacity to help the crew. As Charles Clarke, the lead cinematographer of the film, recalls:

> From then on, every aid the Chinese officials could give was ours: permits to photograph wherever we wished—official guides and interpreters—the cooperation of the Chinese Army for our scenes of the Revolution of 1912—and even relaxation of censorship rulings, so that, instead of having to have all of our film developed and inspected in China, we were able to send the greater part of the film to the studio's own laboratory. . . .[16]

Nevertheless, the Chinese government made MGM agree, at least in part, to several important conditions: (1) the film should present a truthful picture of China and her people; (2) the Chinese government could appoint its representatives to supervise the picture in its making; (3) MGM should accept as many as possible of the Chinese supervisor's suggestions; (4) if the Chinese government decided to add a preface to the picture, MGM would comply; (5) all shots taken by the MGM staff in China would have to be approved by the Chinese censors before their export; and (6) the entire cast of the picture should be Chinese.[17]

These terms were followed by the studio to varying degrees. On the question of casting Chinese actors, MGM seems to have made a half-hearted attempt to find a Chinese actor for the male lead role, but the role's criteria were impossible for a Chinese actor to meet.[18] Anna May Wong, perhaps the best-known Chinese American actress at the time, was approached by MGM to play a supporting role, but she refused because she resented the fact that the studio had given the two leading roles to Euro-American actors.[19] As for the footage MGM took in China, there are conflicting reports. According to one source, the MGM crew ignored the Chinese regulations and shot whatever scenes they wanted. However, when the footage went through customs, the Chinese x-rayed all the containers. A few weeks later, several thousand feet of blank film arrived in Hollywood.[20] This account is supported by two Chinese reports.[21] But an American source indicates that a significant portion of the footage produced in China was used in the final version of the film.[22]

MGM did accept a Chinese government representative during production, but there was an interesting twist. Initially, Nanjing sent Du Tingxiu (Theodore B. Tu), a former member of the National Film Censorship Committee, to Hollywood as the Chinese supervisor. Du's primary mission was to make sure that The Good Earth represented China accurately. Hollywood took advantage of his presence and paid him for consultation on other films dealing with Chinese subjects as well. Apparently, Du's performance at this job was a disappointment both to his superiors in China and to his hosts in the United States. While American producers complained that Du's supervision did not ensure the smooth passage of their films by the Chinese censors,[23] people in China were upset when they found offensive scenes in The Good Earth during a preview.[24] Subsequently, Nanjing recalled Du and appointed Tan Zudian (Tom Gubbins), a member of the local Chinese community in the Los Angeles area, to fill Du's position. This incident suggests that offensiveness, much like beauty, is in the eyes of the beholders. In this case, Du seemed much less sensitive than his colleagues in China. In his report on The Good Earth, he wrote, "I have been a film fan for over thirty years and based on my experience, I am fully convinced that this film is unmatched by any other films in terms of its accurate portrayal of Chinese life, beautiful cinematography, well-written plot and profound moral message."[25] Du's cosmopolitanism and open-mindedness made him an ineffective "supervisor," because films approved by him continued to run into problems with the censors in China, which from Hollywood's point of view defeated the purpose of his presence there.

Though Du was recalled, the production of *The Good Earth* went on. During the final stage of the production, Du's successor, Mr. Tan, visited the studio three times a week, with transportation provided by MGM. The Chinese government appointed a consular official named Huang Chaoqin to aid Tan. Later, Huang would write a lengthy report detailing all the official exchanges between the Chinese government and MGM.[26] At the time, Huang's responsibility was to make certain that the studio used only the location footage approved by the Chinese censors. However, that job became almost impossible when MGM created a Chinese farming village in the suburbs of Los Angeles. Huang reported that he could not tell which scenes in the film were shot in China and which were shot on the studio set.[27]

To what extent MGM was genuinely sensitive to Chinese concerns or motivated by financial concerns is difficult to know for certain, but it did make many efforts to avoid Chinese objections.[28] In some ways, the revisions the studio was forced to make highlight the differences between the Chinese officials and American filmmakers in their visions of China. Hence, these changes deserve a closer look.

CONFLICTS AND ACCOMMODATIONS

To begin with, the film script of *The Good Earth* already made some significant departures from the novel on which it was based. While some changes were made for dramatic reasons, others had to do with the studio's concern about Chinese sensitivities, because there had been a great number of Chinese protests against offensive American films in previous years. From the very beginning, the writers involved in adapting the novel to the screen made deliberate attempts to present "a completely sympathetic portrayal of Chinese life," which, in their opinions, the novel failed to achieve. Their view of the novel seemed to echo some of the Chinese criticism, which charged the author with racism and a slanted view of China. Among other changes, the scriptwriters decided to depict one of Wang's sons as representing the new China, using new methods to fight the locusts, studying at the university, and leading the villagers to prosperity. They also transformed the family from one wracked by quarrels and bitter envy in the novel into a wholesome, affectionate, sympathetic unit, bound together by profound ties. To avoid Chinese objections, they reduced the viciousness of the uncle and cousin and toned down the sexual dimension of the Lotus character, who was changed from a prostitute to an entertainer. Her illicit affair with Wang's younger son was made much less explicit than in the novel. Finally, they eliminated the part in the novel where Wang takes another concubine at an extremely old age.[29]

Since the film was about rural China, MGM studied a Chinese film entitled *Rendao* (*Humanity*, 1932, dir. Bu Wancang), which also dealt with rural life in China, hoping to take some clues as to the way Chinese filmmakers portrayed rural China.[30] But little did the studio know that the film they saw as a model had had its own problems with the government censors. In September 1932, the United Photoplay (Lianhua), the studio that produced the film, requested that the National Film Censorship Committee approve the film's screenings in Los Angeles and San Francisco. In its response, the NFCC stated: "Part of the film shows human beings for sale as the result of famine, which implies the ineffectiveness of political organization, the collapse of the disaster relief system, and the inadequacy of philanthropy work in China. In the context of international criticism of us in those areas, the film exposes the shortcomings of Chinese society and is quite inappropriate."[31] The logic of this criticism is quite remarkable. The government censors do not contest the accuracy of the film's message. Rather, they disapprove of showing the shortcomings of Chinese society in the context of Western criticism of China and they are particularly concerned about the *political implications* of such criticism, which tended to undermine the legitimacy of the regime. These two concerns are important to our understanding of Chinese sensitivity to negative portrayals in foreign films and will be discussed further.

In addition to the studio's own efforts to sanitize *The Good Earth*, the Hays Office, Hollywood's self regulatory agency, also placed a high priority on eliminating potentially problematic scenes and dialogue from the film.[32] After reading the script of *The Good Earth*, Joseph Breen, the chief censor of the Production Code Administration, wrote a letter to Louis B. Mayer, the head of MGM, and suggested a total of twenty revisions, many of which had to do with avoiding problems with the Chinese government censors. For instance, he suggested that the scene of the uncle belching be omitted and that the girls in the teahouse be presented as entertainers rather than prostitutes. The studio quickly made these and other changes specified by the Hays Office.[33]

Yet, despite the sanitizing by the studio and the Hays Office, the Chinese censors continued to find problems in the script and demanded further revision.

Their list of requested deletions includes replacing the word "slave" with "maid-servant," cutting a dialogue that referred to Wang Lung as not having had a bath since the New Year, removing the scene showing soldiers cutting corpses with their bayonets, and deleting a reference to cannibalism in northern China. They also demanded that the scene showing a barber making fun of Wang Lung's queue be dropped and that the length of a segment showing soldiers engaged in robbing be reduced.[34] However, the studio did not comply with all of these de-mands. The word "slave" was used twenty times in the early version of the film. After the Chinese protest, MGM told the Chinese that they had made eighteen cuts to delete that word, but saved its use in two places where deletion would cause problems for the overall structural integrity.[35] As for Wang not having bathed for a year, the studio maintained that the detail was too important to the characterization and refused to delete it. MGM did cut the barber's scene, but kept another scene with which the Chinese found fault.[36]

After the film's completion, MGM gave a preview to the Chinese ambassa-dor in Washington, D.C. The studio also arranged screenings for the Chinese consuls in Los Angeles and San Francisco. MGM hoped that those previews would help the film to pass the censors in Nanjing. As one studio official put it, the idea was "to bring such data to the attention of the Central Film Cen-sorship Board in Nanjing" because, if the Chinese diplomats approved the film and the censors in Nanjing banned it, MGM would have very good grounds for a protest.[37] Apparently, the studio was quite familiar with the bu-reaucratic apparatus of the Chinese government and the relative degrees of sympathy they could expect from different branches of the bureaucracy, and they tried to exploit this to their advantage.

Several leading Chinese intellectuals who happened to be in the United States in 1937 were also invited to the screenings and asked for comments. Their remarks were reported in a Chinese fan magazine. Hu Shi, professor of literature and dean of humanities from Peking University, criticized the film for its inaccurate details as well as its melodramatic banality. He pointed out that Wang's success was due to O-lan's chance discovery of the jewelry purse, which undercut the film's theme of hard work and industriousness. But Hu also reminded his countrymen of MGM's good intentions and the efforts the studio had made to incorporate Chinese concerns. He cautioned Chinese audiences not to overreact to the film's blemishes. Jiang Baili, another well-respected scholar, urged audiences to be more receptive to the film, though he also recognized that American filmmakers tended to focus on the exotic aspects of Chinese life. Lin Yutang, perhaps the best-known Chinese writer in the West during the 1930s and 1940s, seemed most enthusiastic about the film, praising both its realistic portrayal of Chinese life and its superb craftsmanship.[38] But given Lin's personal debt to Pearl Buck, who had helped Lin launch his literary career in the West,[39] one has to take Lin's remarks with a grain of salt.

By contrast, critics in China were generally disappointed with the film and found its depiction of rural China superficial. However, they also acknowledged that the film was exceptionally sympathetic to the Chinese, in contrast to the majority of American films featuring China and Chinese locales.[40] Nevertheless, when the completed film was brought to China after its premiere in the United States, Chinese censors made additional deletions before allowing it to be publicly screened. Among other cuts, they deleted a scene showing a refugee lying by the side of the road and a shot of an old woman lying on the ground while vultures are seen in the barren trees. The segment where O-lan teaches her children how to beg and the subsequent begging sequence also were deleted, along with a short scene of a banner that reads, "The world should have equality for everybody."[41]

It is interesting to note that the Chinese censors' approval of this film was contingent on recognition of MGM's good intentions and the efforts it had made. In no way were the Chinese enthusiastic about the film. In fact, some of them made it clear that the film still contained scenes that would be considered offensive if found in other films, but considering the efforts MGM had already made, these scenes could be forgiven and tolerated. Interestingly, MGM officials seemed to be aware of the exception the Chinese censors made for them. In a letter addressed to George Weltner of Paramount and copied to Joseph Breen, an MGM executive acknowledged that the film still contained many of the things that had been objected to in other pictures.[42]

Several sources suggest that MGM cheated the Chinese censors by sending them a cleaned-up version, but distributed a different version outside China. A Chinese American named Huang Wencong reported that he saw *The Good Earth* in the Astor Theater in Los Angeles and found scenes that were supposed to have been deleted. Huang believed that MGM had sent to China a different version of the film for censorship.[43] Two Hays Office documents lend support to Huang's speculation. A report from China to the Hays Office indicates that in early 1938, when *The Good Earth* was shown in Chinese territories occupied by the Japanese, the Japanese censors deleted some scenes and dialogue that the Chinese had specifically requested that the studio eliminate. Another letter to the Hays Office dated November 1938 indicates a similar problem,[44] suggesting that the actual film copy in circulation was different from the one approved by the Chinese censors. This evidence brings into question MGM's sincerity in complying with the Chinese requests and illustrates the intriguing and complex dynamic of the negotiations between the studio and the Chinese government. In one sense, perhaps the Chinese government had limited success in getting MGM to toe its line. But by demonstrating its seriousness about China's screen image and its determination to use its power to combat a negative representation of China, the Nationalists made American filmmakers more sensitive to Chinese feelings. In this sense, the significance of the Chinese intervention, successful or not, went beyond one individual film.

CONCLUSION: AN UNEQUAL TREATISE OF ETHNOGRAPHY

The Chinese interference in the making of *The Good Earth* is not an isolated case, but represents the government's consistent policy with regard to foreign films. During the 1930s, a large number of American films were banned, censored, or forced to endure cuts by Chinese officials.[45] This seemingly harsh treatment of American films was a response to the exceedingly derogatory portrayals of China and the Chinese people by Hollywood. A Chinese critic observed in the 1930s that in American films, whenever a male Chinese character is introduced, he must be an ugly-looking creature with a queue hanging behind his back and connections with the underworld.[46] Yet, Hollywood's dominance of the international film market meant the supremacy of its vision of the world.[47] The Chinese were concerned that people all over the world would form their views of China based on American films, which perpetuated racist and contemptuous views of China[48] and constituted a "Western style for dominating, restructuring, and having authority over the Orient."[49]

But due to the political fragmentation of China during the first two decades of the twentieth century, there was never a concerted effort by the Chinese to deal with this problem. With the establishment of the Nanjing government in 1927, the new regime took systematic steps to address the national image issue. In early 1930, Harold Lloyd's picture, *Welcome Danger,* caused a public stir in Shanghai because of its caricaturing of Chinese people. In response, the Chinese government banned the film and barred all of Lloyd's films from China. That incident signaled the beginning of Chinese censorship of foreign films.[50] Indeed, the Nationalist government took the matter so seriously that it signed agreements with a number of countries to mutually ban films deemed offensive to national dignity. The result was that a film offending the Chinese would not only be banned in China, but also in other countries that had signed the treaty.

One American film producer commented in 1937, "We seem to rub them the wrong way almost every time we make pictures dealing with Chinese characters or things Chinese."[51] If taken out of context, the Chinese government and its intellectuals may seem, indeed, to have been oversensitive. In some cases, their actions may be perceived as an infringement on the freedom of speech of the American filmmakers. But viewed from a historical perspective, their actions are understandable. In his discussion of the colonial discourse on China, Professor John Fitzgerald suggests a connection between Chinese sensitivity and the colonial ethnography:

> The cumulative impact of European racism, over a century of dialogue between colonial ethnography and nationalist reflection on the nature of Chinese people, contributed to a new kind of racial sensibility that sought desperately to find a "way out" of its predicament. Foreign colonials pointed out what was wrong with John Chinaman, explained how he could rectify his faults, and then promised that if he made the necessary improvements he could have his country back. . . . In the Nationalist Revolution, overthrowing imperialism made as much sense as good manners.[52]

In other words, the Chinese resented the image of China as backward, uncivilized, chaotic, and incapable of self-governance, because such an image was an integral part of the colonial discourse that justified foreign dominance of China. That discourse was supported by the West's military, economic, political, and cultural dominance over China, constituting "the unequal treaties of ethnography."[53] In this context, the Nationalist government's effort to censor *The Good Earth* and to project a more positive image of China to the world was in line with its anti-imperialist agenda.

The story about Chinese intervention in the making of *The Good Earth* raises many complex issues. As the controversies concerning *Red Corner, Seven Years in Tibet,* and *Kundun* show, many people in the West tend to view Chinese censorship of American films dealing with Chinese subjects as infringements on American filmmakers' freedom of speech.[54] Such a view is too simplistic and ignores the larger context of the unequal power relationship in which the New World's representation of the Old World takes place. Hollywood is becoming the most powerful force in the world, next only to the U.S. military.[55] As such, Hollywood can easily mass-produce images of other countries and peoples, but other countries cannot produce images to counter

Hollywood's. In this regard, the American monopoly on public perception and "knowledge" constitutes a form of cultural hegemony. As the recent discussion about hate speech suggests, not all voices have equal opportunity to be heard, hence the predominance of certain voices often means the silencing of other voices. From this perspective, government censorship functions as an attempt to create a level playing field.[56] This perspective may help us understand the Chinese government's attempt to restrict Hollywood's freedom when it comes to representing China. Until the Chinese are able to compete with Hollywood to provide alternative truths, knowledge, and aesthetics through cinematic images, it is perhaps inevitable that they will resort to other means to contest Hollywood's cultural dominance.

For individual American filmmakers who see their choice of subject materials as a matter of artistic freedom, it is important to bear in mind that when the overall output of Hollywood's "Chinese pictures" shows an unmistakable preference for certain subject material, it is difficult for the Chinese to see the issue from the perspective of artistic freedom. One conscientious American film producer pointed to this problem decades ago: "What if the Chinese make a movie with an American theme and center the action around the 'speak easy' of the prohibition days? And how would Americans feel if the Chinese distort things so badly as to make it appear to those not familiar with things American that American life generally revolves around the speak easy?"[57] As Hollywood prepares to expand into China in the twenty-first century, it is perhaps useful to heed the lessons of history.

NOTES

I wish to thank Professor Susie Lan Cassel, Joseph Esherick, Paul Pickowicz, Yingjin Zhang, and Yi Sun for their careful readings of earlier drafts of this chapter and the many helpful comments they made. I am also grateful to Professor Barry Saferstein for proofreading the paper and making editorial changes.

The research for this paper is funded by a California State University, San Marcos, Faculty Development Grant.

1. For representative works, see Harold R. Isaacs, *Scratches on Our minds: American Images of China and India* (New York: Day, 1958); Dorothy Jones, *The Portrayal of China and India on the American Screen, 1896–1955* (Cambridge, Mass.: MIT Press, 1955); Richard Oehling, "Hollywood and the Image of the Oriental, 1910–1950," *Film and History* 9, no. 3 (1978); Blaine T. Browne, *A Common Thread: American Images of the Chinese and Japanese, 1930–1960* (Ph.D. dissertation, University of Oklahoma, 1985), chapter 1; and Gina Marchetti, *Romance and the "Yellow Peril": Race, Sex, and Discursive*

Strategies in Hollywood Fiction (Berkeley: University of California Press, 1993). See also Allen L. Woll and Randall M. Miller, *Ethnic and Radical Images in American Film and Television: Historical Essays and Bibliography* (New York: Garland, 1987); and Chen Ruxiu, "Haolaiwu mopian shiqi de Zhongguo xingxiang" (The image of China in American silent films), *Dianying xinshang* (Film appreciation), no. 92 (1995).

2. Peter Conn, *Pearl S. Buck: A Cultural Biography* (Cambridge: Cambridge University Press, 1996), 141.

3. Peter Ellis, "Review of *The Good Earth*," *New Masses*, 16 February 1937, 167–68.

4. "Review of *The Good Earth*," *Literary Digest*, 13 February 1937, 19–20.

5. John Gassner and Dudley Nichols, *Twenty Best Film Plays* (New York: Garland, 1977).

6. Liu Haiping, "Pearl S. Buck's Reception in China Reconsidered," in *The Several Worlds of Pearl S. Buck: Essays Presented at a Centennial Symposium, Randolph-Mason Woman's College, March 26–28, 1992*, ed. Elizabeth J. Lipscomb, Frances E. Webb, and Peter Conn, Contributions in Women's Studies, no. 144 (Westport, Conn.: Greenwood, 1994), 61.

7. *Dianying jiancha weiyuanhui gongzuo baogao* (The National Film Censorship Committee's news bulletin) (Nanjing, 1934), 102–3.

8. *Dianying jiancha weiyuanhui gongzuo baogao.* For details concerning the National Film Censorship Committee, see Zhiwei Xiao, *Film Censorship in China, 1927–1937* (Ph. D. dissertation, Department of History, University of California, San Diego, 1994).

9. Letter dated 8 May 1937, by H. B. Howard, assistant trade commissioner, MGM correspondence with the Hays Office, Code Administration File, Margaret Herrick Library, Beverly Hills, California.

10. "China Refuses Permission to Film *Good Earth*," *China Weekly Review*, 3 February 1934.

11. Zhou Zhenhuan, "Sai Zhenzhu Dadi de fanyi jiqi yinqi de zhengyi" (The translation of *The Good Earth* and the controversies it caused), *Minguo chunqiu* (Republican forum), no. 4 (1992): 21–23.

12. "Greater Shanghai Municipality Puts Ban on *Good Earth*," *China Weekly Review*, 25 March 1933, 158.

13. Paul K. Whang, "Will *The Good Earth* Be Filmed in China?" *China Weekly Review*, 17 February 1934, 450.

14. "Filming of Pearl Buck's *Good Earth* Proceeds," *China Weekly Review*, 5 May 1934, 381.

15. Charles G. Clarke, "China Photographically Ideal," *American Cinematographer* (September 1934).

16. Clarke, "China Photographically Ideal."

17. See Howard letter, 8 May 1937.

18. "Migaomei she Dadi pinqing Zhongguo juwuba" (MGM looking for Chinese giant), *Dian sheng* 4, no. 6 (February 15, 1937): 118. According to Peter Conn, Pearl S. Buck herself proposed to the studio that Wang Lung be played by a Chinese actor, but MGM ignored her advice. See Conn, *Pearl S. Buck*, 194.

19. "Huang Liushuang tan Dadi, jujue ren peijiao" (Anna May Wong on *The Good Earth*, refused supporting role), *Yule zhoukan* (Entertainment weekly) 2, no. 7 (1936): 140.

20. Conn, *Pearl S. Buck*, 159.

21. "Huaqiao danren Dadi de yaojiao" (Overseas Chinese play important roles in *The Good Earth*), *Yule zhoubao* (Entertainment weekly) 2, no. 21 (1936): 422. See also footnote 18.

22. "Review of *The Good Earth*," *Time*, 15 February 1937, 55.

23. Studio documents, Margaret Herrick Library, Beverly Hills, California.

24. "Zewen Wang Yuanlong, Du Tingxiu" (Questioning Wang Yuanlong and Du Tingxiu), *Dian sheng* 3, no. 44 (November 1934): 863.

25. "Guan yu Dadi yingpian" (Concerning *The Good Earth*), *Dian sheng* 6, no. 11 (March 19, 1937): 515. See also Mary Ann Dhuyvetter, *China Reconsidered: The Realistic Portrayal of Chinese People in the Novels of Pearl S. Buck and Alice Tisdale Bobart* (master's thesis, Department of English, San Diego State University, 1998), 150.

26. "Caojiu Dadi yingpian shencha baogaoshu" (Drafting the report on *The Good Earth*), *Dian sheng* 6, no. 11 (1937), 516.

27. "Zhongxuanhui dui Dadi zhidaoyuan xunshi yaodian yu Dadi yingpian shezhi zhi shiji qingxing" (Central Publicity Department's major concerns about *The Good Earth* and the making of this film), *Dian sheng* 6, no. 12 (1937), 558.

28. "Jing wo zhengfu kangyi, Dadi neirong chong jia xiuzheng" (After our government's protest, *The Good Earth* is revised), *Dian sheng* 6, no. 3 (March 1937): 209.

29. James L. Hoban Jr., "Scripting *The Good Earth*: Versions of the Novel for the Screen," in *The Several Worlds of Pearl S. Buck: Essays Presented at a Centennial Symposium, Randolph-Macon Woman's College, March 26–28, 1992*, ed. Elizabeth J.

Lipscomb, Frances E. Webb, and Peter Conn, Contributions in Women's Studies, no. 144 (Westport, Conn.: Greenwood, 1994).

30. "Migaomei *Dadi* yingpian yi *Rendao* wei shezhi lanben" (MGM's *The Good Earth* models after *Humanity*), *Dian sheng* 6, no. 18 (1937): 810.

31. *Dianying jiancha weiyuanhui gongbao* (The National Film Censorship Committee's news bulletin) 1, no. 6 (1932): 3.

32. John Harley, *World-wide Influence of the Cinema: A Study of Official Censorship and the International Cultural Aspects of Motion Pictures* (Los Angeles: University of Southern California Press, 1940).

33. See Breen's letter to Mayer, 11 March 1936. Production Code Administration File, Correspondence File, Margaret Herrick Library, Beverly Hills, California.

34. "Jing wo zhengfu kangyi, *Dadi* neirong chong jia xiuzheng" (Under our government's protest, more changes were made to *The Good Earth*), *Dian sheng* 6, no. 3 (1937): 209.

35. In the current video release version of the film, the word "slave" is used at least five times, which raises questions about the credibility of MGM's account.

36. "Huang zong lingshi yijianshu yu gongsi fuwen" (Consul General Huang's advice and MGM's response), *Diansheng zhoukan* (Motivetone weekly) 6, no. 12 (1937): 560.

37. Letter dated 10 June 1937, Studio document, Code Administration File, Margaret Herrick Library, Beverly Hills, California.

38. "Hu Shi, Jiang Baili, Lin Yutang deng dui yingpian *Dadi* yijian" (Comments on *The Good Earth* by Hu Shi, Jiang Baili, and Lin Yutang), *Dian sheng* 6, no. 11 (1937): 516–17.

39. Lai Feng, "Sai Zhenzhu zhu Lin Yutang chengming" (Pearl S. Buck helped Lin Yutang's career success), in *Minguo Zhanggu* (Anecdotes of Republican history), ed. Shen Xiaoyun et al. (Shanghai: Shanghai Renmin chubanshe, 1997), 117–18.

40. Luo Caiqing, "Guanyu Dadi" (Regarding *The Good Earth*), *Dian xing zhoubao* (Star weekly) 1, no. 3 (1937): 14–15.

41. *The Good Earth* file, Margaret Herrick Library, Beverly Hills, California. Again, in the current release version, all of those "problematic" scenes are included.

42. See note 37. Studio document, Code Administration File, Margaret Herrick Library. It is not clear who is the author of this letter.

43. "Zhengming *Dadi* weijia xiuzheng" (An eyewitness's account of the unmodified *The Good Earth*), *Dian sheng* 6, no. 14 (1937): 644.

44. A document dated April 1, 1938, cites a report revealing the details of the censored scenes and dialogue. See Code Administration File, Margaret Herrick Library, Beverly Hills, California.

45. See *Dianying jiancha weiyuanhui gongbao* (The National Film Censorship Committee's news bulletin), published between 1932 and 1937.

46. Paul Whang, "Boycotting American Movies," *The World Tomorrow* (August 1930): 339–40.

47. For a more detailed discussion on Hollywood's international dominance, see Ian Jarvie, *Hollywood's Overseas Campaign: The North Atlantic Movie Trade, 1920–1950* (Cambridge: Cambridge University Press, 1992).

48. Blaine T. Browne, *A Common Thread: American Images of the Chinese and Japanese, 1930–1960* (Ph.D. dissertation, University of Oklahoma, 1985), chapter 1.

49. Edward W. Said, *Orientalism* (New York: Vintage, 1979), 3.

50. For a more detailed discussion of this incident, see Zhiwei Xiao, "Anti-imperialism and Film Censorship in China, 1927–1937," in *Transnational Chinese Cinemas: Identity, Nationhood, Gender,* ed. Sheldon Hsiao-peng Lu (Honolulu: University of Hawaii Press, 1997).

51. Letter to Joseph Breen, 16 April 1937, Production Code Administration File, Correspondence File, Margaret Herrick Library, Beverly Hills, California.

52. John Fitzgerald, *Awakening China: Politics, Culture, and Class in the Nationalist Revolution* (Stanford, Calif.: Stanford University Press, 1996), 104.

53. Fitzgerald, *Awakening China,* particularly chapter 3.

54. Lisa Atkinson, "What's Entertainment," *China Business Review* 24, no. 2 (March/April 1997).

55. Quoted in "The Hollywood Love Affair with Tibet," *New York Times,* 19 March 1997.

56. Robert C. Post, ed., *Censorship and Silencing: Practices of Cultural Regulation* (Los Angeles: Getty Research Institute for the History of Art and the Humanities, 1998).

57. Letter to Joseph Breen, 16 April 1937.

V

Establishing a Chinese American Identity

16

The "In Search of Roots" Program: Constructing Identity through Family History Research and a Journey to the Ancestral Land

Albert Cheng and Him Mark Lai

The "In Search of Roots" program has brought me one step closer in the course of discovering who I am. In a process that began only four years ago, this has been a year long, life changing experience that has redefined who I am and forever changed my perspective on life as a Chinese in America.

—*Ryan Kwok, 1999 intern*

Every summer since 1991, a group of young Chinese Americans like Ryan Kwok embark on a journey to search for their ancestral villages in China after they have researched family and archival records in the United States. The interns, ages sixteen to twenty-five, are part of the "In Search of Roots" program sponsored by the Chinese Culture Foundation of San Francisco (CCF), the Chinese Historical Society of America (CHSA), and the Overseas Chinese Affairs Office in Guangdong Province, People's Republic of China. After eleven years of experience, the program coordinators (the authors of this chapter) have discovered that the interns, during the course of searching for their family heritage, were inevitably changed by the experiences. Many reached a realization that even though they are ethnic Chinese, their identities are indisputably Chinese American and different from Chinese in China. Additionally, the program provides the interns an opportunity to deconstruct America's damaging portrayals of the Chinese and to construct their own cultural definers and identities.

This chapter focuses on five areas: namely, an overview of the program, its evolution and history, the program structure and curriculum, the journey to China, and the program coordinators' findings about the impact on the interns.

PROGRAM OVERVIEW

The program involves a year-long commitment to researching one's Chinese American family history and genealogy. After exploring their Chinese roots in America, participants explore their roots in China through searching for and visiting their paternal and/or maternal ancestral villages in the Pearl River Delta region of Guangdong Province, home to the majority of Chinese who have migrated to the United States since the mid-nineteenth century. The program culminates in a Chinese New Year exhibition of the interns' research at the Chinese Culture Center in San Francisco, where the participants share what they have learned with family, friends, and community.

The overarching intent of the program is to provide the participants with an awareness and appreciation of the totality of the Chinese American experience through research on family history and genealogy. Consequently, they can gain a better understanding of their heritage, which ultimately helps them to better understand their identities as Chinese Americans.

The program has five major outcomes: at the conclusion of the project the interns construct a family tree with related familial history (including an essay, photographs, and artifacts) to be included as part of a group family history and genealogy exhibit; interns expand their knowledge of the historical development of China and the Guangdong Province, with emphasis on the peoples of the Pearl River Delta region; they deepen their understanding of the history of the Chinese in America; they explore research facilities, such as the records of the National Archives; and ultimately they visit their paternal and/or maternal ancestral villages in China.

In October of each year, the CCF circulates recruitment brochures and applications to all the major high schools, colleges, universities, community organizations, and other public facilities in the San Francisco Bay area. Applicants are interviewed and screened and approximately ten candidates are chosen at the beginning of the year. In the spring, the selected interns attend a series of nine Saturday seminars. They also begin gathering materials to write their individual family histories, under the guidance of the program coordinators.

In July the group goes on a guided two-week trip to China to search for and visit their ancestral villages under the auspices of the summer camps program of the Guangdong Province Overseas Chinese Affairs Office of the People's Republic of China. Since the program's inception, interns have visited ancestral villages in the counties and county-level municipalities of Guangzhou, Panyu, Huadu (formerly Huaxian), Foshan, Nanhai, Shunde, Zhaoqing, Dong-guan, Bao'an, Shenzhen, Huizhou, Zhongshan, Zhuhai, Doumen, Xinhui, Taishan, Kaiping, Enping, and Heshan. Over one hundred interns have gone through the program, visiting more than one hundred fifty villages.

EVOLUTION AND HISTORY OF THE PROGRAM

There is an ancient Chinese adage, *yinshui siyuan* (when drinking water, remember the source). As an expression of this spirit, the Chinese people have one of the world's oldest continuous literate genealogical traditions, the beginnings of which can be traced more than 3,500 years back, to the Shang period, when the kings frequently appealed to their ancestors for guidance in important undertakings. Over the centuries Chinese reverence for their forebears developed into a scholarly discipline, resulting in a rich and voluminous body of genealogical literature. However, despite this tradition of scholarship, interest in family history and genealogy was not widespread in the Chinese American community until years after the end of World War II.

A major factor was that genealogical research necessarily had to take second place to the Chinese Americans' constant struggle to survive in a hostile American environment, where they were regarded as undesirable and were oppressed by Chinese Exclusion Laws and other discriminatory legislation and practices. Another factor contributing to this development was the fact that before World War II the Chinese American population in the United States was small and overwhelmingly first- or second-generation. Many had families in China but led sojourner bachelor existences in this country. Family genealogy, if it came under consideration at all, would merely be a simple extension of the family tree in China with some addenda for American-born generations, if they existed.

Chinese Americans emerged from World War II with a somewhat improved political, social, and economic status in American society. The relaxation of immigration restrictions allowed the growth in the proportion of families in the Chinese American community. America's postwar prosperity fostered the growth of a Chinese American middle class of professionals, technical personnel, and business people, who began to participate in mainstream society in increasing numbers and who pressed for recognition as equal partners in America's pluralistic society. The common interests and goals of this middle class rooted in America fostered kindred feelings of community. These were often expressed by bonds of ethnic identity. Some of the manifestations of these sentiments were an increased interest in the history and culture of the common ethnic community and the deeds of their forebears.

In 1963, a group of Chinese Americans founded the Chinese Historical Society of America (CHSA), the first community-formed group to document and disseminate information on the history of the Chinese in America. In 1965 the Chinese Culture Foundation of San Francisco (CCF) was founded to provide a forum for Chinese and Chinese American culture. By the seventies and eighties similar groups began to appear in other major Chinese American communities.[1]

As researchers began to develop and accumulate Chinese American historical materials, especially oral interviews and biographies, it became apparent that there was much in common between historical and genealogical research. During the late 1960s and early 1970s CHSA made some desultory attempts at oral interviews and also collected a few genealogies, but inexperience and lack of a clear objective led the effort to falter. For the moment genealogical research remained an individual undertaking.

In Hawaii, however, there were already many Chinese families who had been several generations in the islands, and this history gave impetus to greater participation and institutionalization of Chinese American family history research. The founding of the Hawaii Chinese History Center (HCHC) in 1971 provided a contact point for those interested in the history of the Chinese in Hawaii. During the seventies the HCHC organized a number of field trips led by Irma Tam Soong, Douglas Chong, and others to local historical sites and to tape record oral interviews. In 1973 the HCHC sponsored its first major work, *The Chinese in Hawaii: An Annotated Bibliography*, providing a useful reference tool for researchers.[2] By the mid-1970s the HCHC had redefined its objectives to include encouraging genealogical and biographical research and the compilation of family histories.[3]

The HCHC published Jean Ohai's *Chinese Genealogy and Family Book* in 1975 and became the first Chinese American historical organization to sponsor a genealogy seminar, which was held at the United Chinese Society. In 1978 the HCHC became active in arranging for microfilming of Chinese clan genealogies by the Genealogical Society of Utah. The same year another genealogical seminar was announced and Dr. Timothy David Woo made available his family history, *To Spread the Glory: A Thousand Years of Heritage* (1977), through the HCHC to further stimulate family history research.[4]

In the continental United States, however, the first Chinese American family history workshop did not occur until the 1980s, although, as was the case in Hawaii, individuals had been working on their own family histories. In 1978 the Chinese Historical Society of Southern California (CHSSC), founded in 1975, cosponsored an oral history project with the Asian American Studies Center of the University of California, Los Angeles (UCLA), to capture the experiences of Chinese people in southern California, and was in the process of editing the materials into the book, *Linking Our Lives* (published in 1984). In 1983 the two groups cooperated again to hold a workshop, "Family History for the Chinese American," at UCLA. The program introduced the methodology of genealogical research and included presentations on Chinese American family trees and Chinese kinship terms, resources for family history research, oral history techniques, and highlights of Chinese American history.[5] However, there were insufficient responses after the workshop to warrant CHSSC to embark on a family history research program.

The HCHC continued to take the lead in promoting Chinese American family history research. It sponsored more genealogical seminars. In 1985 the center, in cooperation with a number of Hawaiian Chinese groups, organized a highly successful "Researching One's Chinese Roots" conference, which attracted 335 paid registrants.[6] The conference proceedings, edited by Kum Pui and Violet Lai and published as *Researching One's Chinese Roots* (Honolulu: HCHC, 1988), became a resource book for Chinese American family history research, especially in Hawaii. The conference was followed by a genealogy exhibit in 1986. During the late 1980's the HCHC also copublished several family histories.

During the 1970s, relations between the People's Republic of China and the United States had begun to relax after two decades of hostile confrontation. By the late seventies the mainland Chinese government had changed to an open policy, allowing more investments from abroad and interchanges with other countries. Chinese Americans resumed communications with relatives and friends in the ancestral land. Some visited their ancestral villages in search of their roots. In 1982 the Overseas Chinese Affairs Office of Guangdong Province inaugurated a summer camp program for Chinese American youth in Kaiping County in the Pearl River Delta region. In subsequent years various travel agencies and organizations in Chinese American communities recruited groups of participants. Although the programs were little more than vacation jaunts, they opened the possibility of in-depth activities in search of roots.

In 1989 Chinese Americans in San Francisco launched a family history conference, when the CHSA, CCF, and Cheng Society of America jointly sponsored the "Chinese American Family History and Genealogy Symposium/Workshop."[7] Benefiting from the experience of HCHC and CHSSC and receiving the generous support of these sister societies, the symposium/workshop focused on giving guidance in areas deemed unique to Chinese American family history research.

Some of the topics of the presentations covered the history of the Chinese in America, resources of the National Archives, Chinese research materials at the Family History Library in Salt Lake City, and the historical development of Guangdong Province and the Pearl River Delta region. Additionally, the symposium provided lectures on oral history techniques, surnames as clues to family histories, Chinese genealogies, and the construction of one's family tree. Handouts included maps and essays made available through the generosity of CHSSC and HCHC. Despite the fact that the event took place only nine days after the Loma Prieta Richter scale 7.1 earthquake, which rocked the San Francisco Bay area, eighty interested people attended the event. Most of the presentations were subsequently published in the 1991 issue of the CHSA journal *Chinese America: History and Perspectives*.

Finally, in 1991, the CCF and Community Education Services, in conjunction with CHSA, followed up on the 1989 symposium/workshop with the inauguration of the "In Search of Roots" program.

PROGRAM STRUCTURE AND CURRICULUM

Given geographic, time, and cost constraints on visiting China, the program had to make a number of difficult decisions. It so happens that a great majority of Chinese immigrants settling in the San Francisco Bay area, especially those arriving before 1965, came from the Pearl River Delta region of Guangdong Province, an area approximately the size of the San Francisco Bay area. For logistical and economic reasons, the program elected to select as interns Chinese Americans who can trace their ancestries to that region; nevertheless, similar programs can be developed for other regions. Also, due to the intensive nature of the program, participants are limited to those who live within commuting distance of San Francisco.

In the early years, interns were asked to select one ancestral village to visit, because of the poor conditions of the roads in the region. Typically it took a whole day to complete one village visit. The rapid economic developments in southern China during the mid-1990s resulted in greatly improved travel conditions. By 1997 all the major cities were linked with well-paved multi-lane highways, thereby allowing the interns to visit two ancestral villages if they elected.

A requirement of the program is for each intern to develop his or her paternal and/or maternal family tree. The intern is also required to submit an essay about his or her family history, starting from the generation that emigrated abroad, as seen against the context of historical developments. Initially, articles and handouts from the 1989 symposium/workshop served as basic reference materials, but eventually additional reference notes were developed for the participants as new sources became available and as the coordinators reassessed the needs of the program.The series of nine seminars, from February through June, begin with a public presentation by the interns from the previous year. This provides the new interns an opportunity to learn about what they may expect out of the program, to ask questions, and to network with interns from previous years.

At the second seminar, interns are given guidance on the key elements of family history and genealogy. Additionally they are coached on oral history techniques so that they can begin immediately to interview parents and relatives to gather genealogical and family history information. They are also encouraged to find old family photographs and documents and search for genealogy records, with coordinators also giving help where needed to interpret or identify documentary materials.

At the third seminar, the participants visit the National Archives in San Bruno.[8] They are given an orientation by the director on the use of this important resource and a tour of the facility. Additionally the interns receive valuable information on the history of Chinese immigration to America, the development of the Chinese American community and the effect of immigration laws and American conditions leading to changes in Chinese surnames, and the process of accessing family records. This knowledge aids the researchers in appraising the reliability of the information found in the archives.

The fourth, fifth, and sixth seminars dwell at some length on the historical and geographical background of China. These lectures help the interns to better understand and evaluate information elicited from their oral interviews and from Chinese genealogies, to sift myths and exaggerations from historical realities, to place the materials in the proper historical context, and to prepare them for the trip to China. Since the interns' ancestral villages are in the Pearl River Delta region, the provided background information focuses on regional, geographical, and historical developments, as well as their relations to Guangdong Province and all of China.

Seminar seven is dedicated to the history of Chinese immigration to America and how it affects names and genealogical research. After gaining an understanding of the history of Chinese in America, the interns embark on a day-long trip, in seminar eight, to the recently declared national historic site, the Angel Island Immigration Station, located in the San Francisco Bay. From 1910 to 1940, Chinese arriving to San Francisco were detained, interrogated, and processed through this station as part of the enforcement of the Exclusion Laws. It was here that the massive immigration records were created, and it was also here that many endured painful experiences, as evidenced by the countless Chinese poems carved into the wooden walls of the barracks.[9]

The last seminar prepares the interns for their journey to China. By this time, interns have obtained the appropriate visas from the consulate of the People's Republic of China, made all the necessary travel arrangements, received traveling tips and instructions, and provided to the best of their ability the pertinent information for the search of their ancestral villages. Frequently interns from previous years join the session to share their learning and experiences. The interns also have the opportunity to view video documentaries of earlier Chinese American trips to the Pearl River Delta region, such as *The New Americans: Chinese Roots* (Donald Young), *China, Land of My Father* (Felicia Lowe), or *Separate Lives, Broken Dreams* (Jenny Lew).

For two weeks in July the interns journey to southern China. Each intern has the option of searching and visiting two ancestral villages if he or she desires. Additionally they attend the Guangdong Overseas Chinese Youth Festival, where they meet young people of Chinese heritage from other parts of the world, such as Germany, Japan, France, Hong Kong, Canada, Malaysia, Madagascar, England, Indonesia, and Fiji. The 1999, 2000, and 2001 interns also visited Beijing as part of the summer youth program that was sponsored by the Beijing Overseas Chinese Affairs Office.

THE JOURNEY TO CHINA

The climax of the program is the trip to China, where each intern visits his or her ancestral village(s). Under optimal conditions with ten interns, twenty villages can be visited within a ten-day period. In spite of the crammed schedule, interns achieve a higher feeling of accomplishment and fulfillment in the knowledge that they have successfully pursued the histories of both sides of the family or, in a few cases, of two different ancestors on one side of the family. In preparation for this endeavor, the program coordinators start early in the program, usually during the interview process, to obtain the names of the ancestral villages of each intern in order to map out the group's travel itinerary, and to gather pertinent information on the Chinese names of parents, grandparents, and other relatives, which can serve as clues to locating the correct sites.

The final search for the ancestral village begins well before the journey. It starts with finding out the written Chinese name of the village, the township and county that govern it, and the municipality that has jurisdiction over the township and county.[10] It also requires the written Chinese names of the relative or relatives who last resided in the village before emigrating. This information is then provided to the Guangdong Province's Overseas Chinese Affairs Office, which sends the data to the regional and local Overseas Chinese Affairs offices. They, in turn, locate the village, the village leaders, elders, and relatives, if any are there. The Pearl River Delta region houses thousands of villages. In a great majority of the cases, the only way to locate the villages is through the township and village Overseas Chinese Affairs offices, which seek out the knowledgeable village folks to guide in the search. This is because there are no detailed maps that clearly pinpoint the location of many of these villages. The way to the villages resides in the minds and memories of the locals.

If complete and accurate information has been forwarded in advance, preferably two months ahead of time, and if the local offices have done their groundwork, the search is relatively simple. For the most part, the local authorities will simply confirm the data with the intern, bring in a relative or two, and guide the intern to the village and ancestral home, if it is still in existence. Should the local officials fail to research ahead of time, an on-the-spot search in the village can be tedious and frustrating. In a few instances, the elders who would have known the intern's ancestors have all died and no connections are made. The search concludes only with the finding of the village.

In cases of incomplete or inaccurate information, the search is invariably more complicated and difficult. The ancestor's name, for example, may turn the search into a strange puzzle. Every now and then the name does not match the local records. This results from several possible factors. Conceivably, the ancestor may have changed his or her name in the United States. During the sixty-one oppressive years of the Chinese exclusion period (1882–1943), many immigrants arrived in this country as "paper sons" of other people, and thus carried with them surnames that were not their own. Another possibility is the use of names other than the given name recorded in the village. In the conventional Chinese tradition, men commonly have up to three names: the first, *ruming* or *xiaoming*, given at birth; the second, *xueming*, created by his teacher when he begins attending school; and the third, *zuming*, adopted after his marriage. Sometimes all the names are recorded or known to the village elders. As for the younger generations, names other than the given ones are usually not known. Accordingly, accurate identification of the names is essential. Equally important is the accurate identification of the village. Having the wrong village name makes it almost impossible to proceed with the search.

Once inside the village, the Chinese officials take great care in reconciling the facts with the interns to certify that they are indeed the "real" descendants. These officials will frequently ask the same question in different ways to ensure that the answers match the data they have on record. For example, they may ask, "when did your ancestor leave the village?" The same question may be phrased, " how long have your ancestors lived in America?" What they fear most is to usher the interns to the wrong ancestral home. This, to them, is a grave ethical violation! A mistaken identity not only can be embarrassing but also can permanently damage the lineage records of the intern and the family. Virtually in every case, the officials will summon several elders and village historians to join in the discussion for validation.

A case in point, 1994 intern Albert Chan had to return to his mother's ancestral village a second time to complete his search. During the interim, several discussions took place with the local officials to verify certain information. The difficulty with this search was that his maternal grandfather had changed his name in the United States, and this new name was unknown to any of the village elders and Albert did not know of his grandfather's original name. Although Albert provided the officials with the address (street and number) of the ancestral home, they were not fully convinced of this information and were very hesitant to take him to the house. According to the officials, the ancestral home itself had been sold and demolished, and a new home now stood on that site. The officials told Albert that the best they could do for him was to show him the location, but they could not take him into the new home. It was not until an elder showed up, a man who once knew Albert's grandfather, that the whole tone of the search changed. The elder looked at Albert and said, "you look exactly like your grandfather when I last saw him in Guangzhou some fifty years ago!" That statement instantly created a new trust. Albert confirmed that he was a mirror image of his maternal grandfather. "There's no way to fake a face!" remarked one of the local guides. The rest is history. Not only did Albert enter the new home, but he also discovered that part of the ancestral home still stood unchanged and still belonged to his family. He also was treated to a wonderful official banquet where the best of the local Shunde cuisine was served!

Cooperative officials in the regional and local Overseas Chinese Affairs offices play a key role in creating the conditions for a successful search. Virtually all of the officials who have worked with the program have treated this search in a serious manner, and they have gone out of their way to assist the interns in their quests. There have been very few instances in which officials were reluctant, and in these cases they would diplomatically say, "It's been too long. Everyone has emigrated. No one here knows about your family. It's very difficult. We no longer have any one who can help us help you." In cases like this, the search requires going into the village itself and asking the local residents directly, as in the case of 1992 intern Hamilton Chang, who through this method finally located his paternal grandfather's ancestral home.

From time to time, productive searches may yield genealogical records that go back twenty-five to thirty generations; ancestral portraits and photographs; stories (lore and legends) of the village and ancestors; artifacts like ceramic bowls, double-gourd water containers, teapots, or other items that were used by the ancestors; or newly discovered relatives. At the public presentation, 1999 intern Warren Lei remarked, "I woke up with a few butterflies in my stomach hoping that perhaps someone would know of my ancestors. . . . [S]uddenly my fears were calmed as the city officials informed us that I had relatives that still lived there!" In 1992, intern Lily Wong wanted to postpone her search, because she was afraid that she would find nothing—no relatives, no ancestral home, or even no village. Her fear stemmed from the fact that her family emigrated from the village over one hundred years ago, first to Burma and then to the United States, and through the years had lost contact with the village. Lily, after some coaching, decided to continue the search. To her amazement, not only did she find the village, she discovered relatives who closely resembled her grandfather, an ancestral home, and most valuable of all, a genealogy book that recorded over twenty-five generations of her family.

IMPACT ON THE INTERNS: THE PROGRAM COORDINATORS' FINDINGS
The majority of the interns were overwhelmed when they first encountered their histories. Many were moved to tears. It was a highly emotional moment, not only for them, but also for the people around them. Audrey Low, a 1997 intern, cried for days after uncovering the mystery that shrouded the history of her family for over half a century. She learned, as she was standing on the empty lot where her ancestral home once stood, that during World War II, the Japanese military occupied and destroyed a majority of the village's residences, including her family's. This caused the sudden exodus of the village residents, who scattered and found refuge elsewhere. Among them were Audrey's American ancestors, who had died and never told the story to anyone. Audrey no longer carried the burden of not knowing what happened to her ancestors. The visit instead brought clarity and understanding. It made Audrey whole again.

Sixteen-year-old 1999 intern Jason Lew sobbed as he stood alone inside his ancestral home. He wrote, "After I closed the door I broke down and cried. This was home. This was where everything started. This wasn't a place to visit. It was not the history of a country, nor was it the history of a person. It was my history. These were the walls that knew my family's stories. This was the roof that kept my ancestors alive. This was the ground I came from. These were my roots." At long last he succeeded in reestablishing the long-lost connection between his family in the United States and their ancestral beginnings. The journey gave meaning to his existence. It created for Jason a sense of belonging, a sense of history, and a sense of pride.

At the same time, the interns witnessed the hardships, the sweat-soaked and bone-weary farmers, the poor living conditions of the less-affluent rural villages, which had open sewers, no running water, no electricity or sanitary facilities, barefooted children, old clothing, and labor-intensive work such as manual tilling, irrigating, and harvesting. Georgette Wong, a 1992 intern, wrote, "The trip to my village was incredible. I didn't know what to expect when I got there. I felt very emotional as we arrived at the village, seeing how different my life would have been, had I been born there." The experience made Georgette appreciate what she had in America. It also validated that she, though ethnically Chinese, was different from the Chinese in China.

Finding their roots has caused the interns to reflect upon who they are and where they come from. In doing so, they begin to redefine or construct their identities as Americans of Chinese heritage. In 1994 intern Phyllis Yang wrote, "One year ago, I never imagined I would know so much about my family history. Searching for my family roots not only taught me a lot about my ancestry but enabled me to better understand myself as well." Like Georgette and many other interns, Phyllis saw herself as an American of Chinese ancestry. She understood the Chinese values that she practiced, but at the same time Phyllis knew that she was unlike her counterparts in China.

The interns become closer to their families as a result of extensive interaction with family members to gather oral histories and anecdotes, family records and documents, and genealogical information. In 1992 Tina Tom wrote, "In many ways this trip was not so much about finding my roots as it was about making sure that my relationships with my family take root." What the interns also found out were the origins of the beliefs, values, and practices of their family members in the United States who began their lives in the villages.

The interns understand more about the Chinese rituals, heroes and heroines, history and culture, cuisine, language, and customs, all of which instill great pride in each of the interns. Consequently, the interns start to "deconstruct" the negative stereotypes that have long haunted their mental constructs. A passage in the April 19, 1999, issue of *Time* magazine reads, "'I grew up feeling ashamed of a big part of my identity,' says Julia Fong (1997 intern) of Berkeley, Calif. After gathering details about her family's life in China, she visited the ancestral villages. 'A large part of what I gained is feeling proud of who I am,' she says, 'It makes me glad that I am Chinese.'"

For some interns, the experience has inspired them to explore more deeply their Chinese heritage. Several interns, like Albert Chan (1994), Andrea Louie (1992), Kevin Gee (1998), Linda Cheu (1992), May Wong (1998), Ryan Kwok (1999), and Petrina Chi (1998), have returned and stayed in China to teach or study. Kevin Gee, who studied and taught in China for two years, wrote, "I now realize that the work I have started through Roots is just a beginning. The search for my family history and identity as a Chinese American is a continual process."

Others have made stronger connections with the community and, in many cases, are emerging as leaders. Jeffrey Ow serves as a member of the board to preserve the Angel Island Immigration Station. Tony Tong (1994) was and Linda Cheu (1992) is a board member of the Chinese Culture Foundation of San Francisco. Julia Fong was the secretary of the board for the Chinese Historical Society of America. Lisa Mar (1991) is a leading scholar on the history of Chinese Canadian women. Donald Young (1993) has produced several significant video documentaries on Asian Americans and is active with the National Asian American Telecommunication Association.

This program has impacted the personal lives of the interns in a very powerful way, not only in terms of developing their identities, but most importantly in placing this development within the context of a much broader understanding and appreciation of the Chinese American experience. Tina Tom sums it up in a March 4, 1994, interview with *Asian Week:* "I think that the 'Roots' program can be instrumental in helping Chinese Americans discover their heritage and in bringing about a greater awareness and interest in the Chinese American community. For many Chinese Americans like myself, who do not feel like a part of the rest of the Chinese American community, going back to their ancestral village gives one insight into the Chinese American experience. It provides us all with a common experience that connects us to the rest of the community."

Another important consequence of the program are the lasting friendships and relationships that have been forged as a result of the interns studying and traveling together as a team. The program provides the opportunity for the interns to build strong ethnic bonds among themselves. They continue to meet

and socialize several times a year as part of the Roots Alumni activities. For instance, on February 24, 2001, the alumni hosted a ten-year anniversary celebration honoring the founding visionaries of the program. The alumni also
maintain a comprehensive mailing list of all interns and, from time to time,
publish a *Roots Newsletter.*

About one-third of the interns are high-school students and the rest are
undergraduates or graduates from the local universities; a few have finished
college and are working. A point of interest is that more than two-thirds of the
high-school students are in their senior year, while about six-tenths of the university students are seniors or graduates, suggesting that when people are entering a transitional period in their lives, they may be more receptive to new
commitments, such as the Roots program. Moreover, the current movement
of Asian Americans seeking equal participation in American mainstream society also plays an important role in awakening a sense of ethnic consciousness that motivates the participants to inquire into their roots as part of a
process to affirm their individual identities.

After eleven years of experience, the coordinators find that the program is an
effective means to help young Americans of Chinese heritage discover more
about themselves. The interns come away with an increased awareness of their
legacies in America and China. The program is about discovering more about
one's self against the backdrop of developments in Chinese American and Chinese, particularly Guangdongese, societies. It is about searching for, discovering,
interpreting or reinterpreting, making meaning of, and constructing one's identity through family history research and a journey to the ancestral land.

The quest for one's identity is very much a part of the American experience. Lynn Pan, in her scholarly work *Sons of the Yellow Emperor: A History of
the Chinese Diaspora* (1990), aptly writes, "We are told by historians that root-
lessness and the search for identity have always been features of American life,
and we are not surprised that, of all Chinese settlers abroad, it is the ones in
America who feel most keenly what Simone Weil, in her tormented wartime
exile among the English, called 'perhaps the most important and least recognized need of the human soul'—the need to be rooted." (295)

NOTES

1. Him Mark Lai, "Chinese American Studies: A Historical Survey," *Chinese America:
History and Perspectives* (1988): 11–29.

2. Irma Tam Soong, *The History of the Hawaii Chinese History Center, 1970–1980*
(Honolulu: Hawaii Chinese History Center, 1980).

3. *Hawaii Chinese History Center Newsletter* 8, no. 4 (November 1978).

4. *Hawaii Chinese History Center Newsletter* 8, no. 2 (June 1978).

5. Announcement, "Family History for the Chinese American: A Special Workshop," University of California, Los Angeles, and Chinese Historical Society of Southern California, 1983.

6. *Hawaii Chinese History Center Newsletter* 14, no. 1 (December 1985).

7. Announcement, "Chinese American Family History and Genealogy Symposium/Workshop," Chinese Culture Foundation, San Francisco, October 1989.

8. From 1882 through 1943 the United States passed a series of Chinese Exclusion Acts, which severely limited Chinese entry into this country. Due to the enforcement of these racist immigration laws, the Immigration and Naturalization Service and the federal courts left a vast body of official documents concerning the Chinese. From the nineteenth century through the greater part of the twentieth century the majority of the Chinese immigrants landed in this country at San Francisco and, to a lesser degree, Honolulu. Moreover, large Chinese communities existed in central and northern California as well as in Hawaii. Thus many federal government documents connected with the Chinese, especially Chinese immigration, are stored in the National Archives and Records Administration-Pacific Region, located conveniently in San Bruno near San Francisco. It also houses federal archival documents for Northern and central California, Nevada (except Clark county), Hawaii, America Samoa, and the Pacific Trust Territories. Examples of these records include Chinese Exclusion Act case files, arrival investigation case files, Chinese partnership case files, passport and control files, return certificate application case files, certificates of identity for Chinese residents, index of Chinese partnerships in and outside of San Francisco, passenger lists of vessels arriving in San Francisco, records of foreign-born and U.S.-born Chinese departing and returning to the United States, records of war brides with children, and more. This body of documents, not usually considered a major source for genealogical research for other Americans, is an important and fairly easily accessed resource for many Chinese American researchers.

9. Him Mark Lai, Genny Lim, and Judy Yung, *Island, Poetry and History of Chinese Immigrants on Angel Island, 1910–1940* (San Francisco: Chinese Culture Foundation of San Francisco, 1980).

10. An extremely useful reference for locating ancestral villages is the *Index of Clan Names,* compiled for the Toishan (Taishan), Hoiping (Kaiping), Sunwui (Xinhui), and Chungshan (Zhongshan) districts (counties) by the American Consulate General in Hong Kong during the 1950s to aid detection of immigration fraud.

17

Ah Quin: One of San Diego's Founding Fathers

Murray K. Lee

There is no other person in the early history of the Chinese in San Diego, California, who is more deserving of being included among the founding fathers of the city, along with the likes of Alonzo Horton and George Marston, than Ah Quin. The early immigrant Chinese are mostly a nameless group of men who have never been fully acknowledged for their contributions to the development of California and the West, but Ah Quin is an exception. He was a man respected by all, a successful entrepreneur, a community leader and patriarch, who bridged the gap between the Chinese and the white establishment of his day. In 1880 Ah Quin was asked to come to San Diego to be the Chinese labor broker for the building of the California Southern Railroad. This job also opened the door for him to become a successful merchant with interests in farming, real estate, and mining. He raised a large family, was a leader in his community, and had the unofficial title "Mayor of Chinatown." How Ah Quin came to be such a success in America is a story of his drive to succeed, coupled with his unique ability to adapt to an alien and oftentimes hostile culture.

Success as a patriarch and entrepreneur was not the only thing that distinguished Ah Quin from other early pioneers; his diaries, written almost entirely in English, are his most unique legacy (see Cassel, chapter 3 in this volume). Ah Quin's diaries provide the backbone of sources for the story of his life. Unfortunately, there are only ten diaries covering a span of twenty-five years (1877–1902); therefore there are many gaps. However, the years covered happen to be during the most significant and productive period of his adult life. Most of his early years followed the typical pattern of life for his Chinese immigrant contemporaries who were not involved in mining or contract labor, such as those who worked on the railroads or in agriculture. He worked at service-type jobs that were open to Chinese at the time, such as houseboy and cook. The later years of his life (not recorded in his diaries) are fairly well known because of what he achieved, what his descendants and friends recall, and local newspaper accounts. While working with the railroad as a labor broker, he used the small standard diaries that could easily fit in his coat pocket. The diaries resemble a day-to-day log of his activities, except when they are spiced with some unusual event. Unlike a typical diary, his don't give us a lot of personal opinions and inward feelings, which is very typical of a busy, hardworking Chinese father. Unfortunately, Ah Quin stopped writing his diaries after 1894 for reasons unknown. There is a list in the diaries, however, of all his children and their birthdays, which includes the birth of his last child, on August 21, 1900.

ORIGINS

Ah Quin was born on December 5, 1848, in a small village in the Hoiping (Kaiping) District of Guangdong Province of southern China.[1] He was the eldest son of parents who were farmers. The family name was *Tom*, which can also be Romanized as *Hom*, but as is often the case with Chinese immigrants, his name was misinterpreted by government officials and he became known as Ah Quin.

When Ah Quin was young, his parents moved to Canton (Guangzhou), the provincial capital. This gave him the opportunity to grow up in the city with the greatest exposure to the West. Canton was opened to trade with the West in 1757 and for almost a century was the only seaport in China available for such trade. Canton's monopoly on foreign trade created a boon for local merchants and they took advantage of it. The "Canton System" prevailed, and the trade was concentrated in a handful of "Hong" merchants (from *gunghong*, a merchant guild). This system of dealing with the Western traders provided a balance of payments entirely in favor of China, which resulted in the British introduction of opium into China from India. When China attempted to halt this trade, the first Opium War resulted, and in 1842 English naval power forced the Chinese to open several other treaty ports and to surrender Hong Kong. The colony of Hong Kong and the Pearl River Delta area played major roles in the emigration of Chinese to Southeast Asia and America.

By living in Canton, Ah Quin had opportunities much greater than those offered in his family's village. It provided him with the chance to receive an education at an American missionary school, to learn English, to learn to read and write Chinese, and to broaden his education through exposure to one of the most cosmopolitan Chinese cities of the period.[2] This early training proved important for Ah Quin in gaining future opportunities in America.

EMIGRATION TO AMERICA

In the mid-nineteenth century, no doubt, Ah Quin's family found itself suffering along with all the Chinese in the area. The series of wars, rebellions, floods, and famine were the necessary "push" factor that led many families in the Pearl River Delta area to send a son or sons to California, or "Gold Mountain," as they called it. Word had filtered back to China from the early immigrants to the gold fields that there were opportunities for mining and other employment. This was the lure, or "pull" factor. Fortunately, Ah Quin's family was able to pay his passage to San Francisco, unlike the families of most Chinese immigrants. If the fee of $50 was not paid, the immigrant had to buy a ticket on credit, thus the "credit-ticket system," and have the money deducted from the wages he would earn. The ticket usually took about three years to repay.

EARLY YEARS IN AMERICA

At age twenty Ah Quin followed many of his countrymen to Gold Mountain to help in the survival of the family and to seek his fortune. In 1868, when his ship landed in San Francisco, he was most likely met by clan members who took him to Chinatown and provided him with lodging and employment. San Francisco's Chinatown was where most of the early immigrants got their orientation and start in America. It provided a safe haven and a place to learn the system before venturing into unknown places or jobs. Ah Quin contacted the Chinese mission in San Francisco and continued his religious study. In the late nineteenth century, the American Protestant denominations gave high priority to missionary work in China. When Chinese began immigrating to California, the missionary movement thought that this provided them with an even greater opportunity to Christianize them and to instill Euro-American cultural values.[3] The Chinese missions were familiar to him and he was comfortable at the missions in Chinatown. They provided him with a place to add to his knowledge of English, continue his religious studies, and develop contacts with Americans. His time at the missions proved mutually beneficial to the goals of both Ah Quin and the missions. He remained in San Francisco for about six years, employed in a variety of jobs, which included serving as a houseboy and cook.

Early Years: Santa Barbara

In about 1873 Ah Quin moved to Santa Barbara, where he had an opportunity to learn merchandising from an uncle. Santa Barbara had a small Chinese community (234 in 1880) where the Chinese worked as servants in the homes of white families or were employed in the fields. Santa Barbara also had a Chinese mission, which Ah Quin joined. The mission provided him with additional instruction in English and the opportunity to establish contacts with other Chinese and prominent members of the Congregational Church. He became a friend of Judge Charles Huse, one of the founders of the church, and even after he left Santa Barbara he visited the judge whenever he passed through the town (figure 17.1).[4]

What did Ah Quin gain from going to Santa Barbara other than a chance to learn a trade from his uncle? Most likely, his stay provided a more conducive environment to integrate into the American lifestyle, as he began to wear American clothing and adopt some customs. Santa Barbara was a small town with a small, nonthreatening Chinese community. Unlike San Francisco, the Chinese had a more intimate relationship with the local people. He also began to write his diary while here, and the first entry was in June 1877.

Early Years: Alaska

The Santa Barbara company of E. J. Gourley and Stearns had coal-mining interests in Coal Harbor, Alaska, and Ah Quin signed on as the cook. His ship stopped in San Francisco on the way and there Ah Quin's uncle, Tom On, lectured him about leaving California.[5] Evidently his uncle believed there were better opportunities in California. Ah Quin may have looked at this job as a way to see Alaska and make a try at being on his own. Anyway, he was determined to fulfill his obligation and arrived in Alaska on July 26, 1877, after experiencing a bad case of seasickness. Conditions for cooking at first were quite inadequate, yet he had to prepare two meals for the miners every day. In December he wrote, "I get up about 3 o'clock this morning put some coal in the stove—have one little sparky fly in my right eye and hurt me very badly in that time and clean about 70 sculpions fish, or may be another name called sturgeon—and cut my both fingers two places—and the thermometer in the even[ing] at five oclock is very low—18—very sorry my boiler water kettle had three hole in it—cannot use longer—soonest broke them, I no more kettle"[6]

After improvements were made to the living quarters, Ah Quin found enough time to explore the island, which was part of the Shumagin group. Even though Ah Quin was homesick and had concerns for his aging parents, Gourley convinced him to stay on longer. Ah Quin used his time during the long Alaskan winter nights to write letters, read the Bible, and make records in his diary. He wrote and received many letters from California and China, and as was customary for Chinese in America, he sent money to his family.

While in Alaska, Ah Quin decided to cut off his queue. This was not a decision to be taken lightly. The Chinese had been required to wear queues

FIGURE 17.1
Ah Quin in Santa Barbara, California, 1873 (Copyright © San Diego Historical Society
Research Archives, Photograph Collection. Reprinted with permission.)

from the time of the conquering Manchus and their removal brought a loss of dignity. Perhaps for Ah Quin it was a matter of practicality, because in the isolated site maintenance was too difficult, or perhaps the act was a demonstration of his commitment to adopt America as his new country. He says, "I called Mr. E. J. Gourley and cut off my queus —it just look like the white people—not like china any more—and Gourley and Mr. A. K. Thompson, another workman, very glad and laugh at me."[7] He gave them a few strands as a memento, and they graciously accepted. Ah Quin completed his contract in July and returned on the steamer to Santa Barbara. Alaska provided him with an adventurous interlude in his career and financial benefits. The additional money no doubt allowed him to send more money back to his family, which may have been one of the motivating factors in taking this job. Cutting off his queue, adopting Western clothing and customs, and practicing his English were further evidence that he planned to remain in America. The next step was to find an occupational pursuit more suitable to his talents.

Early Years: Visit to San Diego

Ah Quin returned to Santa Barbara in 1878 and was welcomed back to the mission. He evidently had progressed in his knowledge of English to such an extent that he was allowed to teach and conduct classes in English. In Santa Barbara, Ah Quin began using his bilingual ability when his friends sought him for advice, especially in legal matters. Thus he began his role as a mediator and an adviser on legal problems common to new immigrants, sometimes providing assistance in finding lawyers to represent them in violations of local ordinances or immigration compliance. In many cases, he would be asked by the court to assist as a translator.

Ah Quin went to work for Colonel William Hollister on his large ranch, but this was work similar to what he already had been doing and he began to survey the job possibilities elsewhere in California. He contacted friends in San Francisco and also considered San Diego. After contacting friends in San Diego, he decided to make a short visit and left with his friend Shin Sha on the steamship *Senator* on September 28, 1878.[8] Ah Quin was welcomed by his relatives on the dock in San Diego and was housed in the Sam Kee washhouse near Chinatown. While attending the Presbyterian Church during his visit he met George Camp, the minister, and George Marston, owner of a dry goods business. Marston was later instrumental in founding the Chinese mission. Before leaving San Diego, Ah Quin visited with Wo Sing, a Chinese landowner, herb doctor, and owner of several fishing junks. This was an important contact for him and eventually led to a significant friendship and business association. Ah Quin, with another friend, Ah Tom, returned to Santa Barbara on the *Orizaba*, one of the side-wheeler steamships that would play a significant part in the transportation of Chinese laborers to San Diego.

Early Years: Back to San Francisco

Ah Quin spent two years in San Francisco with the primary goal of job hunting. He lived with his uncle, Tom On, and performed odd jobs while continuing his job search. He also continued his association with the Chinese mission and there met William Pond, a minister, who would later take charge of the San Diego Chinese mission at the request of George Marston. Ah Quin even went to Stockton in search of employment, but could find nothing suitable. Soon he had to fall back on his cooking ability and took a job at the Presidio as cook and servant for two officers. His salary was only $25 per month, but he had his own room in the building. It seems that the Chinese of that period could only find jobs in the service industry, doing contract labor on the railroads, or working in the fields.

By 1855 the use of Chinese as cooks, houseboys, gardeners, and laundrymen became a thriving business in San Francisco. In 1865, when Charles Crocker was trying to solve the shortage of labor in building the Central Pacific portion of the transcontinental railroad, he suggested to his foreman, Strobridge, the use of Chinese. Strobridge thought the idea preposterous and, in his opinion, the Chinese were only good at raising vegetables, doing laundry, and serving as cooks or houseboys for the wealthy. To build a railroad over the Sierra with these "rice-eating weaklings" was rank nonsense.[9] With so many jobs closed to the Chinese immigrants it must have been frustrating for a young man with ability and potential such as Ah Quin to be caught in this stereotype. Crocker disagreed with his foreman, because he had a Chinese servant, Ah Ling, who had proved himself a marvel of endurance. He also confronted his hard-nosed foreman with the argument: hadn't the ancestors of these "weaklings" built the Great Wall of China? The use of Chinese railroad labor proved so successful that eventually Crocker employed twelve thousand Chinese on the Central Pacific.

Therefore, when the construction of a railroad in San Diego was anticipated, there was no hesitation in seeking Chinese labor, and the possibility of Ah Quin serving as the labor broker was suggested. In the fall of 1880, letters from George Marston and Reverend Camp in San Diego arrived. This opportunity was what Ah Quin was looking for, and it didn't take him long to make a decision. He terminated his job at the Presidio, after providing his employ-

ers with a young replacement, and left on October 25 for San Diego. The
steamer made a stop at Santa Barbara and Ah Quin was met by Gourley at the
dock, and he visited his friend, Judge Huse.[10] These friendships with the white
establishment, which Ah Quin maintained throughout his life, were likely why
he was considered for the job in San Diego. Even though previously he had
only a short stay in San Diego, he had met George Marston and Reverend
Camp and impressed them with his Christian training, his bilingual ability,
and his adaptability, which would serve him well in the role for which he was
hired.

GETTING ESTABLISHED IN SAN DIEGO

When Ah Quin arrived in San Diego in late 1880, he had to acquire a base of
operations for his new assignment, so he chose a store location in the Stingaree District on Fifth Street, between I and J. By then Alonzo Horton's "New
Town," or "Horton's Addition," had supplanted Old Town as the center of San
Diego. Ah Quin ordered a variety of stock that would appeal to both Chinese
and American clientele. He remained in this location until 1882, and then relocated to a permanent residence on Third Street in the heart of Chinatown
(figure 17.2).

San Diego, unlike San Francisco, had a small Chinese community. The 1880
census of San Diego showed a population of 8,618, of which only 229 were
Chinese. The occupations of the Chinese were similar to those of other California cities. There were 118 men working in the service industry as cooks,
laundrymen, gardeners, and servants. There were forty laborers, only four
merchants, and two herbalists. There were only eight women and they were
listed as "keeping house." There were twenty-eight fishermen, who by 1869
had located in two villages, one along Point Loma at Roseville and one along
San Diego Bay at the foot of Third Street.[11]

The fishermen were probably the first Chinese immigrants to establish
themselves in San Diego. They had also developed a shipbuilding industry and
made some of the best seagoing junks along the California coast. The fishermen at the foot of Third Street lived in redwood shacks erected over the water on stilts, with their junks anchored in the waters nearby. They fished from
Monterey Bay to lower Baja California and specialized in the harvest of
abalone, which they dried and shipped to San Francisco for export to China
and other Chinese settlements.[12]

The Stingaree District was adjacent to the harbor, where all the ships
docked and all the sailors came ashore, therefore it became the red-light

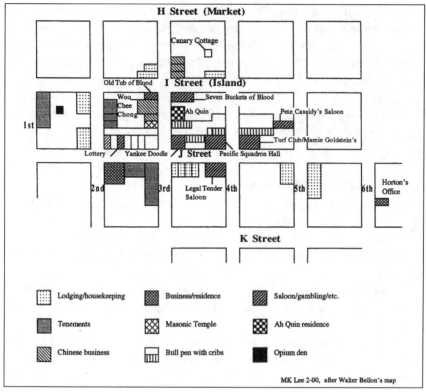

FIGURE 17.2
Map of the Stingaree District and Chinatown, San Diego, early 1900s (Copyright ©
Murray K. Lee. Reprinted with Permission.)

district of San Diego, much like the Barbary Coast was for San Francisco.
The city of San Diego confined these activities south of Market Street, an
area that included the city's Chinatown. There were saloons, brothels, gambling halls, and cribs catering to lonely sailors and others who were out
looking for "action." Although the Chinese operated many legitimate businesses in the area, they too operated gambling halls and the Chinese lottery
was prevalent. This is the environment that Ah Quin found himself in: not
altogether unfamiliar because of his period in San Francisco, but with
greater opportunities for him to establish a new merchandising business
and to invest in the growth of the city. He recognized the importance of
working with the city's white establishment and the railroad job offered
him the challenge of working with whites. Success would establish his rep-

utation and allow him to attain the rewards that all his countrymen desired in coming to Gold Mountain.

THE CALIFORNIA SOUTHERN RAILROAD

San Diego had been trying to get a railroad connection for years in order to compete with Los Angeles and San Francisco. San Diego had a natural harbor, much like San Francisco's, but did not have the links to the hinterland that were needed to develop as a major port. The only alternative was to link up with the rest of the country anywhere possible. Frank Kimball, National City founder, was instrumental in convincing the directors of the Atchison, Topeka, and Santa Fe Railroad to put the terminal in National City. After much negotiation, on October 12, 1880, the California Southern Railroad was chartered, with Benjamin Kimball as president. From National City, the line would run through San Diego, following the coast north through Rose Canyon to the San Luis Rey River, then inland along the Santa Margarita River via Temecula Canyon to San Bernardino, a distance of 116 miles. In 1881 an additional eighty miles was chartered to link up with the Atlantic and Pacific Railroad near Barstow. The goal of completing the railroad by the summer of 1882 depended upon finding sufficient labor.[13]

In National City, Ah Quin began negotiating with the railroad officials on the number of Chinese laborers to be used. He knew that many Chinese laborers would be necessary, and since there were insufficient numbers of laborers in San Diego, he had to negotiate to procure most of the labor elsewhere, which sometimes required him to make recruitment trips north. Customarily, the Chinese laborers required their own food; therefore, he also had the task of supplying them, which gave him the opportunity to develop a produce business. In early 1881 Chinese began to arrive by steamer from the north. As many as one hundred came on one trip by the steamship *Senator,* which docked in San Diego on March 5. The newspapers of the day always carried announcements of the arrival of the steamships, their cargoes, and passengers.[14] Although some of the contractors on the railroads refused to hire Chinese, the bulk of the labor force was Chinese and they always were assigned to the most difficult and dangerous sections.

The various contractors divided the line into sections and in May of 1882 there were six contractors supervising a total of fourteen gangs of Chinese and white workers. The wages were $1.75 per day.[15] Ah Quin was kept busy dividing his time between the construction sites and his San Diego store and most likely had to rely on the customary gang foremen to supervise the construction tasks. Since he also had logistic responsibilities, he shipped great quantities of food and supplies up the line to the work gangs. The Chinese diet included rice, potatoes, and fish, and the laborers undoubtedly consumed many gallons of tea, as their predecessors on the Central Pacific had done in the 1860s. Fortunately, the San Diego Chinese fishing fleet was capable of providing a steady supply of seafood products. There was no record of complaints about the food, although the costs of supplies were on the high side. Tents and makeshift huts were the principal living quarters in the camps, which had to move periodically as the construction progressed.

In the summer of 1881 construction began in the Temecula Canyon area, the toughest stretch of terrain along the route (figure 17.3). This was the location of a large Chinese camp, which housed over two thousand laborers who were working at cutting and blasting a right of way through the canyon. The cuts were not sloped, but were dug vertically as much as fifty feet deep and two hundred feet long.[16] The dust became so heavy and conditions so bad that at times the Chinese refused to work. Their apprehensions proved justified when a number of injuries and even a fatality occurred in this area from falling rocks.

FIGURE 17.3
Chinese railroad workers constructing the roadbed of the California Southern Railroad along Mission Bay, ca. 1881 (Copyright © San Diego Historical Society Research Archives, Photograph Collection. Reprinted with permission.)

The railroad construction pace picked up after passing through the Temecula Canyon area, and over a mile of track was laid every day. Trains began to run in the spring of 1882 to Encinitas and by late summer all the way to San Bernardino, although the railroad was not officially declared completed until September 13, 1883. As reported by the *San Diego Union*, Ah Quin was one of those who celebrated with an excursion on the train to San Bernardino in October 1882. As the railroad construction wound down, many of the Chinese workers returned to San Francisco, but several work gangs were retained for maintenance. Ah Quin was responsible for a number of the crews, kept them staffed and supplied with provisions, and also delivered their wages on his frequent trips on the train.

It wasn't long before Ah Quin was back recruiting Chinese labor once more, because heavy rains in early 1884 began to undermine the new railroad bed. When the railroad owners saw that the threat of damage was imminent, they asked Ah Quin to speed up efforts to recruit labor, and he traveled to Riverside and Los Angeles in search of men. While he was on this assignment, the rains reached their peak and the Santa Margarita River became a deluge, washing away many portions of track and forcing Ah Quin to return by steamship rather than by rail. The engineers who had planned the route didn't take into consideration the potential for flooding on this ordinarily placid river, which the railroad crossed many times. Locals had warned that occasionally there were unusually heavy winter rains and it wasn't long before this proved to be the case. Thirty miles of track had been washed out, especially in the Temecula Canyon area, and it was reported that railroad ties could be seen far out to sea. Ah Quin got stranded while up the line and on February 2 reported, "no train home to SDC then back to Colton . . . rain—cannot have train home because in Temecula Valley is brook [broke]."[17]

Ah Quin spent a considerable amount of time recruiting labor for the railroad repairs. He had to compete with the demand for Chinese labor in agriculture in the California Central Valley. No labor could be obtained directly from China after the Chinese Exclusion Act of 1882, but due to his efforts the railroad was able to get most of the men it needed. By the end of 1884, most of the repairs were completed and men could be transferred to the extension beyond San Bernardino.

MERCHANT, PATRIARCH, AND ENTREPRENEUR
Without any mention in his diaries, Ah Quin took leave from his railroad construction duties to travel to San Francisco to be married. Apparently, he had

met Sue Leong at the Chinese Presbyterian Mission in San Francisco. She was a ward of the mission and also had been taught English. At twenty, she was thirteen years younger than Ah Quin. Ah Quin had reached a significant milestone in his life; he had found an occupation suitable to his skills, at a place where he was accepted and where there was potential for growth. He had just turned thirty-three and he was ready to raise a family and remain permanently in San Diego. On December 14, 1881, he returned to San Diego with his wife on the steamship *Ancon*, the arrival of which was reported by the *Union*.[18]

Despite the prevalence of vice in the Stingaree area, some members of the Chinese community were able to endure and to begin to raise families. The Chinese settled in this area because of the proximity of the harbor, their fishing fleet, and the wharves. The Chinese were restricted to "below H (Market) Street" as were the activities of the Stingaree. Like other Chinese communities, the San Diego Chinese were bolstered by a support system that included family, benevolent associations, and the Chinese mission.

Ah Quin and his wife Sue in their two-story home on Third Street were able to raise a family of twelve children (figure 17.4). Beginning with Annie in 1883, the birth of a child was almost an annual occurrence until the turn of the century. George, the first of five boys, was born next, and it was noted in the newspaper that he was the first Chinese boy to be born in San Diego.[19] He was followed by Mamie, Tom, Margaret, Lily, Franklin, Minnie, Henry, Mary, Mabel, and McKinley. The children would be brought up as citizens of the United States, although Ah Quin was not able to realize his own desire for citizenship because Chinese were not allowed to become naturalized until 1943, when the Chinese Exclusion Laws were repealed.

Ah Quin believed in education, and the Chinese Mission School, established in 1885, provided this opportunity for his children. The mission was originally located at Eighth and D streets, but after several temporary moves it moved closer to Chinatown, on First Avenue, on land donated by George Marston. A new building and dormitory was constructed and dedicated on First Avenue in 1927.[20] The only children at the early Mission School were those of Ah Quin. Annie learned how to play the organ and George studied violin, and they all joined in the singing.

Ah Quin would take his children throughout the city to see the sights and events. On April 22, 1891, his diary says, "today hung up some flag in the front of the store because President Harrison and parties come tomorrow morning." On the following day with Tom he was able to see the president at the Horton House. He was "near me by 4 or 5 feet," he said in his diary.[21] There is no question as to Ah Quin's acculturation process, considering his participation in

FIGURE 17.4

Ah Quin and Family, 1900 (*Rear, left to right:* Tom, Annie, Mamie, George; *middle:* Margaret, Franklin, Sue [wife], Ah Quin, Lily; *front:* Minnie, McKinley [on Sue's lap], Mabel, Henry, and Mary) (From "The Ah Quin Story, Part II," *Chinese Historical Society of San Diego Newsletter* [fall 1996]. Copyright © Murray K. Lee. Reprinted with permission.)

American historic events and the naming of his boys after prominent American political figures, beginning with George and ending with his last son, McKinley.

When Ah Quin's railroad job was completed, his effort to expand his merchandising business and his real estate holdings began to occupy most of his time. The business had profited by his earlier railroad connection, which gave him the opportunity to develop the means to provide food and supplies to the workers. This included the growing of food crops locally as well as the importing of food and supplies from elsewhere.

He acquired property around the city and county. Many of the plots were used for farming and he hired workers to cultivate them. He had farmland on San Miguel Mountain, in National City, and in Bonita, along the Sweetwater River. His diary states that he sold his potato ranch in Bonita to See Fung and Tom Hin in June 1894 for $300.[22] He also owned land as far away as Los Angeles and San Bernardino.

FIGURE 17.5
Third Street in the heart of Chinatown, opposite Ah Quin's home, early 1900s (Copyright © San Diego Historical Society Research Archives, Photograph Collection. Reprinted with permission.)

Earlier, when Ah Quin was in Santa Barbara, he had developed an interest in gems and picked up the fundamentals of gemstone cutting and assaying from James Shedd, an assayer. In San Diego, he became acquainted with another assayer and chemist, Walter S. Young, who had an office on nearby Fourth Street. This renewed interest in gems was most likely stimulated by gold and the rich gem deposits found in San Diego County's mountains. In 1891, Ah Quin translated a book on the subject by Pierre de P. Rickett into Chinese, which evidently impressed the *Union*, which described his accomplishment as a "literary curiosity." Ah Quin tried to encourage his son Tom to learn the art of gem cutting from his friend Fred Rynerson, but to no avail. However, many years later Tom and Rynerson became partners in the ownership of the Himalaya Mining Company. The Himalaya Mine, located in the Mesa Grande area, became the richest of all the gem mines in San Diego

County and its pink tourmaline was exported to China, since it was desired by the empress dowager.[23]

COMMUNITY LEADER AND SPOKESMAN

From the time Ah Quin arrived in America, he had a knack for making friends and establishing valuable contacts. Besides his early friendships with those men he had met and worked for in Santa Barbara, such as Judge Huse and E. J. Gourley, he knew Reverend William Pond, who was one of the founders of the Chinese missionary movement. He was acquainted with judges, lawyers, and businessmen. Men like Frank Kimball and, especially, George Marston were friends, and their addresses were listed in the back of his diary. He also had Hong Kong contacts and contacts with his fellow Chinese throughout the country. For example, besides those California cities where he had once lived, he had contacts in Los Angeles, Fresno, Marysville, Salt Lake City, New York City, and Baltimore.[24]

One of Ah Quin's closest friends and confidants in the 1890s was Tom A. Yark, owner of a Chinatown business that sold Japanese goods, and who, like Ah Quin, was a Christian and could speak English. Since their stores were close together, they visited each other frequently, had long conversations, and played games of Chinese checkers. There are many entries in Ah Quin's 1891 diary that say briefly, "go up to Tom A. Yoke [Yark] Japanese store play the Chinese checkers with him." They also had business relationships and borrowed money from each other. Later, when Yark went to Arizona, they corresponded.

In 1887 Ah Quin brought an eleven-year-old girl named Wong Hin to San Diego as a servant to the family. He made the arrangement through the Chinese mission in San Francisco. This was a practice common among the Chinese. The girl was later accepted as a member of the family. The procedure was misunderstood by Walter G. Smith, the pugnacious and sharp-tongued editor of the San Diego Sun, and in 1889 he accused Ah Quin of holding her in slavery. The rival San Diego Union came to Ah Quin's defense, vouching for his character and noting that "Ah Quin is known as a straightforward businessman and has the confidence and trust of those who know him." They might have also noted that Ah Quin was a true patriarch and a man who loved his children and may have been thinking of how he could help his wife and also help this girl. He hired a lawyer and sued the newspaper for $20,000 for slander, but after a year of inaction he became frustrated with the issue and withdrew his suit, in spite of his lawyer's advice. Three years after the charges, in August 1892, Wong Hin, whom Ah Quin's family had treated like a daughter, was married to a Los Angeles merchant in a Chinatown ceremony.[25]

The use of the American judicial system whenever Ah Quin felt it necessary was a right he freely exercised as he became more acquainted with the system. He also never hesitated to contact the *Union* if he felt his reputation might be at stake as a result of one of their articles. On October 4, 1892, the *Union* printed a statement by Ah Quin in response to a report that someone named Ah Quin had been arrested for selling lottery tickets. He was quoted as saying "I never gamble or deal in lottery tickets and being the father of eleven children I do not want people to think I am the Ah Quin under arrest."

One of Ah Quin's roles as community leader was as a middleman or spokesman. He helped his fellow Chinese prepare their certificates of identity, which were required as a result of the Chinese Exclusion Laws. Ah Quin's bilingual capability also put him in demand as an interpreter. The local courts called upon him often to interpret for them in cases involving Chinese. Many of the violations at that time involved fishing or gambling. At one time he was requested to act as an interpreter for a judge in Riverside. In 1890, during a U.S. congressional investigation into the effects of Chinese immigration to America, Ah Quin was called to appear before the committee when it was holding hearings at the Hotel Del Coronado in San Diego. The reasons for these hearings were most likely apparent to Ah Quin. At this time the committee was trying to justify extending the Chinese Exclusion Law of 1882 and was inquiring about gambling in Chinatown. He did not want to portray his community in a bad light, but he admitted that it did exist, but was conducted by men who were not permanent residents.[26]

One of Ah Quin's accomplishments during his final years involved his cooperation with Walter Bellon, a health inspector, hired by the city. Bellon began surveying conditions around the Stingaree District and Chinatown and found many unhealthy and substandard conditions. Of course, the residents did not welcome him, and many of the landowners were absentee and unwilling to invest in the necessary improvements. Ah Quin was the exception; he introduced himself to Bellon and offered his help to improve the conditions in the area. In fact, he became one of the earliest in Chinatown to install plumbing in his house. Bellon gave Ah Quin much credit for his success in bringing improvements to the area. He said, "Ah Quin was a living example of good citizenship, thrift and integrity, and did not indulge in the accepted traffic of his community." Police Chief Keno Wilson added, "He was without exception the finest Chinaman I have ever known."[27]

One of the motivating factors in the cleanup of the Stingaree was the forth-coming Panama-California Exposition in Balboa Park in 1915. In 1912 the area was purged of much of its substandard housing, saloons, gambling dens, and prostitutes. Although many of these elements relocated or reappeared in other forms, the area never regained the notoriety of its early days.

THE AH QUIN LEGACY

Ah Quin prepared his sons to assume his duties as a merchant and entrepre-neur by involving them in his business activities. They often accompanied him on his rounds of inspection on his properties and his farming plots. George took over the family produce business at 431 Third Avenue (figure 17.5) and operated the Santa Margarita Ranch, which later became Camp Pendleton. After George's death in 1930, Georgia, his eldest daughter, kept the business going until her brother, Joseph, graduated from high school and could man-age it. The building remains in the family and is managed as a rental property by Madeline Quin, daughter of Joseph.

Tom became the most influential Chinese in the community and inherited the title of "Mayor" from his father. He ran the Monkey King lottery house, was involved in local politics, and owned the Fifth Avenue Restaurant (Nanking Café), which served as a meeting place for many city councilmen. Later, Tom's lottery operation included the Central Valley, and he was known to offer a tourmaline crystal as a special premium to lottery winners. Tom and his younger brothers had joined with Fred Rynerson in acquiring a fifty-year lease on the Himalaya tourmaline mine. Frank had studied mining engineer-ing at the University of Southern California, a field Ah Quin had encouraged his sons to pursue.[28] In 1935 the city began to raid all of the gambling estab-lishments in the area and Tom's business, along with many others in China-town, never recovered.

Four of Ah Quin's seven daughters married Chinese and three married Euro-Americans. Mamie married Royal Rife, Mary married Joseph Farina, and Mabel married Willie West Kennerly. Mamie and Mary had no children. Kennerly, who became a police officer, married Mabel, in spite of the opposi-tion of her mother and his friends. They had to be married in Tijuana because of California's miscegenation laws.[29] There are six generations of descendants of Ah Quin and his wife Sue. Their numbers have reached 143 and are grow-ing.[30] The children made significant steps in achieving the acculturation process fostered by their parents. But unfortunately Ah Quin did not live to see his grandchildren grow up, because on February 8, 1914, at age sixty-six, he died from a fatal accident. The prior evening he was crossing the street on the way to a banquet in honor of his first grandson and was struck by a motorcycle driven by Charles Mundell. He was seriously injured and taken to his home, where he fell into a coma and died the next morning.[31]

Chinatown was shocked by the news and went into mourning. Ah Quin was given a Christian burial, as he had stipulated. As reported by the *Union*, Reverend W. H. Noble came out of retirement to give the funeral address at Mt. Hope Cemetery, praising Ah Quin for being a fine friend, community leader, and family man. Six American and six Chinese pallbearers carried the casket to the gravesite as the band played "Nearer, My God, to Thee."[32] The estate was valued at over $50,000, with the store and real estate holdings in Los Angeles and San Bernardino, a considerable sum in those days.

Ah Quin certainly must be included among the prominent founders of San Diego, not only for his accomplishments as an entrepreneur and labor broker for San Diego's first railroad, but for his leadership and his ability to use his influence to improve the community and help his countrymen. Ah Quin's role as unofficial "Mayor of Chinatown" gave the community someone who was highly regarded and trusted by the white establishment. This role was vital when the area was under pressure during the cleanup campaign by the city, and when there were residents who needed a voice and legal guidance. He used the American justice system when he felt he was wronged and set an early example in the Chinese immigrant's fight for rights. When considering the period in which he lived, Ah Quin's accomplishments during his life were remarkable—his mastery of English, his Christian conversion, his ability to learn and adapt to his environment, and his keeping of a diary in English. The latter, in itself, is a most unique contribution and a boon for historians. And considering that he was able to raise a family of twelve children in the midst of the notorious Stingaree District, Ah Quin also must be ranked as one of San Diego's most noteworthy patriarchs.

NOTES

1. Andrew R. Griego, *Mayor of Chinatown: The Life of Ah Quin, Chinese Merchant and Railroad Builder of San Diego* (master's thesis, San Diego State University, 1979). Although Griego indicated that Ah Quin was born on December 8, 1848, in Toishan (Taishan), his gravestone lists a village in Hoiping (Kaiping) as his birthplace, on December 5, 1848. It may be noted that when Ah Quin mentioned that it was his birthday in his diaries, e.g., December 20, 1884, and December 21, 1892, it was the fifth day of the eleventh month of the Chinese (lunar) calendar;

therefore there is some doubt as to the actual date, as often occurs with those who use the Chinese calendar.

2. Griego, *Mayor of Chinatown*, 8.

3. Karl Fung, *The Dragon Pilgrims: A Historical Study of a Chinese-American Church* (San Diego: Providence, 1989), 18–19.

4. Griego, *Mayor of Chinatown*, 26.

5. Ah Quin Diary, San Diego Historical Society Archives, June 14, 1877.

6. Diary, December 13–14, 1877.

7. Diary, June 1, 1878.

8. Diary, September 28, 1878.

9. Oscar Lewis, *The Big Four* (New York: Knopf, 1938), 70.

10. Griego, *Mayor of Chinatown*, 38.

11. Judith Liu, "Birds of Passage," *Gum Saan Journal* 10, no. 1, (June 1987).

12. Murray K. Lee, "The Chinese Fishing Industry of San Diego," *Mains'l Haul* 35, nos. 2–3 (summer 1999).

13. Richard F. Pourade, *The Glory Years, Vol. 4: The History of San Diego* (San Diego: Union Tribune Publishing Co., 1964), 158.

14. *San Diego Union*, 5 March 1881.

15. *San Diego Union*, 11 May 1881, 8 January 1882.

16. R. P. Middlebrook, "The Chinese at Sorrento," *San Diego Historical Society Quarterly* 10 (January 1964).

17. Andrew R. Griego, in his article "Rebuilding of the California Southern Railroad," *Journal of San Diego History* 25, no. 4 (fall 1979), says that "brook" meant that the valley was filled with rushing water, but what Ah Quin really meant was that the railroad was "broke." This is substantiated by an article written by Liz Yamaguchi of the Fallbrook Historical Society, "Floods, Fall Brook and Fallbrook," as a letter to the editor of the *Fallbrook Enterprise* newspaper, 4 March 1993. The article says that on the second day of February the train was delayed when rain softened the canyon walls and brought boulders crashing down on the rails along the Santa Margarita River. Occasionally Ah Quin's spelling caused some confusion.

18. Griego, *Mayor of Chinatown*, 48.

19. *San Diego Union*, 10 February 1885.

20. Centennial Book Staff, *Chinese Community Church: One Hundred Years of Leadership and Service* (San Diego: Chinese Community Church, 1985).

21. Diary, April 23, 1891.

22. Diary, June 30, 1894.

23. Griego, *Mayor of Chinatown*, 70–71.

24. Diary, "Addresses," 1891. Listed among the addresses in this diary was one for my grandfather's store in Baltimore, Maryland: "Hop Lung Co.; 108 Park Avenue, Baltimore, MD." Alongside was the Chinese character for "Lee."

25. Griego, *Mayor of Chinatown*, 60–61.

26. Griego, *Mayor of Chinatown*, 64.

27. Walter Bellon, "Memoirs," manuscript, San Diego Historical Society.

28. Peter Bancroft, "The Sickler Family: Historic San Diego County Gemstone Miners," *Wrangler* 29, no. 1 (1996).

29. Rosemary Eng, "Chinatown: Now a Memory," *San Diego Tribune*, 22 September 1970.

30. Murray K. Lee, Ah Quin family tree, July 2000.

31. *San Diego Union*, 9 February 1914.

32. *San Diego Union*, 10 February 1914.

18

Contesting Identities: Youth Rebellion in San Francisco's Chinese New Year Festivals, 1953–1969

Chiou-ling Yeh

On May 8, 1969, an editorial in the *Chinese World*, a San Francisco Chinese American community newspaper, questioned the usefulness of the Chinese New Year Festival. "Sure there's a big [Chinese New Year] parade every year. That's nice. But what has anyone done to alleviate the problems [in Chinatown]?"[1] This criticism focused on a central question in Chinatown: why were Chinese American leaders busy promoting Chinatown as a tourist center while ignoring its social, class, and racial problems? These problems were also the major factors in the increase in Chinese American juvenile delinquency. Meanwhile, the college-educated Chinese Americans, drawing on past experience with grassroots social movements, began to challenge their elders and address the plight of Chinatown.[2] The Chinese New Year Festival, the biggest event in the community, was used by the festival committee to promote commercialism and showcase Chinese American ethnic and gender identities. Yet various Chinese American youth groups used the festival to protest social injustice and the indifference of Chinese American leaders to community problems. The Chinese New Year Festival gave rise to competing definitions of ethnic and gender identities constructed, on the one hand, by festival organizers and, on the other hand, by different groups of youth protesters.

Using mainstream and Chinese American community newspapers, festival publications, and oral histories, this chapter investigates this conflict between Chinese American identities promoted by the festival organizers and those upheld by the different groups of community youth. It employs the concept of "everyday resistance" used by James Scott in *Weapons of the Weak* to examine criticism, disruptions, alternative celebrations, and counter rituals in the Chinese New Year Festivals.[3] The festival organizers were part of the Chinatown establishment, a term used by Victor and Brett de Bary Nee that refers to Chinese entrepreneurs in Chinatown who often played important roles in family associations and community affairs. Even though they were subordinate in relation to white elites who controlled the larger society, the Chinatown establishment held a privileged "local" position because it controlled community economic resources and were the spokespersons for Chinatown.[4] In contrast, other Chinatown residents did not possess these resources to use against the Chinatown establishment. They, however, were able to use what Scott refers to as "everyday resistance" to destabilize the Chinese New Year festivals. This chapter focuses on three examples of resistance: criticism of the Miss Chinatown U.S.A. beauty pageant, the production of an alternative celebration, and youth violence. My contention is that the resistance presented in the festival destabilized the authority of Chinatown leaders. Organizers incorporated the alternative celebration into the festival but failed to respond to social issues raised by the working-class youth. The decision to integrate one form of resistance into the festival while ignoring others transformed both the festival and Chinatown itself.

EAST MEETS WEST

The "loss" of mainland China to Communists in 1949 and the outbreak of the Korean War (1950–1953) created a difficult political and economic situation for San Francisco's Chinese Americans. Anti-Communist hysteria and the war between China and the United States forced Chinatown to distance itself from "Red China" and to form a stronger bond with the Nationalist government of Taiwan.[5] In addition to changes in the political structure, Chinese Americans faced resentment from non-Chinese. Shopkeepers and restaurateurs along Grant Avenue, a tourist thoroughfare, noticed that white visitors were hostile to Chinese. As Betty Lee Sung, a Chinese American woman, recalled, "People would look at you in the street and think, Well, you're one of the enemy."[6] Later, tensions ran so high that non-Chinese visitors seldom frequented Chinatown, a change that contributed greatly to business decline.

The Cold War climate drove Chinatown leaders to attempt to boost business by transforming Chinatown into a tourist center. The Chinese New Year Festival was created as a strategy that Chinese American community leaders used to regenerate their declining economic and political resources. H. K. Wong, Chinatown businessman and public relations executive, initiated the idea of a public celebration in 1953. The Chinese Chamber of Commerce

(CCC), sponsor of the festival, was candid in explaining that the main purposes of the festival were to promote community business and to draw tourists to Chinatown.[7] In addition to economic motives, festival organizers sought to create an image of Chinese Americans as happy, submissive, and law-abiding citizens. The festival committee combined Chinese traditional practices, such as Chinese art exhibitions, Chinese music, Chinese opera, martial arts, lion and dragon dances, and American styles of celebration, such as the Golden Dragon Parade, sports, fashion shows, late-night street dancing, and a Miss Chinatown beauty pageant. The combination of Eastern and Western customs demonstrated that Chinese American values and ideals were perfectly compatible with those of the American culture.[8]

To attract outside tourists, festival organizers often included activities and images in the festival that could be seen as inconsistent. On the one hand, it emphasized the "exotic" and "foreign" elements in Chinatown to attract non-Chinese onlookers and to promote its commercial agenda. For instance, the president of the Chinese Consolidated Benevolent Association (CCBA), better known as the Chinese Six Companies, urged women and children to dress in Chinese-style clothes to provide more "oriental color" during the festival period.[9] On the other hand, the festival organizers often promoted the theme of the compatibility of East and West. St. Mary's Drum Corps and other Chinese school bands played Western instruments but dressed in Chinese-style uniforms. The Miss Chinatown beauty contest was another good example of the combination of East and West, and attracted hundreds of thousands of Chinese and non-Chinese spectators to the annual Chinese New Year festivities.[10]

Miss Chinatown was deliberately designed to embody Eastern beauty and Western intelligence. Festival organizers integrated Miss Chinatown beauty pageants into other New Year's events from 1953 to 1957. Initially, beauty contest candidates were mainly judged by their fund-raising abilities. In 1958, Wong, after a trip to Atlantic City's Miss America pageant, came up with the idea of a nationwide "Miss Chinatown U.S.A." He then changed the judging criteria to beauty, personality, and talent. As Wong pointed out, the contenders for the crown should have the "looks that made China's beauties so fascinating" and represent "the typical Chinese girl in America." The event, he suggested, would trigger "the elusive memory of ancient China's greatest beauties [that] might lurk in the judges' minds as they ponder their decision. Their thoughts might linger on the centuries-old Chinese concept of beauty such as melon-seed face, new moon eyebrows, phoenix eyes, peachlike cheek[s], shapely nose, cherry lips, medium height, willowy figure, radiant smile and jet black hair." In addition to this Chinese standard of beauty, the contestants also needed modern American qualities such as "adequate education, training and the versatility to meet the modern world."[11] The beauty queen contestants, who were required to wear a one-piece cheong-sam dress (Chinese long gown), also needed to show their ability to answer questions in Chinese and in English.[12] This combination of an exotic Eastern appearance and modern Western characteristics was intended as a symbol of American pluralism.

According to H. K. Wong, Miss Chinatown U.S.A. represented all Chinese in America. The beauty queen symbolized both an "ideal" Chinese American woman and Chinatown itself. The use of a symbolic woman to represent Chinese Americans as a whole might have two meanings. First, as historian Judy Wu suggests, the incorporation of the increasingly popular beauty pageant with the larger society demonstrated the assimilation of Chinese Americans.[13] Second, since Chinese women were in a lower position in the gender hierarchy of Chinese culture, the use of a submissive woman to represent Chinese Americans implied their acceptance of the existing social order. Evidence supports the latter. In 1956 reports, in the San Francisco Chronicle and the Chinese World stressed that the Chinese beauty queen had been reared in the three degrees of obedience (to father, to husband, and later to son), and that she possessed the four virtues: good behavior, discreet speech, a serene spirit, and industriousness. "Miss Dong fills a modern role in an ancient tradition," wrote the San Francisco Chronicle.[14] The emphasis on the obedience of the Chinese American woman to her father, husband, and son symbolized the obedience of Chinese Americans to the new fatherland.

Pageant organizers also wanted to use Miss Chinatown U.S.A. to promote the acceptance of Chinese Americans within the larger society. Chinese American women often were portrayed by the mainstream media as exotic prostitutes or victims of footbinding. By introducing beautiful, charming, and intelligent beauty queens, the pageant gave the public a modern image of Chinese American women and informed the larger society about the demographic changes, as the Chinese American community went from "a bachelor society" to "a family society." Moreover, the contestant's high heels and makeup symbolized the adoption of middle-class American consumer values.[15]

By using the Chinese New Year Festival and Miss Chinatown U.S.A. to construct an assimilated, law-abiding, submissive, and middle-class Chinese American identity, Chinatown leaders successfully promoted Chinatown as a tourist center in the 1950s and 1960s. San Francisco city officials recognized the potential economic boon created by the festival and treated Chinatown as a municipal moneymaking machine for the city.[16] Instead of requesting that city hall improve the deplorable social conditions in Chinatown, community leaders chose to focus on economic gains and thus cooperated with city hall to exploit the community.[17] By the late 1960s, with the rise of social and ethnic consciousness, this profit-pursuing and antireform attitude became a target of criticism for community activists. The commercial- and tourist-oriented celebrations became a contested ground between Chinatown leaders and community youth.

BEHIND THE GILDED CHINATOWN

The Chinese New Year Festival presented visitors with a picture of a happy, noisy, and affluent Chinatown by deliberately downplaying its social problems. Based on what J. K. Choy, assistant vice president and manager of the Chinatown branch of the San Francisco Federal Savings and Loan, experienced at the festival, no tourist would know that most Chinatown residents suffered from substandard living and working conditions. He pointed out that "Behind the fancy bright neon signs, gold-leaf dragons, expensive shop fronts and tempting restaurant entrances are sweatshops, over-crowded apartments and—in recent years—neglected children."[18] As an ethnic ghetto, Chinatown had the characteristics of a slum. Changes in U.S. immigration laws between 1962 and 1965 brought in tremendous numbers of new immigrants, making conditions even worse. Chinatown had been notorious for its dense living quarters, even before the arrival of the new immigrants. In 1965, the density figure was nine hundred persons per acre—ten times the city average.[19] In 1968, 72 percent of Chinatown housing was substandard, a factor that no doubt contributed to the highest tuberculosis rate in San Francisco in the 1960s.[20]

In addition to the poor living environment, Chinatown residents were frustrated with the limited employment opportunities and poor earnings resulting from insufficient English skills and discrimination. In 1960, the unemployment rate in Chinatown was 12.8 percent, while it was 6.7 percent for the city. Those who did have jobs were fortunate if they made a substandard living. In the same year, the incomes of Chinese males in San Francisco were only 68 percent of those of white males, while those of Chinese females were 36 percent.[21] Even though many immigrants came to this country with higher education and job skills (see Liu, chapter 1 in this volume), such experience did not guarantee success. On the contrary, their credentials were not recognized by most San Francisco employers and their insufficient command of English often prevented them from finding jobs commensurate with their abilities. Most immigrants ended up in jobs far below their skill level. Men often acquired jobs in restaurants while women worked in sweatshops.[22]

Chinatown residents attempted to confront these socioeconomic problems while fending off racial discrimination from the larger society. As mentioned earlier, the anti-Communist hysteria and the Korean War created racial tensions between Chinese and non-Chinese Americans. The Chinese New Year Festival successfully created business opportunities for Chinatown, but did not fully reduce racial tensions. Right after the 1956 Chinese New Year celebration, for instance, a federal grand jury subpoenaed twenty-six Chinatown family associations, creating the impression that the entire community engaged in assisting the illegal entry of Chinese immigrants. This obvious discrimination forced Chinese Americans to fight back. Eventually, they won the case.[23] This incident, however, did not drive Chinese Americans to consider an overall strategy to deal with such racial issues.

While institutional racism in housing and employment declined between the 1950s and 1960s due to gains from the civil rights movement and ethnic movements, Chinese Americans nonetheless experienced popular prejudice. Tourists expected to experience "the color" of Chinatown—to see cute little children, quaint shops, and other exotic features. One twenty-seven-year-old acculturated Chinese American pointed out that white tourists "come into the Chinese meat store with their cameras, and they touch things. . . . Sure, you feel you're in a zoo." Merchants had mixed feelings toward tourists, who provided "the next bowl of rice," but at the same time, who often "look at the indigenous people with no more feeling or empathy than they would extend to animals in a zoo."[24] Oftentimes, the rowdy behavior of tourists created resentment in the people of the community. Recalling the night of the 1969 Chinese New Year parade, George Chu, a middle-class Chinese American, said "I . . . watched well-dressed couples stroll through Waverly Place, tearing posters and paper lanterns from the booths for souvenirs. . . . When asked politely to put things back, they handed over the decorations without a word of apology or any sign of shame; they acted as if Chinatown was theirs for the picking. I was beginning to understand the bitterness which lies just below the surface of this supposedly well-assimilated community."[25] Some of the whites liked to throw firecrackers carelessly into the crowd. The parade route became a very dangerous zone that many American-born Chinese dared not enter.[26]

Nonetheless, merchants and the Chinatown establishment often kept silent about the condescending and patronizing attitudes of white visitors for fear of offending them and driving off business.

To attract non-Chinese visitors, the Chinatown establishment purposely exploited the ethnic ghetto and downplayed these economic, social, and racial problems. Benevolent associations, trade guilds, and tongs constituted the informal political power in Chinatown. Among them, the CCBA always claimed to be a spokesperson for the Chinese American community and an organization devoted to the rights and welfare of Chinatown. Yet, the CCBA and other traditional groups were mainly concerned with the interests of factory owners, merchants, and landlords, instead of the welfare of general members.

As sociologists Paul Takagi and Tony Platt suggest, the changes in the immigration laws in 1965 brought in significant numbers of fresh laborers to replace the aging pre-1925 workforce. The new immigrants provided the labor that maintained Chinatown as a tourist center. Takagi and Platt state: "Chinatown is not a racial community in the traditional sense. It is glued together and sustained because of its importance to the tourist industry, with linkages to the nearby chain hotels, airlines and the San Francisco Chamber of Commerce."[27] In order to attract tourists, Chinatown's stores and restaurants kept prices down by using cheap labor. Business people in Chinatown thus deliberately exploited their counterparts to maintain their economic and political success. Yet, as the following example shows, a growing awareness of ethnic, social, and class inequality in the late 1960s fostered critiques of the Chinatown establishment.

CHINESE AMERICAN YOUTH

Ethnic and class struggles started in the form of a youth movement that responded to the unequal racialized relations and substandard material conditions of Chinatown. In 1968, the Chinatown establishment began to receive tremendous criticism from Chinatown youth. Many youth groups burgeoned in the 1960s and these can be roughly divided into three categories: Chinese-born immigrants, American-born Chinese high-school dropouts, and college-educated, American-born Chinese.[28] Some members in the latter group contributed to the establishment of Asian American studies and social activist organizations, while the first two groups formed "delinquent" and political gangs in Chinatown to vent their frustration and protest social inequality. The larger society was shocked by the youth rebellion in Chinatown, because Chinese American youth had been depicted as hardworking, achievement oriented, and well disciplined.

The post-1965 new immigrants, not unjust social conditions, were blamed for this problem.

The reason for the low occurrence of juvenile crimes before the 1940s was demographic. There were simply very few Chinese Americans born in the United States. Before repeal of the Chinese Exclusion Act in 1943, Chinese immigrant women, with only a few exceptions, were not allowed to enter the country. After the repeal, Chinese American families started to grow. Youth crimes, in fact, emerged before the influx of new immigrants. Between 1943 and 1949, 184 Chinese American juvenile delinquents were sent to San Francisco juvenile court. From 1958 to 1964 a noticeable crime wave struck Chinatown.[29] From 1967 to 1970, according to scholar Stanford Lyman, the pattern shifted from petty crime to quasipolitical incidents (see also Zhang, chapter 13 in this volume).[30]

Wah Ching (China Youth) was the group blamed by Chinatown leaders and mainstream society for the increasing crime rate.[31] Begun in 1963, Wah Ching was a group of young immigrants from Hong Kong. By 1968 there were two hundred to three hundred Wah Ching in San Francisco, mostly males from seventeen to twenty years old. Some of them came to the United States after 1962 under family reunion provisions, but the majority came after 1965, when immigration laws were relaxed. Very few Wah Ching had steady jobs, and those who did lamented wages that were often less than one dollar an hour. Their deficiency in English prevented them from continuing school and seeking work outside Chinatown. Many of them turned to petty crime to survive.

Tired of living in despair, Wah Ching finally cried out for help at a meeting of the city's Human Rights Commission hearing on February 26, 1968. They proposed a comprehensive, two-year program of classes so that students could earn high-school diplomas and receive vocational training. They requested funds for a recreational clubhouse that would serve as a springboard for job training. Even though the Human Rights Commission recognized the problem, it asked for community help. Unfortunately, the CCBA refused to help these youth, claiming: "They [the Hwa Ching] have not shown that they are sorry or that they will change their ways. They have threatened the community. If you give in to this group, you are only going to have another hundred immigrants come in and have a whole new series of threats and demands."[32] The CCBA also regarded the request as a challenge to its authority, since Wah Ching's request exposed Chinatown problems to outsiders, tarnishing the reputation of Chinatown and its leadership.

The failure to solve youth problems pushed some young people to consider violence. One youth commented: "Some of these kids are talking about getting guns and rioting. And I'm not threatening, the situation already exists." Wah Ching resorted to crimes and disruptions in the 1968 and 1969 Chinese New Year parades to vent its anger and frustration when it got no help from the Chinese American elite or the city. Youth gangs thus became one of the biggest problems in Chinatown and often attracted attention in newspaper headlines, further contributing to the decline of Chinatown's tourist business in the 1970s.[33]

Leway (an abbreviation for "legitimate ways") was another major youth group in Chinatown. Originally formed by seventeen American-born Chinese in 1967, it grew from two hundred to four hundred in early 1968. Leway tried to stem juvenile delinquency in Chinatown by running a pool hall to generate funding for a job-training program. The pool hall became a gathering place for the youths and more than two hundred persons often congregated there. However, its agenda could not be accomplished, because it used the earnings to pay for rent and legal assistance. In addition, its members suffered police brutality and harassment, especially when its treasurer, LeLand Woo, became a major figure in a conflict between Chinatown celebrants and the police during the 1968 Chinese New Year parade. Police harassment and brutality toward Chinese American youth were major factors leading to the 1968 and 1969 Chinese New Year riots.[34]

Several youths from the Leway formed the Red Guard Party in 1969. It was influenced by Mao Tse-tung and the Black Panther Party, which was founded in nearby Oakland in 1966.[35] The Red Guard Party published its own newspapers declaring its determination to fight white supremacy, police brutality, and the Chinatown elite.[36] Yet its grassroots activity—a free breakfast program for children and free lunch for elders—did not succeed. The Red Guard Party also engaged in other antiredevelopment activities, such as preventing the Chinese Playground from being torn down to build a garage, protesting when the Kwong Chow Temple was destroyed, and fighting against the tearing down of the International Hotel, a residential hotel whose inhabitants were mostly seniors.[37] Like other community activists, the Red Guard Party challenged the authority of the CCBA and paved the way for other community organizations.

Chinese American college students also actively worked to solve social problems in Chinatown. A group of Chinese American students at San Francisco State College formed the Inter-Collegiate Chinese for Social Action to work on the problems of the community, especially those that affected youths.

It established a tutorial program in Chinatown to teach English to Wah Ching members.[38]

They also went to the streets to raise class and ethnic awareness in the community by criticizing the Chinatown establishment's tourist orientation. On August 17, 1968, the Concerned Chinese for Action and Change (CCAC), an organization of college students and young professionals, formed a picket line along Grant Avenue during peak tourist hours to make sure that the public became fully aware of the socioeconomic problems in Chinatown. In addition, it criticized the CCBA for not helping to solve the deplorable conditions in Chinatown. On August 28, the CCAC requested that the CCBA stop work on the Chinatown gateway, which was designed to attract more tourists; however, the protest did not bring a successful result.[39]

A CONTESTING SITE: THE CHINESE NEW YEAR FESTIVAL

The Chinese New Year Festival was the biggest celebration in Chinatown, often attracting huge crowds. As a result, the festival became a site of criticism for its use of community resources that promoted tourism without benefiting the community. The festival often brought trouble to the community, since outside hoodlums swarmed the area while the police force was unable (or unwilling) to intervene. Furthermore, people in the community felt that "If we can mobilize the community for the Chinese New Year celebration, then we should be able to equally mobilize the community concerning social problems."[40] However, the power center in Chinatown was not interested in solving these social problems.

In addition, the festival staged by the CCC further exposed its intention to cater to non-Chinese Americans and to exclude Chinatown residents. One reader of the *Chinese Pacific Weekly*, a San Francisco Chinese American community newspaper, expressed discontent that the festival was targeted more at non-Chinese than Chinese. He pointed out that the Miss Chinatown U.S.A. beauty pageant, coronation dance, and fashion show were held in an upscale hotel or restaurant. Tickets were so costly that ordinary Chinese Americans could not afford to attend.[41] Starting in 1959, the Miss Chinatown U.S.A. pageant was held in the three-thousand-seat Masonic Auditorium located outside Chinatown. The limited seating often prohibited people from observing the beauty contest. The editor of *East/West*, a San Francisco Chinatown community newspaper, suggested that the pageant should move to the twelve-thousand-seat Civic Auditorium because "the pageant belongs to the people, the man on the street."[42] Gilbert Woo, editor of the *Chinese Pacific Weekly*, argued that the fashion show was only for rich women who had money and leisure time.[43]

While the parade seemed to be the only event that ordinary Chinatown residents could attend, its route was changed in 1965 due to the fear of fire hazards.[44] (Since then, the parade has started near the civic center and few floats even enter Grand Avenue.) Symbolically, the Chinese New Year parade became a celebration less for the community and more for the city, even though it was the most visible event of the Chinese American community.

The burgeoning criticism of the Chinese New Year Festival in the late 1960s signified the attempt to counter the ethnic and gender identities imposed on the event by the festival organizers. The criticism of the Miss Chinatown USA beauty pageant, the production of an alternative celebration, and the outbreak of youth riots symbolized the attempt of reformers and protesters to redefine these identities.

Criticism of the Beauty Pageant

As aforementioned, to diffuse political hostility in the 1950s and 1960s, festival organizers successfully used beauty pageants to present Chinese Americans as an assimilated, law-abiding, nonthreatening, middle-class model minority. Yet, such gendered ethnic representation became controversial in the late 1960s. Chinese American college students and community pageant protesters began to question the notion of a submissive and conforming beauty queen. Inspired by Chinese female revolutionaries in China, college activists criticized the emphasis on Confucian values as ideals for Chinese American women, and as the most appropriate representation of Chinese American ethnicity. Instead, they sought to promote the image of China's "Iron Girls," who were revolutionary women in Communist China, as role models. In addition, they questioned the idea of Miss Chinatown U.S.A. as the representation of Chinese American women. In fact, an American college-educated Miss Chinatown with fluent command of English was quite different from her non-English speaking immigrant counterpart. Donned in beautiful evening gowns with heavy makeup, the beauty queen symbolized affluent middle-class purchasing power at a time when most Chinatown women were toiling in the sweatshops and hardly making ends meet. The commercialized, assimilated, middle-class Chinese American female identity created by the pageant organizers was exactly what college-educated Chinese American youth criticized and sought to change into an image of "Iron Girls."[45]

Influenced by the women's liberation movement, community feminists questioned the seductive and submissive representation of Miss Chinatown

U.S.A. because it ironically reflected the stereotypical image of Chinese American women in the mainstream media. Although the pageant supporters and contestants claimed that Miss Chinatown was not a sex object, since she did not wear a bathing suit, this defense proved disingenuous when a bathing suit contest was adopted in 1967. The contest also changed the floor-length cheong-sam to mini-length to be more appealing. In addition, beauty contestants often intended to project themselves as sex objects. For example, the 1967 beauty queen used performance to simulate a strip show, even though she only took off a scarf.[46]

Using white beauty standards to select a representative of Chinese American women elicited criticism from the community. Alice Kong, a beauty contestant, commented that "It was obvious those girls with height had it."[47] One Chinatown resident further pointed out that the beauty contest "shows that the closer you look like the Whites, the prettier you are. For example, the longer the nose, the prettier."[48] The African American cultural movement of the 1960s, especially the notion of "black is beautiful," inspired Gilbert Woo to suggest that the pageant committee should establish an "oriental" standard of beauty to build ethnic confidence rather than undermine it.[49]

In fact, the conflicts over the Chinese and white standards of beauty were not new. The beauty standard suggested by H. K. Wong emphasized a merger of Chinese beauty and modern American qualities. However, from the start of the Miss Chinatown U.S.A. contest, judges were criticized for placing too much emphasis on the Western ideal. The critics had a point; the 1958 queen, June Gong, placed second in the 1957 Miss New Hampshire contest—suggesting that the pageant committee employed "American" standards in choosing a Chinatown queen. The beauty standard was again a point of controversy in the 1959 contest, when the winner was more statuesque than average Chinese American women (she was 5'6").[50] Beauty standards reflected an internal anxiety within the community; that is, should beauty be defined by Chinese or American culture?

An Alternative Celebration

Community activists and Chinatown residents also criticized the commercial purpose of the Chinese New Year celebration. In order to get funding for the festival, the CCC allowed carnival operators in Waverly Place, a Chinatown street, even though the rides and games had no cultural attachment to the Chinese New Year observance. The carnival often disturbed regular business and created parking and crime problems. Moreover, Chinese children wasted *li see* on games offering shoddy, cheap, and unattainable prizes.[51]

In 1969, the Chinatown-North Beach Youth and Recreation Committee and the Concerned Chinese for Action and Change organization successfully forced the CCC to sponsor a Chinese New Year Street Fair. Since the carnival had received so much criticism from youth groups and the media, the CCC decided to use the fair to eliminate the game booths while retaining the rides. Reflecting the influence of a newly ascendant ethnic movement, the fair was designed to educate the public about Chinese culture, history, and tradition. As part of an effort to improve interracial relations, youth groups invited African Americans to have four booths in the fair. In the beginning, the CCC did not want the Street Fair to include African American booths, but it relented later.[52] This cooperation, on the one hand, showed the continual effort of the CCC to control the definition of Chinese American identity by regulating the fair's content. The reason that the CCC agreed to sponsor the Street Fair was to control these youth groups so they would not engage in any political or undesirable activities in the festival. In fact, the Red Guard Party distributed Mao Tse-tung's Red Book in the Street Fair in defiance of Chinatown leaders, who had a history of associating with the Nationalist government in Taiwan. On the other hand, the fair also demonstrated that the voice of the youth groups could not be ignored.

Youth Violence

Not all youth groups considered the alternative celebration an effective way to vent their anger and frustration at community problems. So some youth resorted to violence to protest racial injustice and social problems.[53] Such violence reached its high point during the Chinese New Year festivities. A reader of the *Chinese Pacific Weekly* reported that he saw fighting among Chinese American, African American, and white youths during the 1963 Chinese New Year period.[54] Fourteen assault cases were reported in the one-week Chinese New Year period in 1968 and a small-scale riot broke out during the parade. Two days later, a group of Chinese American youth had a violent confrontation with police. The Tac Squad was called in to restore order. College-educated Chinese Americans also used violence as a form of protest. On February 27, 1969, two days before the Chinese New Year Parade, the Concerned Chinese for Action and Change had a violent confrontation with a school superintendent about insufficient educational programs for Chinese Americans.[55] City hall and the police were afraid that interracial fighting would break out during the festival period in 1969—a fear that indeed became a reality.[56]

A riot broke out during the 1969 Chinese New Year parade. On March 1, violence occurred as the Chinatown Task Force of Youth for Service attempted to prevent a full-scale riot between Chinese and whites. According to reports, eighty-nine people were injured, including nine police officers, and more than seventy people, mostly whites, were arrested. During the day, at the Street Fair, several Chinese American youths had already had an argument with their white counterparts in which Joe Louie, leader of the Raiders (a Chinatown gang) even beat the white leader.[57] After 10 P.M. most Chinese American families had left the parade routes. Grant Avenue was left to tourists and crowds of Chinese youth—Raiders, Wah Chings, Junior Raiders, Baby Wah Chings, and others. The first fights started around 10:30, between Chinese American youth and whites. Strings of firecrackers were thrown at the injured Chinese American youth by whites.

Even though policemen were nearby and were supposed to control the situation, they were reluctant to do so and worked ineffectively to prevent trouble.[58] With a racist attitude, the police tended to ignore the whites who threw firecrackers randomly at the festival. In addition, law enforcement officials often received false information regarding Chinese Americans, which created "a great possibility of continued police harassment and police violence against the citizens of Chinatown."[59] Besides, since few police knew the Chinese language or understood Chinese American culture, they could not handle community affairs effectively. As a result, the police often used excessive force against Chinese American youth. The simmering animosity between the police and Chinese American youth finally erupted into large-scale conflict. The student movement in the 1960s also generated great animosity between the police and youth from other racial and ethnic groups. This animosity, ironically, averted a race riot.[60] But even though this incident turned out to be a battle with the police, the underlying racial problem could not be ignored—a point well understood by Chinese American youths who used violence to address social and racial issues.

Yet the incident did not compel Chinatown leaders or city hall to pay attention to youth issues and racial problems. After the incident, the police department only remarked that "the disorders may have started simply because there were 'too many people in one place.'"[61] Chinese American community leaders were fearful that the lucrative Chinese New Year Festival would be prohibited. Eight days after the riot, Mayor Joseph Alioto told a press conference that the city would take steps to control "rowdyism, fireworks and characters who cause trouble." He said that he had no intention of discontinuing the Chinese New Year parade, since it was "an event that rivals the Mardi Gras for national and international attention."[62] In order to attract more tourists and promote business, both the city and the Chinatown establishment again chose to downplay racial and social problems.

Chinese leaders and the mainstream media often attributed youth violence to class issues rather than racial issues. In the 1960s, African Americans had articulated racial problems clearly, while Chinese American leaders often regarded relations between themselves and whites as based on "class distinctions."[63] In other words, they thought people must "earn" their position rather than question an unjust racial system. However, the riot did encourage the mainstream media to pay attention to Chinatown's problems. The *San Francisco Chronicle* wrote a series of articles about the "real" Chinatown, including coverage of housing shortages, low pay, youth delinquency, and other immigrant problems.[64] The CCBA, on the other hand, was busy with a cover-up, claiming that "there [were] very few problems in Chinatown, if any."[65] The failure to solve the structural deficiencies in the late 1960s led to more problems in the 1970s. The inability to solve youth problems led Wah Ching to divide into three groups in mid-1969: one group conducted more violent behavior on the street while the other two were adopted by the Suey Sing and Hop Sing Tongs, thereby creating more gang warfare in the 1970s.[66]

CONCLUSION

The Chinese New Year Festival was a stage for Chinatown leaders to define Chinese Americans as part of a loyal, assimilated, and law-abiding model minority. Their production of ethnic and gender identities, however, tended to silence class divisions within the community and racial divisions with the outside. By setting economic profit as the primary goal, community leaders downplayed social problems in Chinatown and encouraged racial discrimination. Alternative celebrations, beauty pageant critics, and street violence presented different voices from the community. These critics and protesters created various Chinese American identities that were different from the one defined by the festival committee. Street fighting and riots destroyed the flow of the "happy" Chinese New Year celebration, and forced tourists to see the "real" Chinatown behind the celebratory scene. It pushed Chinatown leaders to face social, class, and gender problems.

Dissenting voices compelled the CCC to make changes in the 1970s. In response to criticism from Chinese American feminists, it began to encourage Chinese American female organizers to become involved in the pageant leadership. The continuation of using Miss Chinatown, U.S.A. to represent

Chinese Americans, however, indicated that the organizers still intended to define Chinese Americans as a nonpolitical, law-abiding, and happy minority population quietly conforming to middle-class American expectations and values.

This monoethnic definition, however, could not continue to resist internal and external pressures to change festival traditions and Chinese American identity. Youth gangs adopted more violent resistance in the 1970s and 1980s that permanently damaged the image upheld by festival organizers. This led, in part, to the long recession of Chinatown business. Moreover, the normalization of U.S. relations with the People's Republic of China created a different political dynamic in the community. In addition, due to rising ethnic consciousness, the CCC no longer had the privilege of dominating the ethnic definition of the Chinese. The Chinese Culture Center's Spring Festival created different types of Chinese New Year celebrations that were identified with working-class Chinatown residents.

NOTES

My thanks to those who shared their experiences with San Francisco's Chinese New Year Festival. I thank Robert Johnson and Tim Kelly for their willingness to read an earlier draft. In addition, I thank referee readers and editor Susie Lan Cassel for pushing me to think more clearly. I also thank Yong Chen, Thelma Foote, and Mike Masatsugu for their valuable suggestions. Finally, I thank Susan Schober for proofreading this paper.

1. *Chinese World,* 8 May 1969, 1.

2. The younger generation I refer to here came from both middle class and working class. They were often divided by national origin and education, not class background. Native-born Chinese often could not get along with "fresh-off-the-boat" immigrants, nor did these two groups share many ideological beliefs. Even though I roughly divided Chinese youth into three categories for this study—Chinese-born immigrant groups, groups of American-born Chinese high-school dropouts, and college-educated, American-born Chinese—many factions, in fact, existed.

3. James C. Scott, *Weapons of the Weak: Everyday Forms of Peasant Resistance* (New Haven, Conn.: Yale University Press, 1985).

4. They often operated import-export companies, garment shops, and real estate or insurance agencies. Victor G. Nee and Brett de Bary Nee, *Longtime Californ': A Documentary Study of an American Chinatown* (Stanford, Calif.: Stanford University Press, 1972), 228.

5. Because the United States recognized the Chiang Kai-shek regime, Chinese Americans were forced to pledge their ancestral allegiance to the Nationalist government. The Nationalist government also seized the opportunity created by anti-Communist hysteria to become a dominant political power in San Francisco's Chinatown for twenty years by cooperating with the Federal Bureau of Investigation and the Immigration and Naturalization Service to oppress the leftist support. Him Mark Lai, "To Bring Forth a New China, to Build a Better America: The Chinese Marxist Left in America to the 1960s," *Chinese America: History and Perspectives* (1992), 42–52.

6. Betty Lee Sung, quoted in Judy Yung, *Chinese Women of America: A Pictorial History* (Seattle: University of Washington Press, 1986), 83.

7. The CCC was founded in 1910. In order to maintain Chinatown as a tourist center, the chamber advocated the preservation and perpetuation of an oriental motif along Grant Avenue. Ngai Ho Hong, "In Order To Serve" (San Francisco Chinese New Year Festival Souvenir Program, 4–7 February 1960).

8. As with other ethnic festivals in the high Cold War, the Chinese New Year Festival adopted the ideology of conformity and integration. See John Bodnar, *Remaking America: Public Memory, Commemoration, and Patriotism in the Twentieth Century* (Princeton, N.J.: Princeton University Press, 1992).

9. *Chinese World*, 31 January 1957, 6. The Chinese Six Companies was founded in 1882 in response to the hostile political climate after the passage of the Chinese Exclusion Act in 1882. This organization played an important role in looking after the interests of the Chinese American community and mediating relations between Chinatown and the broader society before World War II. Thomas Chinn, *Bridging the Pacific: San Francisco Chinatown and Its People* (San Francisco: Chinese Historical Society of America, 1989), 3–7.

10. Chinatown had a long history of using its pageants to raise funds. Beginning in the 1910s, San Francisco's Chinatown organizations sporadically sponsored community pageants to raise funds for social services, such as a Chinese Hospital. From 1948 to 1952, the Chinese American Citizens Alliance and San Francisco Lodge annually selected Chinese beauty contestants for the Fourth of July. *Asian Week*, 12 February 1981, 2.

11. H. K. Wong, "Chinatown USA Pageant" (San Francisco Chinese New Year Festival Souvenir Program, 4–7 February 1960); H. K. Wong, "Concept of Beauty," in *San Francisco Chinatown on Parade* (San Francisco: Chinese Chamber of Commerce, 1961), 79.

12. In order to serve the purpose of the pageant, the organizers emphasized its side-slit area, creating "the 'poured-in' look so highly desired." Judy Tzu-Chu Wu,

"'Loveliest Daughter of Our Ancient Cathay!': Representations of Ethnic and Gender Identity in the Miss Chinatown U.S.A. Beauty Pageant," *Journal of Social History* 31 (fall, 1997): 1, 4. I am grateful to the author for allowing me to see her article in manuscript.

13. Wu, "Loveliest Daughter," 7, 8.

14. *San Francisco Chronicle*, 12 February 1956, 2; *Chinese World*, 16 February 1956, 2; Wu, "Loveliest Daughter," 8.

15. Wu, "Loveliest Daughter," 8.

16. The success of the Chinese New Year Festival led San Francisco Mayor George Christopher to build a Chinatown gateway to attract more tourists. In 1963 the San Francisco Convention and Visitors' Bureau began to cosponsor the festival.

17. Ivan Light and Charles Choy Wong aptly characterize Chinatown as an ethnic ghetto that was vulnerable to outside sanctions. With the fear of antagonizing their patrons by disclosing the social problems in Chinatown, Chinese leaders thus deliberately understated the dilapidated conditions. Light and Wong, "Protest or Work: Dilemmas of the Tourist Industry in American Chinatown," *American Journal of Sociology* 80, no. 6 (May 1975): 1342–65.

18. *Los Angeles Times*, 11 February 1965.

19. In 1965, 40,800 Chinese Americans lived in San Francisco, or about 5.4 percent of the city's total population. *San Francisco Department of Public Health Statistical Report* (San Francisco: Department of Health, 1963), 1; Min Yee, "Cracks in the Great Wall of Chinatown," *Ramparts* 11 (October 1972), 36. The plumbing in these houses was generally quite defective and inadequate. James Wilbur Chin, "Problems of Assimilation and Cultural Pluralism among Chinese-Americans in San Francisco" (master's thesis, University of the Pacific, 1965), 17; *Chinese Pacific Weekly*, 25 January 1968, 1.

20. In 1962 the tuberculosis rate was 104.0 per 100,000. It climbed to 164.2 in 1963, then leveled to 153.3 in 1964 and 146.8 in 1967. The citywide rate for 1967 was 51.5. Ling-Chi Wang, "Politics of Assimilation and Repression: History of the Chinese in the U.S., 1940 to 1970," manuscript, University of California, Berkeley, photocopy, 509. In 1964, the tuberculosis rate was 4.4 per 100,000 in the nation. According to the *Merck Manual of Diagnosis and Therapy*, "high rates persist in congested areas of low living standards." Robert Berbow, ed., *The Merck Manual of Diagnosis and Therapy*, 11th ed. (Rahway, N.J.: Merck Sharpe and Dohme Research Laboratories, 1966), 1335.

21. Ronald Takaki, *Strangers from A Different Shore: A History of Asian Americans* (New York: Penguin, 1989), 424.

22. *Chinese Pacific Weekly*, 25 January 1968, 1; Yee, "Cracks in the Great Wall," 36; *Chinese World*, 24 January 1969, 1.

23. Shih-shan Henry Tsai, *The Chinese Experience in America* (Bloomington: Indiana University Press, 1986), 135.

24. Quoted in Chin, "Problems of Assimilation," 94.

25. *San Francisco Sunday Examiner and Chronicle*, 9 March 1969, 21.

26. Joan Lowe [pseud.], interview by the author, San Francisco, 14 July 1998; Beverley Lee, interview by the author, San Francisco, 4 June 1999; Hilary Wong [pseud.], interview by the author; San Francisco, 11 June 1999; *East/West*, 18 February 1970, 1.

27. Paul Takagi and Tony Platt, "Behind the Gilded Ghetto: An Analysis of Race, Class and Crime in Chinatown," *Crime and Social Justice* 9 (spring-summer, 1978): 6, 8.

28. See note 2.

29. Kurt Robert Durig, "Social Change in San Francisco Chinatown" (master's thesis, San Francisco State College, 1961), 97.

30. Stanford Lyman, *Chinese Americans* (New York: Random House, 1974), 162.

31. Wah Ching is also spelled Hwa Ching.

32. *East/West*, 13 March 1968, 1.

33. *East/West*, 24 January 1968, 1; 28 February 1968, 1; 13 March 1968, 1, 2; 20 March 1968, 1; *Chinese World*, 17 May 1968, 1; *San Francisco Chronicle*, 18 March 1968.

34. *San Francisco Chronicle*, 19 March 1968, 48; *East/West*, 20 March 1968, 1.

35. *Chinese Pacific Weekly*, 3 April 1969, 1. Racial relations between African Americans and Chinese Americans were very tense in the 1960s. Interracial fighting often broke out between the two. Stanford Lyman, *The Asian in the West* (Reno: Western Studies Center, Desert Research Institute, University of Nevada, 1970), 105.

36. "Red Guard, Black Panther and Chinese American Society," *Chinese Pacific Weekly*, 27 March 1969, 1.

37. *Chinese Pacific Weekly*, 21 August 1969, 1; "Activities of the Red Guard Party," *Getting Together* 2 (March 1973): 4.

38. *Chinese World*, 20 May 1968, 1; *East/West*, 5 June 1968, 4; Yee, "Cracks in the Great Wall," 38.

39. *Chinese Pacific Weekly*, 22 August 1968, 7; Wang, "Politics of Assimilation and Repression," 576; *East/West*, 28 August 1968, 1. The editorial in the *East/West* called for funding from the Chinatown gateway to be diverted to build a recreational or educational center for immigrant youth, or even to relieve housing shortages in Chinatown. *East/West*, 1 April 1967, 2; *Chinese Pacific Weekly*, 29 August 1968, 1. The Chinatown gateway was completed in 1970.

40. *Chinese Pacific Weekly*, 29 August 1968, 81.

41. *Chinese Pacific Weekly*, 2 March 1967, 14.

42. The first Miss Chinatown U.S.A. was held at the Great China Theatre in Chinatown. *East/West*, 1 March 1967, 2.

43. *Chinese Pacific Weekly*, 2 February 1967, 4.

44. Nee and Nee, *Longtime Californ'*, 161.

45. Wu, "Loveliest Daughter," 13, 17.

46. *Chinese Pacific Weekly*, 21 February 1958, 1; *San Francisco Chinatown*, 20 February 1967, 3.

47. *East/West*, 20 February 1974, 5. Up to 1987, "the average height of Miss Chinatown U.S.A. is 5 feet 3 inches." "Miss Chinatown U.S.A. Pageant" (San Francisco Chinese New Year Souvenir Program, 1987).

48. She also commented, "The contest just shows that the Chinese aren't good enough for the White's beauty contest, so they have to have their own." Interview, *East/West*, 27 January 1971, 9.

49. Abiola Sinclair, "Black Hair and the Cultural/Political Movement of the 1960s," in *The Harlem Cultural/Political Movements, 1960–1970*, ed. Abiola Sinclair (New York: Gumbs and Thomas, 1995), 69–72; *Chinese Pacific Weekly*, 13 February 1969, 10.

50. *Chinese World*, 5 February 1958, 2; *Chinese Pacific Weekly*, 12 February 1959, 7.

51. The CCC received $3,000 from the carnival. *East/West*, 10 January 1968, 2; 28 August 1968, 2; 7 August 1968, 2; *Chinese Pacific Weekly*, 22 August 1968, 7; 20 February 1969, 1. *Li see* was money given at Chinese New Year in a red envelope.

52. *East/West*, 4 September, 1968, 1; 19 February 1969, 1; 19 March 1969, 2; *Chinese Pacific Weekly*, 27 February 1969, 4.

53. The three groups of youths mentioned above used various degrees of violence to reach their goals.

54. *Chinese Pacific Weekly*, 14 February 1963, 9.

55. *East/West,* 8 May 1968, 15; *Chinese Pacific Weekly,* 23 June 1968, 1. The *Chinese Pacific Weekly* had already addressed the interracial youth problem in 1962. *Chinese Pacific Weekly,* 1 March 1962, 3; Buck Wong, "Need for Awareness: An Essay on Chinatown, San Francisco," in *Roots: An Asian American Reader,* ed. Amy Tachiki, Eddie Wong, Franklin Odo, and Buck Wong (Los Angeles: Continental Graphics, 1971), 170; "Editorial: We Are Not Barbarians," *East/West,* 5 March 1969, 2.

56. *Chinese Pacific Weekly,* 27 February 1969.

57. Nee and Nee, *Longtime Californ',* 343.

58. *San Francisco Chronicle,* 2 March 1969, 2; *San Francisco Sunday Examiner and Chronicle,* 9 March 1969, 18.

59. State Attorney General Evelle J. Younger's office issued a confidential article that was full of false and racist statements about Chinese Americans. *East/West,* 10 October 1973, 1, 7.

60. An article in the *San Francisco Examiner,* writing about the history of the Chinese New Year Festival, called this incident "a race riot between young Chinese American gangs and bands of white thugs." The author indicated that it was "political radicals from S.F. State" who diverted the race riot into a fight with the police. *San Francisco Examiner,* 6 February 2000, 3.

61. *San Francisco Chronicle,* 3 March 1969, 2; The Chinese American community newspapers had no in-depth discussion about the 1969 Chinese New Year riot. *Chinese Pacific Weekly* only translated George Chu's article "A Wild Night in Old Chinatown" from the *Chronicle. Chinese Pacific Weekly,* 20 March 1969, 5, 6.

62. *San Francisco Chronicle,* 11 March 1969, 2.

63. *East/West,* 11 March 1967, 5.

64. *San Francisco Chronicle,* 11 August 1969; 12 August 1969; 13 August 1969, 2; 15 August 1969, 7; 20 August 1969, 3.

65. *San Francisco Chronicle,* 15 August 1969, 7.

66. Tong means "hall" in Chinese. In the United States, the term referred to, according to Sucheng Chan, "fraternal organizations that bound [their] members together through secret initiation rites and sworn brotherhood." Chan, *Asian Americans: An Interpretive History* (New York: Twayne, 1991), 67. Some of the Wah Ching members were adopted by Suey Sing Tong and Hop Sing Tong, while some refused to be associated with tongs and formed "Chung Yee," which the media often referred to as Joe Fong Gang or "Joe Boys." The adopting of the tongs' names by some of the Wah Ching did not mean that they obeyed tongs' orders. Sometimes,

warfare broke out between tongs and youth gangs. Calvin Toy, "A Short History of Asian Gangs in San Francisco," *Justice Quarterly* 9, no. 4 (4 December 1992): 655–59. "The Gangs of Chinatown," *Newsweek*, 2 July 1973, 22. The number of crimes annually in Chinatown increased significantly: 2,549 in 1970 and 2,652 in 1971. Even though the dramatic increase reflected the different methods of defining larceny, including petty theft in addition to grand theft, the number of crimes was indeed quite large. *East/West*, 1 March 1972, 1.

19

Mothers' "China Narrative": Recollection and Translation in Amy Tan's *The Joy Luck Club* and *The Kitchen God's Wife*

Yuan Yuan

Many critics, including Amy Ling and Sau-ling Cynthia Wong, have previously addressed the issue of authenticity in Chinese American narratives and specifically focused on interrogating the authenticity of "Chineseness" in the novels produced by Chinese American writers. Apparently, this issue of "nativeness," or the representation of the native Chinese in Chinese American literature, is both intriguing and perplexing. However, I have noticed that to date critics tend to engage issues of authenticity in these ethnic narratives without taking into full consideration the intricate role played by the narrative in configuring nativeness, especially in terms of narrative agencies and narrative strategies. That is to say, the whole issue of nativeness in ethnic literature requires careful examination in the context of the historical and cultural displacement of the narrative subject, and in relation to the function of narration in literary representation. In this chapter, I will explore the complicated nature and complex structure of the mother figures' narratives of their experiences in China in terms of "China narratives" within the context of Amy Tan's novels *The Joy Luck Club* and *The Kitchen God's Wife*.

In both *The Joy Luck Club* and *The Kitchen God's Wife*, Tan tells us the stories of the mothers of daughters in America and the daughters of mothers in China, that is, the mother-daughter relationship across three generations and two continents. In this context, I will only focus on the hermeneutic space, which I call the "China narratives," that emerges in a dialectical process between the Chinese mothers' recollection of their past experiences in China and the American-born daughters' translations of their mothers' stories of China. Therefore, it is not the purpose of this chapter to investigate the authenticity of those mother figures' accounts of China in reference to China;

instead, this chapter attempts to explore the nature, the constitution, the theme, and the function of China narratives in relation to the current position and strategies of narrative agency in American society. Specifically, I will examine the following issues in regard to mothers' China narratives: how they are created by the mothers' recollections of past memory and reconstituted by their daughters' translations; the purpose of this reflective process for marginal characters—immigrants—in American society; the central theme of loss, which forms the essential "plot"; and the function of China narratives for the mothers as either defensive instruments for self-empowerment or discourse strategies with which to dominate their daughters. In the last part, I will analyze China narratives as the bicultural and bilingual site of contention between dominating mothers and their rebellious daughters.

First of all, the mothers' China narratives involve an intricate process of the recollection of past memory. To a certain extent, the narrative structures of both *The Joy Luck Club* and *The Kitchen God's Wife* are partly based on the mothers' recollections of their past experiences. Therefore, in Tan's novels, the mothers' experiences in China all emerge as narratives of reflection—which means, in Tan's novels, different mother figures reconstruct various narratives of their experiences in China against the background of American society and within the context of American culture. For immigrants, recollection is an important strategy used to negotiate a marginal position in an alien society. Specifically for Amy Tan, by retelling her mother's story of the past, she is able to explore the nature and the function of memory and recollection, especially how recollection functions in a bicultural context and how it affects the recreation of individual identities.

Generally speaking, all recollection entails one's conscious negotiation with and active reconstitution of the memory of the past. Put another way, all memories are socially and culturally reconstituted within a specific historical and cultural context and emerge in the form of narratives. This self-reflexive narrative initiates a process of construction of new stories and new histories in search of new identities. Thus, all memory exists in a form of narrative—recollection—and this narrative recollects by preserving, revising, erasing, and recovering past memories, involving both reproduction and repression, inclusion and exclusion. Hence, recollection is a complicated reading of and way of coming to terms with the past, depending on the specific purposes of recollection and the present position of the recollecting subject. Generally, it is through a self-reflexive narrative that memory, especially the repressed memory of the past, finds its way to articulate itself, like in dreams or fables or fiction. Possibly it is only through fables, fictions, or dreams that repressed memories can be expressed. Therefore, the mothers' China narratives, that is, their recollections of past experiences in China, are necessarily constituted partly through the collective cultural history (i.e., myth, folklore, and legends) and partly through personal memories of the past.

For instance, *The Joy Luck Club* begins with a mother's recollection. Tan writes: "the old woman remembers a swan she had bought many years ago in Shanghai for a foolish sum. . . . Then the woman and the swan sailed across an ocean many thousands of Li wide, stretching their necks toward America. . . . Now the woman was old. And she had a daughter who grew up speaking only English and swallowing more Coca-Cola than sorrow."[1] Clearly, memory here involves a cultural reproduction within the American context instead of pointing to the real past in China. So, the mother's China narrative emerges in the United States, the "other" cultural territory, informed by a complex process of translation, translocation, and transfiguration via fairy tales, imaginations, and fictionalization of the original experiences in China. In this retelling/recollecting, the memories of past experiences are recast in the form of a fable or folktale and the real-life experiences in China have been transfigured into a mythical narrative.

In fact, mothers' experiences in China are generally transfigured into China narratives only after they have lost their reference to China; thus they are related more to the present American situation than to the original context of Chinese society. Hence, recollection becomes a dialectical process in which the past and the present engage each other in a continuous dialogue, each revising and configuring the other endlessly. Perhaps, only under such circumstances of loss of origin can experiences in China emerge as a China narrative—a text reconfigured within other contexts. Said differently, it is not so much the reality of the past that is crucial to the formation of China narratives. Instead, it is the present American context that provides meaning and determines the content of the mothers' stories of China. China narratives, therefore, differ from the experiences in China because they signify a specific kind of self-reflexive discourse that is reinscribed within another cultural context to serve specific goals: self-affirmation or self-negation, remembrance or repression. Eventually, China as the memory of personal experiences is translated into a semiotic space of recollection, and China as a geographical location is reconfigured into a variety of discourses: myth, legend, history, and fantasy. No wonder in their China narratives that the mothers themselves turn into mythical figures who forever haunt the lives of their daughters.

China is recollected or recreated somewhere between memory and imagination. That is why the daughters tend to dismiss the tales of their mothers'
past experiences in China as either unreal fairy tales or didactic fables or impossible and incomprehensible stories conjured up to control them. That is
why Pearl, the daughter in The Kitchen God's Wife, is confused and frustrated
about her mother's China narratives. As she observes, "To this day it drives me
crazy, listening to her various hypotheses, the way religion, medicine, and su-
perstition all merge with her own beliefs."[2] So the mothers communicate to
the daughters in a specific form of discourse that is both real and unreal, both
personal and cultural; it sounds like, in Pearl's terms, "a Chinese version of
Freud."[3]

Furthermore, sometimes the mothers' China narratives are based on the
recollections through other narrative agencies that further complicate the
credibility of the mothers' personal stories. For instance, Suyuan, a mother in
The Joy Luck Club, does not directly tell her daughter June about her past. The
mother's China narrative is not passed on to the daughter until after the
mother's death. Put another way, Suyuan's personal narratives of her past experiences in China are re-collected by her daughter, June, who gathers her
mother's fragmented and varied stories partly from her mother, partly from
her joy luck aunties, and partly from her father who, in turn, learns many of
the stories from his wife's friends and family in China years later. Personal stories, when mediated by various narrative agencies, tend to develop into legends. Such is the case with Winnie, the mother in The Kitchen God's Wife.
Winnie reveals to her daughter Pearl the essential part of her hidden past only
after Winnie is convinced she is going to die. Part of her China narrative is further complicated by a dialogical structure maintained by Winnie's recollection
and her friend Helen's remembrance—the two versions of the same past experiences in China, for various reasons, not only complement, but also contradict each other. So in both novels, the mothers' China narratives are linked
to the death of the mothers; otherwise both mothers' tales of China would re-
side in silence, the unspeakable silence that points to a horrible memory of the
past. Apparently, recollection through various agencies eventually lends the
memory a status of folk tale or legend.

According to Hayden White in Metahistory, all historical narratives are
"emplotted." That is to say, all histories are written (recollected) around specific themes or plots, depending on the narrator's point of view or the purpose
of narration. History as a form of cultural recollection can be written in the
genres of comedy, tragedy, farce, or romance and using certain moral justifi-

cations or utopian desires as main themes. In both *The Joy Luck Club* and *The Kitchen God's Wife*, the mothers' recollections are also organized around certain recurring tropes, to use Hayden White's term, or certain plots. I believe that the plot at the center of the mothers' recollection is loss—a tragedy of loss.

In both *The Joy Luck Club* and *The Kitchen God's Wife*, loss functions as the dominant metaphor and the recurring theme for the mothers' China narratives. It is also the central code through which to decipher their existence. Each mother's story of her experiences in China eventually develops into a story of loss. Hence, moving to America means to them a loss of identity, center, home, and the reality of existence—they feel themselves being reduced to "ghosts," as in an alien territory. Even though mothers and daughters interpret China with different codes and from different positions, they are all overshadowed by a prevalent sense of loss. To quote Ying-Ying St. Clair in *The Joy Luck Club*, "We are lost."[4] The daughters seem to be lost between cultures, whereas the mothers appear to have lost everything. As June says about her mother, "She had come here in 1949 after losing everything in China: her mother and her father, her family home, her first husband, and two daughters, twin baby girls."[5] Lena St. Clair shares June's position regarding her own mother: "My mother never talked about her life in China, but my father said he saved her from a terrible life there, some tragedies she could not speak about. My father proudly named her in her immigration papers: Betty St. Clair, crossing out her given name of Gu Ying-ying. And then he put down the wrong birthyear, 1916 instead of 1914. So, with the sweep of a pen, my mother lost her name and became a Dragon instead of a Tiger."[6] Their previous identities are deleted with immigration: the mothers become the others.

In *The Kitchen God's Wife*, the mother's China narratives are based on Winnie's recollection of her horrible experiences in China. In fact, the pain and suffering that are central to Winnie's recollection of her past invite repression rather than recall. The recollection process becomes extremely painful because it resurrects a traumatic past that has been buried and muted in Winnie's memory. Due to the repression of the past memory, Winnie's China narrative is subject to constant postponement, revision, and erasure in order to conceal the unspeakable pain. As Winnie says, "Now I can forget my tragedies, put all my secrets behind a door that will never be opened, never seen by American eyes. I was thinking my past was closed forever."[7] Memory for Winnie embodies loss or pain; her China narrative requires concealing instead of unfolding. Remembering inevitably entails pain and, eventually, desires for repression transform into the necessity of repression. In short, Winnie's experience in

China is transfigured into a discourse of repression and her recollection of experiences in China is translated into a narrative of loss.

It is interesting to note that most mothers in Tan's novels share a similar form of speech about their past—a silence that attempts to repress the painful memory of the past. Generally speaking, the mothers in Tan's novels do not want to share their past memories with their daughters and the past is simply something they are not able to talk about to their daughters directly, as both June and Pearl are made aware. Hence, narrative and silence, seemingly opposed to each other, actually tell the same story—the repressed memory of the past. If narrative is one strategy of dealing with the past via recollection, silence is the other via repression: one attempts to affirm the present self and the other tries to negate the past memory. Recollection functions as a defensive contraction of the self, as Beng Xu observes: "The memory itself has become a psychic defense."[8] A coherent memory reconstituted through the process of recollection ensures the continuity of identity in the alien environment.

However, despite the fact that recollection of one's past has been reconfigured as a discourse strategy for self-affirmation and self-construction, it is interesting to note that mothers' recollections of their past experiences in Tan's novels sometimes demonstrate more loss of memory rather than recall of the past. Ironically enough, forgetting plays an important role in the process of recollection. In *The Joy Luck Club*, June complains of her mother repeating the same Kweilin story to her in various versions and with different endings. She says: "I never thought my mother's Kweilin story was anything but a Chinese fairy tale. The endings always changed. . . . The story always grew and grew."[9] Eventually Suyuan's Kweilin story becomes a fairy tale, more connected to imagination than remembrance. In *The Kitchen God's Wife*, Winnie, failing to recall her mother, provides us with contradictory versions of her mother's image. Winnie believes her mother is pretty, strong, educated, and comes from a good family. But later she admits that "maybe my mother was not pretty at all, and I only want to believe that she was."[10] Winnie's mother becomes a fairy tale figure, conjured up by her imagination, rather than her memory: she becomes a beautiful mother she never sees nor remembers in the first place. That is why Winnie keeps repeating to herself: "Now I no longer know which story is the truth, what was the real reason why she left. They are all the same, all true, all false. So much pain in everyone. I tried to tell myself. The past is gone, nothing to be done, just forget it. That's what I tried to believe."[11] Because of loss of memory, there is simply no prior text present in her mind to be re-collected. Hence, recollection transforms into a creative process. In short, mothers' China as a historical reality lies at a remote distance from their present remembrance, irretrievably lost beyond recall; it is made present only through a narrative that involves forgetting instead of remembering. The mothers' recollection of China signifies nothing less than the lost memories of the past. It is inevitable that their accounts of the past are multiple and contradictory, imaginative and illusive.

Ironically, China, lost or otherwise, functions as the locus that more or less defines the mothers' sense of present reality. American experiences, by contrast, only characterize their marginal existence and alien position. They feel themselves to be out of place, exotic if not outlandish, from their daughters' points of view. Mothers tend to have their homes and identities centered elsewhere—in China. If life in America is too disappointing to be real, their experiences in China, at least, can be transliterated into a body of ideas and vocabulary that give them a unique sense of reality and presence. In the preface to *Memory, Narrative, and Identity: New Essays in Ethnic American Literature,* the authors write, "Memory in this context shapes narrative forms and strategies toward reclaiming a suppressed past and helps the process of re-visioning that is essential to gaining control over one's life and future."[12] Hence, China narratives retroactively create multiple imaginary texts of China that are both defining and defined by the mothers, with their displaced mentality and exile consciousness, conditioned by a paradoxical desire of both repression and nostalgia.

In "Daughter-Text/Mother-Text: Matrilineage in Amy Tan's *The Joy Luck Club*," Marina Heung remarks, "Storytelling heals past experiences of loss and separation; it is also a medium for rewriting stories of oppression and victimization into parables of self-affirmation and individual empowerment."[13] Hence, recollection turns into an active process of negotiation with the past, constantly translating and revising the past into a narrative that grants reality to present situations. In a displaced context, the mothers have imaginatively constructed various China narratives out of their experiences in China for themselves and for each other. One mother, Helen, in *The Kitchen God's Wife,* comments on the past to Winnie: "She and I have changed the past many times, for many reasons. And sometimes she changes it for me and does not even know what she has done."[14] It is indeed ironic that at the end of the novel both of them are compelled to tell the truth that they no longer remember, and continue to "recollect" the stories, even though they have lost the memory. That is why Pearl, Winnie's daughter, complains: "I laughed, confused, caught in endless circles of lies. Or perhaps they are not lies but their own form of loyalty, a devotion beyond anything that can ever be spoken, anything that I will ever understand."[15] The past, paradoxically, is lost in the process of recollection. I agree with Debra Shostak when she says: "In general, memory is about absence. It concerns itself with the pastness of time past and with filling gaps in the known continuum of experience. The imaginative capacity of memory to recover and reinvent images and ideas of absent places bridges the locales, supplying a crucial sense of self."[16] Recollection becomes an imaginative process of self-creation despite a "loss of memory."

China is, so to speak, a "mother land," a repository of history with haunting memories and extraordinary experiences—a repository positioned for reproduction. The mothers constantly revise their China narratives in terms of their present conscious needs and unconscious desires, asserting them in the context of American culture for self-empowerment. Tan made the following remark regarding her own mother's China narrative: "It was a way for her to exorcise her demons, and for me to finally listen and empathize and learn what memory means, and what you can change about the past."[17] The experiences in China, or the past in general, even though forgotten to a certain extent, have always been reconstituted by mothers into narratives that carry out a special mission: to control the fate of their "American-made" daughters. Thus, the loss narrative is transformed into a discourse of control. In *The Kitchen God's Wife*, Winnie says to her daughter Pearl: "In China back then, you were always responsible to somebody else. It's not like here in the United States—freedom, independence, individual thinking, do what you want, disobey your mother. No such thing."[18] In this case, she has transformed an imaginary text of China into a powerful narrative for the purpose of domination. She uses China narratives to establish and reinforce her present authoritative position in America. At least she believes she has the entire knowledge of China, an alternative cultural space to which only she has access.

Lacking ontological stability and lost in constant recollection, China narratives are fabricated and manipulated in various forms. Possibly, the power of China narratives resides precisely in their "loss of reality." The mothers in Tan's novels, assuming the absolute authority of the culture of China, transform China into a semiotic space wherein they can continue to exercise the power that they have lost in the American society. Collectively, they have constructed another cultural territory, actually an alternative cultural space within American society. Eventually, the experiences in China that are channeled through the mothers' narratives are translated into a mode of discourse, a style of domineering, a tongue for control, and a posture for having authority over their daughters' lives. China becomes less a geographical location than a cultural extraterritory that the mothers have created in order to construct or deconstruct the subjectivity of their "American-made" daughters. Collectively, mothers construct this alternative history with their China narratives to empower marginalized positions and combat and control their rebellious daughters.

The mothers' experiences in China become a cultural repository of potential power from which the mothers reproduce excessive China narratives for the purpose of control. As Wendy Ann Ho correctly points out, "The personal stories of the Joy Luck Club mothers do battle through gossip, circular talking, cryptic messages/caveats, dream images, bilingual language, and talk story tradition."[19] Through various discourse strategies, the mothers employ many different China narratives to redeem, if not to combat, their American-made daughters. Ying Ying St. Clair, in The Joy Luck Club, has the following observation about her daughter Lena: "All her life, I have watched her as though from another shore. And now I must tell her everything about my past. It is the only way to penetrate her skin and pull her to where she can be saved."[20] Sometimes, they turn their China experiences into a disciplinary lesson that reinforces restrictive cultural values (An-Mei Hsu's story of recognition of one's worth and value); sometimes they translate their personal memory into a fantastic tale with powerful seduction (Suyuan Woo's Kweilin story of the beautiful Kweilin ladies in an exotic wonderland); and sometimes they transliterate China into a secret text where daughters are excluded, and to which only the mothers themselves have direct access (Winnie's story of the horror of betrayal and abuse by her husband in China).

Lena St. Clair also says: "When we were alone, my mother would speak in Chinese, saying things my father could not possibly imagine. I could understand the words perfectly, but not the meaning.[21]" That is, only the mothers possess the keys to decode the meaning of their China narratives. Hence, Chinese, a secondary language to the daughters, becomes the mothers' primary discourse strategy to manipulate their daughters. As one mother in The Joy Luck Club reminds her daughter about The Book of the Twenty-Six Malignant Gates, which is written in Chinese: "You cannot understand it. That is why you must listen to me."[22] Daughters, for their part, resist their mothers' China narratives by reminding their mothers that their stories are out of context because, as June asserts, "this wasn't China."[23] It is not surprising that June has the following remark about her mother's China narrative: "Over the years, she told me the same story, except for the ending, which grew darker, casting long shadows into her life, and eventually into mine."[24] Even after the death of her mother, those stories continue to haunt June throughout her life.

Marie B. Foster remarks: "Tan's characters are of necessity story tellers and even historians, empowered by relating what they know about their beginnings and the insufficiencies of their present lives. . . . The storytelling, however, is inundated with ambivalences and contradictions which . . . often [take] the form of blame in mother-daughter relationships."[25] So, the daughters, not good listeners in the first place, have to translate their mothers' China narratives within the American context. As Rose Jordan complains of her mother: "More than thirty years later, my mother was still trying to make me listen."[26] The daughter's reception or reconstitution of the China narratives informs a process of translation into a different linguistic system and cultural space. That is to say, the daughter's cognition of China seems to be always already structured, mediated, and overdetermined by the semiotics of the (m)other tongue that serves as the first order symbolic signification. Clearly, the ambiguous nature and intricate structure of the mothers' China narratives make it impossible for the daughters to identify what is Chinese and what is not. Just as Lindo Jong says to her daughter in *The Joy Luck Club:* "How do you know what is Chinese and what is not Chinese?"[27] And it seems that the mothers often enjoy the narrative ambiguity they have created in order to maintain a superior position as the authorities on China.

Therefore, the daughters' reconstructions of their mothers' China narratives are based on the signifier of the first linguistic order (mothers' stories), which assumes somewhat of a historical reference to China. The mothers' China narratives function as the ultimate interpretative frames of the daughters' reconceptualizations of China. It is actually the absolute horizon of the daughters' cognition of China. That is to say, not only do the mothers' stories of their experiences in China provide the daughters with China narratives, but the mothers themselves function as the China narratives to a certain extent, marking the limit of their daughters' perceptions and conceptions of China. Hence, China narratives inform a process of displacement, transformation, and absence in regard to the representation of China. In the (m)others' tales, this China narrative is inevitably a translation, a displacement, and a transformation of the past for present usage. That is exactly why when June, in *The Joy Luck Club,* compares her own observation of Chinese activities with her mother's China narratives, she finds a revealing difference between her mother's fascinating China narratives and her direct social reality at home: "Eating is not a gracious event here. It's as though every body had been starving. They push large forkfuls into their mouths, jab at more pieces of pork, one right after the other. They are not like the ladies of Kweilin, who I always imagined savored their food with a certain detached delicacy."[28]

I argue that the China narrative in Tan's novels serves as an undercurrent but central text that structures the present relationship between mothers and daughters because of the specific roles this narrative plays in their lives. Therefore, the cross-cultural hermeneutics of China are conducted within this domestic space, generally between two generations and, more specifically, between the Chinese mothers and their American-born. Here is Lindo's comment on her daughter Waverly in The Joy Luck Club: "she didn't look Chinese. She had a sour American look on her face."[29] "Only her skin and her hair are Chinese. Inside—she is all American-made."[30] As products of different cultures and histories, mothers and daughters abide by different cultural values and possess different codes of interpretation. In fact, they speak entirely different languages whenever they talk about China: "My mother and I spoke two different languages, which we did," June says in The Joy Luck Club, "I talked to her in English, she answered back in Chinese."[31] The bilingual conversion turns into a game of translation, and in this translation meaning is transfigured, displaced, and occasionally, lost. June remarks, "We translated each other's meanings and I seemed to hear less than what was said, while my mother heard more."[32] With the power of China narratives, the mothers hope to ensure some continuity of their cultural heritage with their daughters, as Huntley notes: "Tan's Chinese mothers have a sense of generational continuity; they feel connected with their own mothers and their mother's mothers, and they feel equally linked with their daughters."[33] Nevertheless, their daughters feel differently about this connection or disconnection. In a bicultural context, the generational dialogue turns into a site of contention between the diasporic mothers and the culturally displaced daughters in this mother-daughter dyad.

Both mothers and daughters have to constantly reevaluate their respective versions of China narratives that are grounded in entirely different cultural contexts, with different historical references and subject positions. For the mothers, China narratives inform a process of recollection (history or loss of it) whereas for the daughters, who have never been to China, China narratives become a text of culture. In other words, experiences in China become semiotic texts that are reconstituted through two different modes

of discourse: historical recollection and cultural reproduction. And this di-
chotomy is dramatized essentially through the dialectic structure between
mothers' historical recollection and daughters' cultural reproduction
(translation). China narratives, eventually, become a semiotic site where
culture and identity are fought over, negotiated, displaced, and transformed. Instead of the static ontological presence of a unitary category, the
China narrative becomes a hermeneutic space for articulating identity and
difference, a dialectical process that initiates the cultural and historical reconstitution of the subjects.

China in mothers' stories resides in a domain of memory based on the personal recollection of a social reality in China, whereas China for the daughters
indicates a territory of dream and fantasy. The daughters' experiences of
China are entirely based on the tales of China via the narratives of their mothers, which have already been translated in a new cultural context and with reference to their American experiences.

NOTES

1. Tan (1989, 3).

2. Tan (1991, 27).

3. Tan (1991, 27).

4. Tan (1989, 64).

5. Tan (1989, 141).

6. Tan (1989, 107).

7. Tan (1991, 81).

8. Xu (1994, 263).

9. Tan (1989, 12).

10. Tan (1991, 120).

11. Tan (1991, 130).

12. Singh et al. (1994, 2).

13. Heung (1993, 607).

14. Tan (1991, 69).

15. Tan (1991, 524).

16. Shostak (1994, 234).

17. Lyall (1995, C6).

18. Tan (1991, 162).

19. Ho (1996, 339).

20. Tan (1989, 274).

21. Tan (1989, 109).

22. Tan (1989, 87).

23. Tan (1989, 152).

24. Tan (1989, 7).

25. Foster (1996, 210).

26. Tan (1989, 208).

27. Tan (1989, 228).

28. Tan (1989, 21).

29. Tan (1989, 288).

30. Tan (1989, 289).

31. Tan (1989, 23).

32. Tan (1989, 27).

33. Huntley (1988, 62).

REFERENCES

Foster, M. Marie Booth. 1996. "Voice, Mind, Self: Mother-Daughter Relationships in Amy Tan's *The Joy Luck Club* and *The Kitchen God's Wife.*" In *Women of Color: Mother-Daughter Relationships in 20th Century Literature,* ed. Elizabeth Brown-Guillory, 209–27. Austin: University of Texas Press.

Heung, Marina. 1993. "Daughter-Text/Mother-Text: Matrilineage in Amy Tan's *The Joy Luck Club.*" *Feminist Studies* 19 (fall): 597–608.

Ho, Wendy Ann. 1996. "Swan-Feather Mothers and Coca-Cola Daughters: Teaching Tan's *The Joy Luck Club.*" In *Teaching American Ethnic Literature: Nineteen Essays,* ed. John R. Maitino and David R. Peck, 327–45. Albuquerque: University of New Mexico Press.

Hune, Shirley, Hyung-Cha Kim, Stephen S. Fugita, and Amy Ling. 1991. *Asian Americans: Comparative and Global Perspectives*. Pullman, Wash.: Washington State University Press.

Huntley, E. D. 1988. *Amy Tan: A Critical Companion*. Westport, Conn.: Greenwood.

Ling, Amy. 1990. *Between Worlds: Woman Writers of Chinese Ancestry*. New York: Pergamon.

———. 1991. "'Emerging Canons' of Asian American Literature and Art." In *Asian Americans: Comparative and Global Perspectives*, ed. Shirley Hune, Hyung-Cha Kim, Stephen S. Fugita, and Amy Ling, 191–98. Pullman, Wash.: Washington State University Press.

Lyall, Sarah. 1995. "In the Country of the Spirits: At Home with Amy Tan." *New York Times*, 28 December, C1, C6–C7.

Rubenstein, Roberta. 1987. *Boundaries of the Self: Gender, Culture, Fiction*. Chicago: University of Illinois Press.

Shostak, Debra. 1994. "Maxine Hong Kingston's Fake Books." In *Memory, Narrative, and Identity: New Essays in Ethnic American Literature*, ed. Amritjit Singh, Joseph Skerrett Jr., and Robert Hogan, 233–60. Boston: Northeastern University Press.

Singh, Amritjit, Joseph Skerrett Jr., and Robert Hogan. 1994. *Memory, Narrative, and Identity: New Essays in Ethnic American Literature*. Boston: Northeastern University Press.

Tan, Amy. 1989. *The Joy Luck Club*. New York: Ballantine Books.

———. 1991. *The Kitchen God's Wife*. New York: Ballantine Books.

White, Hayden. 1973. *Metahistory: The Historical Imagination in Nineteenth-Century Europe*. Baltimore: Johns Hopkins University Press.

Wong, Sau-ling Cynthia. 1993. *Reading Asian American Literature: From Necessity to Extravagance*. Princeton, N.J.: Princeton University Press.

Xu, Beng. 1994. "Memory and the Ethnic Self: Reading Amy Tan's *The Joy Luck Club*." In *Memory, Narrative, and Identity: New Essays in Ethnic American Literature*, ed. Amritjit Singh, Joseph Skerrett Jr., and Robert Hogan, 261–77. Boston: Northeastern University Press.

20

Finding the Right Gesture: Becoming Chinese American in Fae Myenne Ng's *Bone*

Vivian Fumiko Chin

In the field of Asian American literature, ideas regarding the formation of Asian American identities have been contradictory. On one side, the editors of the *Aiiieeeee!* anthology, an early collection of Asian American literature, have expressed a desire to claim an authentically Asian and yet distinct Asian American identity. For the *Aiiieeeee!* editors, a singular and correct Asian original exists, and thus Asian American representations of Asia, can be classified as either "real" or "fake."[1] Of particular importance, here, is the belief that descriptions of Asian and Asian American cultural practices are correct only when these practices can be traced to origins in Asia, and thus authenticated. Other critics have suggested that Asian American identities need not be so rigidly bound to an Asian original. Tracing back to an Asian original, or determining what is real or fake, becomes less relevant when identity can be considered a dynamic process.[2] According to critic Elaine Kim, Asian American identity can be "fluid and migratory,"[3] migrating beyond Asia and America in a manner that can disrupt ideas of static origins. This concept of identity suggests that origins, and what is considered original, may have the ability to change, and may not always be amenable to exact reproduction. If we agree with Kim and consider identity an ongoing process that is "the site of contending, multiple meanings,"[4] we can shift our focus. Rather than simply wondering about *who* we are, we can begin to consider *how* we are becoming. Moreover, in this interrogation, we may ask: what does it mean to say that someone "acts Chinese," and how does acting or being Chinese take place within the United States? The acts that occur in *Bone* illustrate how its characters perform Chinese American identities in ways that may differ from "original" Chinese models, thus producing new approaches to the category "Chinese American."

Fae Myenne Ng's novel *Bone* demonstrates that Chinese American identities exist because of the performance of certain acts. The acts that one performs, or more simply, the things that one does, are not merely the result of one's racial, ethnic, or cultural identity, but also take part in shaping that identity. Chinese American identity within *Bone* is diverse. It ranges from those who live outside Chinatown and do not understand or engage in practices that, for others, define Chinese American culture, to those who live inside of Chinatown and assume a certain power to define Chinese American culture. For example, a seemingly assimilated character, cousin Dale, who attends a predominantly white school, cannot understand why, according to Chinese American practices, family members do not pay each other for services rendered.[5] Other characters have no wish to emulate this "whitewashed" cousin because they have no desire to stop acting in ways they consider Chinese American. This refusal is one of many processes that engender Chinese American ways of being. The processes that work to produce Chinese American identities within *Bone* include acts of resistance against cultural extinction by reinventing rituals that provide ways to remember, and by reinventing through storytelling.

Acts can function as a language within which racial, ethnic, or cultural meanings are produced. What critic Judith Butler calls the "performative" has the power to create and re-create identity, or subjectivity. However, this creative power is not fully controlled by an individual. Butler explains, "the performative is not merely an act used by a pregiven subject; rather, it is one of the powerful and insidious ways in which subjects are called into social being. . . . In this sense the social performative is a crucial part not only of subject *formation* but of the ongoing political contestation and reformulation of the subject as well."[6] Characters in *Bone* engage in performances such as telling a particular story or participating in funeral rites in order to convey messages or to enact meanings that in turn constitute their cultural identities. As French philosopher Louis Althusser notes, "Pascal says more or less: 'Kneel down, move your lips in prayer, and you will believe.'"[7] By acting like a believer, one becomes a believer. In this manner, performances have the power to create identities, just as specific performances within *Bone* have the power to create Chinese American identities. Moreover, these identities can persist despite and because of a history of anti-Chinese legislation and other forms of racism and exclusion. Such conditions have the power to call Chinese Americans into social being. With these points in mind, *Bone* yields ways of approaching questions of genealogy, legitimacy, and the "American" origins of Asian American practices. Ng's novel chooses to "ignore ancient

China" and the China of the immigrant generation's past. Instead, *Bone* focuses on the Leong family's experiences "within the American landscape,"[8] a landscape where becoming Chinese American can involve an "ongoing political contestation."

Many of the practices that occur in *Bone* involve a self-reinvention. This self-reinvention is different from an explicitly unraced, but implicitly white, "American" ideal that promises the reinvention of the self-made man.[9]

One popular belief contends that *anyone* can become an American who is the same as all other Americans; however, such a homogeneous identity may be neither desirable nor possible. In "Decolonization, Displacement, Disidentification: Writing and the Question of History," published in her collection *Immigrant Acts*, Lisa Lowe argues that *Bone* proves that "the 'conversion' of Chinese into 'Americans' . . . can never be completed."[10] Accordingly, despite claims that all Americans can assimilate into a single entity because America is a melting pot, people of Chinese ancestry who live in America can never become simply "Americans." Indeed, in *Bone*, an assimilationist model that demands a linear progression from Chinese to American is superceded by a model in which the ultimate goal is *not* to become a generic American, but to become a certain kind of Chinese American.

Historically, Chinese American reinvention has occurred within a framework of exclusion. For example, in *Bone*, in order to avoid exclusion from the United States, Leon Leong must become a paper son and reinvent himself. Reinvention differs from invention in that it does not make something "from scratch." Instead, reinvention takes something that already exists and makes it into something new. Leon's reinvention takes a Chinese life and remakes it into a Chinese American life. His invented genealogy is a story that changes family histories. Like scores of Chinese immigrant men of his generation, Leon takes what he has been given—legislative exclusion—and creates an identity as a paper son. On the record, his past is completely fictional. In Leon's case, the forced constructedness of identity is obvious.[11]

Another reinvention of the past, and a way of reconfiguring origins, occurs in the telling of Leon's life story. An "old-man hotel on Clay Street" in San Francisco (the San Fran hotel) marks the starting point of the Leong family's history in the United States. After Leon returns to the hotel after living with Mah, Leila notes, "Leon's got the same room he had when he was a bachelor. . . . Our Grandpa Leong lived his last days at the San Fran, so it's an important place for us. In this country, the San Fran is our family's oldest place, our beginning place, our New China. The way I see it, Leon's life kind of made a circle."[12] The

family's "New China," the San Fran hotel, is located in Chinatown, and Chinatown is located in the city of San Francisco. In name, then, the city is both inside and outside of Chinatown. In this way, the boundaries of Chinatown are
not impermeable, nor is Chinatown as Jade Snow Wong describes, "the heart
of Old China."[13] In contrast, a "New China" does not suggest a captured essence
of an ancient thing, but a reproduction that will be different from the original.
Leon returns to the family's "beginning place . . . kind of"[14] making a circle—
he cannot go back to being exactly the way he was, but he must once again
reinvent himself. Additionally, the origin—China—is displaced by a new origin, San Francisco.

Origins are also reconceived in *Bone* by the altering of traditions such as
burial practices. Fae Myenne Ng has remarked that an interest in burial customs influenced the writing of her novel: "The whole ritual of sending the
bones back to China was fascinating to me. Bone is what lasts. And I wanted
to honor the quality of endurance in the immigrant spirit."[15] The practice of
returning the remains of Chinese immigrants to China is a practice that carries much meaning. Two idioms refer to the burial practices of Chinese immigrants. One, *luo ye gui gen,* "falling leaves return to the root," describes the
tradition of sending remains to be buried in China. Such a tradition supports
the belief that the remains of the immigrants belong with the ancestors in the
"true" home, which is the country of origin. Another saying, *Luo ye sheng gen,*
"falling to the ground, growing roots,"[16] applies to the alternate practice of
keeping the remains in the United States, or place of immigration. When the
remains of Chinese immigrants are not returned to their origin, to China, and
are instead interred in the "chosen" land, continuity is disrupted and the origin is displaced. New "roots" take hold in the place of immigration. Although
both immigration and the keeping of remains in American soil may not have
always occurred out of choice, the second idiom, "falling to the ground, growing roots," suggests a transference regarding the notion of homeland, a recon-
sideration of the place of belonging, and the creation of a new origin. Matters
of origin inform practices; a certain ritual is said to be traditional if it has been
enacted and reenacted in the past. In the case of Chinese American practice,
one might conclude that a practice must have originated in China in order for
it to be traditional or "correct." However, *Bone* does not call for a return to
strictly traditional practices. The United States can be the origin of Chinese
American practices, and the United States can become a new origin.

Such a repositioning of origins occurs when Leon's paper father, Grandpa
Leong, dies and his remains are lost before they can be sent to China. By fail-

ing to return Grandpa Leong's remains to China, Leon forestalls the completion of a ritual. Losing Grandpa Leong's body is tantamount to losing the ancestor: the actual loss of his body corresponds to the loss of history that can accompany emigration, and the loss of early immigrant history. When Grandpa Leong's remains are kept in the place that excluded him, and China is not named as the proper home, a return to the origin is prevented. Leon's forgetfulness repositions the rightful place of burial, the true home, as the United States. Leon's neglect can be redeemed if his "forgetting" about Grandpa Leong's bones is read as an act of resistance against the idea that the United States cannot be the true home of Chinese immigrants. The Chinese cemetery in Colma becomes, like the San Fran hotel, a "New China." Because Leon cannot correct this mistake and send the remains to China, he must come up with an alternative practice. A benevolent association man cannot recover Grandpa Leong's individual remains, but he offers practical advice to Leila, counseling her to perform a specific gesture, telling her to "[b]ow to the family headstone." He reassures her that "the right gesture will find your grandfather."[17] Most relevant to Leila is the man's affirmation that the *right* gesture will find Grandpa Leong. This claim provokes a question: how can she know, recognize, and perform the *right* gesture?

For Leila and for Leon, the right gestures can require adapting practices to suit their present needs. This process of invention, or reinvention, resembles a method that anthropologist Claude Lévi-Strauss calls *bricolage.* In Lévi-Strauss's usage, "The bricoleur is adept at performing a large number of diverse tasks. . . . [T]he rules of his game are always to make do with 'whatever is at hand,' that is to say with a set of tools that is always finite and is also heterogeneous."[18] Bricolage occurs "in the continual reconstruction from the same materials, it is always earlier ends which are called upon to play the part of the means."[19] When Leon makes do with what is at hand, and becomes like a father to Leila, he improves upon the original circumstances. He is able to play the role of Leila's father better than her biological father, who has relocated to Australia. In this way, Leon invents a father for Leila. Leon is limited by a system, and yet he is not completely subordinate to it. He can make the best of a bad situation in a way that is more meaningful than this cliché might suggest.

Leon engages in various forms of bricolage that parallel his self-invention. As Leila tells it, "Leon was a junk inventor. Very weird stuff. An electric sink. Cookie-tin clocks. Clock lamps. An intercom hooked up to a cash register hooked up to an alarm system."[20] Leila recalls that Leon has always been an inventor, but his ability to complete projects suffers following the death of his daughter, Ona. "After Ona died Leon still talked up new ideas, but he hardly ever started anything."[21] Mah complains that Leon is "All head and no tail."[22] This complaint agrees with a description of the bricoleur: "The 'bricoleur' may not ever complete his purpose but he always puts something of himself into it."[23] Despite his difficulties finishing or even starting projects, Leon is able to invest "something of himself" into his inventions. His talents lie in his ability to take junk, other peoples' discards, and reconstruct this junk into a functional object. Additionally, because the bricoleur sees potential use or value in all things, "elements are collected or retained on the principle that 'they may always come in handy.'"[24] Leila notes that "Leon was a collector, too."[25] He collects takeout containers, aluminum tins, styrofoam cups, canned food, and tin cans to hold incense and to store string and rubber bands. Leon invents by combining parts to make "very weird stuff," and simply finds new uses for preexisting objects. His methods of recycling express frugality and creativity—he doesn't need to purchase containers for his string and rubber bands, and he is able to make something new, to produce unconventional hybrids that are not merely decorative, but serve some practical purpose. Leon does not reuse objects for their original purposes. In this way, his recycling does not return an object to its origin, but "kind of" makes a circle. Although in part made necessary by poverty, Leon's practice of collecting and inventing constitutes an unconventional value system. He can transform what is devalued by others as junk into something that works, just as he can transform what has been excluded by law into a viable identity.

Following a bricoleur's commitment to collecting, Leon also saves written documents. A collection of papers that Leon has kept in a suitcase reveals to Leila the extent of Leon's false reportage, how he has invented an alternate history. The papers tell an alternate story, a story of rejection and exclusion that contradicts the stories he has told his family. When she reads the papers, Leila realizes that "Leon had made up stories for us; so that we could laugh, so that we could understand the rejections."[26] The documents reveal a lack of correspondence between writing and speech, facts and story, and history and memory. Leila comes to understand that the decades' worth of papers "marked his time and . . . marked his endurance."[27] Because he has saved the suitcase of records, the past, and versions of the past, will not be forgotten. Leon's bricolage makes it possible to reconstruct a history that counters his invented history, and exposes how his self-invention was determined by attempts to exclude him.

History and story act together and both have power. In an interview, Gayatri Spivak remarks that "history is a storying." In other words, history requires story or narrative. When history and story are told, identity and agency become possible. Spivak further explains that "This alternate storying doesn't give you an identity, if you think of identity as something intimately personal which lets you know who you are. It gives a whole field of representation within which something like an 'identity' can be represented as a basis for agency."[28] History, or the "alternate storying" that constitutes Leon's and Leila's narratives, does not simply provide an identity. Instead it both limits and provides a way that identity can be enacted, invented, or reinvented. As a paper son, Leon is able to reinvent himself and give himself an identity that begins with his arrival in the United States. His history is a storying that makes his identity changeable and somewhat untraceable.

The Leong family is a family that in part results from tactics used to avoid deportation. A family can be created in a way that resembles bricolage—by taking preexistent conditions and producing something new. Leon stresses that "it's time that makes a family, not just blood,"[29] acknowledging that the passage of time and shared experiences constitute a family. Leon neglects to mention that anti-immigrant legislation also makes a family. The effects of this legislation are played out when Mah marries Leon, at least in part for "convenience," for a green card, and when Grandpa Leong becomes the grandfather because Leon pays him for the Leong name. As narrator, Leila provides this information, contrasting it against her own "choice" to marry Mason. Leila's conceit that "Family exists only because somebody has a story, and knowing the story connects us to a history,"[30] implies that story can be more binding than name or blood. Listening to the story, learning the story, enables one to become a member of a family, and a subject of history, linked to a common past.

Leila's telling of her family's story defines certain kinds of Chinese American identities. She discusses a personality trait or way of being that involves a willingness to speak and reveals the silence around her sister's death, "After Ona jumped off the Nam. . . . It was a bad time. . . . We don't talk about it."[31] What is not talked about in the family is what Leila "talks about" as the narrator of *Bone*. Comparing herself to her future husband, Leila explains, "One thing I liked about Mason: he *said* things. I mean, I thought about a lot of things, but I never actually *said* them."[32] Leila considers the ability to articulate one's thoughts an admirable and desirable trait, but identifies herself as someone who thinks rather than speaks. In acting as the narrator, however, Leila must "say" things, or at least expose her thoughts as if speaking to the reader. She is compelled to tell. Leila tells the story that memory provides, and tells the story of the interrelation of the past and the present. Leila's story is not a "universal" story, but one that is specific to her place, time, race/ethnicity, and economic class. The message Leila recovers from her memory of Grandpa Leong—"the best way to conquer fear is to act. *Open the mouth and tell*"[33]—promises that to tell is empowering. Telling is an act that can deliver Leila from fear. Telling is a ritual that has a healing power because it can help remember the past. Leila's story recounts a specifically Chinese American history when it shows how the Leong family has been affected by specific personal and political conditions.

Leila is not the only character who tells stories of the past. According to Leila, Leon recites at least two stories: the story of his immigration and the story of his failed business, the Ong & Leong laundry. Of Leon's arrival in America, Leila complains, "I knew the story. One hundred and nine times I've heard Leon tell it."[34] Leila also hears Leon repeat the story of his failed laundry: "Leon always brought up the Ong & Leong laundry. . . . Leon talked about it to anyone who asked. He told the long and embarrassing story again and again."[35] Leon's telling of these stories may be read as ritualistic. Leon repeats the story of becoming a paper son, both describing and enacting a self-invention. Each re-telling retraces this process, as if making it indelible. Leon's recitation of his story resembles Pascal's performed prayer—repeating the story might help Leon believe that he has become his paper identity. Why does he re-tell the same old stories? Leon's experiences show that he is still subject to various forms of exclusion. The papers in the suitcase testify that Leon repeatedly had difficulty finding employment and a place to live. Leon stresses that he did what was necessary to become an American, so this matter should be resolved. At the same time, Leon's re-iteration of the story of his immigration suggests that this is an ongoing process, and the telling is never complete. Similarly, repeating the story of the laundry business, and how its failure led to his daughter Ona's suicide, shows how his grieving over her death is not finished. In re-telling these stories, the past is not done and gone, but continually resurfaces in the present. Through Leon's re-telling, and through the papers in the suitcase, history is not lost.

Leon invents an alternative practice regarding Grandpa Leong's remains, in part because of their loss, and in part because he needs a ritual that will be relevant for himself. Leila also seeks her own rituals. She explains: "What I wanted was to forget. The blame. The pressing fear. I wanted a ritual that forgave. I wanted a ritual to forget."[36] Despite expressing a wish to forget, Leila notes, "I never forget."[37] Like Leon, Leila chooses to remember: "I thought I'd forgotten: with Mason. Nina thought she'd forgotten, with her new guy. Mah wanted to forget, with her gold mine of gossip. But nobody'd forgotten about Ona. And here was proof: Leon's altar. He'd found a way to live with his grief."[38] In the apartment, Leila notices "Ona's ashes. The brass urn sat on the card table next to the sewing machine. . . . Leon had made a whole little altar: a teacup with grains of rice, a teacup full of water."[39] As a bricoleur, Leon is able to take what is on hand and create a space where a ritual for the dead can be enacted. Leon also recites stories from his past and collects materials that he can reuse in new ways. Following this practice of the bricoleur, Leila recollects her memories to narrate her own story, her family's story, and a story of Chinese American immigration. As she narrates the story of *Bone*, she struggles to find "the right gesture." Ultimately, the telling itself becomes the right gesture and the past is recovered and remembered.

The acts of storytelling in *Bone* occur in interlinking layers between author, narrator, and characters. *Bone* begins with Leila's admission, "We were a family of girls. By Chinese standards, that wasn't lucky. In Chinatown, everyone knew our story."[40] In Leila's Chinatown, her family's story has already circulated. Telling the story again allows the story to travel outside of this Chinatown. Leila positions herself within Chinatown and within her family. From this center, Leila speaks as a Chinese American storyteller. For Leila, family, story, and history are intertwined. Leila's task is to tell these stories and connect her readers to her history. The history that she is compelled to recover is the history of her family's losses and power to endure.

Some readers expect a written work, even a work of fiction, to be an authoritative text that will teach them about other people's ways of life. These expectations lead readers to believe that all texts function as ethnographies that explain and let them consume another culture. In this light, a non-Chinese American reader might expect *Bone* to provide something of a "guided Chinatown tour: by providing explanations on the manners and mores of the Chinese-American community from the vantage point of a 'native.'"[41] Although *Bone* does at times explain Chinese American practices, it also leaves certain practices unexplained. A case in point occurs when Leila scolds her sister for wearing red, but does not explain that her dress is inappropriate because red is a Chinese and Chinese American color of celebration.[42] Leila tells her family's story, but she declines to tell all. The reader must approach the text in a way that is similar to the characters' processes of identity formation: readers must reinvent the text according to their own familiarity with the acts that the characters perform.

The acts of bricolage and reinvention that take place in *Bone* demonstrate how Leon and Leila are able to be Chinese American. Moreover, as readers encounter Leila's story, their interpretive acts make the identities of Leon and Leila a continuing process. The Leong family exists because history and story can produce acts. Although Leila and Leon encounter potentially destructive experiences and powers, through forms of reinvention, both Leila and Leon are able to find the right gestures that enable them to endure.

In the schema of Asian American identity, *Bone* enables a reconceptualization of identity formation. To return to preexisting concepts of Asian American identity, the *Aiiieeeee!* editors provide useful examples. They reject the "goofy" idea of "dual personality,"[43] in which an Asian American is imagined to be caught in an eternal struggle between Asia and America. In this paradigm, Asian American identity comes into being as "Asian" elements battle against "American" elements. Furthermore, the *Aiiieeeee!* editors dispute the notion that Asian Americans have access to ancient Asian, or specifically Chinese, cultural knowledge. In their eyes, such a belief is a fallacy. "The myth is that Asian Americans have maintained cultural integrity as Asians, that there is some strange continuity between the great high culture of a China that hasn't existed for five hundred years and the American-born Asian."[44]

Another insidious myth upholds Asian Americans as model minorities who can overcome all obstacles, including racism, by virtue of their hardworking nature. *Bone* challenges these conceptions of Asian America by telling a story in which characters are not torn between Asia and America; where Chinese traditions are not written in stone; and in which the Leong family cannot always succeed. *Bone* is also not a story of "depoliticized self-healing"[45] in which the politics of being Asian in America are ignored or dismissed. While demonstrating how Leon and Leila continue to create within the parameters forced upon them by, for example, poverty and racism, *Bone* provides a stage on which the Leong family can perform, produce, and reinvent ways of being Chinese in America.

NOTES

1. *Aiiieeeee! An Anthology of Asian American Writers* (Washington, D.C.: Howard University Press), edited by Jeffrey Paul Chan, Frank Chin, Lawson Fusao Inada, and Shawn Wong, was first published in 1974, while the lesser-known *Asian American Authors* (Boston: Houghton-Mifflin), a collection edited by Kai-yu Hsu and Helen Palubinskas, was published in 1972. The *Aiiieeeee!* editors' conception of an Asian American who has no direct ties to Asia seems to contradict their simultaneous call

for a faithful adherence to a Chinese literary or heroic tradition. See also, Frank Chin, "Come All Ye Asian American Writers of the Real and the Fake," in *The Big Aiiieeeee!* ed. Jeffrey Paul Chan, Frank Chin, Lawson Fusao Inada, and Shawn Wong (New York: Penguin, 1991).

2. Elaine Kim, preface to *Charlie Chan is Dead*, ed. Jessica Hagedorn (New York: Penguin, 1993), xii.

3. Kim, preface, xi.

4. Kim, preface, xiii.

5. See David Leiwei Li, *Imagining the Nation: Asian American Literature and Cultural Consent* (Stanford, Calif.: Stanford University Press, 1998), 138–39.

6. Judith Butler, "Performativity's Social Magic," in *The Social and Political Body*, ed. Theodore R. Schatzki and Wolfgang Natter (New York: Guilford, 1996), 44.

7. Louis Althusser, *Lenin and Philosophy*, trans. Ben Brewster (New York: Monthly Review Press, 1971), 168.

8. Fae Myenne Ng, talk at Mills College, fall 1995.

9. I am grateful to Sarita Echevez See for pointing this out.

10. Lisa Lowe, *Immigrant Acts* (Durham, N.C.: Duke University Press, 1996), 125.

11. David Leiwei Li notes that as "A paper son himself, Leon's life story is a necessity of invention, part of an interventional oral tradition against the written documents of exclusion laws." Li, *Imagining the Nation*, 136.

12. Fae Myenne Ng, *Bone*, (New York: Hyperion, 1993), 2.

13. Jade Snow Wong, *Fifth Chinese Daughter* (Harper, 1945), 1.

14. Ng, *Bone*, 2.

15. Fae Myenne Ng, *New York* 26 no. 4, 43.

16. I thank my father for bringing these idioms to my attention. I accept responsibility for any mistranslations that may occur here.

17. Ng, *Bone*, 2.

18. Claude Lévi-Strauss, *The Savage Mind* (Chicago: University of Chicago Press, 1966), 19.

19. Lévi-Strauss, *The Savage Mind*, 21.

20. Ng, *Bone*, 5.

21. Ng, *Bone*, 49.

22. Ng, *Bone*, 49.

23. Lévi-Strauss, *The Savage Mind*, 21.

24. Lévi-Strauss, *The Savage Mind*, 18.

25. Ng, *Bone*, 5.

26. Ng, *Bone*, 5.

27. Ng, *Bone*, 58.

28. Gayatri Chakravorty Spivak, "Interview with Alfred Arteaga, 'Bonding in Difference,'" in *The Spivak Reader*, ed. Donna Landry and Gerald Maclean (New York: Routledge, 1996), 26.

29. Ng, *Bone*, 3.

30. Ng, *Bone*, 36.

31. Ng, *Bone*, 3.

32. Ng, *Bone*, 184.

33. Ng, *Bone*, 21.

34. Ng, *Bone*, 57.

35. Ng, *Bone*, 103.

36. Ng, *Bone*, 54.

37. Ng, *Bone*, 61.

38. Ng, *Bone*, 102.

39. Ng, *Bone*, 101.

40. Ng, *Bone*, 3.

41. Sau-ling Cynthia Wong, "Autobiography As Guided Chinatown Tour? Maxine Hong Kingston's *The Woman Warrior* and the Chinese-American Autobiographical Controversy," in *Multicultural Autobiography: American Lives*, ed. James Robert Payne (Knoxville: University of Tennessee Press, 1992), 248–79.

42. Ng, *Bone*, 154.

43. Chan et al., *Aiiieeeee!*, xii.

44. Chan et al., *Aiiieeeee!*, 7.

45. David Palumbo-Liu, *Asian/American: Historical Crossings of a Racial Frontier* (Stanford, Calif.: Stanford University Press, 1999).

REFERENCES

Althusser, Louis. 1971. *Lenin and Philosophy.* Trans. Ben Brewster. New York: Monthly Review Press.

Chin, Frank, Jeffrey Paul Chan, Lawson Fusao Inada, and Shawn Wong, eds. 1991. *Aiiieeeee! An Anthology of Asian American Writers.* New York: Mentor.

Kim, Elaine. 1993. Preface to *Charlie Chan is Dead,* ed. Jessica Hagedorn. New York: Penguin.

Lévi-Strauss, Claude. 1966. *The Savage Mind.* Chicago: University of Chicago Press.

Li, David Leiwei. 1998. *Imagining the Nation: Asian American Literature and Cultural Consent.* Stanford, Calif.: Stanford University Press.

Lowe, Donald. 1995. *The Body in Late-Capitalist USA.* Durham, N.C.: Duke University Press.

Lowe, Lisa. 1996. *Immigrant Acts.* Durham, N.C.: Duke University Press.

Jean-François Lyotard. 1984. *The Postmodern Condition.* Trans. Geoff Bennington and Brian Massumi. Minneapolis: University of Minnesota Press.

Ng, Fae Myenne. 1993. *Bone.* New York: Hyperion.

Ng, Fae Myenne. 1995. Informal talk at Mills College. Fall.

Palumbo-Liu, David. 1999. *Asian/American: Historical Crossings of a Racial Frontier.* Stanford, Calif.: Stanford University Press.

Payne, James Robert, ed. 1992. *Multicultural Autobiography: American Lives.* Knoxville: University of Tennessee Press.

Spivak, Gayatri Chakravorty. 1996. "Interview with Alfred Arteaga, 'Bonding in Difference.'" In *The Spivak Reader,* ed. Donna Landry and Gerald Maclean. New York: Routledge.

Wong, Jade Snow. 1945. *Fifth Chinese Daughter.* Harper.

Wong, Sau-ling Cynthia. 1992. "Autobiography as Guided Chinatown Tour? Maxine Hong Kingston's *The Woman Warrior* and the Chinese-American Autobiographical Controversy." In *Multicultural Autobiography: American Lives.* Knoxville: University of Tennessee Press.

VI

Chinese America: Settled

21

Archaeological Investigations of Life within the Woolen Mills Chinatown, San Jose

R. Scott Baxter and Rebecca Allen

In the last half of the nineteenth century, San Jose was a growing agricultural and horticultural community. Located in the rich Santa Clara Valley, the city was based on an agrarian economy that required cheap labor to be viable. During much of the latter nineteenth century that labor was primarily provided by Chinese. This is a story of a Chinese community occupied while San Jose was in transition from an agricultural to an industrial urban center. The community lifestyle is interpreted through historical documents and the material remains its residents left behind. Archaeological evidence demonstrates that the Chinese were not the stereotypical dirty, backward people often portrayed in contemporary newspapers and popular literature. San Jose's Chinese population was a well-organized community, well established and integral to the region's well-being. This story presents the archaeological history of Woolen Mills Chinatown.

CHINESE IN THE SANTA CLARA VALLEY

As did many early immigrants, the Chinese came to California because of the lure of the gold rush and desperate circumstances at home. The majority of Chinese mining in California were peasants from villages in southern China in the Kwangtung, or Guangdong Province. They were mostly single men seeking to find gold and good wages to support their families in their home villages. Few found success in California's gold mining fields. Many found work in agriculture and new industries that were forming in California. Even more Chinese found employment building the transcontinental railroad in the 1860s. With the railroad's completion, Chinese workers sought new employment in the labor market of the western United States. Some found work constructing other railroads, but most looked to other regions of California, including the Santa Clara Valley.

By the 1860s, the Santa Clara Valley was moving away from ranching and grain farming to horticulture, a labor-intensive industry. Fruit trees and vegetables had to be planted, weeded, harvested, and processed by hand. Industries necessary to sustain horticulture quickly appeared in San Jose. Once harvested, products had to be packed for shipment to market. Early on this consisted of wrapping and boxing fruits and vegetables. With ever-improving canning technology, foods were given longer shelf lives, increasing the value and importance of the valley's products. Though increasingly mechanized, canning required extensive manual labor for cutting, soldering, filling, and sealing cans. Completion of new railroad lines opened up new markets by providing rapid shipment of products in refrigerated cars. Produce could be shipped to points further east than had been previously dreamed possible. Advances in the canning and shipping processes opened global markets to Santa Clara Valley fruit and vegetable growers. The result was a thriving industry focused not only on the planting and harvesting of agricultural products, but their processing (canning) and the manufacture of the machines used in the canning process. Many Chinese found their way into San Jose's fruit packaging industry.

San Jose's industries extended beyond those directly related to horticulture. Refinement of animal products was one of California's earliest industries, and manufacturing companies involved in this task appeared early on in San Jose's history. One enterprise, the G. H. Farthing Company, reduced leather to finished hand coverings. Another, the San Jose Woolen Mills, refined raw wool to finished clothing. Both companies made extensive use of Chinese labor.

The Chinese were a presence in San Jose and surrounding areas from the early 1850s.[1] Census information from 1860 gives the Chinese population in Santa Clara County as twenty-two. By 1870, their number had grown to 1,525. Separate work camps were set up to house Chinese on job sites. San Jose's first separate Chinese community, the Plaza or Market Street Chinatown, was located in what is today modern downtown San Jose. This area provided the Chinese with a home base, where the men could find contacts for jobs, pick up their mail, buy provisions, celebrate feast days, gamble, and worship at the local Joss houses. This Chinatown burned in 1870. Local Chinese temporarily moved to the area of Vine Street, close to the Guadalupe River. By 1872, the Chinese had rebuilt Plaza Chinatown. Ng Fook, a wealthy merchant from San Francisco, provided funds to construct several brick buildings.[2]

From the 1870s to the 1880s, Santa Clara County continued to attract growing numbers of Chinese because of demands for their labor in the fruit- and vegetable-growing industries. The 1890 census reported an all-time high of 2,723 Chinese in the county. Census information likely underestimates the population, especially of the itinerant workers. Santa Clara County's Chinese population swelled during planting and harvest times. Residents of temporary work camps constructed on farms, ranches, and industrial areas may not have been counted by census officials, depending upon when the census was taken. The numbers of Chinese in a particular area varied with the season. Chinese women and children were rarely counted in the census.

AN ENVIRONMENT OF DISCRIMINATION

Almost from the beginning of their immigration, the Chinese faced hostility in California's mining districts and fledgling towns. When California began to experience an economic decline in the late 1860s, reactions against the Chinese by the Euro-American population became more pronounced. A serious anti-Chinese action occurred in 1867, when an "anti-coolie club" attacked Chinese laborers working on the Potrero Railway in San Francisco. A crowd of several hundred injured a dozen Chinese men, destroyed barracks and a shed at the job site, and threatened to storm nearby industries that employed Chinese. Historian Alexander Saxton labeled the Chinese the "indispensable enemy."[3] They were a cheap, expendable labor force that West Coast producers could exploit to successfully compete with East Coast industries. During the 1870s and 1880s, the Chinese represented approximately 8 percent of the total population, but were a much larger portion of the actual labor force, as they were primarily adult men of working age.[4] Saxton estimated that one-quarter of the wage earners in California were Chinese during this time, although that figure seems inflated.[5] Chinese immigrants, no matter how necessary their labor, frequently proved a ready target of discrimination and racial hatred. Similar to the experience in the rest of California, Chinese in San Jose were frequently met with prejudice and hatred, and sometimes with violence. As early as 1870, San Jose's city council had passed several ordinances that were directly aimed at harassing the Chinese community.[6] Some local manufacturers, riding the wave of anti-Chinese labor sentiment, refused to hire Chinese.

Anti-Chinese sentiment in the United States resulted in the Chinese Exclusion Act, signed on May 8, 1882. This law suspended the immigration of Chinese laborers into the country for ten years and forbade all Chinese from becoming citizens. Only merchants, scholars, diplomats, American-born Chinese, and their families were allowed entry into the country. President Grover Cleveland signed the Scott Bill in October 1888, which reinforced the Exclusion Act. In 1892, the Geary Act was passed, extending the exclusion act for ten additional years. The Geary Act required all Chinese living in the United States to carry certificates of residency that included a photograph. Merchants were also required to register their stores and prove that all partners listed were indeed legitimate, and not "paper merchants" only. These laws were aimed at restricting the movement of Chinese and discouraging them from settling in the United States permanently. The Chinese Exclusion Act and similar laws resulted in declining numbers of new Chinese immigrants.

THE WOOLEN MILLS CHINATOWN

On May 4, 1887, firelight illuminated the skyline of San Jose. An arson's torch brought an end to San Jose's second Plaza Chinatown. Many local officials praised the passing of the Chinatown. They had considered it a blemish on an otherwise promising San Jose. "Chinatown is dead. It is dead forever," rejoiced the *San Jose Daily Herald* of May 5, 1887. The *Daily Evening News* of April 17, 1888, declared that "we have a right to be proud, gentlemen, of the fact ... [of] the eradication of Chinatown which for twenty years depreciated the value of the neighboring property." The establishment was soon to be disappointed. While the coals of Plaza Street Chinatown cooled, plans were being laid for not one but two new Chinese communities in San Jose.

Working with a German immigrant named John Heinlen, part of San Jose's Chinese community made arrangements to build a new town at Taylor and 6th Streets. Working against public sentiment, Heinlen leased the land to the Chinese, with whom he identified as a new immigrant himself. Connie Young Yu's book, *Chinatown San Jose U.S.A.*, documents the history of this town. Founded in 1887, Heinlenville existed until the 1930s, when Heinlen's descendants went bankrupt.

Also in 1887, some of San Jose's Chinese community planned for the construction of the Woolen Mills Chinatown, across the street from the Woolen Mills factory, on Taylor Street, adjacent to the Guadalupe River. The Woolen Mills Chinatown was built upon land leased by local entrepreneur Mitchell Phillips to Ng Fook, a prominent San Francisco merchant who was very active in San Jose's Plaza Chinatown. Several Euro-American men were involved in the transaction including W. T. Wheeler, who was noted as the "business agent for the Chinese."[7] Local newspapers variously refer to the new town as Mitch Phillips's Chinatown, Phillipsville, Wheeler's Chinatown, Ng Fook Chinatown, or Ah Fook Chinatown.

As a result of the exclusionary acts, Chinese businessmen frequently had to rely upon Euro-American "front men" such as Mitch Phillips to officially conduct their business, represent them in court, and purchase the property upon which the Chinese lived and operated their stores. While many of the front men may have truly been sympathetic to the Chinese, others were likely simply taking advantage of a business opportunity. The result is that documentary accounts of the relationships between Chinese and Euro-American businessmen are vague and sometimes contradictory, and the history of Woolen Mills Chinatown is no exception.

The San Jose press advocated the Chinese settling in the Woolen Mills Chinatown rather than Heinlenville.[8] A newspaper reporter interviewed Mitchell Phillips, an associate with the real estate firm of Bailey & Phillips. Apparently acting as the leasing agent for Ng Fook, Phillips stated that "In regard to the lease of the Hoefler property below the Woolen Mills, I have been informed that a fruit orchard will shut off the town from the view of the people living on San Pedro street. The nearest house will be 1,000 feet away."[9] In their minds, the town had the advantage of being away from the center of San Jose. The proposed town would be close to only a few landowners, and in an industrial enclave of the Woolen Mills and G. H. Farthing Glove Company. The prevailing sentiment of the local press was that if the Chinese could not be evicted, burned out, or otherwise forcibly removed, they should be as far out of sight as possible. A news article in the *San Jose Daily Mercury* summarized why the Woolen Mills Chinatown was considered the more desirable option: "No buildings will be erected within 300 feet of San Pedro street, and Chinatown will not be visible from this thoroughfare."[10]

A local councilman, Mr. Dunlop, informed the *San Jose Daily Mercury* that at the next meeting of the city council he would "offer a resolution providing that no Chinatown shall be established on the Hoefler tract unless the lessees lay a stone-pipe sewer to connect with the main sewer, at their own expense, and also make the proper house connections before occupying this town."[11] Dunlop reveled in the fact that the connection to the main sewer was nearly 1,000 feet away, so that the expense of the work would be considerable, and he suggested laying other "aggravating" costs upon the Chinese as well. The news article went on to speculate that Ng Fook controlled only one-fourth of the local Chinese and would not be successful in completing his plan for a new

Chinatown. Dunlop's resolution went before the city council two days later, on June 27, 1887. The mayor of San Jose declared the resolution to be out of order.[12]

Determined Chinese went ahead and built their town anyway, primarily backed by Ng Fook, one of the financiers of the Plaza Chinatown. What happened in the interim to the previously "out of order" resolution is not clear from the documentary records, but on October 3, 1887, the "City Engineer was instructed to prepare plans and specifications for a sewer on Taylor Street from 1st Street to the Guadalupe River." Further, a deputy was appointed to notify the property owners that they were to connect with the sewer.[13] On October 31, 1887, R. Ferrell received the contract for the sewer construction on the basis of his low bid of $790.[14]

Although relatively expensive, the sewer system was only part of the overall cost. When all was said and done, it was estimated that construction of the Woolen Mills Chinatown "cost about $15,000."[15] The sewer system alone accounted for more than 5 percent of those costs. An 1887 Sanborn Insurance Map shows other constructions in the new Woolen Mills Chinatown: five tenement buildings (two of brick and three of wood), a wood-frame storage building, and two wood-frame "Chinese tenements." The "tenements" were wood-frame row houses that also likely housed several merchants.

Over the next decade, the Chinatown continued to grow and apparently prospered, despite the death of Ng Fook the year after its construction. By 1889, a theater and two-story temple had been constructed. Dupont Street served as the commercial center of the Chinatown. Four rows of brick buildings lined the southern end of Dupont and two rows of wood-frame buildings lined Dupont north of Taylor. These buildings housed Chinese stores and "tenements" with several storefronts for general merchants. Merchants frequently lived in their stores, on the top floor if one existed, or at the back of the store. Two rows of wood-frame tenements also fronted Stockton. The Garden City Cannery, owned by another of the town's leaders, Chin Shin, provided the anchor for the northeast end of town.

An 1891 Sanborn Insurance Map depicts the town at its height (figure 21.1). Shown is the temple ("Joss house"), the theater, two restaurants, a barbershop, a laundry, stables, a cook house, several warehouses, the Garden City Cannery, roasting kettles, "tenements," and "gaming and sleeping rooms." The gambling houses apparently had rear doors as well as entrances facing the street. A news article notes that a would-be assassin escaped local policeman by running through the rear entry.[16]

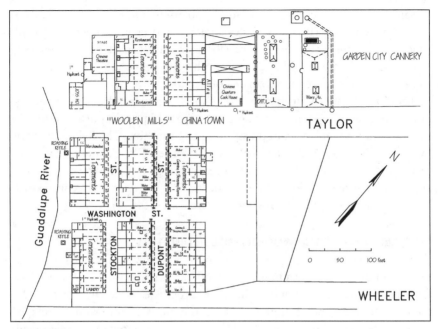

FIGURE 21.1
Map of Woolen Mills Chinatown, San Jose (Drawing adapted from 1891 Sanborn Insurance Map.)

Like many of the American West's early frontier towns,[17] the Woolen Mills
Chinatown catered to a primarily single men's society. At least one set of immigration papers indicates that women and children were living in the
Woolen Mills Chinatown, but their numbers were few. In part this was due to
the restrictive immigration laws for Chinese women. In addition to the merchants' stores, dwellings, barber shops, and restaurants, the community may
have supported gambling and prostitution, for which stores may have served
as fronts. The Chinatown also likely supported opium shops, which were not
made illegal until the early 1900s. Gambling was illegal, but persisted because
many officials looked the other way, although local police frequently publi-
cized their raids to appease local critics.[18]

By the turn of the century, Woolen Mills Chinatown was nearing the end of
a slow decline. The 1900 census shows that manufacturing jobs were few in the
Chinatown by this time. Only six Chinese were listed as laborers in the Woolen
Mills. More than half of the population (forty-seven) was listed as farm laborers. Other occupations for town residents were housekeeper/servant (three),

servant (five), fruit picker (one), head of a boarding house (ten), merchants of general merchandise (two), vegetable peddlers (two), chair mender (one), cook (one), laundry men (six), and general laborers (nine). Census records generally listed a head of household and several other residents, indicating anywhere from three to sixteen men in a single household.

The 1901 Sanborn Insurance Map shows a much-reduced community, only a shadow of the once thriving town. Chin Shin, an important leader in the community, had left around 1897 to return to China. The Kelley Laundry, owned by an Anglo-American, replaced his Garden City Cannery. Having already survived the death of one of its leaders, Ng Fook, the town could not apparently survive the loss of a second. In 1902, the already declined town burned to the ground under mysterious circumstances.

ARCHAEOLOGY AT THE WOOLEN MILLS CHINATOWN
Contemporary documents present two contrasting views of San Jose's China-towns and their residents. On the one hand, the Chinese were viewed as dirty, foreign undesirables who undermined the "progresses" made by American labor. On the other hand, they were an industrious people who persevered against severe discrimination to build a comfortable home in a foreign land. How is it possible to find the "truth" about the residents of Woolen Mills Chinatown?

Archaeology offers one way to look at the past without the cultural bias and prejudices so frequently exhibited in historic documents. Material remains of the past can be interpreted, but they cannot be changed. Information about diet, customs, recreational activities, and a sense of the local economy is all contained within the earth. During the late spring and fall of 1999 archaeological excavations were carried out at the Woolen Mills Chinatown site (CA-SCL-807H). Excavations were prompted by the widening and realignment of the Guadalupe Parkway in San Jose. New construction undertaken by the California Department of Transportation (Caltrans) has now completely destroyed the site of the Woolen Mills Chinatown. Prior to that occurrence, Caltrans funded data recovery excavations at the site.

Using historic maps as a guide for the town layout, archaeologists directed two backhoes to remove several feet of fill that had accumulated on the site since the town's abandonment. When the ruins of the town were revealed, careful hand excavation began. Using shovels, trowels, brushes, and picks, archaeologists slowly peeled back the layers of rubble and soil in search of intact deposits and features that would provide information on how these people lived. When the digging stopped in the fall, what was exposed was a substantial, well-organized community.

Buildings and Streets

Building foundations were some of the first things uncovered. Most of the foundations had been disturbed. Scavenging (robbing) of brick from the abandoned town and later land-development activities impacted the remains. Despite these alterations, there was still enough of the foundations left to orient further excavation. Once the outlines of some key buildings were established, it was possible to accurately project where other important features should be located. Building footprints were evidence of the substantial structures that once stood there. The business district along Dupont Street, composed of brick buildings, presented to the public (Chinese, white, or otherwise) a substantial, lasting presence.

A number of wooden posts were identified in the backhoe exposure areas that corresponded to lot lines within each block. The wooden posts likely indicate fence lines dividing the areas behind the structures into individual yards. These yards provided residents space to conduct outdoor activities, such as tending gardens and drying clothes.

Archaeologists exposed several brick piers in the center of Dupont Street. It is possible that the piers served as supports for a canvas shade cover on this commercially oriented street. Awnings along storefronts were common at this time. They provided patrons some protection from the elements. This arrangement can still be seen in many modern Chinatowns. Though no historical records describe awnings in Woolen Mills, an 1884 map of the earlier Plaza Chinatown indicates wooden awnings that covered nearly all of the space between buildings. There may be a correlation with the Woolen Mills. If such is the case, the location of the brick piers indicates that the entire street was covered. This, in addition to the gravel laid down on the road bed, would have provided for a street passable in all weather. Overall, visitors to the Woolen Mills Chinatown would have encountered graveled streets that were a vast improvement over the nineteenth century's typical muddy quagmires.

Sewers and Water

Historically, San Jose was always troubled with annual flooding and dozens of free-flowing artesian wells. This problem was only compounded by regularly flooded outhouses. During the latter part of the nineteenth century, the importance of sanitation was being realized, and great leaps in technology were being made in waste removal. San Jose was on the cusp of this technology, making rapid progress in the design of sewerage systems. When the Woolen Mills Chinatown was proposed, the city made clear that it had no intention of letting them build without a proper sewer system, although not all of San Jose's contemporary neighborhoods were so blessed. Excavations at the Woolen Mills Chinatown identified and documented an elaborate sanitation system.

The system was constructed of a combination of redwood drains and ceramic pipe. Wood drains carried waste out of the house. They flowed into another wood main running along the rear lot lines. These connected into a large ceramic pipe that then flowed into the main under Taylor Street. This sewer main carried effluent to the city line on San Pedro Street and out to the bay. Woolen Mills's sewer was a state-of-the-art system at the time of its construction. The use of wood instead of all ceramic pipes brought the cost of construction down. The result was an efficient, cost-effective system that met the needs of the community and the city alike.

The Woolen Mills Chinatown also boasted a new hydrant system. Fire was always a danger, with the combination of wooden buildings and oil or gas lighting. Earlier fires at the Plaza Chinatown illustrated this hazard and provided a lesson for town builders. To battle any future threat of fire, several hydrants were constructed in the Woolen Mills Chinatown. These were linked to a well and pump, providing a reliable source of water.

Communal Cooking Feature

Figure 21.1 shows two "roasting kettles" west of the residential buildings, along the Guadalupe River bank. Excavation exposed the remnants of one of these roasting structures (figure 21.2). Archaeologists uncovered a round, brick structure resting on a flat, brick floor and filled with layers of ashy loam and artifacts. Bricks were laid with an opening at the bottom that served to clean out ash and debris. Adjacent to the structure, dirt around the bricks contained a great deal of large mammal bone, mostly pig. Inside, it was filled with ash, sandy soil, and many artifacts, including ceramics, more bone, and glass. Remains of three redwood posts were found in the dirt spaced around the brick floor, at the corners. These may be remnants of a rack that supported things hanging over the brick cooking feature, or a shade awning over the structure.

Archaeologists are uncertain exactly how this feature functioned. A notation for a pork-roasting furnace appeared on the 1884 Sanborn Insurance Map for the Plaza Chinatown that used the same mapping symbol as the 1891 Sanborn map of the Woolen Mills Chinatown. The cooking feature was likely

FIGURE 21.2
Excavated cooking feature west of Block 1 (Photograph by Jerry Doty. Copyright ©
Jerry Doty. Reprinted with permission.)

used for roasting animals such as pigs. Alternately, it may have functioned
more like a smoker. During different times of the year, a large kettle may have
sat on a grill and provided a heating place for ceremonial community stews.
Certainly the cooking feature indicates community food preparation and
meals, as does the notation of a Chinese cookhouse on the 1891 map (figure
21.1).

A Community Dump

During the nineteenth century and well into the twentieth century, urban residents usually disposed of their garbage in the most economic fashion available. This meant dumping or burying it in the back yard or dumping it in the
outhouse, especially when a new pit was being dug. Since the Woolen Mills
Chinatown was hooked up to an elaborate sewer system, using outhouses for
garbage disposal was not an option. Apparently, dumping refuse in the back
yard was not appropriate in this case either. City Council Minutes indicate
that during the late 1880s San Jose was working on developing organized
garbage pickup. While the city council was debating this, the residents of
Woolen Mills organized their own system of waste disposal.

Archaeologists encountered a large deposit of garbage adjacent to the Guadalupe River. This dump proved to be the largest intact deposit of artifacts recovered from the site. This feature is important not only for the quantity of artifacts it produced but for its concentration. Typically, in urban situations archaeologists find small backyard trash pits and privies full of garbage. In contrast, almost all of the refuse at Woolen Mills was concentrated in this one dump. This shows a level of organization contrary to the image of the Chinese portrayed in contemporary newspapers. The dump was sensibly located behind the main buildings, away from the center of town, removing garbage from the center of activity. Archaeological excavations suggest each dumping of refuse was covered with a layer of soil. This would discourage rodents and help seal in some of the smell generally associated with food dumps. Woolen Mills was not the rancid, garbage-strewn community so worrisome to San Jose's Euro-American residents. Archaeological excavations revealed a relatively clean community for its time, with organized waste removal.

Table settings and food preparation and storage items found in the community dump demonstrate residents' ties to their homeland, but also the influence of their settling in California. These remains show the sophistication of Chinese merchants in supplying town residents, and the town's ties to the greater local and national economies. Chinese pottery appears throughout the artifact assemblage. Numerous spoons and bowls used for individual servings appeared in numerous styles, including Bamboo ware, Celadon, and the polychrome Four Flowers pattern (figure 21.3). This pottery varies in its relative cost, from inexpensive to costly. Bamboo ware, the least expensive variety, was the most common ceramic type found. Brown stoneware imported from China carried familiar foodstuffs and also provided for storage of food after its initial use. Spouted jars, wide-mouth jars, large globular jars, and liquor bottles appeared in great numbers in the trash dump and in the areas surrounding the nearby cooking feature. Table settings manufactured in the United States and England expand the portrait of meals in the Woolen Mills Chinatown. Plain white earthenware and more elaborate transfer-printed platters, cups, and bowls illustrate the availability of Euro-American table settings. While the Chinese must have liked using objects familiar to them, they were also expanding their patterns of consumer behavior to include non-Chinese items. This may have been a matter of practicality (dependent upon trade routes and availability) or a matter of desire to try out new things in a new land.

Bottles from the community dump illustrate a similar pattern. A variety of spice and condiment bottles and jars indicate the continuation of Chinese

FIGURE 21.3
Chinese ceramics, Four Flowers pattern, arranged in a conjectured place setting (Photograph by Jerry Doty. Copyright © Jerry Doty. Reprinted with permission.)

food preparation patterns, as well as the incorporation of Euro-American spices into the diet. Some were likely used to approximate familiar flavors, while other spices were probably new to the Woolen Mills residents. From the proportion of Chinese liquor bottles, it is obvious that town residents still had a taste for hard liquor from the homeland. The presence of Bass Ale and Guinness Stout bottles demonstrates an adaptability of that palate for lighter refreshments (figure 21.4). A variety of American-made sodas are also present, indicating a newly acquired taste for something bubbly and nonalcoholic. Woolen Mills's residents were filling their needs with locally produced items, such as soda from the Golden West Soda Works and cream from the American Dairy in San Jose. These were complemented by regionally produced commodities, such as soda from the San Francisco Soda Works and medicine from the Rexall Drugs in Gilroy.

Items such as medicinal bottles give clues about the relative health of the population (figure 21.5). The variety of health-related artifacts also speaks to the continuation of Chinese patterns, but again the incorporation of new ideas and products. Medicine bottles containing locally produced liquids reputed to cure consumption and Chamberlain's Colic medicine imported from

FIGURE 21.4
Bass Ale, Chinese liquor, and American liquor bottles (from left to right) (Photograph
by Jerry Doty. Copyright © Jerry Doty. Reprinted with permission.)

New York provide direct evidence of serious ailments. Contents of a Laxall
bottle (also imported from New York) provided relief for temporary discom-
fort. Small vials filled by the town's pharmacy indicate the continuation of
Chinese herbal medicine. These bottles were intended for single dosage use.
Opium tins and pipe fragments show the use of this familiar drug for recreation, but also perhaps to help ease aches and pains.

FIGURE 21.5
Variety of Chinese and American medicine vials and bottles (Photograph by Jerry Doty. Copyright © Jerry Doty. Reprinted with permission.)

The community dump also produced substantial quantities of bone. Represented in this material are cow, pig, and a variety of birds and fish. As is common on many Chinese sites of the period, pork seems to have been the preferred food source. Fish is also highly represented in this collection. Some fish were caught in the adjacent river, others were shipped in from nearby ocean trade points, and yet more was dried and shipped to the town from China in brown stoneware jars. Archaeological remains of shellfish and other foods from the ocean included bay clams, oysters, abalone, pismo clams, crabs, and crayfish. Other fragments such as bits of eggshell and peach and plum pits round out a picture of dietary patterns and behaviors.

So What Does All This Tell Us?

The historical archaeology that took place at this site illustrates a lesson that has been learned before, but is different for every community. Stereotypes infrequently hold up under careful scrutiny. Many of the existing documentary accounts portray an isolated, unclean, cluttered Chinatown that Euro-American locals avoided whenever possible. The archaeology of Woolen Mills brought to light a well-planned, well-kept, sanitary Chinatown with wide, graveled streets, a hydrant system in case of fire, and a complex sewer system.

Contemporary documents such as newspaper accounts also frequently portray Chinatowns as isolated communities filled with strange and exotic items from China. Archaeology expands this picture. Residents of the Woolen Mills Chinatown were an integral part of San Jose's economy and social life. Historical documents note that the Chinese worked at many of the local farms, businesses, and factories. Many artifacts point to trade with the local Euro-American community. Chinese Merchants were linked to local, regional, national, and international trade networks. Woolen Mills Chinatown residents had access to a variety of consumer goods, and, like the rest of the San Jose community, they had choices in fulfilling their needs and wants. Overall, the artifact assemblage points to a complex material culture and diet of Woolen Mills Chinatown residents.

Archaeology holds a special place in the tale of San Jose Chinese community history, awareness, and activism. Archaeology at the Plaza Chinatown, San Jose's earliest Chinese community, occurred in 1986. A report was never written, but this excavation sparked an interest in local community heritage that continues today. A Chinese temple was rebuilt in Kelly Park, Connie Young Yu wrote the story of Heinlenville,[19] and the Chinese Historical and Cultural Project has been holding Chinese Heritage Festivals and exciting and educating locals about Chinese history and culture in San Jose ever since that time.

Excavations at the Woolen Mills Chinatown continued this pattern, contributing to community awareness and a sense of a past rich with history. Many of the Chinese who lived in the Woolen Mills community were recent emigrants, sojourners who intended to return to China. Others were second-generation Chinese Americans. Although the existence of the Woolen Mills Chinatown ended in 1902, its story did not. Many town residents either left for China or moved on to other California Chinatowns. Others stayed in San Jose, moving to Heinlenville, continuing the story at that location. San Jose's Chinese community today is thriving, testimony to the determination of San Jose's earliest Chinese American residents.

ACKNOWLEDGMENTS
The California Department of Transportation, District 4, provided funding for excavations and write-up. We would like to particularly acknowledge the assistance and encouragement of Mark Hylkema. We also benefited from the input and efforts of Connie Yu, Annemarie Medin, and Julia Costello.

NOTES

1. Yu (1991).

2. Yu (1991, 22).

3. Saxton (1971).

4. Daniels (1988, 15).

5. Saxton (1971).

6. Laffey (1993, 27).

7. *San Jose Daily Mercury,* 18 May 1887; 5 June 1887.

8. *San Jose Daily Mercury,* 20 June 1887.

9. *San Jose Daily Mercury,* 21 June 1887.

10. *San Jose Daily Mercury,* 20 June 1887.

11. *San Jose Daily Mercury,* 25 June 1887.

12. City Council Minutes (1887, 490).

13. City Council Minutes (1887, 544–46).

14. City Council Minutes (1887, 561–62).

15. *San Jose Daily Mercury,* 1 January 1888.

16. *San Jose Daily Mercury,* 24 September 1888.

17. Baxter (1997).

18. McLeod (1947).

19. Yu (1991).

REFERENCES

Baxter, R. Scott. 1997. "The Rise and Decline of Gold Hill: An Anthropological Look at the Changing Demographics of a Nineteenth-Century Boomtown." Paper presented at the Fifth Biennial Conference on Nevada History.

City Council Minutes. 1887. Various citations, given in text. Santa Clara County Recorder's Office, San Jose.

Daily Evening News (San Jose). 1888. Citation given in text. California History Room, San Jose Public Library.

Daniels, Roger. 1988. *Asian America: Chinese and Japanese in the United States since 1850.* Seattle: University of Washington Press.

Laffey, Glory Anne. 1993. *The Early Chinatowns of San Jose. Archives and Architecture, San Jose.* Manuscript on file with the author and KEA Environmental, Inc., Sacramento.

McLeod, Alexander. 1947. *Pigtails and Gold Dust.* Caldwell, Idaho: Caxton Press.

San Jose Daily Herald. 1887. Various citations, given in text. California History Room, San Jose Public Library.

San Jose Daily Mercury. 1887–1888. Various citations, given in text. California History Room, San Jose Public Library.

Sanborn Fire Insurance Company. Maps of Plaza Chinatown, Woolen Mills Chinatown, cited in text. On file, California State Library, San Jose History Museum, San Jose Public Library.

Saxton, Alexander. 1971. *The Indispensable Enemy: Labor and the Anti-Chinese Movement in California.* Berkeley: University of California Press.

Yu, Connie Young. 1991. *Chinatown San Jose U.S.A.* San Jose: San Jose Historical Museum Association.

22

The Chinese Immigrants in Baja California: From the Cotton Fields to the City, 1920–1940

Catalina Velázquez Morales

This chapter will discuss the routes and the process of arrival of Chinese immigrants to Baja California between 1920 and 1940. Analyzing the moment of arrival and the type of work that these immigrants did allows us to observe three waves of Chinese migration: the first, from 1899 to 1920, made up largely of farmers and renters of the Colorado River Land Company; the second, from 1921 to 1930, made up of merchants, political refugees, and clerks displaced from other states by anti-Chinese policies; and the third, from 1931 to 1945, made up predominantly of owners and employees of small shops, some of them already Mexican citizens. Focus will be placed on commercial, agricultural, and sociocultural activities that permitted the Chinese to climb the social ladder and integrate into the most important economic and political groups in the region.

THE MIGRANTS

The Chinese immigrants' situation was very difficult due to the harsh conditions in China at the beginning of the twentieth century. Many of these workers who left parts of Guangdong Province in southern China were forced to emigrate as a means of improving their economic condition. In some cases, it was their will to survive that pushed them. The farmers, who had only their knowledge of agriculture upon which to build a livelihood, sometimes signed contracts that were not in their best interests, hoping to achieve better living conditions for themselves and their families. In some cases, once they left their hometowns, they never saw their families again.

In the international treaties signed between China and powerful Western countries, there were no provisions to protect the Chinese workers from the exploitation to which they were submitted. On the contrary, the rule was to accept the entry of Chinese workers only to cover the areas of labor that were not currently filled by the local workforce. In the case of Mexico, the Chinese labor force advanced the development of the sisal hemp fields, cotton plantations, mining, and railroads, activities that acquired special relevance during the regime of Porfirio Diaz, when the entry of foreign capital was encouraged in an attempt to modernize the economy.

The Chinese, beginning in the middle of the nineteenth century, immigrated to work in places like Peru, Brazil, Cuba, Mexico, and the United States. They entered these countries by way of Mexican ports, such as Salina Cruz, Manzanillo, Mazatlán, Guaymas, Mexicali, and Ensenada, among other places (figure 22.1). Mexico's border was an important entry point for these migrants. According to the immigration service of Mexico, besides Baja California, there were large Chinese populations residing in the states of Sinaloa, Sonora, Tamaulipas, Veracruz, and Yucatan.

Due to the Exclusion Act of 1882 in the United States, the border region of Baja California became a pole of attraction for Chinese who were trying to evade deportation. Mexicali operated as a center of concentration for Chinese expelled by U.S. government officials in the city of San Francisco. Most of these Chinese did not know Asia; they were born in the United States and they were American residents. They did not wish to go to China and sought refuge in Baja California,[1] from where they might reenter the United States. To this group of migrants were added others who came directly from China through networks organized to transport them to the American continent.

At the beginning, the transportation of Chinese to the United States and Mexico was carried out by English and Chinese shipping companies; afterwards, the American companies, to protect their investments, would continue transporting the Chinese groups. A great number of Chinese immigrants who arrived at the Mexican coast were transported by American boats, although official communiqués tried to minimize this fact, or plainly denied it. A frequent route used by the Chinese immigrants was China-San Francisco-Mexico. By this time, one of the objectives of the American consular officials was to verify that the Chinese workers who were crossing their territory arrived in Mexico, the country that, according to the contractors, was their final destination.

These Chinese arrived in Baja California in different ways. Some were introduced as contraband from San Felipe to Valle Banderas.[2] Others were picked up by smugglers in San Diego or San Francisco and sent in small boats

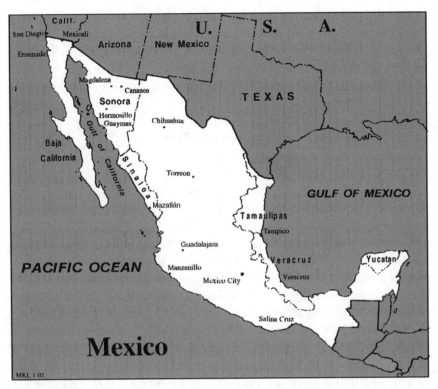

FIGURE 22.1
Map of cities of Chinese immigration, Mexico (Copyright © Murray K. Lee. Reprinted with permission.)

that rounded the peninsula to be off-loaded in the Colorado River Delta.[3] They also arrived on ships of the Compañía de Navegación del Golfo de California that called on the river port of El Mayor, located on the Colorado River.[4] This service was used by those who were in charge of conducting the Chinese all the way to the Mexicali Valley. The sea routes were complemented by multiple roads and trails that entered and exited the territory of Baja California.[5]

The immigration of the Chinese to Mexico was very profitable, regardless of whether the Chinese planned to stay in Mexico or were in transit to the United States, for the members of networks that organized the transportation of hundreds of workers, including recruiters, immigration officials, transport companies, public servants where Chinese settled, and especially, the companies that hired them.

The National Register of Foreigners lists the names of the regions in China that Chinese migrants left to settle in Baja California. Among those that appear most frequently are Boy San, Chung Shan, Foy San, Hoy Ping, Hoy Sang, Nam Hoi, Toi Sang, and Ying Ping.[6] All of these are situated in southern China, in Guangdong Province.[7] This province was the scene of constant economic and political upheaval, which may have contributed to the fact that, in the 1920s–30s, a great number of its population migrated to countries like the United States, Mexico, Costa Rica, Cuba, and Peru.

THE PROCESS OF ARRIVAL

Among the Chinese who entered Mexico during the first wave of immigration (1899–1920), we find that the farmers comprised two groups: those who possessed only their abilities as laborers and those who, in association with other Chinese, had the resources to rent a piece of land from the Colorado River Land Company.[8] In the former category, there is a correlation between the place of origin and the type of activity that the immigrants performed in Mexico. The laborers who came directly from China were assigned the hardest agricultural jobs in the Mexicali Valley, while the Chinese migrants who came from the United States arrived with the intent to rent land to plant cotton and to establish businesses in the city. Some Chinese farmers grew vegetables in their own plots and sold the produce in shops or through vendors who traveled through the agricultural camps, offering these products to the workers.

The success of these migrants can be attributed, in part, to a very solid bond between land, agriculture, commercial centers, and businesses situated within incipient urban zones of the Northern District of Baja California. These migrants created a foundation that later allowed the Chinese to have important measures of control over the production and distribution of their products. During this time, thanks to political and social contacts that they developed, they managed to consolidate their financial position, as they transferred their activities from the rural zones to the urban zones. Their participation in services increased. The tendency was to attain legal status in the country with the purpose of obtaining citizenship.

Between 1921 and 1930, the highest number of Chinese immigrants arrived in the region. It is said that between ten thousand and fifteen thousand Chinese arrived in the Mexicali Valley. Some came directly from China and others were displaced from other states of the Mexican Republic as a result of ever-increasing racist measures against them, especially in Sonora and Sinaloa.[9] In those states, the different political stances of the members of the immigrant community, because of the situation in China, manifested themselves in violent clashes. The authorities exploited these circumstances and expelled many from the country. Even those who avoided conflict were affected by the conduct of their fellow countrymen, and many had to close or sell their businesses, sell their other possessions, and retreat to Baja California.

The third and last wave of immigrants (1931–1945) is possibly the hardest to describe and the smallest in terms of the number of entries officially registered. During this period, the Ministry of the Interior (Secretaría de Gobernación) updated the Registry of Foreigners of Baja California. These records, although sporadic, allow us to reconstruct the characteristics of the Chinese of that time and, more importantly, suggest a comparison between the third group of immigrants and the first two groups who settled in the Northern District of Baja California. In this third phase, thanks to the political and social networks that the Chinese developed, they easily eluded the official instruments of control; some requested Mexican citizenship, remade their family life, and reorganized their financial activities. During this period, many Chinese children were born in Mexico.

INITIAL ACTIVITIES

Among the principal activities performed by the first wave of Chinese immigrants upon their arrival in Baja California were those related to fishing. In March 1879, the subprefect of the Central District of the territory noted that there was a Chinese fishing company that specialized in abalone and was located around the Isla de Cedros in the Pacific Ocean. The abalone that the Chinese junks fished in Baja California was transported weekly to San Francisco, via San Diego, on ships belonging to the Pacific Coast Steamship Company (see Bentz and Schwemmer, chapter 8 in this volume). Most of it was then exported to China and other Asiatic countries.[10] The fishing activity of the Chinese junks precipitated the development of the port of San Diego, due to the fact that they were the first fishing boats to go outside the bay.[11] The Chinese were the first to fish on a grand scale, covering the coast from San Francisco all the way to Baja California.

During these years, the number of Chinese immigrants arriving in the Northern District of Baja California was very low. We find only isolated references to illegal fishing by Chinese in the documents.[12]

FIRST DISPLACEMENT

The Chinese left their fishing activities for agricultural work when the Mexicali Valley developed and needed more workers. According to the projections

of the Colorado River Land Company at that time, the valley would be transformed into an agricultural emporium.

With the intention of solving the problem of a lack of laborers in the valley, the Agricultural Chamber of Mexicali became the main association in
charge of hiring workers, using recruiters to find Mexican workers from other
parts of the country. Unfortunately, when they brought small groups of workers to Mexicali, close to the U.S. border, the workers ended up going to the
United States, where they could earn higher salaries.[13] Because of this, General
Esteban Cantu, political chief of the Northern District of Baja California, pub-
licized the need for a large workforce for the cotton plantations of the Mexicali Valley. Once these jobs were open to non-Mexican workers, Chinese
quickly received preferential treatment. Combined with this, the Chinese who
rented land from the Colorado River Land Company preferred to contract
their own countrymen, who were willing to accept very low salaries and bring
their own equipment. According to Ye Can Chan, their working conditions
were familiar:[14]

> [T]he company and colonist gave them room and board and woke them up
> with a bell and in the same way they called them to lunch; in each job the Chi-
> namen had to bring his own tools: if he used a shovel, he had to bring it to work;
> if he used a plow, the same. . . . [T]hey used the same technique that was used
> in China, the plow was pulled by oxen. The tools were built for the most part by
> them.[15]

One Chinese laborer described the work as follows:[16]

> [W]e were dedicated to agriculture; that is, to cultivation of alfalfa and cot-
> ton. . . . [W]e planted it in plots, using a two-wheeled apparatus to plant the
> seeds, which were irrigated through canals, that is, that these canals were fed
> by the Colorado River; that means that these canals were built by my coun-
> trymen, who many of them stayed there, dead from the intense heat, in the
> Mexicali Valley, because most of it was desert, full of tumbleweeds, that
> means that here in Mexicali there was very little rainfall, that is why my coun-
> try men, when they could not take the heat, left for the interior, those that
> stayed had a hard time of it, because the way they lived and were treated they
> did not bear the heat, and one by one they died. There was one doctor, but
> because he charged too much, and because most of us did not make much,
> we didn't have enough to pay the doctor; we only had enough to half eat and
> buy the necessities; our main food was our own, that we bought every time
> that a food truck came to the fields.[17]

Given the difficult working conditions, it is no surprise that in 1923 Manuel Roncal, president of the National Agriculture Chamber of the Northern District of Baja California, informed the president of Mexico that each year the agricultural zone faced a problem of a lack of laborers to pick the cotton crop. Lew Chun, Lee Wing, and Wong Charm asked President Alvaro Obregon for authorization to bring in two thousand Chinese workers to solve the problem. These workers would be used exclusively in the cotton fields of Mexicali, which at that moment had about thirty thousand acres of cotton.

The officials approved and, with the influx of Chinese laborers, the renters of the Colorado River Land Company were able to fill the need "for an expanding agriculture [market], products of which were entering the benefits and drawbacks of a world market."[18]

During the agricultural year of 1915, from a surface of twelve thousand hectares, the Chinese harvested a crop of 20,851 bales of cotton. In a period of five years, the area dedicated to the cultivation of cotton increased to fifty thousand hectares, from which they obtained 79,200 bales of cotton. This level of production was maintained until 1930,[19] fundamentally relying on cheap labor from Chinese workers.

Colonization of this region only started between 1903 and 1905, and thanks to efforts to expand the Colorado River Land Company, alfalfa and barley began to be planted to feed the livestock. To cultivate cotton, the Colorado River Land Company introduced a great number of Chinese, who cleared and prepared the land for cultivation as well as dug canals. The work was intense, so that by 1915 we have the results mentioned above.

Besides their activities on the land, the Chinese involved themselves in local commerce, dedicating themselves to the sale of dry goods, clothing, shoes, and general merchandise. Furthermore, they opened hotels, laundries, and restaurants. Their success was based on hard work and an understanding of the alliances between land, commercial centers, and agricultural business. The fact that they overwhelmingly employed fellow Chinese made them successful in establishing strong networks within a growing ethnic community. The businesses located in Chinatown (La Chinesca) managed to control the dry goods businesses of the Northern Territory[20] as well as restaurants, hardware stores, hotels, and bars.[21]

THE CHINESE AND THEIR RELATIONSHIP WITH THE LAND

Among the best renters of the Ranch of the California-Mexico Land and Cattle Company, we find A. K. Joy, Chos Ming, Say (o Jay) Quan, and Lee Wing, representatives from Chinese companies that had contracts with the Colorado River Land Company. This shows the growth of Chinese investors, most of whom lived in the United States and had the money to invest in the cotton fields. They rented great tracts of land and sublet to colonists and farmers who worked the land according to very specific conditions: "With this system of employment, the dissatisfaction of the employees went directly to the renters, more than to the owners of the ranch."[22] The Chinese worker was employed to work the land, including preparing it for planting cotton and keeping the canals clean.

The Colorado River Land Company rented their lands to other companies, some of them run by Chinese who contracted their countrymen to work those lands. Many times the subletting companies did not pay the salaries agreed upon nor provide the days required for rest. Thus, the Chinese were not only employees of the Colorado River Land Company, but by subletting the land, they became entrepreneurs who hired other Chinese. "For the opening of new land for cultivation, it is not an exaggeration to say that the Chinese farmers have invested no less than one million two hundred and fifty thousand pesos in the last three years, and have on the whole, establishments and buildings that are permanent investments of capital in Mexico."[23] Joseph Richard Werne writes:

> The Chinese had to borrow great sums of money to finance their cotton crops. American businessmen gave them 24% annual interest, stipulating that the debtors should take their cotton for processing to the owner of their mortgage. In general, the habilitator felt that the colonists kept their word, but they felt more secured by the guarantee that Gral. Esteban Cantu gave them, when he offered to use every legal or illegal means to force the Chinese to honor their obligations.[24]

Esteban Cantu offered to use this type of pressure for the benefit of the renters of the Colorado River Land Company, whose partners were practically owners of the whole valley, and had sufficient power to press the authorities of the district to keep their interests safe. Years after the Chinese began working as farmers in Baja California, they organized themselves into farming associations, possibly to gain the capability to pay rent to the Colorado River Land Company and work the land independently. As mentioned above, they combined their agricultural activities with some commercial business in the urban zone, which coupled with their family structure made it easier for them to accumulate capital. This situation permitted them, a few years later, to leave the land and go to the city to dedicate themselves to industry, commerce, and services.

RANCHES

In 1919, according to Eduardo Auyon,[25] there were fifty Chinese ranches that had a combined total of 29,752 hectares of surface dedicated exclusively to cotton. The Chinese organized under cooperatives to sublet lands from the Colorado River Land Company and generally had the financial backing of groups residing in southern California. In 1919, between the ranches and businesses that participated in the cultivation of cotton in Mexicali, strong economic development occurred. It was during this financial bonanza that Wong Co Huen, who lived in the United States, arrived in Mexicali to look for Mexican associates. When the Mercantile Bank S. A. was established in this city, Wong became one of its officials.[26]

The Chinese ranches produced fifty thousand bales of cotton. Lau Jin, known as "the king of cotton," arrived from the United States with $2 million, which he invested in a dry goods store, two Chinese drugstores, and a ranch.[27] G. C. Cudahy, from Chicago, who by 1917 was apparently the third most important landowner of the Mexicali Valley, employed a great number of Chinese laborers to work 1,740 hectares of cotton. The biggest Chinese ranch was owned by Kam Li Yuen, who employed four hundred Chinese workers. The second in importance was owned by Tai Lin Yuen, who had two hundred employees; next were Kon Fou Yuen, Kon Ton Yuen, Kon Chan Yuen, Joi Yee Yuen, and the ranches Chinatown (La Chinesca) 1, 2, 3, 4, 5, and 6.[28] Auyon says that the number of Chinese farmers registered in the census who were thought to work on established small ranches and farms in the valley was very limited, although toward 1921 the census mentioned 1,942 farmers. In reality, the number was closer to ten thousand Chinese farmers.[29] The Chinese paid between one and ten dollars per hectare for the plots, depending on the condition of the tract.[30]

Nonetheless, in the 1930 census no Chinese ranches were registered. The names of the Chinese ranches disappeared. It is possible that they changed names or were affected by agrarian reform. The price of cotton fiber in that year reached fifty-eight cents a pound, and the Chinese ranches harvested thirty thousand bales per year during 1920–1930, each bale weighing five hundred pounds.[31] Even though the Chinese still represented the main labor force and were earning the lowest salaries, by the end of the 1920s, they largely stopped being employees and became merchants and artisans. Many of those who worked in the fields left for the city and changed their activities.

FROM THE FIELDS TO THE CITY

By 1921–1930, there was a second displacement in which the Chinese, after establishing networks in the fields, started to extend themselves toward another level of production. Loyal to their farming origins, they first worked and tilled the land, generally associating in groups, through which they could obtain a certain margin of profit. This allowed them to move toward commerce and small industries in the urban zones. Although the Chinese worked in rented fields, the security that farming gave them permitted them economic, political, and social status in the region. During this period, they consolidated their finances and, evidently, participated in social activities. There were many Chinese businesses that had the trade name "merchants and farmers" and covered the merchandising needs of local Chinese (import and export). Goods, many imported from San Francisco, were distributed wholesale and retail among small businesses. These activities represented a vital force for the development of the region.[32]

In Mexicali, the Chinese correlated commerce with farming. Among the most important companies that were created in this period was the Chinese Mercantile Mexican Company, organized by an association of Chinese merchants living in San Francisco. Likewise, the Casa Colorada (the Red House), with a capital of 300,000 pesos in gold, was represented by Fernando Yee Kee, its main partner. The main business of this company was general merchandise for its workers in the cotton fields.

The Nom Hing Cheung House, made up of merchants and farmers, sold all types of Chinese and Mexican merchandise. It had branches in Guamuchil and San Blas, Sinaloa, and in Nogales, Sonora. The Casa Blanca (White House) was the property of Him Sing and Company. They were general merchandise wholesalers and retailers and also owned a bar and a restaurant. There was also Chong Kee and Company, whose owner was one of the biggest plantation owners in the Mexicali Valley. The manager of this company was Samuel Chong, who at the same time was the representative of the Chinese Commerce and Agriculture Ministry. Other dry goods businesses that were no less important included the Mercantile Company and the John Kong company. At the head of the latter was Lee Wing, a cotton grower who had the most capital in the Chinese colony. The Imperial Hotel was a big investment; its general manager was Pablo Chee. The building was built by a Chinese cooperative society in which each member participated proportionally in buying capital shares. Many of the shareholders of this cooperative lived in San Francisco, in other cities of the United States, and in China.

The Chinese migrants also participated in other economic activities, such as industrial shops where they made shoes, cigars, and cigarettes, and sold most of these goods to their own people. Chinese industry and commerce was developed, on the one hand, to satisfy the demands of the Chinese community living in Mexicali and, on the other hand, to cover the needs of the local population. The first of these two points is related to the fact that the great majority of the Chinese migrants often preferred to buy what their countrymen produced.

The small industrial shops in Mexicali were developed by Chinese and quickly grew, propelled by the opening of the first shoe stores, tanneries, carpenter shops, auto repair shops, dry goods stores, bakeries, and pastry shops by Chinese.[33] Their ease in organizing associations and cooperatives helped Chinese to advance financially in just a few years. In the various places in the country where they settled, they advanced commerce and organized new financial alliances, as well as created mechanisms to provide supplies, even far from supply centers.

FINANCING

What happened with commercial activities, also happened in the financial arena. The Chinese migrants founded their own banks, which allowed them to establish their own rules for bank credit. The Chinese Mercantile Mexican Company (Wa-Mak Sion Mu Kun Si) was one of the most important firms that financed the Chinese farmers of the Mexicali Valley.[34]

About the Chinese, one banker writes:

> They had banks, they paid with papers written in Chinese; there was a bank next to the bar. Did you know El Barrilito? It had a bell, it was full of Chinese, and it was a bank, hardware store and general store, they changed checks and there on the corner, they called it the Red House, that was another Chinese bank, because it was divided in two parts, the land belonging to the Colorado River, for example, a Chinese company, let's suppose 5,000 acres and a green house here, another Chinese planted 5,000 more acres and this one had his bank, and then over here there was one that was called "Centinela," and that one was exchanged in Chinatown, in Chinatown Alley, right on the corner where there's a store that's called Dingo, next to La Malinche, those houses were general stores and hardware stores and all those things that you wanted, and they were banks at the same time.[35]

During this time the main clients of the banks were the farmers; later the banking system continued to develop as the cotton fields expanded.

COMMERCE AND LA CHINESCA

Mexicali's town council restricted the installation of Chinese businesses and homes to one area, near the border. A measure that had as its objective to segregate the Chinese from the rest of the population and to prevent them from prospering in their business activities explains why the Chinese congregated and developed a Chinatown, or "La Chinesca." This area was the center of important financial transactions, because in it the main Chinese businesses were located.

The Chinese did not forget cultural and recreational activities. They had two theaters, the Mexicali and the Loc-Kun, three teahouses, and twenty-eight associations, most of which had their own meeting places.[36] They had a hospital for the mentally ill, a school, and other centers that provided charity for the needy of their community.

One thing that is very clear is that the Chinese community from the very first years of existence built its own administrative, political, and social infrastructure to deal with the problems of its members. They were able to build all of this without neglecting their relationship with the local authorities, with whom they had established a tradition of cooperation in the development of public places, like parks and gardens, that represented a benefit to the general population.

La Chinesca experienced two fires, one in 1919 and the other in 1923. The second fire made clear to the local authorities that they did not have a reliable census count of Chinese businesses or accurate information on the types of activities in which these businesses participated. In addition, they did not know how many Chinese lived in "La Chinesca." But all of this was forgotten when a complex of corridors and subterranean rooms was discovered below the burned building. The local authorities did not have the slightest idea that these underground spaces existed.

The fire and resulting discovery contributed to increased speculation and concern about the habits of the Chinese. The underground spaces were speculated to be opium dens, thus fostering a stereotype of opium-addicted Chinese. The authorities at the time did not understand the cultural practices of the Chinese workers, and their lack of information helped to perpetuate stereotypes.

In hindsight, perhaps we can better understand the life of Chinese field hands from the Mexicali Valley who worked long and tiresome hours in extremely difficult conditions. We know that the city and the Mexicali Valley in the summer can reach temperatures nearing fifty degrees Celsius. It is feasible that the Chinese, after working extensive hours, needed a space that would provide optimal conditions for sleep. During the summer, they surely worked at night and rested during the day. To sleep underground must have been both cheap and convenient. Rather than being used for illicit purposes, the tunnels and spaces may have been sleeping areas for hot and tired workers.

CONCLUSION

Beginning in 1903, the first groups of Chinese workers arrived in Mexicali, brought in by fellow Chinese, farmers who lived in the Mexicali Valley, such as Chan Fuk Chau, Wood York, Ramon Lee, Charles Ung Ham, and the Ma brothers, Antonio, Agustin, and Mariano.[37]

The Chinese of Baja California were an ethnic group that developed a peculiar social dynamic. Unlike other foreign groups, the Chinese managed to incorporate themselves into the commercial and agricultural markets of the region, at the same time that they preserved the links with their place of origin, relationships that helped them to maintain cultural and social enrichment.

The process of immigration and the establishment of the Chinese in Baja California took different forms and followed different objectives, but the movement of Chinese into the area was constant. The first phase was an undulatory movement in which immigrants were pushed from the South of Mexico, toward the Northwest territories, and finally into Baja California. The same thing happened with the Chinese who were forced to abandon American soil (due to the Exclusion Act) and ended up residing on the Mexican border. The movement typically started slowly and gently and then gathered speed and momentum towards the U.S.-Mexican border.

The Chinese arrived, but they remained restless. They settled in fishing, then farming, and soon in business. Some ended their relationships with the sea to dedicate themselves to cultivating the land at the same time that they opened stores where they sold their agricultural products alongside other merchandise. Finally, they went to the city, so that few were still found in the fields, because they had shifted their capital to the urban zones of Mexicali, Tijuana, and on a smaller scale, Ensenada.

The ascending social mobility of the Chinese migrants was the result of their organizational structures. If one had to characterize the labor mobility of Chinese workers in Baja California, one would have to note their displacement from the sea to the fields and from the fields to the city.

The Chinese migrants in approximately fifteen years moved from economic activities of the primary sector toward the tertiary sector, and did so relatively easily. Unlike other ethnic groups, the Chinese managed to integrate themselves into the economically and politically strongest groups of the region. This was largely a result of their tendency to organize into cooperatives and associations, economic and social.

NOTES

1. Alfonso Salazar Robirosa, *Cronología de Baja California del Territorio y del Estado de 1500 a 1956* (Mexico City: Cuadernos Bajacalifornianos, Litografía Artística, 1957), no. 7, 82.

2. See Jose Angel Espinoza, *El Ejemplo de Sonora* (sin pie de imprenta, 1932), 62.

3. Nicole Marie Diesbach, *El proceso de producción agrícola en el Valle de Mexicali* (Ph.D. dissertation, Escuela de Ciencias Sociales y Políticas, Universidad Autónoma de Baja California [hereafter UABC], 1977), 55.

4. Aurelio de Vivanco, *Baja California al día, Distritos norte y sur de la Península* (Los Angeles: Wolf, 1924), 410.

5. Archivo General de la Nación (hereafter AGN), fondo Gobernación, vol. 245, sección s/s, 1906 (9), expediente 1, in Instituto de Investigaciones Historicas, Universidad Autónoma de Baja California (hereafter IIH-UABC), 1906.18 [38.8].

6. The names were registered in a very irregular way because they were written according to sound; there was no standard spelling or transliteration.

7. The southern region is part of the tropical zone and has the highest temperatures and the most rainfall in the country. In this sector, there are no harsh winters and the summer lasts for six months. Ren Meie et al., *Geografía Física de China* (Berseng, China: Ediciones en Lenguas Extranjeras, Colección Biblioteca Básica, 1984), 320–21.

8. Between 1904 and 1905 the Colorado River Land Company, an American firm made up of investors from Los Angeles and the Imperial Valley, bought most of the land that could be irrigated in the Mexicali Valley from Guillermo Andrade, which gave the Colorado River Land Company virtual control of the region. See Antonio Padilla Corona y David Piñera Ramírez, "El surgimiento de Mexicali," in *Mexicali: Una historia*, vol. 1 (Mexicali, Baja California: Instituto de Investigaciones Históricas, 1991), 186.

9. Espinoza, *Ejemplo de Sonora*, 395.

10. *San Diego Union*, 2 March 1872.

11. They were called junks after a similar type of sailboat that was used in the Middle East, on which sails made out of canvas were sewn over enormous bamboo

poles that kept them stiff in the wind. *El Pequeño Larousse Ilustrado. Diccionario enciclopédico* (Bogotá, Colombia: Larousse, 1999), 584.

12. In the third population census, of 1910, about 9,760 inhabitants are given for the rural areas in the territory of Baja California, Northern District, distributed in an area of 75,144 square kilometers, a population density of 0.1 per square kilometer. The foreign population was not registered. *Tercer Censo de Población de los Estados Unidos Mexicanos*, verified on the October 27, 1910, vol. 1 (1918), 33.

13. AGN, fondo Departamento del trabajo 496, file 12, 1922, IIH-UABC [1.31].

14. Fonseca Herrera gives an example of the kind of contracts that were offered to the Chinese, although this one is from Costa Rica, 1872:

Art. 1. Enrique Meigs Keith, Hubve and Grytcell are obligated according to the Supreme Governments concession, published in the Gazette of 15th April, that for 18 months counted from this date bring to Puerto de Pantanas [it does not specify the number] Chinese workers between the ages of 18 and 40. They should be healthy and will come with contracts signed by them or their mandarin. They will be obliged to work for their buyers during 8 consecutive years from the moment they arrive from China.

The contractors have the obligation to give them good food and enough of it, lodging, three changes of clothes. The work shift should not exceed 12 hours. They will have 3 days a year for their religious festivities, and medical care in case of sickness.

Art. 2. Upon landing they will be checked by doctors, who will be paid for by the contractor.

Art. 3. Each person should pay the company 350 pesos in local currency for each Chinese, half when he is told about the arrival and the rest would be paid 3 months later with 1% interest added.

Art. 4. In case the prepayment is not made, the company can sue for damages or keep the Chinese and contract them to somebody else.

Art. 5. The contractor must accept this responsibility from the government, which watches the fulfillment of that contract, especially the treatment they give to the Chinese workers. (Zaida María Fonseca Herrera, *Los chinos en Costa Rica en en siglo XIX* [San José, Costa Rica: Thesis, Facultad de Ciencias Sociales, Universidad de San José, 1979], 26-27.)

15. Ye Can Chan, interview, Archivo de Historia Oral, IIH-UABC.

16. Avilés Ana María, *Antecedentes Históricos de las actividades económicas de Mexicali* (Mexicali, Baja California: Instituto de Investigaciones Sociales UABC, 1983), 22.

17. Chan interview.

18. Humberto Rodríguez, "Salud y muerte en los trabajadores chinos de una hacienda consteña," in *Chinos culies: bibliografía y fuentes documentales y ensayos,* serie Historia, no. 2 (Lima: Instituto de Apoyo Agrario e Instituto de Historia Rural Andina, 1984), 152.

19. AGN, *Tesis resumida de Baja California* (Ph.D. diss., UNAM, 1958), 47.

20. Robirosa, *Cronología de Baja California*, 76–77.

21. *Minerva* (1930), published by the Honorable Chinese Colony. Photocopies are at the archive of IIH-UABC.

22. Edna Aide Grijalva, "La Colorado River Land Company," in *Panorama Histórico de Baja California* (Tijuana, Baja California: Centro de Investigaciones Históricas UNAM-UABC, 1983), 360.

23. AGN, Departamento del Trabajo, caja 1992, expediente 11/10, 1926, IIH-UABC [2.35].

24. Joseph Richard Werne, "Esteban cantú y la soberanía mexicana en Baja California," in *Historia Mexicana* 30, no. 117 (July–September 1980), 16–17.

25. Eduardo Auyon Gerardo, *El dragón en el desierto: los primeros chinos en Mexicali, 1903–1991* (Mexicali: Instituto de Cultura de Baja California, 1991), 50.

26. Auyon, *Dragon en el desierto*, 49.

27. Auyon, *Dragon en el desierto*, 51.

28. Auyon, *Dragon en el desierto*, 51.

29. Auyon, *Dragon en el desierto*, 56.

30. Auyon, *Dragon en el desierto*.

31. Auyon, *Dragon en el desierto*, 51.

32. The businesses included La Casa Colorada of Yee Kee and Company, on Juarez and Azueta streets, represented by Fernando L. Chisau; La Casa Juan Chong Lung y Compañia; the Nuevo París Café, managed by W. Lim Peters; Chong Kee y Compañía, on Juarez Street, represented by Samuel Chong; the International Supply Co. in the lobby of the Hotel Carrillo, today La Popular building; Pablo Chee y Compañía, on Madero Azueta and Ferrocarril (Av. López Mateos today) streets; Compañia Mercantil Mexicana, on Reforma (Teniente Guerrero) Street, represented by Lew Chun; La Casa Blanca, of K. Him Sing and Company, on Reforma and Azueta streets, today the site of the Garcia Merino building; La Casa Him Sang Lung y Cia, on Reforma Street; Hop Lee Restaurant, one door down from the gambling house called El Tecolote; The Palace Café of H. Yuen and Company, on Reforma Street; and the department store called Chewlee Singkee y Compañía, next door to The Palace Café, represented by Samuel León. Archivo Histórico del Gobierno del Estado de Baja California, Colección Peritos, caja 1, no. 60.

33. Vivanco, Baja California al día, 200.

34. Auyon, *Dragón en el desierto*, 52.

35. Carlos Flores Rodríguez, interview by Javier Hernández Gamboa, Archivo de Historia Oral, IIH-UNAM-UABC, M-18; also see Catalina Velázquez Morales, "Los chinos agricultores y comerciantes en Mexicali 1920–1934," *Meyibo* 3, nos. 9–10 (1989).

36. Auyon, *Dragón en el desierto*, 52.

37. *Cuadro Logial*, pamphlet of the Logia Simbólica Che Kung Tung, Archivo Histórico del Gobierno del Estado de Baja California, no. 9.

23

The Urban Pattern of Portland, Oregon's First Chinatown

marie rose wong

CHINATOWNS AND URBAN MORPHOLOGY

American Chinatowns are pieces of the historic ethnic urban fabric of American cities and no single event or trend can claim responsibility for the creation of these places. They have been described as "ghettoes," a term associated with negative images of slum-like districts of a city that are inhabited by a minority group. Like ghetto, the term "enclave" also suggests a specified boundary.[1] Enclaves are more specifically defined as tightly woven geographically and as places where the dominant group is isolated from the peer society. Socially, members of the immigrant population will identify with one another based on common experiences of culture, including race, tradition, relationships, and lifestyles. With respect to Chinatowns, the early social community shared, among other things, common origins, language, the stimulus associated with discrimination, and organizational affiliations that helped them to survive.

Enclave area boundaries are typically defined by a concentration of the common culture residents.[2] The boundaries that created Chinatown enclaves were not abrupt demarcations, such as a fence, but indications in the built environment that separated the enclave from the surrounding community. These indicators included mixed-use home and business structures that were occupied by the community, signs expressing their language, ornaments (flags, banners, statues), use of color to depict meaning and symbolism in ornaments (reds and golds for festive occasions, white for mourning), and kinetic places such as open markets or commercial stands that physically defined the area. Combined, these created symbolic and concrete boundaries that were recognized by both the peer society and the ethnic community over time. This image of enclave holds true of a number of old Chinatowns that formed before the turn of the century.[3]

It appears that in order for an ethnic enclave to be produced, the peer society needs to actively participate in the inhibition of its development, and an element of "external" coercion is most critical in the formula to create this type of urban spatial setting. In the absence of this, the morphology or urban pattern of the ethnic community takes the form of what could be called an ethnic urban "non-clave."[4] Where the enclave is characterized as being geographically territorial, the non-clave has no location restrictions, and the urban growth stages of the community appear diffused or scattered, as was the case with Portland's Chinese district. The term "Chinatown" is still used to acknowledge the ethnic district, but it relies on characteristics that are evident from the presence of the social community or the cultural and vernacular modifications to the buildings, more than the creation of concrete physical boundaries.

Beginning in 1851, and for at least one hundred years, the Chinese of Portland exemplified the non-clave morphology as they continued to partially or completely occupy buildings in numerous blocks throughout the downtown. The community was dispersed further by a second group of Chinese who were farming undeveloped land west of the central city and selling produce as a small farmer's cooperative. Viewed as two distinct communities, the urban Chinese had primarily settled along the flood-prone waterfront of the Willamette River, while their rural countrymen located in a marshy, far less developed area that was identified by Portlanders as the "Chinese Vegetable Gardens."[5] Beginning in the mid-1870s and for at least thirty years, Portland possessed two spatially and economically independent Chinese immigrant non-clave districts, which together were geographically unlike any other Chinese American settlement.

As "place," the American Chinatown was born of necessity, serving as a transient camp for migrant and seasonal laborers in the early 1850s. These areas became permanent and spatially compact urban settlements of businesses and residences, and were characterized by "foreign-looking" residents and an immigrant population of men.[6] With a supportive structure of family and district associations, they provided the source for a social network within the community. As an institution of social support, Chinatown offered an organizational base that supplied a personal and economic foundation for its population, and to some extent provided a substitute for the lack of traditional family life.

Most accounts that describe the morphology or urban pattern of China-towns identify their creation as a result of the escalating prejudice, violence, and unemployment that occurred from 1850 to 1900, in the critical period of geographic formation of the ethnic community. While federal Chinese Exclusion Laws did much to shape the demographic profile of the community, they directly contributed very little to the morphological pattern of Chinatowns. It has also been noted that the Chinese sought refuge in their own urban enclaves because of the need for socializing within the ethnic group and because of the prejudiced imposition of legal and economic sanctions.

San Francisco's Chinatown developed in an enclave pattern, where the beginning node of the community at Dupont (now Grant) and Sacramento streets developed into a ten-block area that has been described as "both a living community and a ghetto prison."[7] This city served as a major immigration station and a first stop for the vast majority of Chinese entering the United States. As the numbers of Chinese immigrants to that city escalated, and as coercion by exclusionists increased to have Chinese remain in one area and limit their potential "contamination" of other parts of the city, the Chinese continued to congregate within a defined geographic area of the San Francisco downtown. By 1885, Chinatown was a fully developed enclave, serving as home, economic foundation, and refuge to an immigrant community.[8]

The history of Seattle's Chinatown also exemplifies an enclave development pattern, but one that gradually shifted its location from the tide flats of the Puget Sound waterfront to a regraded area on the east side of the downtown, near the Union and King street rail stations.[9] Chinatown was an area that provided comfort to the residents in a familiar social setting, and was identifiable to the greater community by the exotic and romantic image of its physical appearance, much like the descriptions that were used for the residents themselves.

Unlike San Francisco or Seattle, Portland's early Chinatown did not follow the spatial pattern of an enclave, even in light of the commonalities or characteristic experiences that were present among all Chinese American settlements. National exclusion legislation was the seminal link for all Chinese, and is most readily observed in the imposed limitations to permissible immigration classes and the resulting demographic profile of a skewed society composed primarily of men and labeled as a "bachelor society." Portland shared the same gender imbalance that was evident throughout the Chinatowns of California, Washington, and Oregon, and between 1880 and 1910 the disparity between the number of Chinese males and females was at its highest for all of these states.[10] The physical environment of Chinese social settlements reflected, and was shaped by, the national demographic pattern of their immigration.

All Chinese immigrants shared in a culture that was significantly different than the pervasive Western and Eastern European backgrounds that formed the dominant white society in American cities. By birth, coercion, and choice, the Chinese were a foreign element within a blossoming identity of "American" culture and were typically thought of as "the most alien of aliens."[11] They were often deemed as unassimilable foreigners because of those distinguishing expressions evident in their race, dress, food, language, and traditions. Regardless of their presence as a majority ethnic group, particularly along the West Coast, or their desire to be a part of the American mosaic of customs, they carried a stigma that impeded their ability to assimilate and make the transition into societal acceptance. These social barriers eventually manifested themselves through geographic separation, first in rural settlements and later in the Chinese districts of small towns and large cities. While Portland's dominant society still perceived the Chinese as unassimilable, the outbreaks of racial violence that had corralled the Chinatowns in Seattle, Tacoma, and San Francisco and forced the expulsion of Chinese residents from downtown areas were absent.

POPULATION, ECONOMICS, AND SETTLEMENT PATTERNS

The greatest concentration of Chinese in the United States from 1870 to 1910 was along the West Coast, with California assuming the largest percentage of the population and Oregon retaining a strong second-place position.[12] The majority of these Chinese entered through San Francisco in the early years, with increasing numbers coming through the Northwest customs ports of Astoria, Oregon, and Seattle, Washington, after 1870.

By 1880, the total number of Chinese in the United States was 105,450, and California and Oregon shared over 80 percent of that total, with 75,132 and 9,510 respectively.[13] According to U.S. Census figures, California's Chinese population continued to decline after this date, while Oregon's population of Chinese steadily increased into the early 1900s. These shifts in population reflect changes in the political, and economic climate and public sentiment in both states, as the Chinese sought employment, personal safety, and a degree of acceptance. Unlike in California, broad-based employment opportunities for railroad work in Oregon lasted into the 1880s. At the same time, there was a strong need for labor in Northwest cannery and lumber industries, and for farm labor in the Willamette Valley. Even the antilabor stance of the exclusion laws did not prevent thousands of Chinese from migrating and entering the labor markets of Oregon. Most importantly, the general public opinion of Oregonians was in favor of using Chinese labor whenever possible, particularly since it contributed to building state and local economies. While labor unions achieved a degree of success in influencing anti-Chinese activities, such as restrictive local residential ordinances, community violence, and eviction from local job markets in neighboring states, Oregonians displayed more resentment at labor union members, who were viewed as outside agitators trying to exact control over local economies.

The economic boom in California associated with the discovery of gold in 1848 was an early attraction for immigrating Chinese, as was contract labor that was available from railroad work on the Central Pacific line from California in 1865. Even before federal intervention in Chinese immigration, objections from political and economic factions in California were surfacing, as the early exclusionists complained about the "foreigners" who were absconding with the state's riches. Miner's taxes were exacted in California and in Idaho, with the latter voiding any Chinese claim to mining land at all. As unemployment escalated and blame was assigned to the Chinese presence, many of them fell prey to robbery, attack, and murder from vigilante justice. Before any national stance was made to legislatively eliminate the Chinese "menace," states in the West Coast and Rocky Mountain regions were using legislative measures to inhibit work opportunities in hope of forcing the Chinese out of employment and their areas of settlement in small towns and mining camps. Even with the passage of exclusion laws, anti-Chinese riots did not stop, and in some areas conditions worsened. Many sharecropping Chinese were evicted from rural areas and sought safety in the growing Chinese quarters of American cities. More than a haven of protection, Chinatown offered the opportunity of an organizational structure that would supply a social and economic foundation for its male population and, to some extent, provide a substitution for the lack of a traditional family structure.[14] Forced from mining areas and left unemployed from the completion of the transcontinental railroad, many Chinese sought other employment in large cities along the West Coast.

When the Central Pacific Railroad was completed in 1870, activity toward building the Northern Pacific Railroad line in the Pacific Northwest was just beginning. Financial setbacks in construction costs slowed the process of completion and in so doing provided employment opportunities for Chinese workers in Washington and Oregon well into the 1880s. On top of an initial hiring of seven thousand contract laborers, an additional six thousand Chinese workers were brought into Oregon in 1883 in order to complete work on the line. Labor was in demand from canneries located along the Columbia River in Oregon and the Puget Sound in northwestern Washington. Work for logging companies, and other labor and service positions, such as farming and domestic, laundry, and restaurant work, provided the mainstay of employment for a majority of these immigrants. Beginning in the 1870s, some Chinese were employed in public works projects with the city of Portland, where they were hired to clear land for housing developments and build roads and drainage systems downtown and in the newly developing areas to the west of the city.

Portland had an immigrant demographic profile similar to other cities in the mid-nineteenth century in that it harbored a sizable population of European foreign-born. What distinguished this city is that by the 1890s, Chinese immigrants comprised a majority ethnic group, second in number only to Germans in the 1860, 1870, and 1910 population profiles. In 1890 and 1900, the Chinese outnumbered Germans and all other ethnic groups recorded in the city, and represented 25 and over 26 percent of the total foreign-born population, respectively.[15] During this same time period, San Francisco's Chinese population had decreased from 25,833 to 13,954, while Portland's increased from 4,539 to 7,841. This phenomenon can be directly linked to steady and consistent employment opportunities and the reputation of Portland as a safe environment for immigrant Chinese.

In their early years in Oregon, the Chinese lived primarily in Baker, Grant, Josephine, Jackson, and Umatilla counties. In the formative pattern of settlement, much like the early draw to California, these areas were the most attractive as they represented the major mining regions of the state and an economic resource for early Chinese. As Oregon's urban and rural economies continued to expand, the opportunities for Chinese immigrants to venture into employment areas other than railroad work and mining increased. As land became available for purchase, Oregon's Willamette Valley drew many migrating Western Europeans who had settled in East Coast and Midwestern cities, while Chinese immigrant workers found employment as laborers in the orchards and hop farms of western Oregon.

As with other cities, Portland had an ample supply of simple and spare boardinghouses, lodging facilities, and single-room occupancy hotels scattered throughout the downtown area. These dwelling units housed thousands

of male transient and migratory workers who represented the seasonal workforce involved in logging, railroad-line maintenance, canneries, and the agricultural work that was available throughout the state. In order to cut the high
cost of renting, a number of Chinese would crowd into a single room. Cities
and towns became temporary stopping places for the wealth of Chinese laborers, who bought supplies and remained for short stays as they traveled between work sites for seasonal and contract employment.

PUBLIC SENTIMENT, LOCAL POLICIES, AND CHINESE SETTLEMENT

In addition to shaping national political actions against Chinese immigration
through the adoption of federal Chinese exclusion laws, San Francisco had an
early and leading position in developing local ordinances intended to restrict
Chinese employment and living conditions, such as laundry and lodging-
house ordinances. Cities in Oregon and Washington enacted similar sanctions, though Portland was the least successful at adopting local discriminatory policies.[16]

Anti-Chinese organizations and labor unions such as the Knights of Labor
and the International Workingman's Party took active roles in voicing anti-
Chinese sentiments through political rallies, meetings, and publications, such
as San Francisco's *WASP* magazine, and the *San Francisco Chronicle*. Labor
party leaders Daniel Cronin and Burdette G. Haskell had led the Chinese riots
in San Francisco and had been successful in the expulsion of over seven hundred Chinese in Washington territory.[17] In Tacoma, the Chinese Quarters had
been burned and the population evicted from the city, with many of those
who fled reported to have relocated to a more tolerant Portland. In 1886,
Cronin and Haskell extended their mission to repeat the tactics and successes
that they had had in neighboring states and territories by gaining the critical
public and political support needed to rid Portland of the Chinese.

Cronin and Haskell advertised and held rallies and had a limited number
of supporters in Portland, but never gained the endorsement of prominent
citizens, nor the local newspaper, the *Oregonian*, and were consequently unsuccessful in leading an expulsion of Chinese from Portland. In general, the
citizen commentaries clearly expressed resentment at the behavior of any outside agitators who would come into the city and attempt to tell local authorities how to handle municipal affairs. Then, too, no one wanted to see a reen-
actment of the violence that had been witnessed in Seattle's and Tacoma's
Chinatowns. Portland mayor Gates had even deputized an additional three
hundred guards to monitor any rallies that Cronin and Haskell organized.

As editor of the *Oregonian*, Harvey Scott sympathized with national popular opinion that the Chinese could not be assimilated, and that they were basically an undesirable people, but he reminded readers that above everything, law and order must always prevail in Portland. After all, the Chinese did provide the city with a valuable service of cheap labor that was important for the economic growth of Oregon and that, in turn, kept the state's goods competitive with similar market goods manufactured on the East Coast. Scott's editorials reasoned with the public that Portlanders would not and should not want to do the menial and hard labor that the Chinese were so well-suited to do. With this in mind, no unemployment problems really existed. The message was clearly received. Haskell's attempts at anti-Chinese rallies were countered by an equally vocal local committee that supported the law and economic platform that the *Oregonian* had championed for Portland. By 1886, the anti-Chinese organizations in Portland had all but dissipated in favor of the bigger goals of continuing to bolster the economy of the state and use the ample Chinese labor that was at hand to build Portland into a world-class city.

Aside from the social profile of the city, the formation of Portland's early Chinatown settlement exhibited unique qualities that are most directly attributable to commitments made by the city toward economic growth. Building a strong local and state economy that was able to compete in national and international goods markets was at the forefront of local politics in the 1880s. This goal combined with a law-and-order platform that was supported by local government officials and popular media. Portland's Common Council members considered mimicking San Francisco as a model for enacting local anti-Chinese discriminatory legislation, specifically with respect to limiting their building occupancy to designated areas of the downtown. Adopting such an ordinance was abandoned because of enticing financial returns from high rental fees that were charged to Chinese tenants, who were willing and able to pay property owners and landlords of commercial buildings and land. The lack of local land-use restriction legislation allowed the Chinese to rent and own property, while local political growth concerns enabled them to participate in developing the community economy.[18]

As early as February 1865, when the Chinese population was at a modest two hundred, the *Oregonian* began an editorial crusade on the "appropriate" locations for the Chinese within the city.[19] Portland's first attempt to officially regulate a Chinese quarter of the city was proposed by the city's Common Council the following September. San Francisco had already defined part of their downtown for the Chinese to congregate. This was the example that *Oregonian* editor Harvey Scott preferred to the contemporary practice in Portland, where the Chinese had random and free selection to occupy almost any building throughout the central city. The prevailing attitude of the editor was that they provided a strong and willing workforce to the city, but that this attribute did not give them free reign to live wherever they chose in Portland. Scott continued to plead that an appropriate place for Chinese living quarters was a critical issue that needed to be decided before their numbers increased in the city.

PORTLAND'S RURAL AND URBAN CHINATOWNS: "NON-CLAVE" AND ENCLAVE

While Portland had not experienced large-scale violence against the Chinese, anti-Chinese sentiments were taking place in small Oregon communities and work camps. Rioting had taken place in the Albina, Oregon City, and Mount Tabor areas located east of the Willamette River. And like the rioting in Washington, these Oregon skirmishes resulted in many of the rural Chinese relocating to the city, in the Portland downtown area, where there was already a burgeoning ethnic community.

As a typical pattern of migration, mob violence that occurred in isolated small towns and rural areas throughout California, Washington, and Oregon led many Chinese to seek the support and safety found in populated urban environments, and most specifically in the area occupied by the Chinese quarters. These shifts in geographic location to leave agrarian and small-town settings for an urban lifestyle were the most obvious changes in the settlement of Chinese immigrants and mimicked the trend of the U.S. population. Prior to the passing of Chinese Exclusion Laws, about 80 percent of the Chinese lived in small towns and rural settings, while after the turn of the century, around half of Chinese Americans lived in metropolitan environs.[20] The Chinese of Oregon mirrored the national trend of people leaving rural areas for the city.

The "Chinese Vegetable Garden Community" occupied an area adjacent to the meandering Tanner Creek on the west side of the downtown (see figure 23.1).[21] The creek and the gully were laced with simple wooden huts or shanties, and the gulch was furrowed for planting. Initially, the Chinese were farming a modest three acres of land, but by the late 1880s they had expanded to an excess of twenty-one acres of fruits and vegetables. Truck gardeners or peddlers were a common sight in the downtown area, as the Chinese sold their wares to residences and businesses in the downtown, as well as the urban Chinese district.

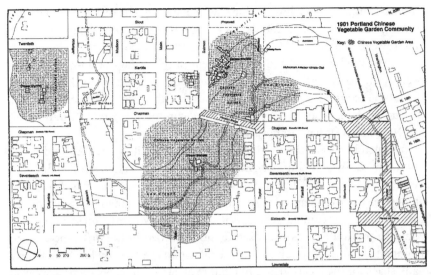

FIGURE 23.1
Map of rural Chinatown, Portland, Oregon (From *Sweet Cakes, Long Journey: A Social and Urban History of Portland, Oregon's First Chinatown*, by marie rose wong. Copyright © marie rose wong. Reprinted with permission.)

In the next twenty years, the city undertook a number of municipal changes to survey and extend urban growth to the part of Portland that was occupied by the rural Chinese community. Construction of the Multnomah Athletic Club and a number of expensive and exclusive neighborhood development projects took advantage of the natural amphitheater setting as a quiet place with large urban lots in a part of the city where affluent residents could escape the noise and bustle of the downtown. The new site opportunities existed because of the construction of culverts that controlled the creek's flooding, and because of the extension of city streets and expanded rights of way. The Chinese garden community responded by shifting the farming areas and shanties to less-developed areas adjacent to the creek. By 1908, a number of shanties were gone and the total number of peddler homes was dramatically reduced, as was the area of cultivation. The garden community now occupied less than eleven acres of land.

With the attrition of garden land due to expanding urban development, the Chinese rural community was also effected by new policies and ordinances that were being adopted for the downtown. In 1897, the Common Council enacted the collection of standard licensing fees, which would be imposed on all vendors within the city limits, along with a subsequent ordinance that pro-hibited peddlers on city sidewalks as a response to the complaints about the overcrowded walkways of the growing city. Any violators of the sidewalk or-dinance would be subject to imprisonment of thirty days or a fine of $50. In essence, the combination of development pressures and the ordinance pro-hibited the economic viability and livelihood of the rural Chinese and caused irreparable damage to the fragile gardening community. After 1910, the Chi-nese Vegetable Garden disappeared from public record.

In September 1865, the Portland Common Council drafted "An Ordinance to Prevent Chinese Using Any Building or Dwelling House for Habitation within Certain Limits." If passed, the law would have made it unlawful for any Chinese to use or occupy any structure without first obtaining written per-mission from the council. The specific locations where Chinese occupancy would be prohibited was purposefully not included in the ordinance. It was the intention of the council to allow for flexibility in the city law by leaving a blank space for the location and filling it in at a later time, depending on what part of the city was viewed as needing protection from Chinese occupation.

After a second reading and approval by the Common Council, and follow-ing review and comment by the city attorney, the ordinance was indefinitely withdrawn from consideration. While the council argued that the Chinese should be treated as any other "nuisance" in the city, the city attorney's decid-ing finding was that the rights of the Chinese to live as citizens of the state of Oregon precluded any possibility of legislation that prohibited them from also living wherever they chose to in the city.

In the years to follow, the *Oregonian* continued to support the position that city officials should try to quarantine the Chinese, as is evidenced in a series of editorials that referred to "the Chinaman disease that was permitted to oc-cupy the heart of town or any prominent quarter of it."[22] There were some in-dividual property owners who agreed that the Chinese population should be contained at the outskirts of the city, and who refused to rent property to Chi-nese as a public service to the community. In the absence of a legal mechanism to "corral" the ethnic population, the choice of where Chinese could live and operate their businesses was left to private market supply and demand. Any hopes of resurrecting an ordinance to prescribe a Chinese enclave in the city was diminished by those people who were anxious to prosper by renting prop-erty to the Chinese. Even the *Oregonian* conceded that no one could complain about the presence of the Chinese as long as there was no consensus on a means of prohibiting their ability to rent wherever they wished.[23] In the absence of a restrictive ordinance, there was little to prevent the Chinese from constructing or owning a structure, or from renting rural land or urban property.[24]

As long as there were landlords willing to rent property and buildings and the Chinese were willing to pay for the privilege, their presence throughout the community was inevitable. The earlier and strongly expressed opinions for advancing the economic interests of the state were more important than debating the right of Chinese to rent property throughout the state, which in turn kept the Chinese community from developing into a coerced spatial location within the city. Forming part of the urban fabric of the city at the height of the Chinese presence, the residences and businesses of the Chinese were scattered across downtown among the rest of the downtown businesses, and clearly did not exhibit the spatial definition of an "enclave."

Rental fees for two-story buildings continued to escalate in price in the downtown. In 1873, the price range for these buildings was from $125 to $500 per month, and by 1880 the Chinese were reported to pay between $800 and $1,000 per month.[25] The ability of the Chinese to pay the asking price was far too enticing for a landlord to turn them away, and it was particularly lucrative to rent or sell land that was near the Willamette River, since the adjacent flood-prone properties were deemed to be unsuitable for "white" occupancy.

Family and district associations helped to locate housing in the typical, communal room and boardinghouse arrangements that were pervasive in Chinatown. This housing type reflected the low numbers of traditional families and responded to the needs of the all-male households of the bachelor society. It was common practice in the West Coast Chinatowns to have a structure rented by a sole proprietor or merchant partners, with business uses located at the street level. Other floors of the structure would then be parceled out into living quarters and boarding facilities for laborers or used for special functions, such as the community's Chinese associations. As in San Francisco, it was not unusual to see overcrowded boarding facilities with as many as thirty men in one small room, as laborers tried to save money on meager accommodations.[26]

In the absence of a restrictive housing ordinance, there was little to prevent Portland's Chinese from constructing or owning a structure, or from renting urban property from whomever they could, irrespective of the cost. Chinese merchants and labor contractors Moy Back Hin and Seid Back both purchased a number of properties in Chinatown, some of which were used for their own mercantile enterprises.[27] After 1923, the ability of Chinese to purchase property was halted when the state followed suit with six other Western states, including California, in forbidding anyone ineligible for naturalization to purchase or own land.[28] But by the time this law had passed, the wealthy Chinese of Portland, along with syndicates backed by merchant memberships, had already established themselves as owners of some of Portland's downtown lots and buildings, making for an urban pattern that in no way resembled a well-defined and contained geographic enclave. Portland's action not to pursue adoption of an ordinance remanding that the Chinese operate businesses within specific locations of town is most evident in their settlement pattern. The community was a shifting settlement in the downtown area and remained so until the 1960s.

Between 1863 and 1926, Chinese-occupied buildings formed a scattered pattern of occupancy within the downtown, with no formation of an ethnic enclave. Unlike in San Francisco and Seattle, what could be identified as a node or center of development of the Chinese community did not begin to form until the Chinese had been in Portland for twenty years. The node, at the intersection of Alder and Second streets, served as the location of the community bulletin board and was the source for news from China and other Chinatowns, and of local events. By 1879, the Chinese had partially occupied structures in forty-nine blocks scattered throughout the downtown, an increase from thirty-four blocks in 1875. The developing node continued to expand and eventually filled in all of the block faces of the intersection.

By 1900, Portland's Chinese population had peaked, as had their residency and business occupancy of the downtown. In a mix of contiguous businesses distributed throughout the central business district, the Chinese were now occupying parts of fifty-six downtown blocks; Chinese buildings included the Chinese Benevolent Association, thirty-eight gambling houses, thirty-six "female" boarding houses, three theaters, and six Joss houses (figure 23.2).[29]

The first two decades of the twentieth century put Portland into another cycle of a building boom, and during this time a few specific events can be credited with the beginning of the decline of the Chinese district and to its subsequent relocation. City officials embraced the then popular nationwide city beautiful movement, and intended to improve the downtown by implementing numerous citywide public works projects that would clear land for redevelopment and improve transportation, sewer, and drainage systems.[30] Downtown redevelopment continued to enhance the escalating property values. A single lot that had sold for $20,000 in 1902 was valued at $350,000 in 1906. The district that served as home and provided the economic livelihood

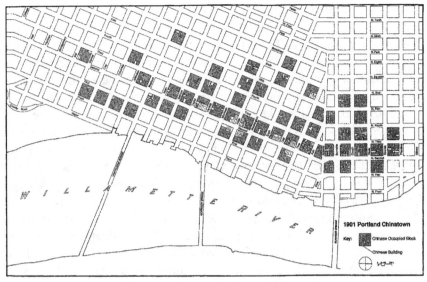

FIGURE 23.2
Map of urban Chinatown, Portland, Oregon (From *Sweet Cakes, Long Journey: A Social and Urban History of Portland, Oregon's First Chinatown*, by marie rose wong. Copyright © marie rose wong. Reprinted with permission.)

for the Chinese community became an attractive place for redevelopment. In the midst of this period of new construction, the Chinese were an important part of the labor force needed for municipal building projects, but were simultaneously losing their business and residences in the old structures in the downtown that were targeted for replacement.

As land values continued to increase, the *Oregonian* reported that the Chinese were continuing to relocate their businesses to a district north of the downtown, in an area that had already become the site of a number of businesses and tong factions. The physical split of the community between the north and south of the Burnside Street axis created separate identities for the two districts, as "Old Chinatown" in the south downtown and "New Chinatown" in the north. In truth, relocation decisions were not that easily accepted by the Chinese community, and there was a lengthy debate in the Benevolent Association as to which area was most suitable. The most notable and established Chinese merchants and property owners preferred the older, southern downtown district, while tongs and newly forming Chinese merchant cooperatives were pooling resources to build mixed-use megastructures in the less-expensive northern industrial area of the downtown. Seid Back and Moy Back Hin had anticipated that the issue of establishing an "official" Chinese district in the city was inevitable and both men implemented their preference by leasing land and constructing properties in an effort to see the Old Chinatown remain. Irrespective of land values, the Chinese in Old Chinatown were not conceding to any quick move, and if anything, the ethnic community was even more scattered throughout the entire downtown.

In 1909, Old Chinatown lost occupancy of its development core at Second and Alder streets because of expired leases and the intentions of local owners to redevelop the area with modern high-rise office structures rather than retain the old two- and three-story buildings. Although a local newspaper reported that the "old and picturesque Chinatown [was] passing away rapidly," the reality was that the transition was a slow and steady decline and that the Chinese community had also spearheaded some of the location decisions, as less-expensive property was being acquired in "New Chinatown."[31] One by one, site redevelopment dissipated the core businesses of the district, and the steady erosion of the ethnic community continued for another thirty years. In the early 1940s, the last of the Chinese buildings and businesses along the Front Street waterfront were demolished and, by 1950, only four buildings were recorded as being leased by Chinese merchants in the Old Chinatown. For the first time since their arrival in Portland one hundred years earlier, the majority of the Chinese were concentrated in one location with discernible visual boundaries that segregated the Chinese and their businesses and homes from the greater Portland community. With no further need to differentiate the two separate districts, north downtown was simply identified as "Chinatown" and finally assumed the pattern of an ethnic urban enclave.

As a place within the city, Portland's Chinese immigrant community epitomized the non-clave description between 1850 and 1940, as there never was a specific district or zone of the downtown that created a perceived barrier between them and the dominant community. Rather, the location of "Chinatown" continually shifted and redefined itself throughout these years. In both the enclave and non-clave urban patterns, the underlying element in the cultural cohesion of the community lies with the social structures, such as the family associations and tongs, and the common bonds of a shared cultural experience.

NOTES

1. In this analysis, the term "enclave" is spatially and visually oriented rather than used to provide an analysis of socioeconomic forces that perpetuate or hinder the

interaction of the cultural group and the spatial setting. This latter discussion of enclave can be found in Peter Kwong, *The New Chinatown* (New York: Noonday, 1987) and in Jan Lin, *Reconstructing Chinatown: Ethnic Enclave, Global Change* (Minneapolis: University of Minnesota Press, 1988). Both of these accounts provide expertise on intercommunity conflict.

2. Mark Abramson, *Urban Enclaves: Identity and Place in America* (New York: St. Martin's, 1996), 13.

3. David Chuenyan Lai, *Chinatowns: Towns within Cities in Canada* (Vancouver: University of British Columbia Press, 1988), 7.

4. This author has developed the term "non-clave" to describe the physical presence of an ethnic community that does not occupy contiguous sites within a geographically contained area.

5. The Sanborn Map Company listed this rural area as the "Chinese Vegetable Gardens" on their maps beginning in 1879.

6. Mark Abramson, *Urban Enclaves*, 13.

7. John Kuo Wei Tchen, *Genthe's Photographs of San Francisco's Old Chinatown* (New York: Dover, 1984), 19.

8. Tchen, *Genthe's Photographs*, 20. The boundaries of Chinatown were roughly between Broadway Street to the north, Kearney Street to the east, California Street to the south, and Stockton Street to the west.

9. The morphological shift in Seattle's Chinatown took about forty years, in what could be identified as three main phases. The first Chinatown settlement originally consisted of a small group of stilted buildings located along the tide flats of the city's waterfront. In the second phase and following a city fire in 1889, the Chinese quarters relocated to brick buildings in a concentrated area at South Washington Street and Second Avenue. Major development projects precipitated the final movement phase to the present location of the core of the Chinatown community at South King Street at Seventh Avenue. The first development project was the 1907 regrading of the area southeast of the second Chinatown location, along with the widening of South King and South Jackson streets. The construction of Union Station (1910) and the King Street Station (1911) made an attractive opportunity for building projects, and specifically hotel buildings that were constructed by Chinese investment companies and entrepreneurs such as Goon Dip. These hotels became the nexus of the Chinese community and consisted of single-room-occupancy hotel and lodging house living quarters for transient workers.

10. According to the U.S. Census, 1880 had the most severe ratio disparity of Chinese males to females for Oregon (57.0:1) and Washington (126.4:1), while

California's highest ratio occurred in 1890, with 22.5:1. Ratio figures for Oregon between 1880 and 1900 steadily improved from an increase in Chinese females. U.S. Bureau of the Census, *Census of Population*, 1880–1900.

11. S. W. Kung, *Chinese in American Life* (Westport, Conn.: Greenwood, 1962), 76.

12. U.S. Bureau of the Census, *Census of Population*, 1870–1920. From the beginning of this immigration pattern, the majority of Chinese newcomers settled along the West Coast, with modest migration into the central United States occurring in the 1880s. From 1870 to 1920, Oregon held the second highest population of Chinese in the western United States, including Idaho, Wyoming, Montana, Colorado, Utah, Nevada, Arizona, and New Mexico.

13. U.S. Bureau of the Census, *Census of Population*, 1870–1920. Washington State's Chinese population was recorded at slightly more than three thousand.

14. Victor G. Nee and Brett de Bary Nee, *Longtime Californ': A Documentary Study of an American Chinatown* (New York: Pantheon, 1973), 63.

15. U.S. Bureau of the Census, *Census of Population*, 1860–1930.

16. Among those they did adopt were the Lodging House or "Cubic Air" Ordinance, which required at least five hundred cubic feet of air per tenement inhabitant, a law that was only enforced in the overcrowded boardinghouse conditions of Chinatown. The Laundry Ordinance imposed higher quarterly license fees for laundry businesses that did not have vehicular delivery than for those that did, a regulation that was clearly directed at laundries owned by Chinese, since they had no such service.

17. U.S. Bureau of the Census, *Census of Population*, 1870–1920. This figure includes an estimated three hundred Chinese from Tacoma and four hundred from Seattle.

18. Lin's account offers an insightful look at the dynamics of local economies within Chinatowns.

19. "The Chinese," *Oregonian*, 16 February 1865, 3.

20. U.S. Census figures. See also Roger Daniels, *Asian America: Chinese and Japanese in the United States since 1850* (Seattle: University of Washington Press, 1988), for his discussion on the shifts from small-town living to living in cities with over 100,000 population.

21. The number of the acres and the name of the "Chinese Vegetable Garden" community are based on data obtained from Sanborn Fire Insurance Company maps, 1879–1926.

22. "Any Chinamen," *Oregonian*, 12 December 1866, 3.

23. "The Chinese Question Ably and Fairly Discussed," *Oregonian,* 22 July 1884, 4.

24. Immigrant Chinese were permitted to purchase property in Oregon until 1923, when the state followed suit with six other states, including California, to forbid property ownership to those people ineligible for naturalization.

25. The typical frontage of these buildings was forty feet.

26. City of Portland, Fire Marshall's Correspondence, Record Series 5000–01, 1925.

27. Both of these men were wealthy and influential in the Chinese community. Hin was reportedly the first Chinese millionaire of the Northwest, and before the turn of the century Back's property interests in downtown Portland were yielding in excess of $200,000 a year. In addition, Hin had been named the Chinese Consulate representative for the Western states in 1905.

28. The other states that enacted similar legislation included California, which held the first such statute, followed by Arizona (1917), Louisiana (1921), New Mexico (1922), and Idaho and Montana, which passed this legislation in 1923, as did Oregon. Dudley O. McGovney, "The Anti-Japanese Land Laws of California and Ten Other States," as cited in the *California Law Review* 35 (1947): 6, 7.

29. The label of "female" boardinghouses was typically used by property assessors to describe houses of prostitution in the city.

30. While much of this movement had been focused in East Coast cities, the overall intention was to get city leaders to think about ways to plan and develop a grand and beautiful urban environment with civic spaces, landscaping, parks, boulevards, and improved streets, and to gloss over the problems that had accumulated from the blight of America's long period of industrialization in the city. For Portland, infrastructure improvements would control the near annual flooding of the Willamette River.

31. "Old Chinese Buildings to Give Way to Structures for White Men," *Portland Daily Abstract,* 10 September 1908, 1.

24

The Diverse Nature of San Diego's Chinese American Communities

Ying Zeng

Since immigration laws were changed in 1965, the immigration of ethnic Chinese to the United States has increased dramatically. Moreover, those who arrive in the United States today are from many different countries and areas, speak disparate languages, and have varying cultural backgrounds. Whereas previously most ethnic Chinese immigrants were from Guangdong Province, China, today they hail from Taiwan, Southeast Asia, every part of mainland China, and elsewhere. Furthermore, whereas most Chinese immigrants used to settle in Chinatown areas, today the majority live outside of Chinatowns. Until recently, scholars focused their efforts on Chinatown communities, thus leaving a growing and important part of Chinese America unaccounted for. This chapter sheds light on the new, diverse Chinese American communities through an examination of two case studies in the Chinese American communities of San Diego. In particular, it will show that the postwar waves of immigration changed the makeup of San Diego's Chinese American population.

BACKGROUND OF CHINESE AMERICAN COMMUNITIES IN SAN DIEGO

San Diego is located south of Los Angeles and just north of the Mexican border. It is a port town and home to a healthy agricultural industry. San Diego County is the second most populous county in the state of California, with nearly three million people. The city of San Diego has the sixth largest population of all cities in the United States (table 24.1).

The first Chinese to appear in southern California drifted down from the Sierra Nevada gold fields, where Chinese were excluded from the best-paying claims (see Valentine, chapter 2 in this volume). Many of them had been fishermen back in their homes in the Pearl River Delta area of Guangdong

Province. The early Chinese immigrants established San Diego's fishing industry, which would later become one of San Diego's most important industries. In the 1870s and 1880s the Chinese supplied all the fresh fish requirements of San Diego and exported dried fish products to other Chinese communities worldwide. During the peak, there were eighteen Chinese junks based in San Diego (see Bentz and Schwemmer, chapter 8 in this volume).

However, good times did not last long. As had already happened in the goldfields, Chinese once again became the targets of exclusion. In 1888 Congress passed the Scott Act. Under the Chinese Exclusion Act of 1882, Chinese laborers already living in the United States had been allowed to return after leaving the country by presenting certificates of residence to the collector of customs at their port of entry. However, the Scott Act invalidated these certificates and denied reentry to any noncitizen laborer who went past the three-mile territorial limit of the United States. The Chinese fishermen were thus barred from exploiting the prime fishing grounds off the Mexican coast. By 1888 Chinese comprised only 52 of a total of 159 fishermen in San Diego. By 1893 there was only one Chinese junk left fishing in San Diego County.[1]

Besides being fishermen, the Chinese were employed as laborers on the railroad and worked in service industries as launderers, cooks, servants, and gardeners. In the 1880s many Chinese were involved in the building of the Hotel Del Coronado. Between 1881 and 1884 some fifteen hundred Chinese laborers in San Diego were employed to build the California Southern Railroad. In 1887 seventeen of the twenty-three laundries in San Diego were operated by Chinese. Later, as their capital accumulated, they became merchants, restaurateurs, and grocers. When the Scott Act brought about the end of the Chinese fishing industry in San Diego, many of the Chinese went into market gardening. By 1900 there were twenty-seven market gardens in San Diego. Chinese farmers introduced a variety of Chinese fruits and vegetables to San Diego.[2]

The early Chinese fishermen established a fishing village at the foot of San Diego's New Town. This small area later became known as San Diego's Chinatown. The community grew with the arrival of the railroad laborers, but many of the residents had left by the end of the century. Since the Chinese community of San Diego never had a chance to grow large enough before the anti-Chinese immigration laws of the late 1800s, the community was never able to solidify a large, centralized Chinatown area.

Chinese immigration, however, increased sharply after the Chinese exclusion laws were repealed in 1943, especially after the passage of the Immigration

Act of 1965. In 1947 the restrictive covenant on real estate was lifted and the Chinese were able to purchase real estate in San Diego for the first time. It therefore became much easier for them to establish families and businesses in places of their choosing. At the end of the 1960s, most of the people in the community had moved out of the small district in the downtown area that had briefly been known as San Diego's Chinatown.[3] Later waves of immigrants hardly knew there was once such an area.

Since the latter half of the 1970s, there has been a surge of immigrants from Southeast Asian countries, owing to the turbulent political situation and unfavorable economic conditions for the ethnic Chinese there.[4] After the Vietnam War, many thousands of refugees escaped from Vietnam, Cambodia, and Laos in old and fragile boats. Most of these "boat people" were ethnic Chinese. A great number of them settled in San Diego, since nearby Camp Pendleton was the biggest of the four receiving centers in the United States. Another immigration wave followed the normalization of relations between China and the United States in 1979, which opened the door for people from mainland China to immigrate to the United States. In 1981 Congress granted a separate immigration quota of twenty thousand people from Taiwan.[5] A large number of students, professionals, and professors from Taiwan have immigrated to San Diego since then.

Table 24.1 The growth of the Chinese American population, 1850–1990

	United States	Growth by decade (%)	California	Growth by decade (%)	SD County	Growth by decade (%)
1850	758	-	-	-	-	-
1860	34,933	4508.6	34,933	-	-	-
1870	63,199	80.9	49,277	41.1	70	-
1880	105,465	66.9	75,132	52.5	229	227.1
1890	107,488	1.9	72,472	-0.03	909	297.0
1900	89,863	-16.4	45,753	-36.9	414	-54.5
1910	71,531	-20.4	36,248	-20.8	430	3.9
1920	61,639	-13.8	28,812	-20.5	N/A	-
1930	74,954	21.6	37,361	29.7	558	-
1940	77,504	3.4	39,556	5.9	479	-14.2
1950	117,629	51.8	58,324	47.4	819	71.0
1960	237,292	101.7	95,600	63.9	1,586	93.7
1970	435,062	83.3	170,131	78.0	3,259	105.5
1980*	812,178	86.7	325,882	91.5	8,618	164.4
1990*	1,648,696	103.0	723,669	122.1	19,686	128.4

Source: U.S. Bureau of the Census, Asian and Pacific Islander Population by State: 1980. PC80-S1-12 (Washington, D.C.: Bureau of the Census, 1983); U.S. Bureau of the Census, 1990 Census of Population: Asians and Pacific Islanders in the United States (Washington, D.C.: Government Printing Office, 1993); U.S. Census, 1850 to 1990.
* The numbers for 1980 and 1990 are underestimated, since a large part of the Vietnamese population and some of those from Cambodia, Laos, and other Southeast Asian countries are also of Chinese descent, yet are not included in the statistics.

Today, the Chinese community in San Diego consists of old-timers; American-born Chinese; new immigrants from Hong Kong, Taiwan, mainland China, and other countries; and refugees from Vietnam, Cambodia, and Laos.[6] Although they all may share the same ancestral roots, they were raised in different cultural environments. The once nearly homogeneous community, which consisted almost entirely of immigrants from Guangdong Province and their American-born descendants, was in the span of a few decades turned into a heterogeneous collection of communities. A native-born Chinese American whose parents were from Kaiping, one of the Sze Yap areas of Guangdong Province, remarked, "I had never heard Mandarin in San Diego until the late fifties or early sixties."[7] He still remembers that when his mother first had dinner at a restaurant serving Sichuan cuisine, she insisted that it was not Chinese food since the spicy tastes were so different from the Cantonese food that used to be the only cuisine in San Diego's Chinese restaurants. This diversification in Chinese American communities is now common throughout the United States.[8]

THE DIVERSE NATURE OF CHINESE AMERICAN COMMUNITIES IN SAN DIEGO

With the growth of the Chinese American population in San Diego, there no longer remains a mostly homogeneous community as there was before World War II. San Diego now contains many Chinese American communities with different language, cultural, and political backgrounds. There are times when the differences between groups can split the communities into factions, for example, when the question of the status of Taiwan is raised. But at other times members of the various communities find it advantageous to act as a cohesive unit, such as when the communities united to build the Chinese Historical Museum of San Diego. There are also certain ties that serve to link these diverse groups, bringing them together in efforts to support, at least on some level, a united entity without a geographic center (Chinatown). The most powerful tie is a shared sense of Chineseness.

Just as in other Chinese communities across the United States, San Diego's Chinese American communities are undergoing rapid change. The diverse backgrounds of the Chinese American population make the community socially and culturally heterogeneous. There are several objective factors that hinder the unity of Chinese Americans, such as language barriers, differences in cultural backgrounds, differences in socioeconomic situations, and the influence of the changing relations between the United States and China.

First is the language barrier. As most early (pre–World War II) Chinese immigrants came from Guangdong Province, Cantonese was the primary language of the community. The next generation after these early immigrants, the native-born Chinese Americans, mostly received their education in public and private schools. Although some of them were sent to Chinese schools and learned to speak Cantonese, their native language is English. However, the new immigrants consist of speakers of different language groups: most immigrants from mainland China and Taiwan speak Mandarin, immigrants from Guangdong Province and many ethnic Chinese from Southeast Asia speak Cantonese; immigrants from Fujian province, Formosan immigrants from Taiwan, and some of the ethnic Chinese from Southeast Asia speak Hokkien; and immigrants of Hakka descent speak Hakka. Although those with higher educational backgrounds generally also speak English, a large percentage of foreign-born Chinese Americans cannot speak English well.[9] An effort to use both English and Mandarin (sometimes both Mandarin and Cantonese) is made in many cases for important community activities and events, but the language barriers still make it difficult to organize members from different groups for a united purpose.

Second, differences in cultural backgrounds also divide Chinese American communities. For example, organizations for Chinese American women demonstrate cultural differences. In San Diego, there are two main Chinese women's organizations. The San Diego Chinese Women's Association was established in 1971. Most of its members are old-timers or native-born Chinese Americans. Because the backgrounds of its members are very similar to those of the Chinese Consolidated Benevolent Association's (CCBA's) members, these two organizations are very close. The Women's Association often raises money to donate to the CCBA, the Chinese Center, or other organizations to support the activities in which its members are interested.[10] On the other hand is the San Diego Women's League, established in 1992. Most of its members are professional immigrants from Taiwan. When a member of the Women's League was asked about the difference between these two women's organizations, she said, "Their education and background is different from ours. They have been here very long, or were born here. But their last generation were mostly from Guangdong; they are mostly descendants of Cantonese people. . . . Our interests are totally different."[11] The length of time spent in the United States, as well as the culture of the area from which an individual immigrated, play significant roles in how that individual defines his/her own "Americanness" or "Chineseness." Such cultural differences also play a factor in the case studies that are discussed below. In sum, cultural background affects the interaction between the various Chinese American communities not only because it establishes familiarity between individuals but also because it shapes their identities as Chinese Americans.

Perhaps the factor contributing most to the separation of Chinese Americans is politics. The influence of the changing relations between the United States and China plays a critical role. Local mainstream society's exclusion of Chinese Americans before World War II led many Chinese Americans to participate actively in China's political struggles, with the hope of building a stronger China as a means to improve their own status in the United States. At that time, China was seen as a weak country and, by extension, the Chinese were seen as a weak people. If the country was made strong, the image of the people would improve. This wish for a strong China can still be seen today, as reflected in the opinions of some of those cited in the example of the Chinese Navy's visit, discussed below.

The question of the status of Taiwan remains the most influential political factor in inter–Chinese American community and individual relations. Although more and more Chinese American organizations declare their intention to remain politically neutral in the Taiwan-mainland struggle, the influence of the struggle is still very strong, particularly on organizations with predominantly immigrant membership. Him Mark Lai notes that, "Just as America's open society allowed pro-PRC and pro-Kuomingtang partisans to coexist, so it also provided an arena for Taiwanese opponents to Kuomingtang rule on Taiwan to organize and to voice their dissent."[12] The supporters of the Taiwan Independence Movement form another group among the diverse Chinese American population. The examples below demonstrate how the Taiwan-mainland split continues to play a major role in shaping the diverse communities.

Despite the many forces tending toward disintegration of the diverse Chinese American community, there are also forces that act to integrate Chinese Americans—forces that cut across diverse subcultural groups, emphasize what is common to most groups, and help maintain a united (although not uniform) community.

For example, external forces acting on Chinese Americans have acted as influential integrative forces. Although the status of Chinese Americans has dramatically improved since World War II, racial and cultural barriers (external as well as internal) still prevent the Chinese and other minorities from full membership in mainstream society. A *San Diego Tribune* survey has shown that, although minorities account for approximately a quarter of San Diego County's total population, there were only two minority representatives in the boardrooms of San Diego's top twenty-five publicly held corporations. The San Diego Police Department, with 448 members from minority groups among its 1,894 officers and support staff, counted only three among its top-ranked officials, including one assistant chief. The San Diego County Sheriff's Department had 423 minority members among its 1,506 employees, but none in high-ranking positions. Out of ninety-nine elected officials on eighteen city councils and the county Board of Supervisors, only five were minorities. Of 240 school and community college board members, only 26 were minorities.[13] As long as this "glass ceiling" exists to distinguish the Chinese from other Americans, it will push Chinese Americans back to their communities. The communities, however, by offering networks of support and sources of mutual understanding, may eventually help provide the means for a collective effort to break through the glass ceiling.

Another factor contributing to a common sense of community is that Chinese Americans share the same ancestral roots. Chinese generally have a strong belief in their common history and origin and common interpretations of the experiences and actions of their mythical ancestors and historical forebears, despite the differences in the cultural environments in which they were raised. Chinese Americans, therefore, to a certain extent are distinguished from fellow Americans by their shared Chinese cultural traditions. Chinese Americans have emphasized familism, one of the essential characteristics of Chinese culture. A Chinese communication network, attaching importance to ties of kinship and friendship, is consciously maintained in Chinese American communities. This informal yet efficient information exchange system unites the communities by cutting across generational and cultural boundaries.[14]

The following two examples offer an opportunity to observe the diversity within the communities as well as the sources of that diversity, such as political orientation. They also demonstrate that, despite differences, a shared sense of "Chineseness" exists. The first example is the visit of the Chinese Navy to San Diego and the second is the return of Hong Kong to China and the communities' reactions to it.

EXAMPLE I. THE FIRST VISIT OF THE CHINESE NAVY TO THE U.S. MAINLAND

On the morning of March 21, 1997, two Chinese destroyers and a support ship arrived in San Diego for a five-day port visit at San Diego's North Island

Naval Air Station. It was the first-ever visit to the U.S. mainland by the Chinese Navy. Like most matters that concern Chinese politics, the Chinese Navy's visit evoked different opinions among different groups within the Chinese American communities.

The visit of mainland Chinese warships to San Diego permits an examination of the role of politics in shaping the relationships among Chinese American communities in San Diego. While many Chinese Americans of San Diego welcomed the ships' arrival, many others, especially natives of Taiwan, Chinese dissidents, and human rights advocates, did not celebrate. Some organizations arranged a tour to Mexico for the same period as the navy's visit and sent invitations to the community leaders of other organizations. The spokesman for the Taiwanese Community Center, which represents the pro-Taiwanese independence movement, declared that they did not welcome the Chinese Navy to the United States. In a written statement, the spokesman further said that they had planned a protest but canceled it out of courtesy to the U.S. Navy, which came to Taiwan's aid during China's missile exercises in the Taiwan Straits in 1996.[15]

Some Chinese American human rights advocates cited the 1989 Tiananmen Square massacre as one of the reasons for their boycott. One of them said, "We support the strengthening of U.S.-Chinese relations, and we support economic and cultural exchanges, but not high-level military relations such as this."[16]

However, one mainland community leader, who represented recent immigrants from mainland China, pointed out, "China has made a lot of progress in allowing its people more freedom. It takes time to bring about fundamental changes." Another community leader, who represented those who were born on the mainland but grew up in Taiwan, remarked, "We should not mix up Tiananmen with this visit. If we keep dwelling on one incident, we will never move forward."[17] While these leaders spoke as individuals, based on interviews and discussions with other members of their communities, I believe their opinions reflect those within their communities.

Over half a dozen organizations formed a welcoming committee to help arrange the welcome activities for the Chinese Navy's visit.[18] The committee consisted of Chinese American members from mainland China, as well as those from Taiwan and Indochina.[19] Among the activities arranged was a welcome reception by Chinese Americans to which fifteen hundred tickets were given out. The tickets were divided among the members of the different groups sponsoring the event.

During the time scheduled for public tours, there were over fifty thousand visitors, most of them Chinese Americans from San Diego and places as far away as Los Angeles, Tijuana, and Phoenix, who went on board the Chinese ships.[20] A retired Taiwanese Navy lieutenant colonel visited one of the ships with his daughter and grandson and said, "This is a first-class ship. China has come of age. I'm proud." Then he added, "I'm not a Communist, but I'm Chinese. As long as China is strong, I'm satisfied."[21] This position appears very similar to the attitudes of pre–World War II Chinese Americans, discussed above. They felt that a strong China reflected well upon them, increasing personal pride and also their perceived status within their new country.

An ethnic Chinese immigrant from Vietnam and his family drove down to San Diego from Los Angeles at four o'clock in the morning. He said, "We're here to welcome our country. We want our children to know where we came from."[22]

The reactions to the visit demonstrate various aspects of Chinese American identity. As the examples show, many ethnic Chinese in San Diego expressed some level of pride in the event. China is not simply a separate government, but their homeland, regardless of whether they immigrated directly from there or not. Even many of those who protested the military nature of the event still expressed hopes for expanded cultural ties. In short, this event brought to the forefront various factors of national, ethnic, and cultural identity. National identity, whether one was pro-Taiwan, anti-PRC, or pro-PRC, served to divide the communities into factions. The uniting factor was a common sense of Chineseness, or a sense of being ethnically Chinese. The man from Vietnam and the officer from Taiwan both emphasized China as a critical source of their identity. China for them was not simply a country or a government, but a culture and an ancient history with which they identified.

EXAMPLE II. CELEBRATION FOR THE RETURN OF HONG KONG

The reaction of San Diego's Chinese American communities to the return of Hong Kong, while demonstrating that the communities can be divided over politics, provides further evidence for how a common sense of Chineseness can help to bring about unified action.

Hong Kong's return to China on July 1, 1997, is considered by many Chinese as the end of China's national humiliation (*guochi*) brought about by events in the nineteenth century. Ethnic Chinese all around the world enthusiastically celebrated this event.

To prepare for the celebration, all the community organizations planned to cosponsor a large evening party. However, as the project began to get down to details, views diverged. Which flag should be hung on the stage, the national flag of the People's Republic of China or the national flag of the Republic of China? Should the PRC national anthem be sung at the party? Who should be invited as special guests? For example, should representatives of the Taiwanese government be invited and, if so, should the consul general of the People's Republic of China also be invited? As a result, the celebration had to be separated into two different activities: an evening celebration party on June 21 and a dinner party on June 29. The evening party was sponsored by pro-mainland groups and the dinner party was sponsored by Taiwanese and politically neutral groups, such as the Chinese Historical Society. The Taiwanese Independence group did not participate in either function. However, as shown below, there was considerable crossover on an individual level.

The consul general and other officials of the Consulate General of the People's Republic of China in Los Angeles, invited as special guests, attended the evening celebration party, cosponsored by many organizations, including four from Tijuana and Ensenada, Mexico.[23] Among the nearly sixty members of the celebration committee, there were community members from mainland China, Hong Kong, and Taiwan, as well as from Southeast Asia and other areas. The president of the San Diego Chinese Association[24] and the representative of the five organizations of ethnic Chinese from Vietnam, Cambodia, and Laos[25] were the cochairs of the committee. Some of the community leaders from organizations not directly sponsoring the event sponsored the celebration party as private individuals.[26] Many of their organizations were responsible for sponsoring the dinner party, or had to maintain political neutrality, such as the Chinese Historical Society. The fact that these individuals were involved in both efforts demonstrates how close the communities were to united action.

The evening party started with the national anthem of both the United States and the People's Republic of China. Community members from different groups appeared on stage and performed. The party ended with a chorus of more than 150 members from various groups and fields.

By contrast, the dinner party was held in a Chinese restaurant and was cosponsored by diverse organizations.[27] The program included awarding of prizes to the winners of an essay contest on Hong Kong's return, showing of a video on the history of Hong Kong and on the ceremony accompanying Hong Kong's return, and a karaoke performance. More than four hundred community members attended the dinner party. The dinner party was marked by a neutral stance. The festivities centered around a common celebration of ethnic, rather than national, pride.

The example of the celebration for the return of Hong Kong shows that despite the great diversity in the Chinese American communities of San Diego, they share a sense of Chineseness that can bring them together to take united action. This shared sense of Chineseness allows the various communities to overcome many regional and political differences and to participate together in major events of this nature.

CONCLUSION

Early San Diego shared a pattern of Chinese immigration similar to northern California and other parts of the United States, with immigrants mainly coming from the Pearl River Delta area and speaking Cantonese. Chinese Americans in San Diego suffered through the same oppressive laws, such as the Chinese Exclusion Act, and were forced out of one business after another, shifting from railroads to mines to fishing to agriculture, as their neighbors to the north. Later, with changes in immigration laws and global politics, came changes in patterns of immigration. San Diego became home to an increasingly diverse number of Chinese American communities. Chinese immigrants and refugees from Hong Kong, Taiwan, Southeast Asia, every part of mainland China, and other countries made their way to San Diego in the latter half of the twentieth century. With each new group, another layer was added to San Diego's history and another stitch to the increasingly complex quilt of Chinese American identity.

With each new wave of immigrants, the Chinese American community of San Diego grew more diverse. The diversity at times gave rise to conflict. The internal conflict among Chinese American communities in today's San Diego, such as in the debates over the Hong Kong celebration party, is by no means the same as the feuds and wars among community organizations in old Chinatowns. The Chinese Americans may split into different groups regarding political events and form various organizations to meet their own cultural and social needs, but in many cases they tend to work together, united around a common ethnicity.

The factors hindering the unity of Chinese Americans are both internal and external. The influences of the changing relations between China and the United States, as well as the changing social, economic, and political situations in both China and the United States, are external factors acting on Chinese

American societies. Perhaps the single greatest contemporary political factor, as demonstrated in the above case studies, is the debate over the status of Taiwan. At the same time, differences of language, culture, educational background, and socioeconomic class, in other words, internal factors, all constitute further obstructions to a unified community.

However, as both of the above case studies show, there are also factors that serve to integrate Chinese Americans. The most dominant factor is a shared sense of Chineseness. "Chineseness" is separate from national identity. It is one's sense of cultural, ethnic, and historical identity with a China that is more than just a geographic location. Chinese Americans are thus drawn together through possessing a belief in a common history and origin, sharing certain Chinese cultural traditions, and facing common social barriers in the larger society; the diverse Chinese American communities, at times, are able to act together as one.

NOTES

1. See Arthur F. McEvoy, "In Places Men Reject: Chinese Fishermen at San Diego, 1870–1893," *The Journal of San Diego History,* Vol. 23.4 (1977); William A. Wilcox, "The Fisheries of the Pacific Coast," United States Commission of Fish and Fisheries, *Report of the Commissioner for the Year Ending June 31, 1893* (Washington, D.C.: Government Printing Office, 1898).

2. Murray K. Lee, "A Short History of the Chinese in San Diego, California," unpublished paper (1996); Suber Joyce, Lanell Alston, and David Vigilante, *San Diego People: The Chinese Pioneers* (San Diego, Calif.: San Diego City Schools, 1982), 23; Karl Fung, *The Dragon Pilgrims: A Historical Study of a Chinese-American Church* (San Diego, Calif.: Providence Press, 1989), 15–16.

3. Fung, *The Dragon Pilgrims,* 75.

4. The treatment of ethnic Chinese in Southeast Asia has been discussed at length in books such as Garth Alexander, *The Invisible China: The Overseas Chinese and the Politics of Southeast Asia* (New York: Macmillan, 1973); David W. Haines, ed., *Refugees as Immigrants: Cambodians, Laotians, and Vietnamese in America* (Totowa, N.J.: Rowman & Littlefield, 1989); Quan Ma, ed., *The Phoenixes: The Story of Ethnic Chinese Immigrants from Indo-China* (Hacienda Heights, Calif.: Leader Publishing, 1998); Leo Suryadinata, *Peranakan Chinese Politics in Java: 1917–1942* (Singapore: Singapore University Press, 1981); Gungwu Wang, *China and The Chinese Overseas* (Singapore: Times Academic Press, 1991). The current situation has been the topic of discussion in many national and international newspapers, especially in 1998 with the increasing anti-ethnic Chinese incidents in Indonesia. Ethnic Chinese, who

were/are often seen as being financially better off than others in South East Asia, are often the subjects of discrimination in economic or political hard times.

5. Betty Lee Sung, *The Adjustment Experience of Chinese Immigrant Children in New York City* (New York: Center for Migration Studies, 1987), 22.

6. Following common practice, in this study "old-timers" refers to Chinese immigrants who immigrated to the United States before 1965, and "new immigrants" refers to Chinese immigrants who immigrated to the United States after 1965.

7. Interview by the author, 25 July 1996. The names of interviewees are not given here in order to protect their privacy.

8. The following table shows the increase in the number of foreign-born Chinese Americans (i.e., new immigrants) since the 1970s.

Table 24.2 Nativity of Chinese American population

	Total	Native-born	Foreign-born	% of Foreign-born
1900	89,863	9,010	80,853	90.0
1910	71,531	14,935	56,596	79.1
1920	61,639	18,532	43,107	69.9
1930	74,954	30,868	44,086	58.8
1940	77,504	40,262	37,242	48.1
1950	117,629	62,343	55,286	47.0
1960	237,292	144,036	93,256	39.3
1970	435,062	229,237	205,825	47.3
1980	812,178	297,789	514,389	63.3*
1990	1,648,696	506,116	1,142,580	69.2*

Source: U.S. Census, 1900 to 1990.
* Since a great number of ethnic Chinese from countries and areas other than mainland China, Taiwan, and Hong Kong are new immigrants who arrived after the 1970s and are not included in the data, the actual percentage of all foreign-born ethnic Chinese in 1980 and 1990 is probably higher than was shown in the census.

9. According to the 1990 U.S. Census, 63.1 percent of foreign-born Chinese Americans do not speak English very well.

10. Interview by the author, 23 August 1997.

11. Interview by the author, 15 August 1997.

12. Him Mark Lai, "Chinese Organizations in America Based on Locality of Origin and/or Dialect-Group Affiliation, 1940s–1990s," *Chinese America: History and Perspectives* (1996): 71.

13. *San Diego Tribune*, 21 November 1991, A-19.

14. Melford S. Weiss, *Valley City: A Chinese Community in America* (Cambridge, Mass.: Schenkman, 1974), 253–56. More research is required on later generations. Due to the limitations of this project, the important question of how understanding of Chineseness changes across generations is not discussed. San Diego's lack of a Chinatown, in which continuity across generations is often strongly promoted, allows a unique opportunity for examining this question.

15. The statement said, "We believe U.S. engagements with the Chinese government should be conducted in a cautious manner, especially in areas of military assistance. Taiwan is not a renegade province of China. We ask that the Chinese Government recognize the sovereignty of Taiwan." Angela Lau, "Chinese Here Differ on Visit of Ships: They Welcome Port Call—or Deplore It," *San Diego Union-Tribune*, 20 March 1997, B-4.

16. Lau, "Chinese Here Differ on Visit."

17. Interview by the author, 19 August 1997, 2 January 1998.

18. The organizations included the San Diego Chinese Association, the Chinese Friendship Association of San Diego, the San Diego Chinese Consolidated Benevolent Association, the Ying On Merchants and Labor Benevolent Association, the House of China, the San Diego Chinese Art Association, and other community organizations.

19. Although neither the major organizations for immigrants from Taiwan nor the largest organization of immigrants from Vietnam, Cambodia, and Laos took part in the activities, some of the community leaders from these organizations joined the welcome committee as private individuals, not as representatives of their organizations. For details, see *American Chinese Times*, 14 March, 21 March, and 28 March 1997.

20. *American Chinese Times*, 28 March 1997.

21. Angela Lau, "First Chinese Navy Visit to San Diego," *San Diego Union-Tribune*, 22 March 1997, A-19.

22. Lau, "First Chinese Navy Visit."

23. These included the San Diego Chinese Association, the Chinese Friendship Association of San Diego, the U.S.-China Entrepreneurial Association, the Fukienese Association of San Diego, the Hakka Chorng Jeng Association of San Diego, the Ying On Merchants and Labor Benevolent Association, the Lien Hwa Chinese Music Society, the House of China, the U.S.-China People's Friendship Association, and other community organizations.

24. San Diego's first and biggest organization for new immigrants from mainland China.

25. There are five organizations that serve the ethnic Chinese from Vietnam, Cambodia, and Laos in San Diego: the Indo-Chinese Association of San Diego (*Shengdiyage Yuemianliao Huaren Lianyihui*), the Chinese Friendship Association of San Diego (*Shengdiyage Huaren Lianyihui*), the Elderly Chinese Association of San Diego (*Shengdiyage Dongnanya Huaren Qiyinghui*), the Hakka Chorng Jeng Association of San Diego (*Shengdiyage Keshu Chongzhenghui*), and the Fukienese Association of San Diego (*Shengdiyage Fujian Tongxianghui*). Although they have their own offices and governing bodies, they usually work together to represent the whole community of ethnic Chinese from Indochina. Whenever there are any events or activities for Chinese communities in San Diego, the five organizations usually participate together and take the same position on any actions. They often call themselves "brotherly bands" (*xiongdi bang*).

26. For example, leading members of the San Diego Chinese Consolidated Benevolent Association, the San Diego Chinese American Science and Engineering Association, the Chinese Historical Society of Greater San Diego and Baja California.

27. For example, the five organizations of ethnic Chinese from Indochina, the San Diego Chinese Consolidated Benevolent Association, the Chinese Historical Society of Greater San Diego and Baja California, and the Friends of the New Party.

Index

acculturation, 248–49. *See also* assimilation

acupuncture. *See* Chinese medicine

Ah Quin. *See* Tom Ah Quin

Aiiieeeee! anthology, 365

Alaska. *See* Tom Ah Quin

Althusser, Louis, 366

Americanization. *See* assimilation

ancestor reverence, 223–24

Angel Island Immigration Station, 299

anti-American boycott in China, 10, 195; backdrop in China, 196; as beginning of modern Chinese nationalism, 195; effects of, 209; U.S. President Roosevelt's response, 209. *See also* Baohuanghui

anti-Chinese organizations: American Federation of Labor (AFL), 127; American Socialist Party, 128; Anti-Chinese League of Unionville, 91; Asiatic Exclusion League in San Francisco, 129; Asiatic Exclusion League in Vancouver, 109; California Workingmen's Party, 128, 156, 170; Gold Hill Miners' Union, 101; International Workingmen's Party,

422; Knights of Labor, 127, 422; Virginia City Miners' Union, 101

anti-Chinese violence, 78–79, 88n3

anti-Communism, 330

Asian American Studies Center of the University of California, Los Angeles, 297

assimilation, 21; as Chinese American goal, 13; Christian conversion, 228–29; funeral and burial practices, 10, 217–30; stereotyping Chinese culture, 22; Tom Ah Quin, 12, 60, 311, 313

Baja California. *See* Mexico

Baldwin, Alexander, 92

Baohuanghui (Chinese Empire Reform Association or Protect the Emperor Society), 10, 196; activities, 198; anti-American boycott role, 196; —, boycott outlined, 204; —, Zeng as leader of boycott, 203–4, 212; chapters and members, 198; Commercial Corporation as business arm, 198; founded in Canada, 196; goals, 197; Los Angeles leader, Tom Leung, 197, 198, 205–6, 207; as new

About the Contributors

Rebecca Allen is a consulting historical archaeologist and historian, and co-owner of Past Forward, Inc. She is currently working with the California Department of Transportation on a large excavation project of the Woolen Mills Chinatown in San Jose. Dr. Allen specializes in the study and interpretation of California's historic past. She is an associate editor for the *Journal of Historical Archaeology* and serves on the California Mission Studies Association Board of Directors. Her most recent publication is *Native Americans at Mission Santa Cruz, 1791–1834: Interpreting the Archaeological Record*, published by the University of California, Los Angeles, Institute of Archaeology.

R. Scott Baxter is a consulting historical archaeologist and historian, and co-owner of Past Forward, Inc. He is currently working with the California Department of Transportation on a large excavation project of the Woolen Mills Chinatown in San Jose. He has an M.A. from the University of Nevada, Reno. He specializes in historical and industrial archaeology of the late nineteenth and early twentieth centuries.

Linda Bentz is a freelance historical researcher. She has worked with the National Parks Service investigating the Chinese presence on Santa Rosa Island and done extensive work in three historic Chinese communities: Ventura, Santa Barbara, and Cambria. Her research interests include Chinese fishermen, California-built Chinese junks, and Chinese American women and families. Her publications include articles in *Ventura County Historical Society Quarterly, Mains'l Haul, Noticias, Asian American Comparative Collection*

Newsletter, Chinese America: History and Perspectives, Gum Saan Journal, and Community Development Department, City of Ventura. She is currently the vice president for the Los Angeles Maritime Museum Research Society.

William M. Bowen received his Ph.D. in medical anthropology from the University of California at Riverside. His research interests include Chinese culture and medicine, Native American shamanism, and alternative health care. His work has been published in Filipino Massage Therapy, Gum Saan Journal, Origins and Destinations: 41 Essays on Chinese America, Yuin Journal, and Natural Health Times. In addition to his formal academic training, Dr. Bowen has been personally involved with Chinese herbology, martial arts, and massage for twenty-five years and is certified to instruct in these subjects by Chinese Taoist grandmaster Share K. Lew, formerly of Gee Lum Kwan Monastery, China.

Susie Lan Cassel is an associate professor in the Literature and Writing Department and chair of the Ethnic Studies Program at California State University, San Marcos. She specializes in Asian American and multicultural American literature and has particular interest in IndoChinese American and Hapa issues. Her work has appeared in the Modern Language Association's Profession, MELUS, Reflections, Frontiers, and JAAS. She is currently transcribing and translating the Ah Quin diaries in preparation for a critical edition.

Albert Cheng, an educator for more than thirty years, is currently the director of administrative services for the California School Leadership Academy at West Ed. For the past eleven years, he has served as a volunteer coodinator for the "In Search of Roots" program of the Chinese Culture Foundation of San Francisco. He serves on the governing board of the foundation and has been elected president for three terms. He has also served as a board member of the Chinese Historical Society of America. Cheng has traced 4,698 years and 124 generations of his family history.

Vivian Fumiko Chin is an assistant professor in the Ethnic Studies Program at Mills College. Her research interests include narrative and performance strategies in Asian American literature. Her publications include "Family, Story, and History: The Power of Chinese American Narrative," in Asian American Literature: Memory and Creation (Osaka: Kyouiku Tosho Press, 2001).

Sue Fawn Chung is an associate professor in the Department of History at the University of Nevada at Las Vegas. She has served as chair of the department and director of international programs. Her research interests include the experiences of Chinese Americans at the turn of the twentieth century and Chinese history in the same period. She has published numerous articles on Chinese and Chinese American history in journals such as *Modern Asian Studies*, *Journal of Popular Culture*, and *Chinese America*, and in collected works, including *Comstock Women*, *Claiming America*, and *Ordinary Women, Extraordinary Lives*. Recently she received the Distinguished Nevadan Award from the Nevada Humanities Committee and the Rita Abbey Outstanding Teaching Award from the College of Liberal Arts. She currently is a member of the Board of Advisors for the National Trust for Historic Preservation.

Victor Jew is an assistant professor in the History Department at Michigan State University. He specializes in U.S. legal and constitutional history and Asian American history and directs graduate training in U.S. nineteenth-century history.

Bonnie Khaw-Posthuma is an assistant professor in the Department of English and Writing at Chaffey College. She received her Ph.D. in English from Claremont Graduate University (and a major in twentieth-century American literature and minors in early American and nineteenth-century American literature). Her research interests include Chinese American, African American, and Native American writing, and film studies.

Him Mark Lai, a 1947 engineering graduate of the University of California, Berkeley, has been a member of the Chinese Historical Society of America since 1965. He is a member of the society's publication committee for *Chinese America: History and Perspectives*, an annual journal cosponsored with San Francisco State University's Asian American Studies Department. In 1969 he taught the first college-level course in America on Chinese American history at SFSU, and he subsequently taught the same subject at UC Berkeley. He has contributed numerous articles and essays to periodicals and books, such as *East-West, Harvard Encyclopedia of American Ethnic Groups*, *Asian American Encyclopedia*, and *Encyclopedia of Chinese Overseas*. In 1980 he copublished *Island: Poetry and History of Chinese Immigrants on Angel Island, 1910–1940*, with Genny Lim and Judy Yung. He has compiled bibliographies on Chinese American newspapers and on Chinese-language materials on Chinese in America. His major work is

From Overseas Chinese to Chinese American, written in Chinese and published in 1992. He is now working on an English version.

Jane Leung Larson is a consultant for nonprofit China organizations, and is currently working in New York City with the Committee of 100 and China Institute in America. From 1980 to 1995, she was executive director of the Northwest China Council in Portland, Oregon. Since 1985, she has done research on the Baohuanghui (Chinese Empire Reform Association), using as primary source materials the papers of her grandfather, Tom Leung, a Los Angeles Baohuanghui leader. Her publications include articles in *Chinese America: History and Perspectives* (1993) and the collection *Origins and Destinations: 41 Essays on Chinese America* (1994), and she has given papers in China and the United States.

Murray K. Lee is the curator of Chinese American history at the San Diego Chinese Historical Museum. He has served on the Board of Directors of the Chinese Historical Society and on the Museum Board of Trustees. His research interests are in Chinese American history, especially in the San Diego area. His publications include articles in the San Diego Chinese Historical Society newsletter; *Mains'l Haul,* the journal of the Maritime Museum Association of San Diego; publications of the Congress of History of San Diego and Imperial Counties; the *Wrangler,* a journal of the Westerners; the *San Diego Gazette;* and other local papers. He has made presentations and conducted museum tours for local schools, universities, and organizations, and presented papers at national conferences.

Nancy S. Lee is a Ph.D. student in the Department of Communication at the University of California, San Diego. She has worked as a freelance writer/editor and communications consultant to several major corporations in British Columbia and she holds a diploma in piano performance from the Royal Conservatory of Music, University of Toronto. Her research interests include the news media, issues of citizenship, and global migration.

Haiming Liu is an associate professor in the Department of Ethnic and Women's Studies at California State Polytechnic University, Pomona. His areas of research include Asian American immigration, social history, family, and Chinese transnational experiences. He has published in *Amerasia Journal* and *Journal of Asian American Studies* on Chinese trans-Pacific family life and Chinese herbalists in America.

Elmer R. Rusco received his doctorate from the University of California, Berkeley, in political science in 1960. He is currently professor emeritus at the University of Nevada, Reno, and has specialized in minority civil rights issues. His book, *Good Time Coming*, focuses upon the African Americans in Nevada, and a recently published article concerns policies regarding Native Americans. He is working on a book manuscript on the political and legal history of the Chinese in Nevada.

Robert Schwemmer is currently the cultural resources coordinator for the National Oceanographic and Atmospheric Administration's Channel Islands National Marine Sanctuary. He serves as a maritime research consultant for federal and state agencies, including private and nonprofit organizations. Past projects have included systematic research in developing shipwreck assessments for the Channel Islands National Marine Sanctuary and National Park, California; the Olympic Coast National Marine Sanctuary, Washington; and the Dry Tortugas, Florida. Deepwater projects include submersible work aboard *Delta* to perform site assessment of the shipwreck *Montebello*, located 900 feet below the surface off Cambria, California. Schwemmer is a charter member and past president of the Los Angeles Maritime Museum Research Society. He is currently vice president of research for the Coastal Maritime Archaeology Resources organization.

Shirley Sui Ling Tam is the editor of *Chinese Christians for Justice*. She earned her Ph.D. in American social policy history from Case Western Reserve University in 1999. Her research interests include Chinese American history, Asian American history, stereotypes and images of minorities, racial discrimination, poverty, and affirmative action issues. Her work has been published in *Origins and Destinations: 41 Essays on Chinese Americans, Chinese Christians for Justice*, and *Ohio History*.

David Valentine is currently working for the U.S. Department of Interior, Bureau of Reclamation, Lower Colorado Regional Office in Boulder City, Nevada. He has worked as an archaeologist for private consultants and the federal government in Arizona, Oregon, Montana, North Dakota, Nevada, California, and Utah. In 1999, he received his M.A. in archaeology from the University of Nevada at Las Vegas. His areas of interest include prehistoric and historic mining, overseas Chinese, contact period Native American sites, and rock art. He

has published in *Halcyon, Nevada Archaeologist*, and *Rock Art Papers.*
Catalina Velázquez Morales is a full-time researcher at the Instituto de Investigaciones Históricas de la Universidad Autónoma de Baja California. She has
a Ph.D. in history from the Universidad Nacional Autónoma de México and
her research interests include the Chinese and Japanese immigrants in Baja
California. Publications include articles in *Visión histórica de la frontera Norte
de México* (Historical overview of the northern border of Mexico), *Mexicali:
una historia* (A history of Mexicali), *Historia de la Universidad Autónoma de
Baja California, 1957–1997* (History of the Autonomous University of Baja
California, 1957–1997), and *Meyibó.*

marie rose wong is a visiting assistant professor in the Institute of Public Service at Seattle University. Her research interests include the history of community development, urban form, and cultural and vernacular architectural
expressions in American Chinatowns. Her articles have appeared in *Arcade
Magazine,* the *Encyclopedia of Vernacular Architecture of the World, Open
Spaces Quarterly,* and *Pacific Historical Review.*

Zhiwei Xiao is an associate professor in the Department of History at California State University, San Marcos. His research interests include film and
popular culture in twentieth-century China. Publications include the *Encyclopedia of Chinese Film,* co-authored with Yingjin Zhang (New York: Routledge,
1998); pieces in *Cinema and Urban Culture in Shanghai, 1922-1944,* edited by
Yingjin Zhang (Stanford: Stanford University Press, 1999) and *Transnational
Chinese Cinemas: Identity, Nationhood, Gender,* edited by Sheldon Lu (Honolulu: University of Hawaii Press, 1998); and articles in journals such as *Twentieth Century China, Asian Cinema, American Historical Review,* and *China Review International.*

Chiou-ling Yeh is a Kevin Starr Fellow in California Studies at the University
of California Humanities Research Institute. She received her Ph.D. in history
at the University of California, Irvine, in June 2001. She is currently revising
her dissertation, titled "Taking It to the Streets: Representations of Ethnicity
and Gender Identities in San Francisco's Chinese New Year Festivals,
1953–2001," for publication. Her research interests include Asian American,
racial, and ethnic history; cultural studies; and gender history.

Dolores K. Young has a Ph.D. in biophysics from the University of Rochester and has taught in the field of physics at various colleges and universities in the United States. She retired in 1992, after teaching at California Polytechnic State University at San Luis Obispo. In the last ten years, she has focused on the regional history of Chinese immigrants and has written articles on the Cuesta Tunnels and stereotypes of Chinese on the transcontinental railroad, which have been published in local papers and delivered at regional conferences.

Yuan Yuan is a professor in and chair of the Literature and Writing Department at California State University, San Marcos. He is the author of *The Discourse of Fantasy: Theoretical and Fictional Perspectives;* translator of Nobel Prize writer Saul Bellow's novel, *The Adventures of Augie March;* editor of the *Journal of the Fantastic in the Arts,* Special Issue on Dream and Narrative Space; and associate editor for the *Journal of the Association for the Interdisciplinary Study of the Arts.* He has contributed articles to *Critique: Studies in Contemporary Fiction, Symposium: A Quarterly Journal in Modern Foreign Literature, Studies in Psychoanalytic Theory, Readerly/Writerly Texts,* and the *American Journal of Psychoanalysis.* He was cofounder, member of the Board of Directors, and secretary of the San Diego Chinese Association, and he also served as member of the Board of Directors and secretary to the Chinese Cultural Association in San Diego.

Ying Zeng is a lecturer at Keio University and a research associate at the Institute of Asian Cultural Studies at International Christian University in Tokyo. She received her Ph.D. in 1999 in comparative culture from International Christian University. Her research interests include Chinese American history, Chinese American literature, and studies of Chinese overseas. Her publications include articles in *Asian Culture, Journal of Japan-China Sociological Studies, ICU Comparative Culture, Chinese America: History and Perspectives,* and *Ethnic Chinese at the Turn of the Centuries.*

Sheldon X. Zhang is an associate professor in the Sociology Department at California State University, San Marcos. His research areas include Chinese organized crime, Asian gangs, juvenile corrections, informal social control, and program evaluation. His work has appeared in journals such as the *British Journal of Criminology; Crime and Delinquency;* and *Crime, Law and Social Change.* He is currently heading a federal project to study the social organization of organized Chinese human trafficking activities across the Pacific Ocean.